Contents at a Glance

Contents

APPENDIX B   Current MySQL Functions   445

About the Authors

Mark Maslakowski is a consultant working for Thor Systems Inc., a company specializing in systems integration. As Senior Solutions Developer, Mark is responsible for developing solutions that fit clients' needs, no matter what the platform. He has been involved in developing large multi-tier applications for several major corporations. Mark started his career in the U.S. Army and has been on the move since. He has filled many roles, including Database Administrator, Senior Developer, and Senior Systems Analyst. Mark can be reached at markm@thorinc.com.

Tony Butcher is a consultant specializing in the design of interactive and database-driven Web sites. As Technology Director for Tribal Internet in the UK, he creates solutions based on MySQL in combination with Perl and PHP3. He has designed Web sites as front-ends to vast data mines searchable by sophisticated user queries and has created dynamic virtual communities of thousands of people with loyalty systems and personalized publishing of information. Although he has had a varied career, he has implemented databases in almost every job he has ever had. "We shouldn't be worried about information overload," he might say, "What matters is how we phrase our questions."

Dedication

I would like to dedicate this book in loving memory of my Father who left this world early but gave those he touched a lifetime of memories and teachings.

—Mark

Acknowledgments

First and foremost I'd like to thank Ken Robertson for giving me the time, the insights, and the opportunity to make this book a reality.

I'd also like to thank Carla Maslakowski. Without her push and direction, I would not have had the career I've enjoyed.

Also, I'd like to thank David Smith of Cornerstone Information Systems, for giving me a chance when no else would.

To all my friends at the club for helping me blow off steam when I needed to the most.

I can't forget my family for being there when I needed them most and for putting up with my bad habits.

I'd also like to thank the team at Sams Publishing, especially Shelley Johnston, for making this experience a pleasurable one.

—*Mark Maslakowski*

Tell Us What You Think!

As the reader of this book, *you* are our most important critic and commentator. We value your opinion and want to know what we're doing right, what we could do better, what areas you'd like to see us publish in, and any other words of wisdom you're willing to pass our way.

As an Associate Publisher for Sams, I welcome your comments. You can fax, email, or write me directly to let me know what you did or didn't like about this book—as well as what we can do to make our books stronger.

Please note that I cannot help you with technical problems related to the topic of this book, and that due to the high volume of mail I receive, I might not be able to reply to every message.

When you write, please be sure to include this book's title and author as well as your name and phone or fax number. I will carefully review your comments and share them with the authors and editors who worked on the book.

Fax:	317.581.4770
Email:	opsys_sams@macmillanusa.com
Mail:	Michael Stephens
	Sams Publishing
	201 West 103rd Street
	Indianapolis, IN 46290 USA

Introduction

Since before the dawn of the computer age, people have been using databases. Before computers, a database may have been a Rolodex containing phone numbers of the important people you knew, or it was a filing cabinet that contained all the personnel records for the company. Today, databases are computer-based and are found virtually everywhere. From desktop databases of your record collection to Web-enabled databases that run large corporations, databases come in all shapes and sizes. Because of this fact, the database industry has grown as fast and as large as the rest of the computer industry.

Until recently, most high-powered databases cost an arm and a leg. They could provide all the tools and functionality to run a business but at a very high price. So most companies would use a database that was cheaper and sacrifice functionality.

Additionally, the Internet has spawned a new need for databases that can be accessed via the Web. This need has led software manufacturers to create products that can take advantage of this technology. Again, price plays a large role. These products are generally very expensive and very platform-dependent, so not all Internet service providers (ISPs) or small companies can take advantage of this technology.

Enter the Linux and Open Source revolution. This cutting-edge idea—to have an operating system and the source code available free of charge—changed the way the industry looked at how it did business. Now that the revolution has finally taken a foothold, people are flocking en masse to see how they can use this newly affordable solution.

MySQL is part of that solution. MySQL was developed by TcX in 1996. They created it because they needed a relational database that could handle large amounts of data on relatively cheap hardware. Nothing out there could provide what they needed, so they created it themselves.

MySQL is the fastest relational database on the market. It outperforms all the leading databases in almost every category. It has almost all the functionality the leading databases have, but it does not carry the hefty price tag that its competitors do. This may seem like a lot of hype and marketing talk, but, after a little time working with MySQL, you will agree.

If MySQL is so good, why hasn't it already caught the attention of the industry? The answer is that until 1999, Linux and the Open Source movement were practically unknown.

MySQL runs primarily on UNIX-based systems—though there are ports for almost every platform on the market. Until the Open Source movement and the availability of UNIX-based operating systems at affordable prices, no one really looked at MySQL as a contender.

Because of the recent success of Linux, MySQL has grown in popularity. Unfortunately, there is not much out there in the form of documentation. That is where *Sams Teach Yourself MySQL in 21 Days* comes in. You'll be introduced to the various components of MySQL, such as installation, administration, and interfacing.

By the time you are finished, you will be well acquainted with these topics as well as others. You will understand why MySQL is one of the best RDBMS available to date.

How This Book Is Organized

This book covers the MySQL relational database management system in 21 days, broken into three separate weeks. Each week covers a different area of MySQL and builds on information learned on previous days.

In the first week, you will learn some of the basics of MySQL components:

- Day 1, "What is MySQL," is the introduction to MySQL—what it is and how it compares to other RDBMs in its class. You will learn about the various components of a database and will be introduced to relational databases.

- On Day 2, "Getting Started," you will learn how to install MySQL on a Linux platform as well as a Windows platform.

- Day 3, "Designing Your First Database," covers the basics of how to design a database. You will design the sample database that will be used throughout the rest of the book as an example.

- On Day 4, "Creating Your First Database," you will create your first MySQL database. You will learn the commands that accomplish this as well as some neat MySQL utilities.

- Day 5, "Making Your Data Normal," covers the topic of normalization—a very important subject when dealing with relational databases.

- On Day 6, "Adding Tables, Columns, and Indexes to Your Database," you'll beef up your database by learning how to add tables, columns, and indexes, which give structure to your design.

- Day 7, "MySQL Data Types," deals with the various data types that MySQL uses.

Week 2 is dedicated to teaching you how to work with your database. You'll cover the various ways to manipulate the data stored inside your MySQL database. You'll learn about MySQL's intrinsic functions and about interfaces, including the popular Perl DBI/DBD interface:

- On Day 8, "Populating the Database," you'll learn the tools and tricks you can use to populate your database.

- On Day 9, "Querying the Database," an SQL primer is given. This basic guide will give you the foundation necessary to manipulate your data.

- Day 10, "Letting MySQL Do the Work—Intrinsic Functions," covers the functions that are available in MySQL.

- Day 11, "MySQL Table Locks and Assorted Keys," introduces you to locks and keys. The uses and reasons for these features will be covered on this day.

- Day 12, "How to Get to the Data—Database Interfaces," starts the topic of interfaces and the various APIs that are available in MySQL. You'll see how the various interfaces share common functions.

- Day 13, "How to Use MyODBC," covers the ODBC driver interface. On this day you'll explore the techniques needed to access a MySQL database using this technology.

- Day 14, "The Perl Database Interface," covers the Perl DBI for MySQL in great detail. You'll build on the previous day's lesson and create your own Perl program to access data via the Internet.

Week 3 introduces some of the more advanced techniques of administrating a MySQL database. You'll cover how to administrate a MySQL database server, including security and optimization techniques. At the end of this week, you'll finish things up by building a Web site using MySQL to build Web pages dynamically and processing user input:

- On Day 15, "MySQL and PHP," you'll learn how to interface MySQL with this hot new technology.

- Day 16, "MySQL and Time," covers how dates are used in MySQL. You'll learn about the various functions that are available to you from MySQL.

- On Day 17, "MySQL Database Security," you'll learn about MySQL security. You'll learn how it is implemented within MySQL, as well as how to keep your database secure.

- On Day 18, "How MySQL Compares," we'll compare MySQL to other databases. We'll take a look at the features that other databases have that MySQL does not have and discuss various workarounds to implement them.

- Day 19, "Administrating MySQL," covers administration in detail. You'll learn about maintaining logs and searching logs for problems. You'll also learn about backing up and recovering a MySQL database.
- On Day 20, "Optimizing MySQL," you'll learn about performance tuning your database engine. You'll learn how to build better queries, as well as some tricks to tweak performance.
- On the last day, "Putting It All Together," you'll use what you have learned in previous lessons to build a working application using MySQL.

About This Book

This book teaches you about the MySQL database management system. You'll learn about a wide range of topics, from creating to interfacing to administrating. By the end of this book, you will be able to install, create, use, and maintain a MySQL database. Along the way, you will learn about database design, as well as how to use a relational database.

Who Should Read This Book

This is book is for you if any of the following are true:

- You have outgrown the database you are currently using and are searching for a good replacement.
- You are developing a Web site that needs database access.
- You have never worked with a relational database before and want to learn how to use one.
- You are moving to a Linux platform and are looking for a proven RDBMS that can support your business.

This book will show you the steps, from start to finish, you'll need to know to use MySQL. Every aspect of MySQL is covered.

If you have never used a Relational Database Management System (RDBMS) before, you may be wondering if this book is for you. It is. It will walk you through the most difficult situations step by step, offering examples and illustrations to help explain and guide you through the toughest aspects of MySQL.

If you have used a RDBMS, such as Microsoft SQL Server, Sybase, or Oracle, this book is also for you. It will give you a chance to see one of the lesser-known systems that can hold its own against the big boys.

If you have used MySQL in the past or are currently using MySQL, this book is for you too. Inside, you will find shortcuts and explanations that you might not find anywhere else. A lot of the questions that you might have asked yourself are answered in this book.

Sams Teach Yourself MySQL in 21 Days assumes that you have no prior experience in database management systems. So take things a little slowly, make sure you understand each lesson completely before you move on. Each chapter builds on previously covered material. You will be able to take what you have learned in one chapter and apply it later.

How This Book Is Structured

This book is intended to be read and absorbed over the course of three weeks. During each week, you read seven chapters and perform the exercises at the end of each chapter.

Conventions Used in this Book

Note

A Note presents interesting, sometimes technical, pieces of information related to the surrounding discussion.

Tip

A Tip offers advice or an easier way to do something.

Caution

A Caution advises you of potential problems and helps you steer clear of disaster.

New terms appear in *italic* in paragraphs where they are defined.

At the end of each chapter, you'll find handy Summary and Q&A sections.

In addition, you'll find various typographic conventions throughout this book:

- Commands, variables, directories, and files appear in text in a special `monospaced font`.

- Commands and such that you type appear in **`monospaced bold type`**.
- Placeholders in syntax descriptions appear in a *`monospaced italic`* typeface. This indicates that you will replace the placeholder with the actual filename, parameter, or other element that it represents.

WEEK 1

At a Glance

As you prepare for your first week of learning how to use MySQL, you will need a few things: a computer, a Web server and this book. If you don't have the first two things, you can still use this book. However, you'll still need to practice these lessons somewhere. You cannot expect to learn something without trying it firsthand. This book will take you step by step through each aspect of MySQL. This book is set up so that each day ends with an exercise. Take advantage of these exercises; they can further help you on your journey to becoming a full-fledged MySQL Database Administrator.

Where You're Going

This week covers the basics of MySQL. On Day 1, you'll learn what MySQL is and some of its uses. Day 2 is where you'll learn how to install MySQL for the Windows and Linux platforms. On Days 3 and 4, you'll learn about designing a database, and then you'll actually create one. Day 5 covers normalization. Day 6 is where you'll learn how to add columns and indexes to your database. The week ends with Day 7's MySQL data types. On this day, you'll learn about the various data types and how they apply to MySQL.

This is a lot material to cover in a week, but if you take your time and follow the exercises, you'll do all right.

1

2

3

4

5

6

7

WEEK 1

DAY 1

What Is MySQL?

Welcome to *Sams Teach Yourself MySQL in 21 Days*. Today, you will start your adventure of discovering one of the best relational database management systems on the market today.

Today, you will learn the following:

- What a relational database is and for what it can be used
- What it means to be on the Enterprise level
- What client/server programming is all about
- Some of MySQL's features

Understanding MySQL

MySQL, pronounced "my Ess Que El," is an open source, Enterprise-level, multi-threaded, relational database management system. That sounds like a lot of sales or marketing hype, but it truly defines MySQL. You may not be familiar with some of these terms but, by the end of today, you will be.

MySQL was developed by a consulting firm in Sweden called TcX. They were in need of a database system that was extremely fast and flexible. Unfortunately (or fortunately, depending on your point of view), they could not find anything on the market that could do what they wanted. So, they created MySQL, which is loosely based on another database management system (DBMS) called mSQL. The product they created is fast, reliable, and extremely flexible. It is used in many places throughout the world. Universities, Internet service providers and nonprofit organizations are the main users of MySQL, mainly because of its price (it is mostly free). Lately, however, it has begun to permeate the business world as a reliable and fast database system. Some examples of commercial use are available on the CD-ROM that accompanies this book.

The reason for the growth of MySQL's popularity is the advent of the Open Source Movement and the incredible growth of Linux in the computer industry. The Open Source Movement, in case you haven't heard about it, is the result of several computer software vendors providing not only a product but the source code as well. This allows consumers to see how their program operates and modify it where they see fit. This, and the popularity of Linux, has given rise the use of open source products in the business world. Because of Linux's skyrocketing popularity, users are looking for products that will run on this platform. MySQL is one of those products.

MySQL is often confused with SQL, the structured query language developed by IBM. It is not a form of this language but a database system that uses SQL to manipulate, create, and show data. MySQL is a program that manages databases, much like Microsoft's Excel manages spreadsheets. SQL is a programming language that is used by MySQL to accomplish tasks within a database, just as Excel uses VBA (Visual Basic for Applications) to handle tasks with spreadsheets and workbooks. Other programs that manage databases include Microsoft's SQL Server, Sybase Adaptive Server, and DB2.

Now that you know where MySQL came from, look at what it is. To begin with, start with the term database. What is a database? You have probably used one in your lifetime. If you've ever bought anything over the Internet or have a driver's license, you can be assured that you have used one. A *database* is a series of structured files on a computer that are organized in a highly efficient manner. These files can store tons of information that can be manipulated and called on when needed. A database is organized in the following hierarchical manner, from the top down. You start with a database that contains a number of tables. Each table is made up of a series of columns. Data is stored in rows, and the place where each row intersects a column is known as a field. Figure 1.1 depicts this breakdown. For example, at your favorite online book store there is a database. This database is made up of many tables. Each table contains specific, common data. You would probably see an Authors table or a Books table. These tables are made up of named columns that tell what data is contained in them. When a record is inserted into a table, a row of data has been created. Where a row and a column intersect, a field is created. This how databases are broken down.

FIGURE 1.1

The anatomy of a database.

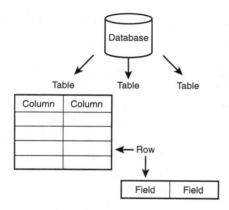

MySQL is more than just a database. It is a system that manages databases. It controls who can use them and how they are manipulated. It logs actions and runs continuously in the background. This is different from what you may be used to. Most people think about Microsoft Access or Lotus Approach when they think about databases. These are databases, but they are not management systems. A DBMS can contain many databases. Users connect to the database server and issue requests. The database server queries its databases and returns the requests to the issuers. Databases, such as Approach and Access, are a step down from this type of system. They share their files with multiple users, but there is no interface controlling the connections or answering requests.

There are many uses for a DBMS such as MySQL. Uses can range from help desk systems to Web site applications. The important thing to remember is that MySQL is large enough and quick enough to function in almost any situation. Where it finds itself most comfortable is the Enterprise.

What Is the Enterprise?

The Enterprise I'm referring to is not a starship or a space shuttle. The *Enterprise* is the area in the business world where many large systems interact with one another to accomplish a common goal. Some applications that are at this level of business include SAP, Microsoft SQL Server, Oracle 8i, and Sybase Adaptive Server. The computer applications that exist at this level of business tend to have certain characteristics. They are usually multiuser in nature—many people can use the same application at the same time. Another characteristic is that they provide some sort of security mechanism. The final characteristic is that applications at this level have to be very flexible.

The first characteristic of an Enterprise-level application is that it can be used by more than one person at a time. This is a requirement at this level of business. More than one person may need to have access to business information at a given time. This is critical for the business to function successfully. MySQL meets this requirement. It can have up to 101 simultaneous connections. This doesn't mean that only 101 people can use this application. It means it can have 101 connections going on at the same time—which is a little different. A connection is the time it takes for a user to receive the data that he or she has requested. In the case of MySQL, this is hardly any time at all. Most database systems in the same class as MySQL allow fewer simultaneous connections. Currently, the only DBMS to offer more connections is Microsoft SQL Server.

The next characteristic that an Enterprise-level application must have is security. When dealing with mission-critical information, only people with the need to know should be allowed to view it. Security keeps malicious people at bay; without it, disasters can happen. MySQL meets this requirement. The security in MySQL is unparalleled. Access to a MySQL database can be determined from the remote machine that can control which user can view a table. The database can be locked down even further by having the operating system play a role in security as well. Very few databases in the same class as MySQL can compare to the level of security that MySQL provides.

One other characteristic of an Enterprise-level application is flexibility. How flexible is the application? Can it change to meet the ever-changing needs of business? How deep can you make those changes? How hard is it to change? MySQL answers these questions very well. It is extremely flexible and easy to use. MySQL can run on almost any platform. If a new CIO wants to change from Windows NT to Linux, fine—MySQL can adapt. MySQL also comes with the source code. If there are any deep-level changes that you need to make, you can edit the source and make these changes yourself. If MySQL is missing a feature that you can't live without, just add it yourself. No other database on the market can offer you

1

that kind of flexibility. MySQL also has several application-level interfaces in a variety of languages. If yours is mainly a Microsoft shop, you can use ODBC to interact with MySQL. If your company is a UNIX shop, you can use C, Perl, or JDBC. There is no end to the flexibility that MySQL has to offer.

In addition to the previously discussed characteristics, databases at the Enterprise level must be able to work together. Data warehousing is a technique that combines all the data in a business. Because of the flexibility and speed that MySQL has to offer, it can work well in any situation.

The Internet has also become a piece of the Enterprise pie. No large corporation is without an Internet presence. These corporations need databases to sell and compete at this level of business. MySQL works well as an Internet-based database server. It has been proven in this arena and is the preferred database of many Internet service providers (ISPs). Because of its speed and multiple application interfaces, MySQL is an ideal choice.

Enterprise applications are the crucial component to a business's decision-making power. Information must be timely and accurate for a business to perform effectively. To do this, applications must work quickly. An application is much like a car. It can look pretty on the outside, but the engine is what gives it its power. The same applies to an application; If its database engine is weak, so is the application. MySQL is clearly the choice for the Enterprise.

What Is a Relational Database?

A *relational database*, simply defined, is a database that is made up of tables and columns that relate to one another. These relationships are based on a key value that is contained in a column. For example, you could have a table called Orders that contains all the information that is required to process an order, such as the order number, the date the item was ordered, and the date the item was shipped. You could also have a table called Customers that contains all the data that pertains to customers, such as a name and address. These two tables could be related to each other. You really couldn't have an order without a customer, could you? You will learn all about relationships on Day 3, "Designing Your First Database."

The relational database model was developed by E.F. Codd back in the early 1970s. He proposed that a database should consist of data stored in columns and tables that could be related to each other. This kind of thinking was very different from the hierarchical file system that was used at the time. His thinking truly revolutionized the way databases are created and used.

A relational database is very intuitive. It mimics the way people think. People tend to group similar objects together and break down complex objects into simpler ones. Relational databases are true to this nature. Because they mimic the way you think, they are easy to use and learn. In later days, you will discover how easy a relational database is to design and learn.

Most modern databases use a relational model to accomplish their tasks. MySQL is no different. It truly conforms to the relational model. This further adds to the ease of use of MySQL.

The Client/Server Paradigm

The client/server paradigm or model has been around a lot longer than most people think. If you look back to the early days of programming, you remember or have heard or read about the large mainframe computer with many smaller "dumb" terminals. These terminals were called dumb for a reason. No logic or processing was done at the terminals. They were just receptacles for the output of the mainframe. This was the dawn of the client/server age, but the term client/server wasn't the buzzword it is today.

As the personal computer became more prevalent, giving rise to the local area network (LAN), the client/server model evolved. Now processing could be done at the client. Clients started sharing data. This data was stored in sharable computers called file servers. Now, instead of all the processing being done at the server, it was all being done at the client. The server or centralized computer was just a large storage device. It did little or no processing—a complete reversal of earlier thinking.

After a couple of years, desktop applications became more powerful. People needed to share more information more quickly. This gave rise to the more powerful server machines. These machines answered requests from clients and processed them. These servers are what you know today as database servers, Web servers, and file servers. This is when people started calling it client/server computing. It is basically a two-tier design; a client issues requests, and a server answers them. All the business logic is at the application level on the client. Two-tier design is still very prevalent today. This is also known as a *fat client* because all the application processing is done at the client level.

After a couple of years, servers became the powerhouses of business organizations because of their duties. They were usually top-of-the-line systems with the best hardware and were tweaked for speed. So, it was just a matter of time before someone came up with the idea of moving the guts of their programs to the server. The client would just be a graphical user interface (GUI), and the main application or business logic would be processed on the server. The server would then make the necessary calls to other servers, such as database servers or file servers, as needed. This gave birth to the three-tier or *thin client* design. In this design, all processing of the business logic is done at the server level. This allows the more powerful machine to handle the logic and the slower machines to display the output. Does this sound familiar? It should—we've come full circle. The heavy processing is again done on the more powerful, centralized machines, while all the client machines do is display the output.

The Internet is a prime example of thin client architecture. A very thin client—the browser—sends requests to a Web server, which sends a response back to the browser. The browser then displays the requested information—completely full circle.

Again, we are on the verge of a new era in computing. Applications are becoming more balanced across the network. Because of a decline in computer prices, very good machines are showing up on the desktop as clients. This allows applications to pick up the slack and perform some processing. Server applications are becoming more advanced as well. You can now run functions remotely and accomplish distributed computing fairly easily. These advancements allow your applications to be more robust in nature and more useful to your business.

Note

> *Distributed computing* allows client programs to interact with multiple server processes, which, in turn, can interact with other servers. The server components can be spread across the resources of the network.

MySQL fits in very well in all these architectures. It performs extremely well in a two-tier or three-tier architecture. It can also perform very well on its own.

Features of MySQL

MySQL is a full-featured relational database management system. It is very stable and has proven itself over time. MySQL has been in production for over 10 years.

MySQL is a multithreaded server. *Multithreaded* means that every time someone establishes a connection with the server, the server program creates a thread or process to handle that client's requests. This makes for an extremely fast server. In effect, every client who connects to a MySQL server gets his or her own thread.

MySQL is also fully ANSI SQL92-compliant. It adheres to all the standards set forth by the American National Standards Institute. The developers at TcX take these standards seriously and have carefully adhered to them.

> **Note**   ANSI SQL92 is a set of standards for the Structured Query Language that was agreed on in 1992 by the American National Standards Institute.

Another valuable feature of MySQL is its online help system. All commands for MySQL are given at a command prompt. To see which arguments the commands take or what the utility or command does, all you have to do is type the command and include the `-help` or `-?` switch. This will display a slew of information about the command.

Yet another feature of MySQL is its portability—it has been ported to almost every platform. This means that you don't have to change your main platform to take advantage of MySQL. And if you do want to switch, there is probably a MySQL port for your new platform.

MySQL also has many different application programming interfaces (APIs). They include APIs for Perl, TCL, Python, C/C++, Java (JDBC), and ODBC. So no matter what your company's expertise is, MySQL has a way for you to access it.

MySQL is also very cheap. For an unlicensed, full version of MySQL, the cost is nothing. To license your copy will currently cost you $200. This is an incredible deal, considering what you are getting for your money. Database systems that provide half the features that MySQL has can cost tens of thousands of dollars. MySQL can do what they do better and for less.

Summary

As you can see, MySQL is a very robust database server. It can fully function in the Enterprise. It has the advanced security measures that need to be in place at that level of business. It also provides speed and flexibility that no other database in its class can match.

MySQL is a relational database. It uses tables and columns to hold data that can be related by keys. It is well suited for this role.

It is also very well suited for various architectures. It can be used in a strictly client/server architecture or as a standalone database. Whatever your needs, MySQL can suit them.

1

Today, you learned about the main features of MySQL. You learned that it is multithreaded and ANSI SQL92 compliant. You also read about the various platforms and APIs that MySQL can use.

Finally, you learned that MySQL is free in most cases (check the MySQL Web site at www.mysql.com for licensing rules). This is hard to believe for such a robust, flexible, and fast RDBMS as MySQL.

Q&A

Q **My mother always said you get what you pay for. If MySQL is so great, why is it so cheap?**

A This is a belief most Americans share. If something is cheap, it isn't any good. For some things this is true, but in the case of MySQL it is not. MySQL is part of the Open Source Movement. It was created by a group of developers who continue to develop on their own time, mostly for free. This allows users to enjoy a truly great product for little or no cost.

Q **If MySQL is everything you say that it is, why haven't I heard about it?**

A MySQL has not enjoyed the popularity of some database products because it does not have a huge company backing it. It was developed by a consulting firm for a client. The firm did not market it. The only reason MySQL has gained popularity now is because of the Open Source Movement and Linux. Hopefully, with this book and the strength of the product, more people will come to enjoy the benefits of MySQL.

Exercises

1. Compare the prices of several other databases that have the same feature set as MySQL. These would include SQL Server, Oracle, Adaptive Server, and DB2. See how much MySQL is really worth.

2. Go to Web sites or test some products that use MySQL. (Some are included on the CD-ROM). Seeing MySQL in action can really change one's mind on open source products.

DAY 2

Getting Started

Today, you will learn about installing MySQL on the Linux and Windows platforms. You will read about licensing MySQL, as well as where you can get MySQL. You will also learn how to change the root password. You will learn about starting and stopping the MySQL server daemon, as well as how to use the command-line—based MySQL monitor.

Licensing

Now that you know what MySQL is and how it fits into the workplace, you can get started working with it. As was stated before, MySQL is an open source application. The source code is available for anyone to view and modify.

However, it is not free in all cases. If you use MySQL for personal, nonprofit use, it is absolutely free on any non-Microsoft platform. However, a license is required if you sell it directly or as part of another service. This means that if you perform services on a MySQL database, the database you are performing services on must be licensed. The current fee (as of this writing) is $200. This is a steal considering the functionality, capability, and speed of this database. The money goes to further development of the product. I strongly recommend visiting the Web site (www.mysql.com) and reading the licensing requirements.

Downloading MySQL

After you have determined whether or not you need to license your version of MySQL, you are ready to download it. At the MySQL Web site, go to Downloads. You will see a list of currently available binary and source code versions of MySQL for a multitude of platforms. Also, for your convenience, various MySQL binaries can be found on the CD-ROM that accompanies this book. This just saves you a step in the installation process. Please refer to your system's documentation on how to access the CD-ROM.

MySQL is always undergoing modifications and enhancements. The newest releases are the Alpha versions. The Alphas contain the newest features of MySQL. They also contain some fixes from the previous versions. They have been tested using TcX's testing modules but have not been tested as thoroughly as possible. TcX recommends using the most current production release. These editions have been tested and are used in production around the world.

MySQL runs on many platforms, and binaries are available for most of them. Binaries are the result of compiling the source code. This is by far the easiest way of acquiring MySQL. The alternative is downloading the source code for your platform and then compiling it. This can get a little more involved. It requires that you have all the right libraries as well as a compiler. This is beyond the scope of this book. If you absolutely must compile the source code, read the documentation thoroughly. If you have any problems, check out the MySQL mailing lists. They are an invaluable information source for MySQL administrators. Members of the development team read the postings regularly and are willing to answer or provide guidance on most of them.

To download the Linux binary, go to a MySQL mirror site. A *mirror site* is an exact replica of an existing Web site that is on another server. This helps distribute the load and traffic of the main Web server and allows others to use the Web server without problems. After selecting a mirror site, click the binary that you need.

This book will cover the installation of the Linux binary as well as the shareware version of the Windows binary.

Installation for Linux

After the download has completed, you will have a zipped tar file named `mysql-3.22.23b-pc-linux-gnu-i686.tar.gz`. It is recommended that you unpack this in `/usr/local`—all the defaults point to this location. You may need to have `root`-level privileges to modify the `/usr` directory. It has been my experience that it is best to install MySQL as `root`; there seem to be fewer ownership problems that way. To unpack the file as explained here, type the following from the command line:

INPUT
```
cd /usr/local
gunzip < mysql-3.22.23b-pc-linux-gnu-i686.tar.gz | tar xvf -
ln -s mysql-3.22.23b-pc-linux-gnu-i686 mysql
```

This is just an example—the filename may change when new versions are distributed. This will unpack the MySQL binary and create the directory structure. The last line creates a symbolic link to that directory. Change to that directory and do a list:

INPUT
```
cd mysql
ls
```

You should see the following results:

OUTPUT
```
ChangeLog          bin  lib mysql-for-dummies
INSTALL-BINARY     configure   manual.htm scripts
PUBLIC             data   manual.txt share
README             include   manual_toc.html sql-bench
Support-files      tests
```

Installation for Windows

The Windows installation is very similar to a Linux installation. Select a mirror site from which to download your Windows binary. The Windows executable is a self-installing WinZip file. After the download has finished, double-clicking the zipped file will begin the extraction/installation routine. After it has installed and performed cleanup, you will be returned to your desktop.

To see the new files, open Windows Explorer and navigate to the `c:\` directory. You should see something similar to Figure 2.1.

The directory structure for both Linux and Windows installations is almost the same.

FIGURE **2.1**

New MySQL Windows installation.

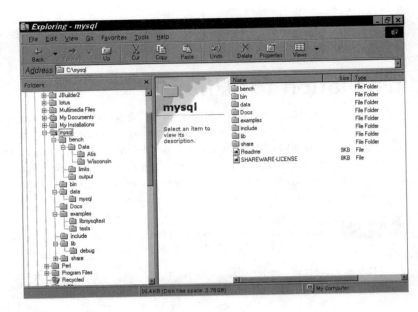

File Contents

Before continuing, examine what you have.

The ChangeLog is a file containing all the changes and fixes for that particular release.

INSTALL-BINARY is an information file explaining how to install MySQL and release notes specific to the platform that is using this binary distribution.

PUBLIC is the copyright and right to use license.

The README file contains useful information on setting up your MySQL server.

The support-files directory contains files to aid in configuring your MySQL server. It also contains a specification file that explains why TcX created MySQL.

The bin directory contains all the MySQL commands, such as mysqladmin, mysqlaccess, and several other important commands. You will study this in depth in later chapters. In the Windows version, there are a couple of extra commands. The MySQLManager (see Figure 2.2) is the graphical user interface (GUI) of MySQL. It shows the current databases and table structure and allows the user to run queries, all within a friendly graphical environment. As with any GUI, some power has been sacrificed for looks. Not all of the features available from the command line are represented. GUIs are nice, but to know the tool, you must know how to use the command line.

FIGURE 2.2

MySQLManager.

The `configure` file contains a script that sets up the `grant` tables in your MySQL server.

The `data` directory is where all the data for the databases is stored. Each database has its corresponding directory, as well as files that store the data, configure the tables, and provide a way to access the data stored in the files.

The `include` directory contains all the C header files. These are used with the C/C++ API. These files are also used in the MyODBC driver.

The `tests` directory contains several Perl scripts to test your MySQL server.

The `lib` directory contains the libraries used in the C++ API.

The `manual.txt`, `manual.htm`, and `manual_toc.htm` are probably the most important tools for a MySQL administrator/developer after the data files. They provide a wealth of information that is invaluable. The `mysql_for_dummies` file is a good starting place for the MySQL newbie.

The `scripts` directory contains the install script for MySQL. It is called by the `configure` command.

The `share` directory contains the error logs and messages.

The `mysql_bench` directory contains the `crash_me` tool. This tool is used to generate comparisons between database systems. The MySQL Web site also contains the benchmarks and comparison information.

Changing Passwords

Now that the directory structure is created and the files have been extracted, you can begin configuring and running MySQL. To create the grant tables, make sure you're in the `/usr/local/mysql` directory and type the following from the command line:

INPUT   `scripts/mysql_install_db`

You will see a flurry of screen output. The script is creating the grant table for MySQL. This determines who can connect to the database. It is a good idea to change the `root` password of your MySQL database now. The database privileges and the file system privileges are two different things. This means that if you have a system user named Mike, you do not have a database user named Mike unless you create one. MySQL's security operates independently of the system's security. You will learn more about security and privileges on Day 17, "MySQL Database Security." For now, just choose a password for `root`.

From the command line, type the following—where *newpassword* is your new password:

`bin/mysqladmin -password newpassword`

This changes the current password (which is empty) to the new password. Security is a high priority in any environment, especially when dealing with the Internet. Make sure that you change your password; if you don't, you are opening the door for anyone to have his or her way with your data.

Starting and Stopping the Server

Like most Database Management Systems (DBMS) in its class, MySQL runs as a service or daemon. A *service* or *daemon* is a program that runs continuously in the background. Generally it doesn't have a user interface and cannot been seen unless you do a `ps` in Linux or look in the Task Manager of Windows (see Figure 2.3). `mysqld` is a server program, which means that its entire purpose is to wait for someone to connect to it and issue a request, and then it responds to that request.

You can think of the server program as an information desk in a mall. It sits there and has no other purpose but to answer questions from inquisitive shoppers. The people who work at the desk and respond to the shopper's requests don't store all the answers in their heads. They look up information from available resources. This is much like the mysqld daemon. It sits there—after it is started—waiting for requests. Depending on the type of request, it will either answer it directly or use the database that was asked for in the request. This is what makes an enterprise-level database different from a desktop application.

FIGURE 2.3

mysqld *running as a*
background process.

Using MySQL in Linux

To use your database, the MySQL daemon has to be running. (If the server program is not running it cannot respond to any requests). To start the server in Linux, make sure you are in the mysql directory and type the following from the command line:

```
cd mysql
bin/safe_mysqld &
```

The safe_mysqld command starts the server. The ampersand, &, forces the program to run in the background. There are several ways to ensure that your process is up and running. From the command line, try the following:

INPUT
```
cd mysql
bin/mysqladmin -p ping
```

You should then see

OUTPUT
```
Enter password: Yourpassword <enter>
Mysqld is alive
```

The ping argument of the mysqladmin command is a quick and easy way to see if the mysql process is running. Another technique is to actually check the system processes. To do this, type the following from the command line:

INPUT `ps -aux |grep mysql`

If mysqld is running, you will see an instance of it here.

The safe_mysqld command is the best way to start your engine. It will automatically restart itself if it goes down. You can start MySQL by using the mysqld command. This is not recommended in production environments because it does not automatically restart itself.

To stop the engine, use the mysqladmin command with the shutdown argument, as shown in the following:

INPUT
```
cd mysql
bin/mysqladmin -p shutdown
```

This will safely shut down the engine. A more drastic way of stopping the engine is to use the kill command. This is not recommended because it can cause corruption of your data.

As with most server daemons, it is recommended that you start this process when the server is started and stop it when the server is stopped. To do this, use the mysql.server script with the start argument (mysql.server start) located in the support files directory. Use this script in the rc.d directory. Refer to your brand of Linux's documentation to do this correctly.

Using MySQL with Windows

Like Linux, the MySQL server runs as a background process. To start the server on a Windows platform, double-click the mysqld.exe file in the \mysql\bin directory. This will start the process.

To stop the service, run the mysqladmin shutdown command from the DOS prompt. This will take the server process down gracefully. The more drastic, possibly harmful way is to use the Task Manager to shut the process down. This could cause data corruption and is not recommended.

It is also worth mentioning that, unlike the Linux daemon, the Windows process has a small memory leak. After time, this small leak will cause problems. The system will lock up and programs will not run. To fix this problem, reboot the machine every couple of weeks. According to the documentation, the TcX development team has fixed this problem and it will be corrected in the next release.

To have Windows NT start this process automatically, go to the Control Panel and click Services. You should see the `mysqld` service. Check it to start automatically. On Windows 95/98, you must place the `mysqld.exe` command in the Startup directory.

Using MySQL—the Command Line

Now that that you have MySQL up and running, it is time to take your database engine for a spin. The command line interface of MySQL can be daunting the first time, especially if you're used to the GUIs that the other databases in the same class of MySQL offer.

To start the command line interface in Linux or in Windows, make sure you are in the `/mysql` directory. In Windows, you must use a DOS prompt. At the command line, type the following:

```
bin/mysql -p
```

You should see the following:

OUTPUT
```
Welcome to the MySQL monitor. Commands end with ; or \g.
Your MySQL connection id is 3 to server version : 3.22.23
Type help for help.
```

After the output is displayed, you are left with an empty prompt (see Figure 2.4). This is where it can get a little scary for the first time MySQL user. For the most part, all commands to manipulate your data are entered here. A good command of the Structured Query Language (SQL) is a must to get around. This can be a bane or a blessing, depending on how you look at it.

With the command line prompt, you don't need a GUI. You may argue that it is nice to have a GUI; it makes things easier. You can, with a few clicks of the mouse, see all your tables and how they relate to each other. With a GUI, you can see permissions and active connections. You can do a lot with a GUI, but what you can't do is remotely administer your database quickly and efficiently. Most Windows administrators use PC AnyWhere or some other similar product to administer the servers under their control. Though these programs are nice, they leave a lot to be desired, especially over slow dial-up connections.

With the command prompt, these inefficiencies are no longer a problem. With a simple Telnet session, you can remotely administer you database quickly and efficiently. With a command prompt, you can create, drop, and populate a database as if you were there. It only takes a few late night calls to fix a problem to fully realize and understand the power that is afforded with this simple feature.

FIGURE 2.4

The MySQL monitor.

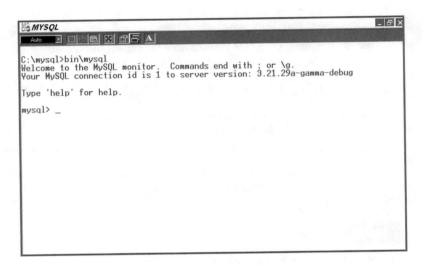

Assuming that you logged in as `root`, take a look at the existing databases in the default installation. To see what databases exist on this server, type the following:

INPUT   `show databases;`

You should see output similar to that shown in Figure 2.5.

To commit the action or SQL statement you have typed, you must end your line with either a semicolon (;) or a \g. This tells the MySQL monitor that you have finished your command and are ready to execute it. Simply pressing the Return or Enter key causes a line feed. This allows you to enter a long SQL string legibly. Another nice feature is the recall button. For Linux users, the up arrow will recall the last lines you have typed, just like the system. It uses a different history file than the operating system, so the only commands that are recalled are the commands that were typed at the MySQL prompt. For Windows users, well, we're just out of luck. There is no history recall key (not even the F3 key—the normal recall key for DOS). The recall key is extremely convenient, especially when you make an error in a long SQL query. There isn't a lot of re-typing.

FIGURE 2.5

Viewing existing databases in the MySQL monitor.

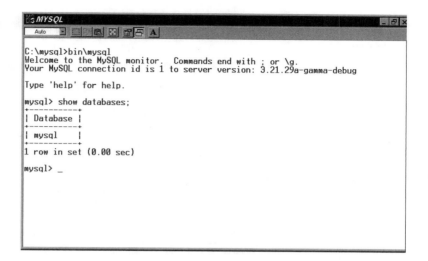

To work with a listed database, you must tell the MySQL monitor which one to use. The command is simple enough. Type the following to use the `mysql` database:

INPUT   USE mysql;

You should see output similar to that shown in Figure 2.6

To see the structure or schema of a database, issue the following command:

INPUT   SHOW TABLES FROM mysql;

The output should resemble Figure 2.7.

This simple command provides a listing of all the tables of the selected database. The following command will show a detailed listing of the columns of your database.

INPUT   SHOW COLUMNS FROM user;

Again, your output should look like Figure 2.8.

FIGURE 2.6

Results of the
USE *command.*

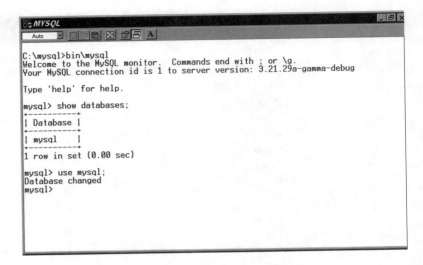

FIGURE 2.7

Viewing the structure of
a database.

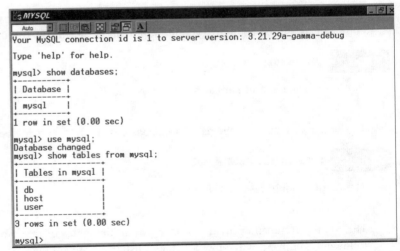

This command displays the descriptions of the fields in the database table. It shows the type, default value, null or not null, and any key fields. This is a very useful command and is used quite extensively.

As you can see, the command line is a great tool when working with your database. It may take some getting used to, but in the end, it is fast, powerful, and reliable.

FIGURE 2.8

Listing the columns of a selected database.

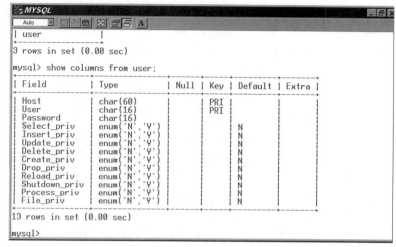

The Built-in Database

With the conclusion of your brief tour of MySQL, you probably noticed that there are already two databases within MySQL. You are probably asking yourself what these tables are and how they are used. The following section describes this built-in database.

The default database is the mysql database. This database stores all the privilege information. An explanation of how the MySQL privilege system works will be covered extensively on Day 17. For now, just know that the mysql database stores all the user, database, and host privileges. Altering or dropping any of these tables will cause problems within MySQL. It is therefore recommended that the tables within this database keep their default structure. Do not change the default types.

Summary

MySQL is a powerful DBMS. It is easy to install, in its binary form, on Windows and Linux systems. The MySQL monitor is a great tool that allows one to access a MySQL database remotely without sacrificing power or speed. Basic administration, such as changing the root password, starting and stopping the server, and displaying database information, is easy to perform. The minimal fee associated with MySQL is a small price to pay for this incredible system. It is the responsibility of the database administrator to ensure that licensing is taken care of properly so that further development of this great DBMS continues.

Q&A

Q **What do I do if I forget the MySQL** root **password?**

A First log in to the system as the same person who is running the mysqld daemon (probably root). Kill the process, using the kill command. Restart MySQL with the following arguments:

```
bin/mysqld -Skip-grant
          USE mysql;
          UPDATE user SET password = password('newpassword')
          ➡WHERE User = 'root';
          Exit
bin/mysqladmin reload
```

The next time you log in, you will use your new password.

Q **How do I change the startup options on MySQL if I use** mysql.server **to start in the** rc.d **directory?**

A mysql.server is a script that contains the mysqld command. To add options such as logging and debugging to the server daemon, you must edit this script. Using your favorite editor, open this file and place the arguments in the appropriate places.

Q **I'm a consultant providing services to a client who uses a MySQL database for a nonprofit organization. Who pays the licensing fees?**

A If you are making money using or providing services for a MySQL database, you must pay the licensing fee. Remember that the fee is relatively small and goes toward further development of this great DBMS.

Q **Where is the data stored in a MySQL database?**

A MySQL uses files to store data. These files are under the data/*databasename* directory, where *databasename* is the name of the database. There are three file types: .ISM, .FRM, and .ISD. The .FRM file contain the table schema. The .ISD is the file that actually holds the data. The .ISM file is the file that provides quick access between the two of them.

Q **Why do I have to pay for the Windows version of MySQL?**

A As stated earlier, MySQL is part of the Open Source Movement, which means that there are a lot of people working on the MySQL project from all over the world.

Most of these people do it for free. Because they are not getting paid, most of these developers use free tools, such as compilers like gcc and IDEs, to help with the development process. Unfortunately, developing for the Windows platform is a little different. To compile a program on the Windows platform, a developer must pay for a compiler, such as Visual C++ or a similar Borland compiler. These programs cost a lot of money. To develop on this platform, TcX must buy these compilers for their developers. This cost is transferred down to the user. That's why you have to pay.

Exercises

1. Using the command line, display all the data in the MySQL database.
2. Check to see if the mysqld daemon is running using two different methods.
3. Telnet to a remote site and start and stop the MySQL server.
4. Use the MySQL monitor remotely.

DAY 3

Designing Your First Database

The most important part of any database is its design. If a database is designed well, it will be a great business tool, giving you the flexibility and the information you need to run your business. Today will cover the following:

- The design process
- The different types of relationships
- Introduction to the sample database

The Design Process

A good design makes or breaks a database. To create a successful database, some thought has to be given to its design. A well-designed database will grow well. Retrieving and maintaining the information in a well-designed database is a breeze. Unfortunately, most people do not take the time to design a database. They just jump in, creating tables and fields for their current needs without planning for the future. This technique leads to a poor structure from which retrieving a single tidbit of information is like getting a tooth pulled, and scaling the poorly-constructed database to fit the needs of the company is a historic event.

Creating a database is a lot like building a house. The builders do not build a house without a plan. An architect comes up with the plan and gives it to the builder. The builder takes the plan and builds the house. The builder pays special attention to the foundation of the house, because without a strong foundation the house will fall. These same basic principles apply to building a database.

You are going to play both roles, the architect and the builder. As the architect, you will come up with the blueprint of the database. You must decide what information you are going to store and track. You must also define the relationships that exist between the tables you are going to build. This is vital to a good, solid relational database.

In the role of the database builder, you will enter the SQL statements that actually create the database. You will have to know what data types to use to store the data efficiently and correctly. This is where the foundation of the database is built. Knowing what types to use and when to use them, as well as building the proper relationships, will help create a solid foundation for your database.

To guide you along the process, I've established a series of steps to help ensure that the design process is performed correctly and thoroughly (see Figure 3.1). The first step is to define the current business process or, in some cases, invent the process. The next step is to define the business objects. After you define the objects, you define the business rules as they relate to these objects. The fourth step is to draw or lay out the database. This helps with the next step, which is to define the table relationships. After the relationships have been defined, you must define the type of data that you are going to store for each field. After all these steps have been taken and you have thoroughly reviewed your work, you can create the database.

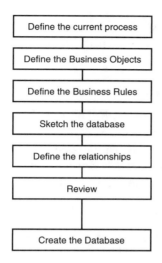

FIGURE 3.1

The database design process.

```
Define the current process
Define the Business Objects
Define the Business Rules
Sketch the database
Define the relationships
Review

Create the Database
```

3

Defining the Business Process

The first step in designing a database is to gain a working knowledge of the current business process. A business process is the way a business performs its duties to meet its goals. For example, an online bookstore might have the following business process:

1. An order is placed for a book by a customer via a Web-based order form.

2. The credit card is verified.

3. The book is deducted from the inventory and the order is placed to the shipping department.

4. The shipping department packages the product, verifies the address, and ships the package out.

In some cases, you will be updating an existing computer-based process, and in others you will be creating a computer-based process based on a paper process.

There are many different techniques to help you gain an understanding of the business process. The most helpful is to interview the people who work with the system everyday. These people should know the inner workings of the process. You may have to interview more than one person to gain a complete and total understanding of the process. How to interview and what questions to ask goes beyond the scope of this book. A really good book that takes you through the entire process is *Database Design for Mere Mortals: A Hands-On Guide to Relational Database Design* by Michael J. Hernandez (published by Addison Wesley).

It is essential that you understand this process fully. From this process, you will gain an understanding of all the objects that are involved. This builds the foundation of your database.

Defining the Business Objects

The next step in the design process is defining the business objects. The business objects are the components that make up the business process. From the previous example, the book and customer would be business objects. The business objects contain the information you want to track in your database. This is really a two-part process; The first part is to identify the object, and the second part is to create fields that describe this object.

 Note

A *business object* is a component of the business process. It is one of the cogs that makes the wheels of business turn.

These objects are usually easy to identify. Most of the time, these components contain the key information that drives the business. Sometimes they are not so easy to see. In the previous example, you could easily point out the book and the customer as definite business objects. But what about the transaction that occurs when a customer actually buys the book? The transaction contains vital information but is not easily recognized as an object. This is why a thorough understanding of the business process is necessary to build a good database.

The second part of this step is creating fields or adjectives that describe the object. Think of the things that are used or are associated with the business object. Continuing with the example, your book object could easily consist of a Title, Publisher, Author, Price, Quantity, and Copyright Date field. The Transaction object might contain a Transaction Date, Amount, Description, and Payment Method. These fields further define your object. They also happen to be the fields you want to track in your database. I find it helpful to write down all the adjectives that describe the object. Later, I eliminate unnecessary ones or add new ones that I might have missed earlier.

Defining the business objects is really the start of building your database. Later, these objects will become tables in your database, and the descriptions will become the fields in your table.

Defining the Business Rules

The third step in the design process is to establish the business rules. A business rule is a statement or series of statements that governs the way a business is run. From the previous example, a sample business rule would be "There are no negative transactions." Obviously, there could be (refunds, for example), but the person running this business might decide that this would be a rule. Another example would be "Every time an order has met the processing requirements, a shipment should occur." This type of rule helps establish the relationships that need to exist between business objects.

There are two types of rules, the *established rule* (a rule imposed by the business) and the *implied rule* (a rule that is based on common sense). For instance, using the example, an established rule would be that a customer can have more than one order. An implied rule would be that every book must have a title. This may seem silly or foolish, but it plays a major role in determining what data types to use for your fields and whether or not a field can be empty.

Note

The *established rule* is defined by the business. An *implied rule* is a rule that may not be defined by the business but is usually defined by common sense.

The best tools to use for this step are a pencil and paper. Write down every rule—whether you think it is silly or not. Have a person that is close to the process help you determine the rules. They will likely give you an insight to the rules that you may not see. Later, this list you have created will save you a ton of time during the actual creation process and will help prepare you for the next stage.

Modeling the Database

The next stage of the design process is sketching out your schema. This may seem like a waste of time at first, but I have found that things make a lot more sense when you can see them laid out in front you. I cannot count the times I have found design flaws just by doing something as simple as sketching it out.

There are many programs on the market today that will display your database. These are great, but in the first draft, I prefer to do it the old-fashioned way. That way I can erase and add things quickly and easily. After the database has been created, the diagrams that are produced by these programs are an invaluable tool when trying to create queries or becoming familiar with a database schema.

After the sketch has been completed, it is time to fill in some of the blanks. You might see some holes that need filling, or maybe now you can see that some of the descriptions you used for one of the objects fit better under another object.

After the dust settles from all the changes that you've made, it is time to start assigning data types to the fields. The types you assign, and whether the field can be null or not null, can be determined, in part, by the business rules you defined in the previous step. The types that MySQL supports are covered on Day 7, "MySQL Data Types." For now, just understand that this is the phase in the design process where data types are assigned.

When you have completed this step, you will see the basic framework for your database. The tables, as well as the columns, for the most part, will be defined. The next step will strengthen the existing structure.

Establishing Relationships

This is the last step before you create your database. Defining the relationships between tables is not always an easy task. First, you have to determine whether a relationship exists. Second, if there is a relationship, you must determine what type of relationship it is.

The easiest way to determine relationships is to look at the diagram that was created in the previous step. Take one table/object and see if it logically relates or will interact with any of the other tables/objects. For example, in the bookstore database, you have a customer, a book, and a transaction object. I would first look at the customer and ask myself if it has any relationships or interactions with the book object. In this example, it does. A customer must buy a book from your store to be a customer, so a relationship does exist. Then I would ask myself the same question, this time with the transaction object. Again, there is a relationship. When a customer purchases a book, it creates a transaction, so there is a relationship. I would then take the book object and see if it has any relationships. It has one with the customer, but it does not with the transaction object. A book will exist without a transaction. The transaction object interacts with the customer, not the book. This all may seem a little confusing at first, but, with time and experience, you will be able to establish relationships quickly and easily.

The next step in this process is to determine what type of relationship exists. There are three types of relationships in a relational database: one-to-one, one-to-many, and many-to-many.

One-to-One

In a one-to-one relationship, a record in table one must have a record in table two, and if table two has a record, a corresponding record must exist in table one. Figure 3.2 demonstrates this.

FIGURE 3.2

A one-to-one relationship.

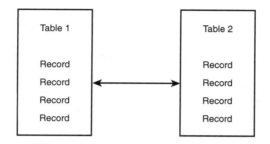

In the bookstore example, a one-to-one relationship might exist between the order and the transaction table. For every order, there must be one transaction, and every transaction must have an order. To create this relationship within the database, you must add a field that will house this relationship. The field that normally does this is called a key field. Key fields are discussed in more detail on Day 11, "MySQL Table Locks and Assorted Keys." For now, just understand that a *key field* helps define relationships, among other things.

The key field is a unique field within the table. No other record will have the same value in this field. The reason behind this is to distinguish a record from all other records in that table (see Figure 3.3).

FIGURE 3.3

Key fields in a one-to-one relationship.

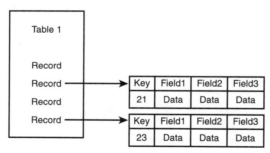

For this reason, most database designers name this field the ID field. For example, the Book table would have a Book_ID field, and the Transaction table would have a Trans_ID.

To establish your one-to-one relationship, you must designate one of the tables as the primary table and the other as the secondary table. This is generally an arbitrary decision in a one-to-one relationship. To make it easy, choose the table that will be affected first when you add a new record to the database. This primary table will contain a key field. In the example, the Order table will have an Order_ID field that is unique to this table.

The secondary table will have its own unique key field, as well as the key field from the table with which it shares a relationship. Both of the fields will be unique within the secondary table. This will create the one-to-one relationship. Figure 3.4 demonstrates this concept.

FIGURE 3.4

A one-to-one relationship in a database.

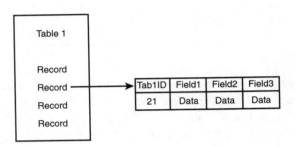

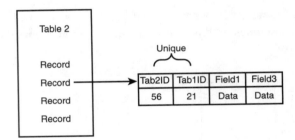

One-to-Many

A one-to-many relationship occurs when a record in table one may have many corresponding records in table 2, and table two has many records that correspond to only one record in table one (see Figure 3.5). At the bookstore, a one-to-many relationship exists between the Customer table and the Order table. One customer can have many orders, but the orders only point back to one customer. Figure 3.6 illustrates this point.

FIGURE 3.5

A one-to-many relationship.

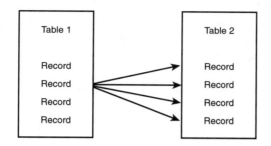

FIGURE 3.6

Here is one customer who has multiple orders.

3

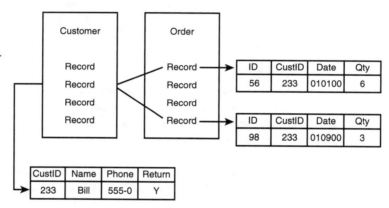

To create a one-to-many relationship inside a database is very similar to creating a one-to-one relationship. Again, it involves using keys. First, you must select a primary table. Unlike one-to-one relationships, there is a definite primary and secondary table. The primary table is the table that contains the single record, and the secondary table contains the multiple records. The primary table's key field will exist in the secondary table, but it will not be unique. The secondary table's key field will be unique, but the foreign key will not be unique. This permits you to add as many records as you want and still be able to distinguish each record individually, as well as relate them to a single record in another table. Look again at Figure 3.6, which illustrates this point.

Many-to-Many

A many-to-many relationship exists when table one has a record that has many corresponding records in table two, and table two has a record with many corresponding records in table one (see Figure 3.7).

FIGURE 3.7

A many-to-many relationship.

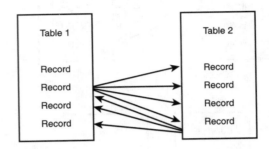

The many-to-many relationship can cause some problems. It might introduce redundant data, which breaks your rules of normalization. Normalization is covered in more detail on Day 5, "Making Your Data Normal." A many-to-many relationship is also hard to maintain. Deleting and adding new records becomes very hazardous. For example, your bookstore has many warehouses across the nation. Each warehouse stores a supply of books. There are many books that might be in a warehouse, and many warehouses might contain a particular book. So what happens if you add a new warehouse? You would have to add every book title again to your table of warehouses. It could get a little hairy. To combat this situation, you would come up with an intermediary table that would link these tables together. This would create two one-to-many relationships (see Figure 3.8). This table would consist of the primary keys of both tables. When a book is placed in a warehouse, this intermediary table would have a new record added consisting of the book's key fields and the warehouse's key fields. If you needed to know which books were in the warehouse, you could query this intermediary table to find out. At first, this might seem like it is adding another layer of complexity to the database. I can assure you it is well worth it. It is very hard to implement a many-to-many relationship without the intermediary table.

After the relationships have been identified, you should add them to your model. This will help remind you to include these relationships when you create the database. You should also add the new key fields that you have created. Remember that a key field is an identifier—it uniquely describes a row of data. It should not be null. After you have completed this process, you are ready for your next step in the design process.

FIGURE 3.8

A many-to-many relationship becomes two one-to-many relationships. This is done to ease maintenance and add flexibility, and to obey the rules of normalization.

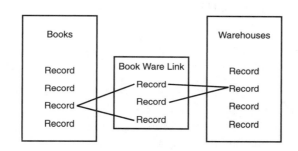

3

The Final Stage—Creating the Database

The final step of the process is actually creating the database. By now, you should have a thorough understanding of the business process, the business objects, and the business rules. You should have a visual model of your proposed database. This is extremely helpful when it is time to modify or query the database. Now is the perfect time to review everything. Go over the business process, see if anything was left out. Review the business objects to ensure that you did not miss any of the implied objects. This is the best time to add or subtract any fields or tables that might make your system better.

After the review is finished, you are ready to assign the data types to each of the fields. The MySQL data types are covered in detail on Day 7. Assigning the proper data types will help enforce the rules you have defined earlier, as well as make your database more efficient. At this time, it is also a good idea to add a key to every table. Every table should have a key field. After you have everything on paper, you can begin creating your database. Make sure you stick to your blueprint. Improvising is not recommended. It can lead to poor design, which is what you are trying to avoid.

After your database is created, you will have to establish privileges, add users, and perform countless other administrative tasks.

Sample Database—The Meet_A_Geek Database

To reinforce what you have learned, you are going to apply today's lesson to a sample project. The project's task is to create a database for an online dating service called Meet-A-Geek. Meet-A-Geek is based on an actual Web site that is using MySQL. The URL is http://www.meetageek.com. I encourage you to visit this site and see what it has to offer. You will continue to build on this project in the following lessons. Now, on with the design.

The first step is to define the business process. After interviewing the client, you might formulate the following plan:

1. A potential Romeo or Juliet comes to the site wanting to place an ad.

2. He or she is first asked to fill out a membership application. This application captures the usual personal information. It also contains a questionnaire with specific questions asking the customer's likes and dislikes.

3. After the customer has successfully completed the application, he or she is allowed to search the database for potential dates.

4. After receiving results from his or her search, a customer can send flowers, a box of chocolate, or some other gift to one of the potential dates he or she found in the database. The customer will click a hyperlink that will take him or her to your catalog of gifts.

5. After the customer has picked out his or her gift, he or she will have the opportunity to purchase this gift via the Web and ship the gift directly to the potential boyfriend or girlfriend with a custom message. The gift giver and receiver must both be members of the Web site to exchange gifts.

From this process, you can easily see some business objects. There is of course the Customer object. There is also a Products object, as well as an Orders and Transactions object.

The second part of this two-part step is to describe your objects. The client Meet-A-Geek has given you the application form for potential customers. This is an excellent starting point to help you describe a customer. Take a look at Figure 3.9.

FIGURE 3.9

Meet-A-Geek application form.

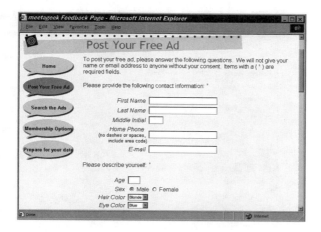

3

From this application, you can describe your Customer object as having the following traits:

- Name—first, last, and middle initial
- Email address
- Home phone number
- Age
- Gender
- Hair Color
- Eye Color
- Race

The questionnaire provides further ways to describe your customer (see Figure 3.10).

From the questionnaire, you gather the following information:

- Favorite activity
- Favorite movie
- Occupation
- Smoker (Yes or No)

After collecting this information, your Customers object would look like that shown in Figure 3.11.

FIGURE 3.10

Meet-A-Geek customer questionnaire.

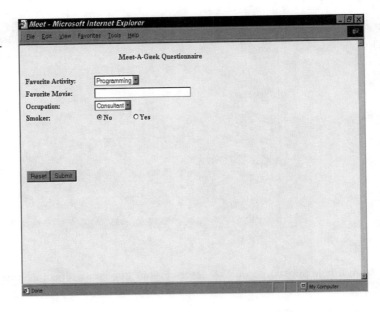

FIGURE 3.11

The Customers *object.*

The other objects will be a little harder to describe. Let's start with the `Products` object. Every product has a price and a name. It would be nice to associate a description with the product, so we'll include one here. Another field you may want to include is the manufacturer. Based on the project requirements, you probably want to include a picture of your product. The end result would look like Table 3.1.

TABLE 3.1 The `Products` Object

Products
Name
Price
Description
Manufacturer
Picture

You would perform the same process on the rest of your objects until you're satisfied with your descriptions. Keep in mind that not only are you describing the objects, you're also looking for information that would help the business accomplish its goal. For instance, you added a picture description to the `Products` table. A picture doesn't necessarily describe your object, but you know you need to have a picture of the item to display on your Web site. This is when you form that association. Take a look at the finished objects in Table 3.2 and see if you would have come up with something similar.

TABLE 3.2 The Completed Business Objects

Orders	Transactions	Shippers	Products	Customers
Order Date	Transaction Date	Name	Name	First Name
Quantity	Shipper	Location	Description	Last Name
Item	Amount Paid	Shipping Method	Price	Address
Customer	Order Number	Active	Manufacturer	City
Custom Message	Ship Date		Picture	State

TABLE 3.2   continued

Orders	Transactions	Shippers	Products	Customers
Amount Due				Zip
				Email
				Age
				Gender
				Eye Color
				Hair Color
				Favorite Activity
				Favorite Movie
				Occupation
				Smoker

We could have added more to this list but I'm going to keep it small and simple. The most important point here is not the contents but the use of the concepts. Hopefully, you will see the importance of good database design.

The next step is to define your business rules. From the analysis of the business process, you can determine some rules. You can also determine the rules from common sense and experience. From the analysis, you know that a person cannot search the database unless he or she is a member. You also know that a gift will not be shipped unless it has been ordered. This may seem quite obvious, but, as I said earlier, even the rules that may seem foolish will help with your overall design. Think of some more rules, and then look at the list of rules I have compiled.

Business rules for Meet-A-Geek:

- A customer cannot search database unless he or she is a member.
- A gift will not be shipped unless it is ordered.
- A customer must have a name and an address.
- A product must have a name and a price.
- A transaction ship date cannot be earlier than the order date.
- A customer's gender can only be male or female.
- The customer is either a smoker or not (a yes or no question).
- The amount paid is equal to the product's price times the order quantity.
- The amount paid cannot be a negative amount.

For the sake of simplicity, stop here. There are many more rules, but stick with what you
have. Now that you have defined your business process, defined and described your
business objects, and have established your business rules, you are ready to model your
database. I have developed a model of your current database. Compare Figure 3.12 to what
you have done and see if they are similar.

Defining Relationships

Let's move on to the next step, which is to define the relationships. To define the
relationships, look at the whole picture you have drawn so far. Right away, you can see a
relationship between customers and orders—a one-to-many relationship. A customer can
place many orders, but those orders all point back to the one customer. Another relationship
exists between the products and orders. This relationship is a many-to-many
relationship—one order can contain many products, and one product can be in many
orders. From what you know about many-to-many relationships, you will have to add
another table to your database. Another noticeable relationship is between orders and
transactions. For every order, there is one transaction. For every transaction, there is one
order. This is a very nice one-to-one relationship.

FIGURE 3.12

The final `Meet_A_Geek`
database model.

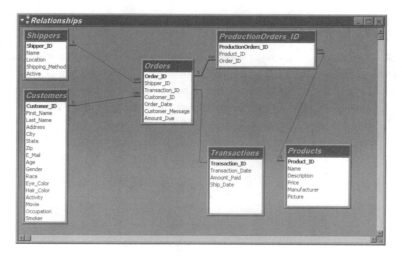

In this step, you are supposed to identify the data types that you will be using. Because you won't cover data types until Day 7, use simple types to express what should be used. Start with the Customers table.

NEW TERM In the Customers table, you have a First_Name and a Last_Name field. From your business rules, you know that these fields are required. To reflect this requirement in the database, you will make these fields NOT NULL. NULL is best explained by telling you what it is not. A NULL value is not 0. It is not an empty string, such as "". It is not a negative number. It is nothing. A field that contains absolutely no value is considered NULL. So, to prevent a field from being empty, you can require it to be NOT NULL. This forces the database to have a value in the field. Because these fields are names, and names are generally letters, you define these fields as character fields. You do the same for the Address, City, State, and Zip fields. You define the Email address field also as a character field. The Age field will be a positive-only number (ages cannot be negative). The Gender, Race, Hair_Color, and Eye_Color fields at first can be defined as character fields. On Day 7, you will learn that it would be more efficient to have these as enumeration types. For now, define them as character fields. The other fields can easily be defined as character fields, except for the Smoker field. You know from your business rules that the Smoker field can be answered with only a yes or no, so you could define this as a Boolean field. A *Boolean* type is a type that is either TRUE or FALSE.

You would perform the same process you performed on the Customers table to each of the remaining tables. Also, remember that this is the time when you will add a key field to each of the tables. After you have finished adding the keys, it is a good idea to model the database again. This will provide you with the blueprint for tomorrow's lesson, which will be to actually create the Meet-A-Geek database.

Summary

Today, you learned the importance of correct database design. A database is like a building. It requires proper planning and designing to stand the test of time. I introduced the database design process. This process is made up of six steps. If this process is followed, the database that is created will be very solid. Each step builds on the previous one. The first step is to define the business process. The next step is to define the business objects. These objects will eventually become the tables that make up the database. The descriptions of these objects will become the fields. The third step is to establish the business rules. These rules govern how the data is stored and how the business objects interact with each other. The next step is to model the database. Modeling helps solidify the structure of the database in your mind. It easily allows you to see the errors and flaws in the design and logic of the database. The final step is to identify the relationships between the objects. You learned that there are three different types of relationships: one-to-one, one-to-many, and many-to-many. You learned what each one does and how to implement this relationship inside the database. Also, today I introduced the Meet-A-Geek project. This project is based on an actual site running MySQL. You practiced the techniques and concepts you learned today on this sample project.

The concepts that were covered today can be applied to any database. They are in this book because, from my experience, there is nothing more important to a database than its design. If you are going to be a MySQL administrator or a programmer writing a program to access the data contained in a MySQL database, it is essential that you know how to design a database.

Q&A

Q **This design process seems like a waste of time. Why should I spend all this time designing when I could spend it actually creating the database?**

A The time spent carefully designing a database will be recouped tenfold when it come to the creating and maintaining of the database. If the database is not well-thought-out or designed correctly, you will spend countless hours adding fields and relationships you may have missed. Extracting the information will also take longer because databases that are hastily put together tend not to be normalized. This results in redundant data, as well as wasted disk space. So the extra hours you spend designing will pay off later.

Q   **What purpose does modeling the database serve?**

A   Modeling the database serves several functions. First, it provides a visual representation of the logic and flow of your design. This will allow you to pinpoint exactly where the flaws or weaknesses exist in your design. Second, it provides a good source of documentation for your database. The model contains all of the tables, their relationships, the fields, and field types. There is no better source of documentation than a good model.

Exercises

1. In the Meet-A-Geek project, you defined several business objects. Can you define any more objects?

2. Come up with the rest of the business rules for the Meet-A-Geek project.

DAY 4

Creating Your First Database

Creating a database is probably one of the most important, yet least used, of all the MySQL functions. There are many ways to accomplish this task in MySQL. Today, you will learn the following:

- The CREATE and DROP commands
- Using the mysqladmin utility
- Adding users to your database
- Creating the Meet-A-Geek database

The CREATE and DROP Commands

When you think of the CREATE and DROP commands, you should envision earthmoving equipment, dump trucks, and cranes, because these are the tools you use to create your database. These commands, though seldom used, are the most important. Hopefully, a lot of thought has gone into the decision making process before either of these commands is issued.

The CREATE Command

There are many different ways to create databases in MySQL. When you create a database, you usually will have the entire layout ready. Normally, you would add the tables immediately after creating the database, but, because this book is a training guide, you will take it one step at a time.

The first way to create a database in MySQL is to enter the SQL (Structured Query Language) command CREATE DATABASE>*databasename* in the MySQL monitor, where *databasename* is the name of the database you are creating. Perform the following steps to create this sample database:

The process of creating a database is the same for most operating systems. When something cannot be done in a particular operating system, I will make note of that fact.

You should have changed your root password for the MySQL database system. To use the mysqladmin command and to start the mysql monitor, you will need to enter this password. For the sake of brevity, I have left that argument (-p) off my commands.

1. Open a terminal.
2. Change the directory to the mysql directory. If you created a symbolic link, you can enter

   ```
   cd mysql
   ```

   If you did not create a symbolic link, you will have to enter the full path, as shown in the following:

   ```
   cd /usr/local/mysql
   ```

   (assuming MySQL was installed to this default directory)

> **Note**
>
> Symbolic links are generally used as shortcuts. They can take a long path name and condense it into one word, making it convenient for the user to use.

3. Ensure the `mysqld` daemon is running. To do this, enter the following:

   `bin/mysqladmin ping`

4. After you are sure the monitor is running, start the `mysql` monitor by entering the following from the command line:

   `bin/mysql`

5. At the monitor prompt, type the following:

   `CREATE DATABASE sample_db;`

Be sure to type it exactly as it appears. Remember that it is necessary to end the line with a semicolon or a \g.

Your results should be similar to those in Figure 4.1.

4

FIGURE 4.1

Results of a successful database creation.

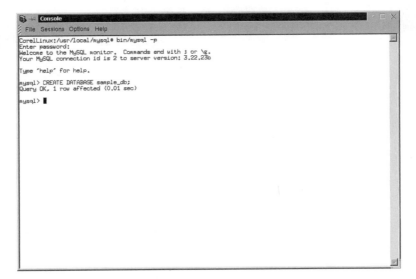

The `mysql` monitor is not case sensitive when it comes to SQL commands. Thus, the following commands are all the same:

```
Create Database sample_db;
```

```
CrEaTe DaTaBaSe sample_db;
```

```
create database sample_db;
```

These commands will all create the same database named `sample_db`. It is a popular convention to capitalize all SQL commands—this book will follow that convention. An important point to remember is that capitalization does matter when it comes to objects within your database. For example, `sample_db` is not the same as `Sample_DB`.

After your database has been successfully created, you can begin to use it. If you recall from Day 1, "What Is MySQL?," the command to do this is USE. To use the `sample_db`, type the following from the MySQL monitor prompt:

INPUT   `USE sample_db;`

The results of your command should resemble Figure 4.2.

FIGURE 4.2

Using the new database.

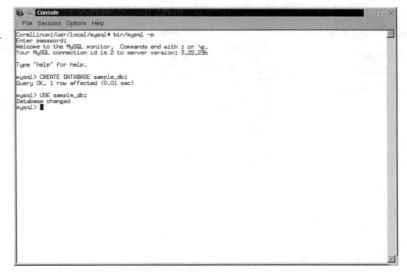

An important point to remember is that MySQL does not automatically make the database you just created the active database. You must implicitly state which database to activate with a USE statement.

The DROP Command

The DROP command is similar to the CREATE command. Where the latter creates a database, the former deletes one. A word of caution, the SQL DROP command is very unforgiving. There are no confirmation boxes asking if you are sure. The DROP command just deletes the database and all the data contained in it. This shows some of the power of SQL commands. Once a command has been committed, there is no going back. (This is not entirely true—you can get your data back from a log file.) Use extreme caution when using the DROP command.

To use the DROP command, complete the following steps:

1. Make sure that the mysqld daemon is running and that you are in the mysql directory.

2. From the command prompt, type

    `bin/mysql`

    This will start the MySQL monitor.

3. From the monitor prompt, enter the following:

    `DROP DATABASE sample_db;`

    This will delete the sample_db database and ALL the data within it.

The output from the previous steps should look similar to Figure 4.3.

4

Figure 4.3

Dropping a database.

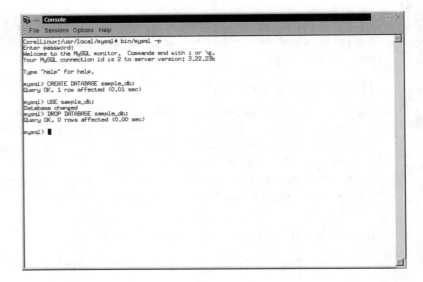

mysqladmin

Like many things in the computer world, there is more than one way to accomplish a task in MySQL. MySQL offers a powerful utility that can help with the creating and dropping of a database—mysqladmin. This utility also provides many other useful functions; you will learn about some of those functions in later lessons. For now, you will create and drop a database using this utility.

Creating a database with mysqladmin is very simple. To create the sample database do the following:

1. Make sure the mysqld daemon is running and that you are in the mysql directory.
2. Type the following command to create the sample database:

   bin/mysqladmin -p CREATE sample_db

Your output should look like Figure 4.4.

Dropping a database is just as easy. To delete the sample database, do the following:

1. Again, make sure the mysqld daemon is running and that you are in the mysql directory.
2. Enter the following command to DROP the database:

   bin/mysqladmin -p DROP sample_db

FIGURE 4.4

Creating a database using mysqladmin.

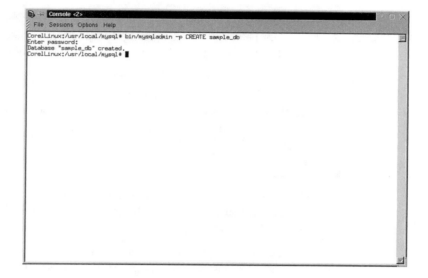

Your output should resemble that shown in Figure 4.5.

FIGURE 4.5

Dropping a database using mysqladmin.

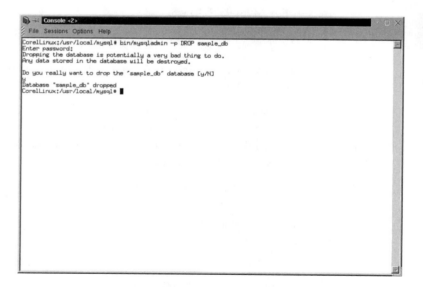

You may have noticed that when using mysqladmin, you are prompted before deleting the database. This is very helpful for the beginning database administrator, as well as the seasoned veteran. It allows one last moment of reflection before all your data is lost.

The CREATE and DROP arguments of the mysqladmin utility are not case sensitive, but the name of the database is case sensitive. Another notable point is that you must have the authority to use CREATE and DROP. As root, you have this authority, but if you are not an administrator, you will not be able to use these commands.

Adding Users

Now that you have your database up and running, you should give other users the ability to use the database. Today, you will learn how to add users; explaining permissions and user privileges are covered in more detail on Day 17, "MySQL Database Security."

To allow a user from your local machine—referred to hereafter as *localhost*—to gain access to your database, the user must exist in several places. The MySQL RDBMS contains a database named mysql. This database holds all the permissions for all MySQL databases. This database consists of the following tables:

- user   The table that holds all the names, passwords, hosts, and privileges of all the users of this MySQL RDBMS.
- db   The table that contains all the users, databases, and hostnames for this MySQL RDBMS.
- host   The table that contains all hostnames, databases, and privileges they hold for this MySQL RDBMS.

For a person to use your database, the hostname of the machine from which he or she will be connecting must exist in the host table. The user must exist in the user table, and the database must exist in the db table. Complete the following steps to give another user the ability to use your database from the local machine.

1. First, make sure the daemon is running and that you are currently in the mysql directory.

2. Add the hostname and database to the host table. To do this, you must use the MySQL monitor.

   ```
   bin/mysql -p
   ```

3. Next, you must make the mysql database the active database. To do this, type the following:

   ```
   USE mysql;
   ```

> **Note**
>
> Remember, commands are not case sensitive, but the database objects are.

4. To add the hostname/database combination to this MySQL RDBMS, you must use an SQL INSERT command. Type the following from the command line:

    ```
    INSERT INTO mysql VALUES('localhost','sample_db',
    'Y','Y','Y','Y','Y','Y','Y','Y','Y','Y');
    ```

Remember that if you do not type a semicolon or a \g, the MySQL monitor will continue your statement on the following line. This is helpful because it allows for easily readable commands, and, if you make a mistake, you can use the history key to bring it back.

Your output should look like that in Figure 4.6.

FIGURE 4.6

Adding a host to the host *table.*

The next step is to make sure you have users to add to your database. You will add a user now.

```
INSERT INTO user VALUES('localhost','TestUser',
PASSWORD('pass123'),'Y','Y','Y','Y','Y','Y','Y'
,'Y','Y','Y','Y','Y','Y','Y')
```

The PASSWORD function is an *intrinsic function*, that is, a function that can be called from within MySQL. You will learn about intrinsic functions in more detail on Day 10, "Letting MySQL Do the Work—Intrinsic Functions." The password function takes a string as an argument and encrypts it. This encrypted word is stored in the database. This prevents prying eyes from easily discovering the passwords of all your users with a simple query to the mysql database. It's best to get in the habit of adding users in this manner.

You are now ready to add your database and users to the mysql database. To do this, enter the following:

INPUT
```
INSERT INTO db VALUES('localhost','sample_db',
'TestUser','Y','Y','Y','Y','Y','Y','Y','Y','Y'
'Y')
```

Let's review what you have done. To allow a person to use the sample_db database from the local machine, several things must be in place. You will need the hostname of the computer the user will be using to connect to your database. In the example, you are going to use the same machine that has the MySQL RDBMS installed. Your machine may have a really cool name, but MySQL only requires the name 'localhost' to describe a local machine. If you were connecting to another mysql database from your machine, your machine's name would have to be in that database. The second thing that needs to be in place is a user. You can add users at any time. Because I'm assuming that you have a fresh installation, I went through the process of adding a user. After the user is added, you could go ahead and give this user permission to use your database. You did this by adding the user to the db table. The advantages of doing things this way will be covered in great detail on Day 16.

Creating the Meet_A_Geek Database

You will create the Meet_A_Geek database using the mysqladmin utility. (You will add users in a later lesson.) You will use this database as an example throughout the book, building upon it in each lesson. To create the database, do the following:

1. Make sure the daemon is active and that you are in the mysql directory.
2. To create the database, enter the following:
    ```
    bin/mysqladmin -p CREATE Meet_A_Geek
    ```

Summary

Yesterday, you learned the importance of proper designing. Today, you took the first step to bringing your design to life. You have achieved an important milestone: You created your first MySQL database. You also learned today that the developers of MySQL give you more than one option to accomplish this task. If you are a command junkie, you can use the `mysqladmin` utility, and if you are an SQL fan, you can use an SQL statement to accomplish the same thing. Either way, you are heading in the right direction to becoming a MySQL DBA.

Q&A

Q **Is there any other way to enter commands into `mysql`? The MySQL monitor can be a little cumbersome, and I have a ton of commands to enter.**

A There is another way, if you are using a UNIX machine. You can pipe a file into the `mysql` program. For example, create a file using your favorite editor (emacs, vi, or gedit). Name the file anything you want. Your commands should appear as they do within the monitor. Make sure they are terminated by a semicolon or an escaped `\g`. When you are finished, you can import the file into MySQL. Make sure the daemon is running and that you are in the `mysql` directory. Type the following:

```
cat /fullpath/filename |bin/mysql
```

This will execute all the statements within the file. This is a great way of adding data or creating a database schema. This also creates a way of storing the schema for transport or for recreating the database if you lose a disk.

Q **How many databases can one MySQL RDBMS contain?**

A Because MySQL uses the file system of the operating system, there really is no limit to the number of databases contained within a single MySQL RDBMS. The size of the database is limited by the operating system. The database tables can only be as big as the OS's file system will allow. For Linux, the maximum size is 4GB.

Exercises

1. Create and drop databases using the `mysqladmin` utility and by using the monitor.
2. Add a couple of users to the database, and try using these accounts.

DAY 5

Making Your Data Normal

When structuring a database, putting the right columns in the right tables can be a daunting task. When you finally accomplish this task, you may find out that you have logic problems within your database, especially if you come from the old world of non-relational databases where everything was contained in the same file. Using the old idea of keeping all your data together in one table in a relational databases is a bad idea. It's almost sacrilegious. A set of rules was established to help database designers. These guidelines lead to the design of truly relational databases without logic flaws. Applying these rules to your database structure is referred to as *normalizing* your data, *normalization*.

Today, you will learn

- What normalization is and the benefits it can provide
- The degrees of normalization

What Is Normalization?

Normalization is a set of rules to help database designers develop a schema that minimizes logic problems. Each rule builds on the previous rule. Normalization was adapted because the old style of putting all the data in one place, such as a file or database table, was inefficient and led to logic errors when trying to manipulate the contained data. For example, look at the `Meet_A_Geek` database. If you stored all the data in the `Customers` table, the table would look like something like the following:

```
Customers
Customer_ID
Last_Name
First_Name
Address
Product_Name1
Product_Cost1
Product_Picture1
Product_Name2
Product_Cost2
Product_Picture2
Order_Date
Order_Quantity
Shipper_Name
```

The table has been abbreviated, but it still portrays the general idea. Now, in your `Customers` table, how could you add a new customer? You would have to add a product and an order as well. What if you wanted to run a report that shows all the products you sell? You could not easily separate products from customers in a simple SQL statement. The beauty of a relational database, if designed correctly, is that you can do just that.

Normalization also makes things easier to understand. Humans tend to break things down to the lowest common denominator. We do it with almost everything—from animals to cars. We look at a big picture and make it less complex by grouping similar things together. The guidelines that normalization provides create the framework to break down the structure. In your sample database, It is easy to see that you have three distinct groups: customers, products, and orders. Following normalization guidelines, you would create your tables based on these groups.

The normalization process has a name and a set of rules for each phase of breakdown/ grouping. This all may seem a little confusing at first, but I hope you will understand the process as well as the reasons for doing it this way. Most people are happy with a spreadsheet that holds all their pertinent data. The time it takes to break down your schema by going through the normalization process is well spent. It will require less time to go through the process than it would to cut and paste your columns of data so they fit the report the boss wants.

Another advantage to normalizing your database is space consumption. A normalized database will take up less space overall than one that is not normalized. There is less repetition of data, so the actual disk space that is consumed holding your data will be much smaller.

Degrees of Normalization

There are basically three steps of normalization. They are First Normal Form (1NF), Second Normal Form (2NF) and Third Normal Form (3NF). Each form has its own set of rules. After a database conforms to a level, it is considered normalized to that form. Say, for example, that your database conforms to all the rules of the second level of normalization. It is then considered to be in Second Normal Form. Sometimes it is not always the best idea to have a database conform to the highest level of normalization. It may cause an unnecessary level of complexity that could be avoided if it were at a lower form of normalization.

5

> **Note**   There are a total of nine different rules of normalization. They are First Normal Form, Second Normal Form, Third Normal Form, Boyce-Codd Normal Form, Fourth Normal Form, Fifth Normal Form or Join-Projection Normal Form, Strong Join-Projection Normal Form, Over-Strong Join-Projection Normal Form, and Domain Key Normal Form. This book will only cover the first three forms of normalization.

First Normal Form

The rule of First Normal Form states that all repeating columns should be eliminated and put into separate tables. This is a pretty easy rule to follow. Take a look at the schema for the Customers database in Table 5.1.

TABLE 5.1   Schema for Customers Database

Customers
Customer_ID
Last_Name
First_Name
Address
Product_Name1
Product_Cost1
Product_Picture1
Product_Name2
Product_Cost2
Product_Picture2
Order_Number
Order_Date
Order_Quantity
Shipper_Name

In Table 5.1, you have several repeating columns. They mostly deal with products. So, according to the rule, you must eliminate the repeaters and give them their own table. That's easy to do. The resulting database tables are shown in Table 5.2.

TABLE 5.2   Eliminating Data Repetition in a Database

Customers	Products
Customer_ID	Product_Name
Last_Name	Product_Cost
First_Name	Product_Picture
Address	
Order_Number	
Order_Date	
Order_Quantity	
Order_Shipper	
Shipper_Name	

Now there are two tables. There still is a problem. There is no way currently to relate the data from the original table to the data in the new table. To do that, a key must be added to the second table to establish the relationship. To do this, add a primary key to the Products table called Product_ID, and add a key to Customers table that relates the Products table to the Customers table. The Product_ID field is an ideal candidate. The resulting tables resemble Table 5.3:

TABLE 5.3   First Normal Form

Customers	Products
Customer_ID	Product_ID
Product_ID	Product_Name
Last_Name	Product_Cost
First_Name	Product_Picture
Address	
Order_Number	
Order_Date	
Order_Quantity	
Shipper_Name	

5

Now, a one-to-many relationship has been established. This represents what the database will be doing in real life. The client will have many products to sell, regardless of how many customers there are to buy them. Also, a customer still needs to have ordered a product to be a customer. You are no longer obligated to add a new customer every time you add a new product to your inventory.

Bringing a database to First Normal Form solves the multiple column heading problem.
Too often, inexperienced database designers will do something similar to the non-
normalized table in today's first example. They will create many columns representing the
same data over and over again. In an electric company in the Northwest, there was a
database that tracked nuclear power plant parts. The table in their database, which
contained the part numbers, had a repeated column that numbered well into the 30s. Every
time a new item was stored for this part, they created a new column to store the
information. Obviously, this was a poorly designed database and a programmer's/
administrator's nightmare.

Normalization helps to clarify the database and break it down into smaller, more
understandable pieces. Instead of having to understand a huge, monolithic table that has
many different aspects, you only have to understand smaller, more tangible objects and the
simple relationships they share with all the other smaller objects. Needless to say, a better
understanding of how a database works leads to a better utilization of your assets.

Second Normal Form

NEW TERM   The rule of Second Normal Form states that all partial dependencies must be
eliminated and separated into their own tables. A *partial dependency* is a term to
describe data that doesn't rely on the table key to uniquely identify it. In the sample
database, the order information is in every record. It would be simpler to use just the order
number. The rest of the information could reside in its own table. After breaking out the
order information, your schema would resemble Table 5.4.

TABLE 5.4   Eliminating Partial Dependencies—Second Normal Form

Customers	Products	Orders
Customer_ID	Product_ID	Order_Number
Product_ID	Order_Date	Product_Name
Order_Number	Product_Cost	Order_Quantity
Last_Name	Product_Picture	
First_Name		
Address		
Shipper_Name		

Again, by arranging the schema in this way, you have reflected the real world in your
database. You would have to make some changes for your business rules to be applicable,
but for illustrating normalization, this is okay.

By now you should be noticing some things. The table that was once hard to read and understand is now making more sense. Relationships between the information that is going to be stored are clearer and easier to understand. Things appear to be more logical. These are some of the advantages to normalizing a database.

One of the major disadvantages of normalization is the time it takes to do. Most people are busy enough, and to spend time making sure their data is normalized when it works just fine is perceived as a waste of time. This is not so. You will spend way more time fixing a broken, non-normalized database than you would a normalized, well-designed database.

By achieving the Second Normal Form, you enjoy some of the advantages of a relational database. For example, you can now add new columns to the Customers table without affecting the Products or the Orders tables. The same applies to the other tables. Getting to this level of normalcy allows data to fall naturally into the bounds for which it was intended.

After you have reached the level of Second Normal Form, most of the logic problems are taken care of. You can insert a record without excess data in most tables. Looking closer at the Customers table, there is a Shipper_Name column. This column is not dependant on the customer. The next level of normalization will explain how to clear this up.

Third Normal Form

The rule of Third Normal Form is to eliminate and separate any data that is not a key. This column must depend on the key for its value. All values must be uniquely identified by the key. In the sample database, the Customers table contains the Shipper_Name column. The Shipper_Name is not uniquely identified by the key. You could separate this data from the current table and put it into its own table. Table 5.5 shows the resulting database schema:

TABLE 5.5   Eliminating Non-Key Data for Third Normal Form

Customers	Products	OrderMaster	OrderDetail	Shippers
Customer_ID	Product_ID	Order_Number	Order_Detail_ID	Shipper_ID
Product_ID	Product_Name	Order_Date	Order_Number	Shipper_ Name
Order_Number	Product_Cost	Order_Quantity	Order_Date	
Shipper_ID	Product_Picture		Order_Quantity	
Last_Name				
First_Name				
Address				

Now all your tables are in Third Normal Form. This provides the most flexibility and prevents any logic errors when inserting or deleting records. Each column in the table is uniquely identified by the key, and no data is repeated. This provides a clean, elegant schema that is easy to work with and easy to expand.

How Far to Take Normalization

The next decision is how far to go with normalization. Normalization is a subjective science. It is up to you to determine what needs to be broken down. If your database is just going to provide data to a single user for a simple purpose and there is little to no chance of expansion, taking your data to 3NF might be a little extreme. The rules of normalization exist as guidelines to create easily manageable tables that are flexible and efficient.

There are times when normalizing your data to the highest level doesn't make sense. For example, suppose you added another address column to your database. It is quite normal to have two lines for an address. The table schema might look like the following:

```
Customer_ID

Last_Name

First_Name

Address1

Address2
```

According to the rules that would make this table compliant with First Normal Form, the address columns would be taken out and replaced with the key for the new table. The following is the resulting schema:

```
Customer_ID     Address_ID

Last_Name       Customer_ID

First_Name      Address
```

The database is now First Normal Form compliant. Your customers can have more than one address. The problem that exists is that you have overcomplicated a simple idea because you were trying to follow the rules of normalization. In the example, the second address is totally optional. It is there just to collect information that might be used for contact information. There is really no need to break it into its own table and force the rules of normalization on it. In this instance, taking it to a form of normalcy defeats the purpose for which the data is used. It adds another layer of complexity that is not needed. A good way to determine if your normalizing is getting carried away is to look at the number of tables you have. A large number of tables may indicate that you are normalizing too much. Take a step back and look at your schema. Are you breaking things down just to follow the rules, or is it a practical breakdown. These are the things that you, the database designer, need to decide. Experience and common sense will guide you to make the right decisions. Normalizing is not an exact science; It is a subjective one.

There are six more levels of normalization that have not been discussed so far. They are Boyce-Codd Normal Form, Fourth Normal Form (4NF), Fifth Normal Form (5NF), Strong Join-Protection Normal Form, Over-Strong Join-Protection Normal Form, and Domain Key Normal Form. These forms of normalization may take things further than they need to go. They exist to make a database truly relational. They mostly deal with multiple dependencies and relational keys. If you are familiar with this level of normalization, you probably don't need this book.

Summary

Normalization is a technique used to create good logical relationships between tables in a database. It helps prevent logical errors when manipulating data. Normalization also makes adding new columns easier without disrupting the current schema and relationships.

There are several levels of normalization: First Normal Form (1NF), Second Normal Form (2NF), Third Normal Form (3NF), Boyce-Codd Normal Form, Fourth Normal Form (4NF), Fifth Normal Form (5NF), Strong Join-Protection Normal Form, Over-Strong Join-Protection Normal Form, and Domain Key Normal Form. Each new level or form brings the database closer to being truly relational. The first three forms were discussed. They provided enough normalization to meet the needs of most databases.

Going overboard with normalization can lead to an inefficient database and can make your schema too complex with which to work. A proper balance of common sense and practicality can help you decide when to normalize and when to let sleeping dogs lie.

5

Q&A

Q   **When is the best time to normalize my database?**

A   Most of the time, normalization takes place after everything gets rolling and your database is ready to move into production. This is not the best time to do it. The best time to normalize is immediately after you have designed your table and have it all diagrammed. That is when you will see some problems and will be able to more readily recognize where normalization needs to occur.

Q   **Should I bring my database to 3NF?**

A   You should only if it makes sense to do so. As shown in today's last example, sometimes it makes sense not to normalize. Normalization breaks things down to their smallest form—small equates to speed. The faster a database performs, the better off you'll be.

Exercises

1. Describe some of the benefits of normalization.
2. Identify areas that may not need to be normalized.

WEEK 1

DAY 6

Adding Tables, Columns, and Indexes to Your Database

Aside from creating the database, adding columns, tables, and indexes are the most important steps in the database creation process. Tables and their columns are what define a database. Today you will learn the following:

- How to create tables and columns
- How to edit existing columns
- What an index is and how it is used

Creating Tables

Creating tables in MySQL is a relatively easy task. Like so many other things, there is more than one way to perform this task. This chapter will cover two ways to add the tables you came up with in your design session. First, you will use the MySQL monitor. The monitor is the primary tool to use when interacting with your database. To create your first table, perform the following steps:

1. Ensure that the `mysqld` daemon is running (using `mysqladmin ping`) and that you are in the `mysql` directory. (`pwd` should return `/usr/local/mysql`, assuming you installed `mysql` in the default directory.)

2. Start the MySQL monitor by typing the following:

   bin/mysql -u root -p Meet_A_Geek

You should be prompted for a password. After you enter your password, you will enter the MySQL monitor with the `Meet_A_Geek` database as the active database (see Figure 6.1).

FIGURE 6.1

Starting MySQL with an active database.

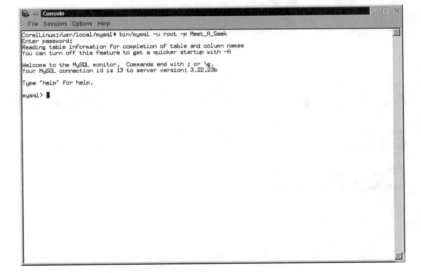

```
CorelLinux:/usr/local/mysql# bin/mysql -u root -p Meet_A_Geek
Enter password:
Reading table information for completion of table and column names
You can turn off this feature to get a quicker startup with -A

Welcome to the MySQL monitor.  Commands end with ; or \g.
Your MySQL connection id is 13 to server version: 3.22.23b

Type 'help' for help.

mysql>
```

From the blueprint that was developed on Day 3, "Designing Your First Database," you will create the Customers table. To do this, enter the following commands exactly as they appear. Remember that pressing the Enter key does not execute the command unless the command ends with a semicolon or a \g.

```
CREATE TABLE Customers (Customer_ID INT NOT NULL
PRIMARY KEY AUTO_INCREMENT, First_Name VARCHAR(20)
NOT NULL, Last_Name VARCHAR(30) NOT NULL,
Address VARCHAR(50), City VARCHAR(20),
State VARCHAR(2), Zip VARCHAR(20),
E_Mail VARCHAR(20), Age INT, Race VARCHAR(20),
Gender ENUM('M', 'F') DEFAULT 'F',
Eye_Color VARCHAR(10), Hair_Color VARCHAR(10),
Favorite_Activity ENUM('Programming', 'Eating',
'Biking', 'Running', 'None') DEFAULT 'None',
Favorite_Movie VARCHAR(50), Occupation VARCHAR(30)
, Smoker CHAR(0));
```

Your output should look like Figure 6.2.

FIGURE 6.2

Creating a new table for the Meet_A_Geek *database.*

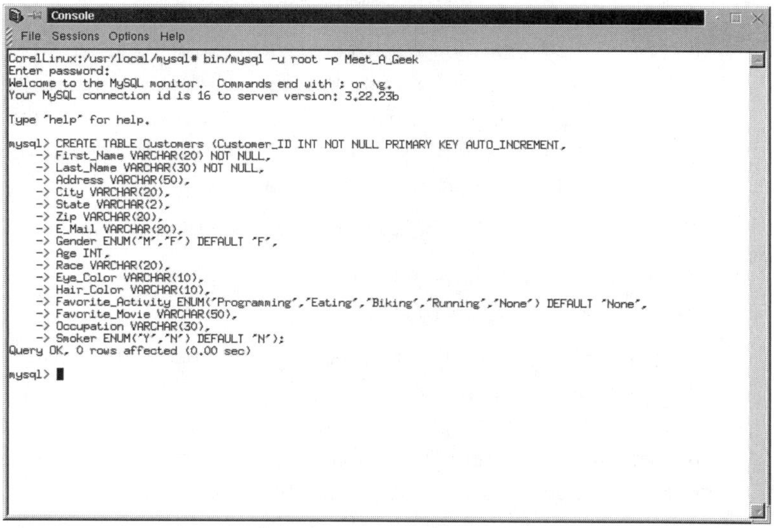

6

1. To verify your actions, type the following:
   ```
   SHOW TABLES FROM Meet_A_GEEK;
   ```

You should see a list of tables available in the Meet_A_Geek database. If you've been following along in the book, there should only be the Customers table.

2. To see a description of the table, you can type in either of the following:

    `SHOW COLUMNS FROM Customers;`

or

`DESCRIBE Customers;`

| Tip | I prefer to use the second command only because there is less to type. Both of the commands return the same information. |

After you have verified your data, you can continue to add tables to the database.

MySQL also enables you to create temporary tables. Temporary tables exist only for the current session and disappear when the connection is dropped. Temporary tables can only be seen by the connection that created them. So if I start up MySQL locally and create a temporary table, Joe, on a remote location, will not see or interact with this table in any way. Temporary tables are useful tools for storing data temporarily, or when you need to store the results of one query and compare them to the results of another. To create a temporary table, issue the following command:

`CREATE TEMPORARY TABLE tablename(columnsname data type);`

As you can see, creating a temporary table is almost like creating a true table, the only difference being the word TEMPORARY.

Another useful function that was recently introduced into MySQL is the ability to create a table based on the results of a query. This is a really nice feature because it allows you to create a table without typing in all the column data. It also allows you to easily create a copy of an existing permanent table. If you wanted to create a temporary copy of the Customers table, you would type the following statement:

`CREATE TEMPORARY TABLE SELECT * FROM Customers;`

If you wanted to create a permanent copy of the Customers table, you could omit the word TEMPORARY and insert the new tablename after the word TABLE. The following is the syntax for this action:

`CREATE TABLE tablename SELECT * FROM Customers;`

Another feature worth mentioning is the IF NOT EXISTS parameter. This statement can be used to check if a table exists before you actually create it. This is extremely helpful when you need to create a table, but don't know if it exists already. The syntax would look like the following:

```
CREATE TABLE IF NOT EXISTS tablename (columnname data type);
```

Remember that the conditional will only create the table if it doesn't exist. Otherwise it will do nothing.

> **Note**
>
> Naming conventions are a necessary evil. They can help the entire project and bring new people up to speed faster.

A word needs to be mentioned about naming conventions. Naming conventions are a good thing. They enable you to have a standardized way of naming objects that you or others may use. By naming things in a certain way, new people can become familiar with a database schema quickly and easily. For example, if you named the table that holds all your customer data Customers and the table that holds all your product data Products, it is much easier for the new guy or girl to learn than if you named the same tables Table_01 and Table_02. The decision is up to you, the database designer. You can name the tables whatever you choose. I prefer to use the following conventions:

- Tables are plural and field names are singular. The table that holds all my customer data is Customers, not Customer. It just makes sense to me. My Customers table, or any table for that matter, holds many different types of the same object. A table is not just a repository for one of my customers but a repository for all my customers. It just makes sense to make tables plural.

- The first letter of a name is always capitalized. This just follows grammar rules. It also looks neater, in my opinion.

- Compound names are separated by an underscore, and the first letter of each name is capitalized (for example, Meet_A_Geek). It may be a pain to type, but it makes things easier to read. Also, spaces and dashes are not allowed in any database object name.

- Use descriptive names and be consistent. When you create a whole bunch of tables, it's nice to know that Last_Name will always be Last_Name, no matter in which table it exists. This is especially helpful when developing programs and queries that access a lot of tables repeatedly.

6

I will use this convention set throughout this book. Feel free to use whatever makes you comfortable. The rules have been tried and tested over many databases and have proven time and again that naming conventions are nice—even if it means a few extra keystrokes.

Entering the commands from the MySQL Monitor prompt is one way to create the schema of a database. Another way to create your schema is with a script. Scripts are text files that contain all the SQL commands required to build your database. This is probably the best way to create your database, because you have the ability to recreate your database (minus the data) at any given time. It also allows for code reuse—because, generally, computer people are a lazy bunch and the less work you have to do, the better.

To start this process, open your favorite text editor. In the text editor, type the following statements:

```
CREATE DATABASE Temp;
USE DATABASE Temp;
CREATE TABLE Test_Table
        (Test_ID INT NOT NULL PRIMARY KEY AUTO_INCREMENT,
        Test_Name VARCHAR(30),
        Test_Date DATETIME,
        Test_Giver VARCHAR(30));
INSERT INTO Test_Table
        (Test_ID, Test_Name, Test_Date, Test_Giver)
        VALUES
                (NULL, 'Test','2000-01-01','Glen');
```

It is common practice to format your SQL statements in this way. I'm not saying that it is bad or good. I like it because of the readability. It takes some getting used to, but it is really clear to see. Of course, you can enter your commands in any way that you like, as long as they are in the same order and end with a semicolon.

In this script, you create a database named Temp. You then make this the active database. After that, you create a table called Test_Table. Add four columns to your table. Then add one row of data. If you were to type this into a monitor session, it would take some time. And, when you end your session, all your statements would be gone. Save this file as Temp.sql. You could use any name here, I chose this name because it is easy to identify what the script does.

Before you can use this script, there are a few things you must do. First, make sure the mysqld daemon is running. Second, ensure that you are in the mysql directory. Finally, to process the script, type the following from the command line:

```
bin/mysql -p </complete path/Temp.sql
```

You will be prompted for a password. Use the root password. You must have CREATE authority to run this script. After your file is processed, start up the monitor using Temp as the active database. Execute a SHOW TABLE command. You should see the Test_Table table. Now type in the following command:

```
SELECT * FROM Test_Table;
```

As you can see, this is a great way to execute SQL statements from a text file.

Altering Existing Tables

Now that you have created your table, what if you need to go in and change something you have done? Changing tables is just as easy as creating them, you just have to know what you want to change. The column name is very different from the table's name. Changing the column's type is different from changing a column's name. Check out the following examples to see how to alter a column's name, type, and the table's name.

Changing a Column Name

Sometimes you may need to change the name of one of your columns. Maybe you misspelled it when you created it and didn't notice until a colleague pointed it out. Or maybe your boss has a naming convention that you need to follow. Either way, changing a column name is pretty painless.

If you need to change the name of a column, do the following:

1. Make sure the mysqld daemon is running and that you are in the mysql directory.

2. Start up the MySQL monitor as you did before, using the Meet_A_Geek database as the active database.

3. To change the name of the First_Name column to FirstName in the Customers table, enter the following from the command line:

```
ALTER TABLE Customers
CHANGE First_Name FirstName VARCHAR(20);
DESCRIBE Customers;
```

You must specify the data type again, or you will get an error. I used the DESCRIBE command to verify the changes. It is not necessary to use that command after you change the table structure—I do it out of habit.

6

Changing a Column Type

Changing a column's type is similar to changing a column's name. You are going to change the Last_Name from a VARCHAR(30) to a VARCHAR(50). Follow steps 1 and 2 of the previous example (changing a column name). Then, instead of typing what is in step 3, type the following:

```
ALTER TABLE Customers
CHANGE Last_Name Last_Name VARCHAR(50);
DESCRIBE Customers;
```

Notice that you must use the column name twice. The reason behind this is that MySQL creates a temporary table to hold your changes. This allows users to continue using the database as you make changes.

Renaming a Table

To change a table's name, make sure the mysqld daemon is running and that you are in the mysql directory. After you are sure that everything is up and running, start the MySQL monitor. From the monitor's command line, type the following:

```
ALTER TABLE Customers RENAME Customer_Table;
SHOW TABLES FROM Meet_A_Geek;
```

Altering an existing table or column is pretty straightforward. A few syntactical gotchas are out there, but it is generally an easy process. The hardest part is in the design. Keep that in mind when you are planning or estimating the length of a job.

Deleting/Adding Columns and Tables

As you can see, when a table or column is created, it is not written in stone and can be changed easily. This even applies to adding columns to an existing table or deleting unwanted columns or tables. The process, again, is pretty straightforward.

Dropping Tables and Columns

To drop or delete tables or columns, make sure the mysqld process is running and that your current directory is the mysql directory. Start up the MySQL monitor with the database you need to make changes to as the active database. After you are up and running, enter the following commands:

To delete an existing table, type

```
DROP tablename;
```

Where *tablename* is the name of the table you want to delete. For example, to delete the Customers table from the Meet_A_Geek database, you would type the following command:

```
DROP Customers;
```

This will delete the entire table and all the data inside the table. Use caution when executing this command. Remember there are no warnings from the monitor. After you drop something, the only way to get it back is through a backup log.

If you need to delete a column from a table, enter the following command:

```
ALTER TABLE tablename DROP columnname;
```

Where *tablename* is the table that holds the column you want to delete, and *columnname* is the column you want to delete.

If you wanted to delete the Last_Name column of the Customers table, you would enter the following statement:

```
ALTER TABLE Customers DROP Last_Name;
```

This will delete the column and all the information that the column stored. Again, exercise caution when using this command.

Adding Columns

We have already covered adding tables to a database. You can only create and drop a table. To add a column, you have to use a variation of the ALTER TABLE command. For example, to add a column to an existing schema, execute the following statement:

```
ALTER TABLE tablename ADD columnname data type;
```

Where *tablename* is the table you need to add the column to, and *columnname* is the name of the column to be added. If you wanted to add the Last_Name column back to the Customer table, you would issue the following statement:

```
ALTER TABLE Customer ADD Last_Name VARCHAR(30);
```

This will add a column to your table. An important point to remember is that the column you add must have a default value. It cannot be a NOT NULL column. It must contain NULL or some other default value. The reason for this is fairly simple. If you add a column that is NOT NULL, how will MySQL know what value to store? It won't, so you must tell it what to store.

6

Using Indexes

An index is a structured file that facilitates data access.

What this means to you as the database designer is this: An index on the correct column will increase a query's speed considerably. An index works much like alphabetic separator folders in a file cabinet. It allows you to skip to the part of the alphabet you're looking for. For example, suppose you needed Glen Brazil's record. You could go directly to the B section without going through every single record before you get to Mr. Brazil's. This makes your searches much easier to accomplish, and you're don't waste time looking at records that are not even close to what you need.

Indexes are wonderful things, but they do have some drawbacks. Too many indexes can have an adverse effect. In the example, you went directly to the B section. What if instead of just having letter separators you separated every name. There would be a ton of separators—almost as many as the number of people you were tracking. This would slow things down instead of speeding them up. So it is best not to have too many indexes.

Another adverse effect is that adding a row to an indexed table can be a little slower than adding it to a non-indexed table. Using the example, it takes a little time to put a record in the correct place. You have to go through the separators and then place it in the right order within the file drawer. This is much slower than throwing the record anywhere in the drawer. Retrieval from indexed columns is much quicker. It is up to you to decide if the good outweighs the bad.

 Note

> Indexes speed up data access for SELECT queries, but they slow it down for INSERT, UPDATE, and DELETE queries.

Deciding Which Columns to Include in the Index

After you have decided to use indexes, you have to choose the column or columns you want to index. This can be a little tricky. You want to place an index on the column(s) that you will use most often as a filter in your queries. These are the columns mentioned after the WHERE clause. For example, in the SQL statement SELECT LAST_NAME FROM Customers WHERE Customer_ID < 10, a potential column to index would be the Customer_ID column. Remember, you are going to index the columns that you use most in your queries. If you perform a lot of queries in which you are looking for the last name of a customer, you might want to index the Last_Name column.

Indexes also work better on columns that contain unique data. That is one of the reasons that keys are usually your best choices for indexes. That could also be one of the reasons that people confuse keys and indexes. A key helps define the structure of a database, whereas an index just improves performance.

One index can be made up of one or more columns. For example, in the Meet_A_Geek project, you can have an index that is based on the Last_Name and First_Name columns. This would be useful if you use both of these as criteria in the WHERE clause of an SQL statement.

You can also have more than one index in a table. In fact, you can have up to 16 indexes in one table. You should never have to use that many indexes. If you do, take a serious look at your database design. You may have some problems. However, using a couple of indexes in a table, based on the criteria I stated previously, is not uncommon.

Creating an Index

By default, MySQL creates an index for you if you declare a column as a primary key. There is no need to create an index on this column; otherwise, you would have two indexes on the same column. The syntax for creating a column looks like the following:

```
CREATE INDEX indexname ON tablename(columnnamelist);
```

The indexname is anything you choose. Again, use something descriptive to help you remember what makes up this index. Notice the keyword ON. Make sure you don't forget this word when creating an index—you are sure to get a syntax error if you do. The keyword ON is followed by the name of the table that holds the column that is being indexed. The columnnamelist is a list of columns that will make up your index. Remember, an index can be made up of one or more columns.

You can also use the ALTER TABLE statement to add an index. For example, if you wanted to add an index to the Last_Name column of the Customers table, you would enter the following:

```
ALTER TABLE Customers ADD INDEX (IDX_Last_Name);
```

This same syntax is used if you want to add a primary key to a table that does not have one. That statement would look like the following:

```
ALTER TABLE Customers ADD PRIMARY KEY (Customer_ID);
```

Creating an index is a simple process. Indexes are one of the key factors to a fast database, and MySQL does a fantastic job with them. Remember not to overuse indexes because, as with all things, moderation is the key.

6

Deleting Indexes

Deleting an index is as simple as creating one. The syntax is the same as deleting a column or a table. You can use either of the following statements:

`DROP INDEX indexname ON tablename;`

or

`ALTER TABLE tablename DROP INDEX indexname;`

They both produce the same effect. Be aware that if you drop a column that makes up an index, that index may be dropped too. If one column of a multi-column index is dropped, only the dropped column will be deleted from the index. If all the columns that make up an index are dropped, the entire index is dropped as well.

If you need to drop a `PRIMARY KEY`, use the following syntax:

`ALTER TABLE tablename DROP PRIMARY KEY;`

Remember that a table can only have one primary key. If you decide that a different column is better suited as a primary key, you must drop the original one first.

Summary

You covered a lot of material today. You learned about the various types of tables that MySQL has to offer, and you learned how to `CREATE`, `ALTER`, and `DROP` these tables. You also learned about the importance of indexes and how they can speed up your database access. You read about the importance of naming conventions and how they can assist you and your colleagues in maintaining and using your database. Most importantly, you learned how to implement the blueprint from the design phase.

Q&A

Q   **I like the idea of temporary tables. What I don't like is that they are invisible to everyone else. Is there a way to make a temporary table viewable by everyone?**

A   There definitely is a way. MySQL provides a temporary table, called a `HEAP` table, that is available to everyone who makes a connection to the server. This table disappears when the server shuts down. This table exists solely in memory and is very fast. However, it has some limitations. Text and blobs cannot be used.

They would take up too many resources and would slow things down. All the data types must be of a fixed length. This, too, is to help conserve resources and speed things up. Also, indexes cannot have NULL values and can only be used in equal-to and not-equal-to comparisons. To create a table like this, you would use the following syntax:

```
CREATE TABLE tablename (columenames columntypes) TYPE=HEAP;
```

You can also convert an existing table to a HEAP table, but remember that the table will be dropped automatically when the server shuts down. The syntax to do this looks like the following:

```
ALTER TABLE tablename TYPE=HEAP;
```

Q I have used other RDBMS like Sybase and SQL Server 7. They have table constraints and checks. Does MySQL have these as well?

A The quick answer is no. However, MySQL can parse this syntax, so you can easily import existing schemas into MySQL without a lot of hassle.

Q How much data can a MySQL table hold??

A This question can be a little tricky to answer. The maximum size of a MySQL table is based on the file system of the OS (operating system). MySQL stores its data in files whose size depends entirely on the operating system. On 64-bit systems, they are so large that there really is no limitation. On a Windows NT platform, you can expect around a 2TB limit.

Exercises

1. Create the schema for the Meet_A_Geek project. Base the schema on the blueprint that was developed on Day 3.

2. Create indexes for the Meet_A_Geek database. Use the lessons you learned here to determine which columns should be indexed.

6

DAY 7

MySQL Data Types

As with most Relational Database Management Systems (RDBMS), MySQL has specific column data types. Today you will learn the following:

- MySQL string and character types
- MySQL numeric types
- Enumerations and sets
- Column modifiers

The MySQL Supported Types

NEW TERM MySQL has various data types that support different functions. A *data type* is the type of data a column will store. There can be many different data types inside a table, but each column will store its own specific type of information. You can think of a data type as a kind of definition for a column. A column defined as an integer column will only hold numeric information, whereas a column defined as a CHAR(10) will hold up to 10 alphanumeric characters. These definitions are the key to a quick and efficient database.

There are basically three groups of data formats. The first is obviously numeric. Numeric data is data that is a positive or negative number such as 4 or -50. Numeric data can also be in hexadecimal format (2ee250cc), scientific notation (2X10^23), or a decimal. The second type is character or string format. This format can consist of letters and numbers, whole words, addresses, phone numbers, and generally anything you have to put quotations around. The final type I like to call miscellaneous. It consists of everything that doesn't quite fit into either of the other two categories. Some, like dates and times, could be alphanumeric but are stored like numbers. There are also some more types that fit this description, and these will be covered in more detail later in this chapter.

As well as data types, MySQL also provides column modifiers. These modifiers further help define a column's attributes. They are AUTO_INCREMENT, UNSIGNED, PRIMARY KEY, NULL, NOT NULL, and BINARY. A more detailed discussion of column modifiers takes place following the coverage of the basic data types.

Numeric Types

Numeric types are meant to store numbers only. You cannot put a letter or a string of characters into a column that is defined as numeric. The numeric type can be broken down further. For example, there are whole numbers and fractions as well as negative and positive values. Different numeric types take up a different amount of space in memory. The reason is that each type has a different range.

You may be asking yourself, why all the complexity? A number is a number. Well yes, but you don't store numbers in memory like a computer does. Suppose you were going shopping for some candy at a bulk candy store. You know, the kind that stores all of their candy in huge drums. Assume that the candy costs $1 a pound. It's Halloween time and you want to get about three pounds of candy out of this drum that probably contains about 50 pounds. You go up to the counter to pay for your candy and the clerk says that you owe $50 dollars. You're shocked, you only needed 3 pounds which should have cost $3 dollars, but you're paying for the whole barrel instead. The reason you should only pay for $3 dollars worth of candy is the same reason why there are different ranges of numeric types. You only have to pay for what you are going to use. If there were no ranges, you would have to use 8 bytes of storage space every time you used a number because MySQL doesn't know what number you are going to store. To save on memory (see Table 7.1), there are ranges.

The names of the different MySQL types and their subsequent ranges are listed in table 7.2.

TABLE 7.1 Numeric Storage

Type Name	Memory Space
TINYINT	1 byte
SMALLINT	2 bytes
MEDIUMINT	3 bytes
INT	4 bytes
BIGINT	8 bytes
FLOAT(M,D)	4 bytes
DOUBLE(M,D)	8 bytes
DECIMAL(M,D)	The value of M + 2 bytes

If the column is numeric and declared UNSIGNED, the range doubles for the given type. For example, if you declare a column that is an UNSIGNED TINYINT, the range of this column is from 0 to 255. By declaring a column as UNSIGNED, you cause that column to have only positive values. The size of the type you are using, (TINYINT, BIGINT) does not change, only the range of values it can hold.

TABLE 7.2 Numeric Types

Type Name	Value Range	Unsigned
TINYINT	-128 to 127	0-255
SMALLINT	-32768 to 32767	0-65535
MEDIUMINT	-8388608 to 8388607	0-16777215
INT	-2147483648 to 2147483647	0-4294967295
BIGINT	-9223372036854775808 to 9223372036854775807	0-18446744073709550615
FLOAT(M,D)	Varies depending on values	
DOUBLE(M,D)	Varies depending on values	
DECIMAL(M,D)	Varies depending on values	

7

FLOATs, DOUBLEs, and DECIMALs are numeric types that can hold fractions. The other types cannot. MySQL gives you the ability to limit the number of digits to the right of the decimal point. For example, suppose you had a value that was 5.6876. You are going to store it in a column whose type is FLOAT(4,2). The number would be stored as 5.69. MySQL rounds the decimal to the number of digits right of the decimal point that is declared in the FLOAT. This same number, declared as a FLOAT(4,3), would be stored and displayed as 5.688. These numbers are the display widths. The first number is the number of digits for the whole number and the second is the number of digits for the fraction. The display values are not required for any numeric data types.

Remember that as a general rule, MySQL processes numeric data faster than other data types. So if you want quicker queries, use a numeric data type with which to search. Also, numeric indexes are generally quicker than character-based indexes.

Nothing is more important than choosing the correct type for the right job. When you define your columns, be sure you take into account the largest possible value you will need. If you don't do this, you could have some serious problems later, especially if your database is used for critical business applications. The following are some general rules for choosing the right numeric types:

- Use numeric types for primary keys. It makes being unique easy, as well as providing a faster way of retrieving data,
- Use DECIMAL for really large numbers. DECIMALs are stored differently and have not limits.
- Use DECIMAL for currency to retain accuracy.
- Use the right data type. Using a number that is larger than needed may lead to inefficiencies later.

When you are transferring data from one database to another, make sure you pick the right types to represent the data. A wrong type could spell disaster. MySQL replaces values that are outside the range with the maximum number for that data type. For example, suppose you had an unsigned TINYINT, whose max range is 255. Suppose you tried to insert a value that was 1000. MySQL would store only the value 255. As you can see, this would be devastating on a mission-critical business application.

The AUTO_INCREMENT, UNSIGNED, and ZEROFILL modifiers can only be used with numeric data types. They perform operations that can only be done with numbers. You have already learned about the UNSIGNED modifier (it makes columns positive—no negative numbers), read on to learn about the other modifiers.

AUTO_INCREMENT

The `AUTO_INCREMENT` column modifier automatically increases the value of a column by adding 1 to the current maximum value. It provides a counter that is useful for creating unique values. The value of a newly inserted row into an `AUTO_INCREMENT` column starts at 1 and increases by 1 for every record that is inserted into the table. For example, you create a table with an `AUTO_INCREMENT` column. You add a row of data. The `AUTO_INCREMENT` column's value is 1. You insert another record, and the value is now 2. You delete the very first row of data, and insert another record. What do you think the value of the new row is? If you guessed 3, you're right. Now you delete the newly inserted row—the row whose `AUTO_INCREMENT` value was 3, and immediately insert another row. What do you think the value of the row is? If you guessed 4, you're right. The `AUTO_INCREMENT` column does not reuse the maximum value if you delete it. It will not reuse a value that is not the maximum value.

To take advantage of the `AUTO_INCREMENT` feature, you must use a NULL, 0, or a blank space in the field that is `AUTO_INCREMENT`ed when inserting a new row. For example, the following will take advantage of the `AUTO_INCREMENT` function:

```
CREATE TABLE Test (Auto_Test int NOT NULL AUTO_INCREMENT);
INSERT INTO Test (Auto_Test) values(NULL);
INSERT INTO TEST (Auto_Test) values(0);
INSERT INTO Test (Auto_Test) values();
```

You can also include a number. If the number already exists, you will get an error. If it doesn't, it will be inserted. If the value is the highest value in the column, the next value that is inserted will be one more than the current value. So, if you wanted to have an `AUTO_INCREMENT` modified column that begins will 9000, your very first record would have to be 9000 and all subsequent records would be incremented by one. You can explicitly declare a starting point by using the following syntax:

```
CREATE TABLE Test
(Test_ID INT NOT NULL AUTO_INCREMENT
AUTO_INCREMENT = 9000,
Another_Column INT)
```

It doesn't matter where you place the `AUTO_INCREMENT`= *nnnn* in your creation syntax. There can be only one `AUTO_INCREMENT` column in a table—MySQL is smart enough to know where to use this value.

7

To get the most recently added sequence number, use the LAST_INSERT_ID() function. This function will return the sequence number that was added last by you. What this means is that this function will return the last record you inserted, not anyone else who may be using the database. This is a handy function to have. Even if someone else inserts a record immediately after you do, this function will return the last record that you inserted. This function is tied to your session, so if you lose your session after you just inserted a record and you try to call this function after you reconnect, you will get a zero, because, according to MySQL, you haven't inserted anything.

One final thing to know about the AUTO_INCREMENT modifier is that it does not start over. So if you reach the maximum value of the data type you picked, you will receive an error. For example, if you select a TINYINT for an AUTO_INCREMENT column, the maximum value it can have is 255. After the 255th record has been added and you try to add another one, MySQL is going to produce an error. To avoid this, use the INT type. You should have more than enough numbers.

The AUTO_INCREMENT modifier only works on integer numbers. FLOATs, DOUBLEs, and DECIMALs cannot be used in an AUTO_INCREMENT column.

ZEROFILL

The ZEROFILL column modifier is used to display leading zeros of a number based on the display width. As mentioned earlier, all numeric types have an optional display width. For example, if you declare an INT(8) ZEROFILL, and the value you're storing is 23, it will be displayed as 00000023. This feature is useful when you need to display the value in its entirety, in sequence numbers or when you need to display information to the user, for example.

Character or String Data Types

The other major group of data types are strings or character types. A string is a set of characters. A string type can store data like Kentucky or 922 Westbrook Ln. Pretty much any value can be stored in a string data type. Again, size is a factor when determining which string type you are going to use. The maximum size and storage specifications are listed in Table 7.3. The storage that is needed for each type is determined by the length of the string.

TABLE 7.3   String Types

Type Name	Max Size	Storage Space
CHAR(X)	255 bytes	X bytes
VARCHAR(X)	255 bytes	X+1 byte
TINYTEXT	255 bytes	X+1 byte
TINYBLOB	255 bytes	X+2 bytes
TEXT	65535 bytes	X+2 bytes
BLOB	65535 bytes	X+2 bytes
MEDIUMTEXT	1.6MB	X+3 bytes
MEDIUMBLOB	1.6MB	X+3 bytes
LONGTEXT	4.2GB	X+4 bytes
LONGBLOB	4.2GB	X+4 bytes

CHAR and VARCHAR

Out of all these types, the VARCHAR and CHAR types are the most used by far. The difference between them is that the VARCHAR is a variable length and the CHAR is not. CHAR types are used for fixed lengths. You would use this type when your values do not change much. If you declare a CHAR(10), all values stored in this column will be 10 bytes long, even if it is only 3 characters long. MySQL pads this value to fit the size that was declared. The VARCHAR type does the opposite. If you declare a VARCHAR(10) and store a value that is only 3 characters long, the total amount of storage space is 4 bytes (the length plus one).

The advantage of using CHAR types is that tables that contain these fixed values are processed faster that those that are made up of VARCHAR types. The disadvantage of using CHAR types is wasted space. The choice is up to you.

As a rule, VARCHAR and CHAR types cannot be used in the same table. MySQL automatically changes the types to VARCHAR when you mix the two. The only exception is when you use small VARCHAR types. Small is defined as values of 4 or less. If you do, MySQL converts them to CHAR types. For example, if you have declared the following:

```
CREATE TABLE Test (Fixed_Col CHAR(5), Var_Col VARCHAR(15))
```

MySQL will automatically convert the Fixed_Col column to a variable length. Conversely, if you declare the following:

```
CREATE TABLE Test (Var_Col1 VARCHAR(3))
```

MySQL will convert the column to a CHAR.

7

TEXT and BLOB

TEXT and BLOB (Binary Large Object) are variable length types that can store large amounts of data. You would use these types when you want to store images, sounds, or large amounts of text, such as Web pages or documents. These types are also good for storing values that vary in size from row-to-row. For example, if you were storing the contents of a <TEXTAREA> from a comments section on a Web page, a TEXT type would be a good choice. The person filling out the form might write a book, while the next person might not write anything. You can think of a TEXT or BLOB as a very large VARCHAR.

The advantage of using a BLOB or TEXT type over other types is the ability to store vast amounts of data. You can store entire files with this type. The disadvantage is that they are processed more slowly, and they take up large amounts of space, which could lead to fragmentation.

In the newest version of MySQL, you can place an index on these types. However, it is not recommended because of the degradation in your database's performance. Indexes on these types can slow things down considerably. TEXT and BLOB types are very large and do not make good candidates for indexes.

Miscellaneous Types

There are basically three miscellaneous types; ENUM, SET, and DATE/TIME types. These are lumped all together here because they do not quite fit in with the previous two types. I will cover the SET and ENUM types today. Day 16, "MySQL and Time," includes information about the DATE/TIME types. That's the day you will learn about all the MySQL date and time features.

ENUM Type

The ENUM type is an enumerated list. Meaning, that this column can only store one of the values that are declared in the given list. The ENUM column can contain only one of these values. The syntax for declaring an ENUM type is as follows:

```
CREATE TABLE Test(
    Return ENUM('Y','N') DEFAULT 'N',
    Size ENUM('S','M','L','XL','XXL'),
    Color ENUM('Black','Red','White')
)
```

You may have up to 65,535 items in your enumerated list. ENUM types make a good choice for combo boxes on Web pages or anywhere where a person must choose from a list of values. Remember, an ENUM type must either contain a value from the list or NULL. If you try to insert a value that is not in the list, a blank value will inserted.

SET Type

The SET type is very similar to the ENUM type. The SET type, like the ENUM type, stores a list of values. The difference is that in a SET type, you can choose more than one option to store. A SET type can contain up to 64 items. SET types are a good choice for options on a Web page where a user can select more then one value. The syntax for creating a SET type looks like the following:

```
CREATE Table Test(
    Advertiser SET('Web Page','Television','Newspaper')
)
```

The column created from this statement would be able to hold the following values:

```
"Web Page"
"Television,Newspaper"
" "
```

When you insert a record into a SET column, you insert the values using one set of quotation marks with a comma separating the values. For example, to insert a record containing two values from the previous example's table, the syntax would look like the following:

```
INSERT INTO Test (Advertiser) values('Web Page, Television')
```

For this reason, never use a SET value that contains a comma because it will definitely mess things up for you.

The reason the SET and ENUM values are grouped into miscellaneous types is because they look and act like strings, but MySQL stores them as numbers. For this reason, they are processed more efficiently than a regular string. They also can be manipulated using numeric operations. For example, you can use the number that MySQL uses to retrieve the values stored in the table. Look at the following example:

```
SELECT * FROM Test WHERE Advertiser = 1
```

This statement will return all values from Test where the Advertiser equals one Web page. To see the values that MySQL uses, you can use the following statement:

```
SELECT Advertiser, Advertiser +0 FROM Test
```

7

The SET and ENUM types are very useful column types and should be considered when designing your database. Remember that ENUM types allow only one choice from the list, and SET types allow more than one choice.

Additional Column Modifiers

MySQL has several key words that modify how a column acts. For example, you have already learned about the AUTO_INCREMENT, UNSIGNED, and ZEROFILL modifiers and how they affect the column in which they are used. Some modifiers only apply to certain type columns. Look at table 7.4 to see what modifiers are available for what type.

TABLE 7.4   Column Modifiers

Modifier Name	Applicable Types
AUTO_INCREMENT	All INT Types
BINARY	CHAR, VARCHAR
DEFAULT	All, except BLOB, TEXT
NOT NULL	All Types
NULL	All Types
PRIMARY KEY	All Types
UNIQUE	All Types
UNSIGNED	Numeric Types
ZEROFILL	Numeric Types

The BINARY modifier causes the values stored in these types to treated as binary strings, making them case sensitive. When you sort or compare these strings, they will also take case into consideration. By default, VARCHAR and CHAR types are not stored as binary.

The DEFAULT modifier allows you to specify the value of a column if one does not exist. The MySQL default value is NULL for all types except ENUM. MySQL uses the first value of the enumerated list as the default. For SET types, MySQL uses the empty string for the default. To specify a DEFAULT value, use the following syntax:

```
CREATE TABLE Test(State char(2) NOT NULL DEFAULT "KY")
```

This will make all records that have a NULL or an empty string value in the State column have the default value, which is "KY".

The NULL and NOT NULL modifiers specify whether a column must have some sort of value in it. For example, if a column is defined as NOT NULL, a value must be placed in that column. Remember that NULL is absolutely no value whatsoever. An empty string (""), even though it looks like it is nothing, is NOT NULL. Using NULL and NOT NULL can force required constraints on the data that is being stored. Review Day 3, "Designing Your First Database," for more information.

The PRIMARY KEY is actually an index that must contain unique values. It cannot be NULL. Every table should have a key, and MySQL allows you to easily create an index by declaring this key as your PRIMARY KEY.

> **Tip**
>
> Even though MySQL does not require you to have them, keys are an essential tool for database performance. Keys are covered extensively on Day 11, "MySQL Table Locks and Assorted Keys."

The UNIQUE modifier enforces the rule that all data within the declared column must be unique. If you try to insert a value that is not unique, an error will be generated.

Summary

As you can see, there are many different kinds of data types. Each type has its own characteristics. It is up to you, the database designer, to associate the correct types with the type of data that you are going to store. This is not always an easy job. But remember this, if you make a wrong choice, you can always change the type with an ALTER TABLE statement.

Today, you learned about all the various types. You learned about numeric types and their ranges, and you also learned about string types. You discovered that there were two groups of string types—variable and fixed length. You learned the advantages and disadvantages of both of these. You also looked at the SET and ENUM types, and saw the difference between these two types and how they were better than ordinary string types. Finally, you read about some of the column modifiers and how they affect the column in which they are used.

7

Q&A

Q   **I want to sort the values of my ENUM and SET columns. How do I do this?**

A   The sort order depends on the order in which the values were inserted. ENUM and SET types are not case sensitive. The value that is inserted reverts to the value that you used when you created the ENUM or SET. For example, if you declared an ENUM with the values "BLACK", "GREEN", "RED", and inserted a row with the value red, it would be converted and stored as "RED".

Q   **I want to store images in my database. What is the best way to do this?**

A   There have been great debates in the discussion groups about this. One argument against storing images or large files within MySQL is that MySQL uses the file system to store its data. Why not let the file system also store the image files and just store the path to the image? That way you don't have to worry about fragmentation inside your database. The problem with this is that if you are operating remotely, you must find some other way of getting the file over to the remote system. There are both pros and cons to both sides of this argument. I will cover how to do this both ways when we get into Interfaces on Days 12-15.

Exercises

1.   Using the knowledge you have gained here, go back and redefine all the column values of the Meet_A_Geek project.

2.   Practice inserting rows into a table using the SET and ENUM column types.

WEEK 1

In Review

At the end of this week, you should feel pretty comfortable working with the MySQL monitor. You also should have a firm understanding of database design. Additionally, you should know how to create a relational database with the proper data types.

1

2

3

4

5

6

7

WEEK 2

At a Glance

You should feel really comfortable working inside MySQL. There are no GUIs to learn—just simple commands. You should also have created a database. You will build on this sample database through each of these lessons.

Where You're Going

This week keeps up the fast pace by introducing you to the various ways to use MySQL. This week also builds on your first week by working with the database you created.

In this week's lessons, the focus is on how to use the database. The week will begin by teaching you how to populate your database with existing data or by transferring data from one database to another. Day 9 covers the SQL programming language. In this lesson, you'll learn how to "talk" to your database. Day 10, "Letting MySQL Do the Work—Intrinsic Functions," you'll learn about the functions that MySQL can perform. Day 11 introduces you to MySQL table locks and assorted keys. The week ends with a series of chapters—Day 12, "How to Get to the Data—Database Interfaces," Day 13, "How to Use MyODBC," and Day 14, "The Perl Database Interfac"—that deal with building programmatic interfaces in your MySQL database.

Again, a lot of information is going to be presented to you. Spend some time looking at the examples and doing the exercises and everything will become clear to you.

DAY 8

Populating the Database

Now that you have designed and created your database, you're ready to put some data into it. You could enter all your data from the command line, but that could be a little tedious, not to mention a waste of time. MySQL offers many ways of importing and exporting data. Let's face it, the most important part of a database is the data, and MySQL has provided many tools for helping with the movement of data in and out of the database.

There are many ways to populate your database. There are also many tools available to help you. The CD-ROM contains some of these third-party tools. Today, you will learn

- Some techniques to import data
- How to import data from a Microsoft Access database
- How to export data from a MySQL database

Methods of Importing Data

There are many reasons to learn how to import data from one database to another. One reason may be because you have outgrown your current database. You need to change database products, but you don't want to loose all the data you have collected over the years. Another reason may be because you don't want to enter in all your data through the command line. This can be a very boring and time-consuming process and can be very error prone. A final reason could be that you are synchronizing your database with another database. The data needs to be transferred, but the databases do not share the same file formats. These are valid reasons for you to understand the many different ways MySQL can aid you in the importation of data.

There are many different ways to import data from an existing database to another database. The most common way of doing it is the Bulk Copy Protocol (BCP). It is an extremely fast way of importing text-based data into an existing data structure. Many databases on the market use this protocol, namely Microsoft SQL Server and Sybase Adaptive Server.

Another common way to import data is through a file conversion process. A file that is written in one format in one database is converted to another format for the new database. You can see this in action when you try to import data into MS Access. The import tool lets you select a file type. After you have selected your file type, it is automatically converted to fit into the new MS Access type. Old Dbase files are converted in this way as well.

Yet another way is to export the data from one database into a format that the other database can read. Comma-delimited files are a prime example. One database exports all of its data into a comma-delimited text file, and the other database reads it in. This is similar to the way BCP works but on a more rudimentary level.

The newest way to transfer data (that's really what we're talking about here) is with Extensible Markup Language (XML). It's a language that resembles Hypertext Markup Language (HTML) but is more robust. It allows programmers to create their own mark up tags, giving developers more freedom than HTML. It offers a way to transfer data across networks easily and reliably. New releases of all the major databases are incorporating this new technology in some way. (For more information on XML, read *Sams Teach Yourself XML in 21 Days*) The developers of MySQL believe that parsing in any way should be done on a level other than the database level. This makes sense. It allows the database to be free of overhead, making it faster and giving the power of choice to the programmer. Programmers are not limited in which format they must output their data—they can simply parse what ever goes in or out of their databases with their own programs.

8

As you can see, there are many different ways of importing data into a database. How you do it is up to you. There are also many helpful tools available. Fortunately, MySQL includes some of them.

MySQL Import Tools

MySQL has a utility that is made specifically for loading data into a table. It is somewhat crude, but very effective. This utility is the `mysqlimport` tool. It resides in the `mysql/bin` directory. It is a command-line utility that takes two parameters plus a number of options. This tool will take a text file and import it into the database and table that you specify. For example, if you wanted to load a file with data into the `Customers` table, you would use the `mysqlimport` command in the following way:

```
bin/mysqlimport Meet_A_Geek Customers.txt
```

This command takes the contents of the text file and loads them into the table specified by the filename up to the first period. In this example, the data in the text file would go into the `Customers` table. If your file had a name like `Cus.to.mer.txt`, the data from this file would go into the `Cus` table. That's why this tool is a little crude, but it does get the job done. Another point worth mentioning is that if the table does not exist or if the data in the file does not match up with that in the table's columns, an error would occur. The data must match in type and in number—just as with an `INSERT` statement. In the previous example, if the table that was receiving the data had `Customer_ID int`, `Last_Name varchar(25)`, `First_Name(15)` columns, and your file had `"I"`, `1`, `"Stan"`, `"Behm"` comma-delimited values, an error would occur. The data does not match in type—the first value in the data file (`"I"`) does not match the data type for that column, which is an integer. The second problem is that the data file contains more entries than the table has columns. To prevent these kinds of mishaps, ensure that everything is correct before trying to insert your data.

`mysqlimport` Options

As mentioned earlier, the `mysqlimport` utility can also take many options. Table 8.1 shows a list of options and what they do.

TABLE 8.1 `mysqlimport` Options

Option	Action Performed
-d or --delete	This option will delete all the existing data in the table before importing the new data.
-f or --force	This option will force `mysqlimport` to continue inserting data, regardless of any errors it may encounter.

TABLE 8.1 continued

Option	Action Performed
-i or --ignore	Causes mysqlimport to skip or ignore rows that share the same unique number. The data from the import file will be ignored.
-L or -local	This option forces mysqlimport to use a file on your local machine, not the MySQL server. This is handy if you want to use a file locally and import it remotely. It is a little slower, but you don't have to FTP it and then run the mysqlimport command.
-l or -lock-tables	This option locks each table before any data is inserted. A good option to use if you are importing a large amount of data on a busy server.
-r or -replace	This option is the opposite of the -I option. It will replace the field in the table that shares the same unique value.
--fields-enclosed-by=char	This specifies what character encloses the data in your file. For example, a lot of products enclose data with quotation marks. You could specify that to the import utility with this option. By default, the mysqlimport utility assumes that there are no enclosing characters.
--fields-escaped-by=char	This option tells the mysqlimport utility what character is the escape character for special characters. Characters that may need to be escaped are the backslash (\) and the newline character (\n). The default is no escape character.
--fields-optionally-terminated-by=char	This option states that data can be enclosed by a special character. Otherwise, it works just like the command of the same name.
--fields-terminated-by=char	This option specifies what character separates the values from one another. In a comma-delimited file, it would be the comma. The mysqlimport utility defaults to the tab character.
--lines-terminated-by=str	This option specifies what ends a line of data. By default, mysqlimport assumes the newline character. A string could be used instead of a single character—a newline and a carriage return, for example.

The mysqlimport command also has the common options, such as -v for version and -p for password.

Importing a Comma-Delimited File

Now, assume that you need to import a comma-delimited text file that you generated from a spread sheet program. Each column of data is separated by a comma and enclosed in quotation marks, as shown in the following:

```
"1", "ORD89876", "1 Dozen Roses", "19991226"
```

Some of the data in the file came from the database and may or may not have been updated. This task must be accomplished by the end of the day on the production system. Your job is to import this data into the `Orders` table in the `Meet_A_Geek` database. You would use the following command:

```
bin/mysqlimport -prl -fields-enclosed-by="
-fields-terminated-by=, Meet_A_Geek Orders.txt
```

This command may look a little bit intimidating, but once you get into it, it's pretty simple. The first part, `bin/mysqlimport`, basically tells the OS what command you want to run. The p option was used because you have learned how to secure your database and must now authenticate yourself before you make any structural changes. The r option is used because you want to replace any records that have the same unique key. You're doing this because you were told that the spreadsheet may or may not have been updated in this scenario. You must assume that your spreadsheet is the most current data, and you want to replace any data in the database with the current data. The l option is used because you want to lock the table while you are inserting records. This prevents a user from selecting or changing any data while you are updating the table. You will learn more about locks on Day 11, "MySQL Table Locks and Assorted Keys." The next couple of options describe the data that is held in your import file. You are telling `mysqlimport` that your data is enclosed by quotation marks and that the fields are separated by commas. Finally, you tell `mysqlimport` what database to use, as well as the table into which to `INSERT` the data. Remember, `mysqlimport` gets the name of the table from the filename. It assumes that everything to the left of the first period is fair game for the table name, so make sure your filename matches your table name.

Import with Batching

Another way MySQL can import data is through batching. Batching is a method of running the `mysql` program passively rather than interactively, as you do with the MySQL monitor, although you still use the same command. To do this, you redirect a file to the `mysql` program. Sound a little confusing? It's not. In fact, it's quite simple.

To do this, you need a text file that contains the same text you would type into the MySQL monitor. For example, suppose that you wanted to `INSERT` some data. You could create a text file that had the following text:

```
USE Meet_A_Geek;
INSERT INTO Customers (Customer_ID, Last_Name)
VALUES(NULL, "Block");
INSERT INTO Customers (Customer_ID, Last_Name)
VALUES(NULL, "Newton");
```

```
INSERT INTO Customers (Customer_ID, Last_Name)
VALUES(NULL, "Simmons");
```

Notice that these commands are syntactically correct—SQL statements are covered in more detail tomorrow—and end in a semicolon, just as they would if you were to type this into the MySQL monitor. The next part is where you will actually import this data into MySQL. Before you can do that, though, the `mysqld` daemon must be running and you must be in the `mysql` directory. Type the following at the command line:

```
bin/mysql -p < /home/mark/New_Data.sql
```

 Note

Daemon is a UNIX term, which equates, for the most part, with Windows NT services.

You will be prompted for a password, and then the file will be routed into the `mysql` program. `mysql` will process every line as if you had typed it into the monitor. This is an extremely fast and effective way of processing SQL statements. As long as your statements are correct, they will be processed.

The `USE` statement is required because the default database was not stated. You could have stated the database and left the `USE` out. It's used here to show you how many commands you could type into the monitor program can be used in a file.

Now you may be asking yourself, "Why in the world would I want to type all those SQL statements into a file and then run them through the program? That seems like a lot of work." Well, you're probably right. But what if you had a log that generated all these commands for you? Now that would be pretty cool, huh? Most databases generate a log of events that occurred in the database. Most of these logs contain the raw SQL commands that were used. So, if you couldn't export the data from your current database to use in your new MySQL database, you could use that log and the batch processing feature of MySQL to import your data easily and quickly. Sure beats typing.

LOAD DATA INFILE

There is one last way of importing data into a MySQL database. It is quite similar to the `mysqlimport` utility, but this method can be run from the MySQL monitor command line. This means that it can also be run from any of the applications that you write using the APIs. That way, you could import data through your application if you wanted.

To begin this process, the `mysqld` daemon must be running and you must be in the `mysql` directory. Start the MySQL monitor. In case you have forgotten, type the following from the command line:

```
bin/mysql -p
```

You will be prompted for a password. After you have successfully started the monitor, type the following command to use the `Meet_A_Geek` database.

```
USE Meet_A_Geek;
```

The monitor will tell you that the database has changed. From the command line, type the following commands:

```
LOAD DATA INFILE "/home/mark/data.sql"
INTO TABLE Orders;
```

Basically, this will take the contents of the `data.sql` file and import it into the `Orders` table, just as with the `mysqlimport` utility. This statement, like the utility, also has some optional arguments. For example, if the file that you needed to import resided on your personal computer and the database server was in another building, you could run the following command:

```
LOAD DATA LOCAL INFILE "C:\MyDocs\SQL.txt"
INTO TABLE Orders;
```

This would take the file's contents and import them into the `Orders` table. No need to transfer the file, MySQL will do it for you.

You can also set the priority of the `INSERT`. If you marked this as a `LOW_PRIORITY`, MySQL would wait until there is no one else reading the table before it `INSERT`s the data. That command would look like the following:

```
LOAD DATA LOW_PRIORITY INFILE "/home/mark/data.sql"
INTO TABLE Orders;
```

You can also specify whether or not you want to `REPLACE` or `IGNORE` items with duplicate key values, much like you could with the `mysqlimport` utility. To `REPLACE` duplicate values, use the following syntax:

```
LOAD DATA LOW_PRIORITY INFILE "/home/mark/data.sql"
REPLACE INTO TABLE Orders;
```

It looks kind of awkward, but that's where the keyword needs to go for the parser to understand what you want.

The next couple of options describe the layout of the file. These same options are available in the `mysqlimport` utility. They just look a little different in this context. First, the keyword FIELDS is used. If this word is used, the MySQL parser expects to see at least one of the following:

- TERMINATED BY *character*
- ENCLOSED BY *character*
- ESCAPED BY *character*

These keywords and their arguments are used in the same way as the `mysqlimport` options. The TERMINATED BY phrase describes what separates the fields in the file. By default, it is the tab character (\t). The ENCLOSED BY phrase describes the encompassing characters. If the fields are enclosed with quotation marks, you would specify that they are using this command. Finally, the ESCAPED BY phrase describes the escape character. By default, it is the backslash character (\). Using the previous example from the `mysqlimport` utility, that same file would be imported the following way using the LOAD DATA INFILE statement:

```
LOAD DATA INFILE "/home/mark/Orders.txt "REPLACE
INTO TABLE Orders
FIELDS
TERMINATED BY ','
ENCLOSED BY '"';
```

One feature that is available in the LOAD DATA INFILE statement that is not in the `mysqlimport` utility is the ability to name specific columns into which to put the data. This is really important if you have a partial import of the data. For example, you are upgrading from Access to MySQL and, in the process, you have added columns to the MySQL database to accommodate some additional requirements. The data that you have in your existing database is still usable but, because the columns don't match in number any more, you can't use the import utility anymore. However, LOAD DATA INFILE can come to your rescue. The following shows how to LOAD DATA into the column that you want:

```
LOAD DATA INFILE "/home/Order.txt"
INTO TABLE Orders
(Order_Number, Order_Date, Customer_ID);
```

As you can see, you can specify as many columns as you want. The column names are also enclosed in parentheses and separated by commas. If you forget either one, MySQL will complain.

Importing Data from Microsoft Access

The next step is to put what you've learned into action. You are going to import data from a Microsoft Access database. There are several third-party tools out there to accomplish this, but you are going to do it the old fashioned way—through hard work and ingenuity.

There are several ways to accomplish this. The easiest way is to create a Data Source Name (DSN) and use ODBC. This is not always the best way. Sometimes, you might need to add a couple of steps to save you time in the long run.

The first way to import data into MySQL from Access is to set up a DSN. Before you can do this, though, you need to install the Open Database Connectivity (ODBC) driver. This is a technology designed by Microsoft to create an environment where data can be shared or dispersed easily between applications without regard to the source of that data. ODBC acts as a layer between any application and any database. It acts as an interpreter from application to database and from database to application. The actual software that acts as the interpreter for the database is called a *driver*. Each database has its own driver.

The ODBC interface and DSN will be covered on Day 13, "How to Use MyODBC." Today, you'll learn how to do it by exporting data into text files and bringing those files into MySQL. This is not the preferred way, but there may be times when you're not able to install an ODBC driver on a machine and use a DSN to point to a MySQL database. It is at that time when doing it this way will be a good experience to have under your belt.

The next section assumes that you have access to Microsoft Access. If you do not, read the section anyway. There are plenty of screen shots to help you understand the techniques that are involved in moving data from one database to another.

To begin, you need a database that has tables you can export. You will find the Northwind sample database on the CD-ROM included with this book. You will export files from this database to your MySQL database.

1. Open the database. You should see all the database objects—tables, queries, reports, and forms (see Figure 8.1).

2. You are going to use the Orders and Customers tables. Open the Orders table; you will see that the dates are stored in dd-mm-yyyy format. This can be a problem when importing data into MySQL. MySQL dates are stored in yyyy-mm-dd. The easiest way to change this is in the Access database. Switch into Design mode and change the format of the dates to match that of MySQL.

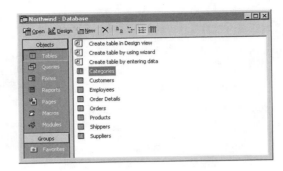

3. You are going to try to export the Orders table to the table with the same name in the MySQL database, but you notice some problems. The NorthWind Orders table is not as normalized and you table is. This is going to require you to do some manipulation to fit your database.

4. The plan is to create a query that will export the data you want to a comma-delimited text file. To do this, click the Queries icon on the left side of the database objects window (see Figure 8.2).

5. You are going to design a query that pulls the data you need to fill the columns in your table. From the query window, click New. The New Query dialog box will open. Click Design View.

6. The Show Table window will appear. Select the tables that contain the data you need here. You need to select the Customers and Orders tables. The Orders table contains the customer name, not the Customer_ID, so you need to pull both tables into your query.

8

7. After you have selected the tables, you need to select the fields to display in your query. Looking at your selection, you can see some of the fields that are in the Meet_A_Geek database, but not all of them. This means that you will have to use the LOAD DATA INFILE command instead of the mysqlimport utility because you have already created your table in the MySQL database. Select the following fields:

   • Select the Customer_ID from the Customers table.

   • Select the Order_ID, Order_Date, Required_Date, and Ship_Date from the Orders table. You should end up with something similar to Figure 8.3.

FIGURE 8.3

The query selection.

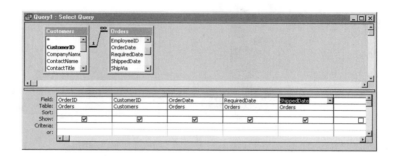

8. After you have selected the fields, run the query. You can do this by clicking the exclamation point on the toolbar. Your screen should look similar to Figure 8.4.

FIGURE 8.4

The query results.

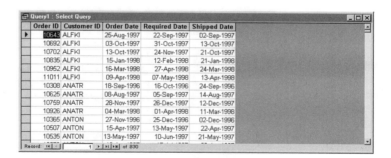

9. Save the query as **OrdersImport**. After you have saved the query, right-click the query's name. A pop-up menu should appear. Scroll down to Export on the menu and left-click.

10. You should now see the Export Query dialog box (see Figure 8.5). The filename should default to the name of the query—OrdersImport. Underneath the filename are your export choices. For now, choose the Text File option and click the Save button.

FIGURE 8.5

The Export Query dialog box.

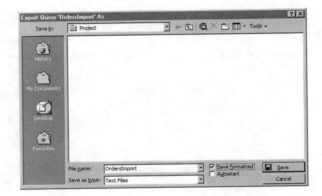

11. The Export Text Wizard will automatically start (see Figure 8.6.). The Wizard helps you format your file. Remember, you want a file where the fields are separated by commas and text fields are enclosed by quotation marks. Make sure the Delimited option is checked, and then click Next.

FIGURE 8.6

The Export Text Wizard.

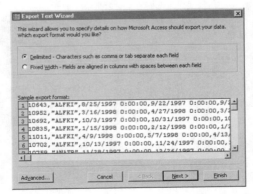

8

12. The next screen (shown in Figure 8.7) lets you choose which character you want as your delimiter. By default, it is the comma. Also by default, the text identifier is the quotation mark. Make sure that these options are selected and click Next.

FIGURE 8.7

Choose your delimiter.

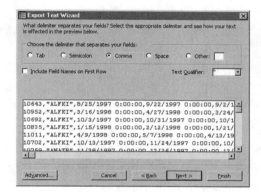

13. The final pane of the Wizard (see Figure 8.8) is the file location. Enter the path where you want to save this file and then click Finish. Barring any unforeseen problems, your file should be created in the directory you specified.

FIGURE 8.8

Choosing the path and filename.

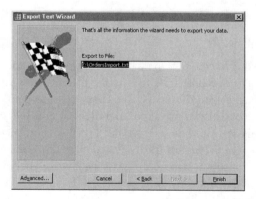

14. You should now have a comma-delimited text file of the data from your query. To double check, navigate to the directory where you have saved the file. Double-click the filename and the file should open. You should see something similar to Figure 8.9.

FIGURE 8.9

The finished import file.

Now that you have your import file, the battle is half over (or half started, depending on your point of view). The second part is to load the data into the MySQL server. This is a pretty simple and straightforward process. The first step is to gain access to the MySQL server. You can do this one of two ways: you can use a Graphical User Interface (GUI) or a Telnet session. For this session, You will use the Telnet session because this will give you the most practice. Because the import file is located on your machine and not your MySQL server (I'm assuming you are using two different machines), you will import the file using the LOAD DATA LOCAL INFILE statement. If your MySQL server and personal machine are one in the same, you can still follow along. You won't have use Telnet, and you won't have to use the LOCAL option in your LOAD DATA statement. Everything else should be the same.

1. Open a Telnet session. The easiest way to do this is from a DOS prompt or command line. Click Start, Run, and then type the following on the command line:

    telnet 10.1.1.50 *(use the name or IP of the machine that is running MySQL)*

8

This should start a Telnet session connecting you to your MySQL machine (see Figure 8.10).

FIGURE **8.10**

A Telnet session.

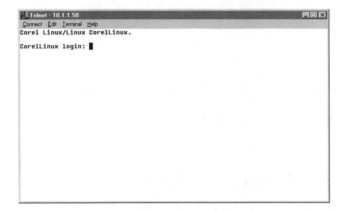

2. Enter your UNIX/Linux username and password. After you get to a command line, change to the `mysql` directory and start the MySQL Monitor.

    ```
    cd /usr/local/mysql
    bin/mysql -p Meet_A_Geek
    ```

    This command will start you in the `Meet_A_Geek` database after you correctly enter the `root` password.

3. After the MySQL monitor is started, issue the following command:

    ```
    DESCRIBE Orders;
    ```

    If you created the database from the CD-ROM, the output should be similar to that shown in Figure 8.11.

4. The next step is where you actually import the data into the database. Enter the following statement at the command line

    ```
    LOAD DATA LOCAL INFILE "E:\\OrdersImport.txt"
    NTO TABLE Orders
    FIELDS
    TERMINATED BY ','
    (Order_ID, Customer_ID, Order_Date, Required_Date, Ship_Date);
    ```

    This should bring all your data in successfully.

Figure **8.11**

Output from DESCRIBE
Orders.

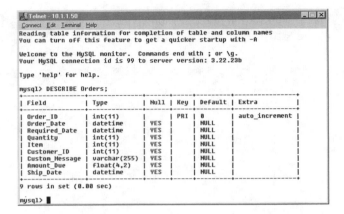

```
Telnet - 10.1.1.50                                              _□×
Connect  Edit  Terminal  Help
Reading table information for completion of table and column names
You can turn off this feature to get a quicker startup with -A

Welcome to the MySQL monitor.  Commands end with ; or \g.
Your MySQL connection id is 99 to server version: 3.22.23b

Type 'help' for help.

mysql> DESCRIBE Orders;
+----------------+--------------+------+-----+---------+----------------+
| Field          | Type         | Null | Key | Default | Extra          |
+----------------+--------------+------+-----+---------+----------------+
| Order_ID       | int(11)      |      | PRI | 0       | auto_increment |
| Order_Date     | datetime     | YES  |     | NULL    |                |
| Required_Date  | datetime     | YES  |     | NULL    |                |
| Quantity       | int(11)      | YES  |     | NULL    |                |
| Item           | int(11)      | YES  |     | NULL    |                |
| Customer_ID    | int(11)      | YES  |     | NULL    |                |
| Custom_Message | varchar(255) | YES  |     | NULL    |                |
| Amount_Due     | float(4,2)   | YES  |     | NULL    |                |
| Ship_Date      | datetime     | YES  |     | NULL    |                |
+----------------+--------------+------+-----+---------+----------------+
9 rows in set (0.00 sec)

mysql> █
```

Database Transfer Tools

As you can see, MySQL has many built-in tools to help transfer data from one database to another. MySQL is also very accepting. Even though it may not use certain features other databases have, such as FOREIGN KEYS, MySQL will not generate an error if it comes across these while importing data. This is because MySQL developers wanted it to be extremely flexible when migrating. To accomplish this, they had to allow for these anomalies.

Because MySQL is from the realm of open source, many people have contributed programs or other useful tools to help work with MySQL. Some of these are GUI interfaces, import wizards, and API wrappers. These tools, along with the ones you can create, are valuable assets to any MySQL DBA.

The MySQL Web site and the CD-ROM that comes with this book have some very useful tools. Explore them and put them to use. There is a very helpful Access export tool called exportsql.txt. It takes the schema and the data from the database and exports them to a text file. The sister script, importsql, does the same thing in reverse, taking a MySQL database and converting it to Access.

Methods of Exporting Data

You can see that MySQL has a rich set of importing utilities. But this is only half of a data transfer. The other half is pulling data out of MySQL. There are a number of reasons for exporting data.

One important reason is for backing up your database. The price of data is always high, and it pays to take care of it. Regular backups can help prevent the loss of precious data. Day 19, "Administrating MySQL," covers the back up process completely. For now, know that backing up your data is one reason for exporting it.

Another reason you may want to export your data is to share it. In the ever growing world of information technology, sharing data is becoming more and more common. For example, Macmillan USA maintains a huge database of potential books. This database is shared among the book stores so they know what books will be published soon. Hospitals are moving closer and closer to a paperless medical record that will follow you where ever you go. The world is getting smaller, and information is being shared more and more and every year.

There are a number of different ways to export data. They are all very similar to importing data, because, after all, it is all just a matter of perspective. Data that is being exported from one database is the same data that is considered an import on the other end. Instead of discussing the various ways other databases export data, you'll learn how MySQL does it.

Working with `mysqldump`

The `mysqldump` utility is a lot like its counterpart, the `mysql` import utility. It shares some of the common options, but this utility does a little more. It takes the entire database and dumps it into a single text file. This file contains all the SQL commands needed to recreate your database. It takes the schema and converts it to the proper DDL syntax (CREATE statements), and it takes all the data and creates INSERT statements out of them. This utility reverse engineers your database. Because everything is contained in a text file, it can all be imported back into MySQL with one simple batch process and the proper SQL syntax. This is incredibly easy and fast. There is no headache at all.

So, if you wanted to dump the entire contents of the Meet_A_Geek database into one file, you would use the following command:

```
bin/mysqldump -p Meet_A_Geek > MeetAGeek_Dump_File.txt
```

This utility also allows you to specify a table you want to dump. If you only wanted to dump the entire contents of the Orders table in the Meet_A_Geek database into a single file, you would use the following command:

```
bin/mysqldump -p Meet_A_Geek Orders >MeetAGeek_Orders.txt
```

This utility is so flexible that it allows a WHERE clause to select only the records you want dumped into the file. To do this, your command would look like the following:

```
bin/mysqldump -p
-where="Order_ID > 2000"Meet_A_Geek Orders > Special_Dump.txt
```

The `mysqldump` utility has a variety of options. They are all explained in Table 8.2.

TABLE 8.2 `mysqldump` Options

Option	Action Performed
--add-drop-table	This option will cause the `mysqldump` utility to add a DROP TABLE IF EXISTS statement before every table. This will ensure an error-free import back into a MySQL database. DROP TABLE IF EXISTS causes MySQL to check and see if the table exists; if it does, it is dropped.
--add-locks	This option causes the utility to wrap the INSERT statements with a LOCK TABLE and UNLOCK TABLE statement. This prevents users from doing anything to the table while these records are being reintroduced to the database.
-c or -complete_insert	This option causes the utility to name each column in the INSERT statement. This can be useful when exporting this data to another database.
--delayed-insert	This option causes the utility to use the DELAYED option in the INSERT commands.
-F or -flush-logs	This option will flush the MySQL server log files before executing the dump.
-f or -force	This option causes the utility to continue dumping, even if errors occur.
--full	This option causes the utility to add additional information to the CREATE TABLE statements. These are the optional statements that were covered on Day 4, "Creating Your First Database."
-l or -lock-tables	This option causes the server to lock the tables that are being dumped.
-t or -no-create-info	This option will prevent the utility from writing any CREATE TABLE statements. This can be handy if you only want the data and not the DDL.
-d or -no-data	This option prevents the utility from writing any INSERT statements. You would use this option if all you want is the DDL.
--opt	This option turns on all the options that will speed up the dumping process and create a faster reload file.
-q or -quick	This option prevents MySQL from reading the entire dump into memory and then executing the dump. Instead, it will write to the file as soon as it reads it.

TABLE 8.2   continued

Option	Action Performed
-T*path* or -tab = *path*	This option will create two files. One file will contain the DDL or table creation statements and the other will contain the data. The DDL file is named table_name.sql and the data file is named table_name.txt. The path argument is the directory where you want these files created. This directory must already exist. To use this command, you must have FILE privileges.
-w "*WHERE Clause*" or -where= "*Where clause*"	As mentioned before, you can use this option to filter the data that will be in the export file.

mysqlimport, like its counterpart, also has file formatting options. You have seen them before, but they are listed again in Table 8.3:

TABLE 8.3   mysqlimport Options

Option	Action Performed
--fields-enclosed-by=*char*	This specifies what character encloses the data in your file. For example, a lot of products enclose data with quotation marks. You could specify that to the import utility with this option. By default, the mysqlimport utility assumes that there are no enclosing characters.
--fields-escaped-by=*char*	This option tells mysqlimport what character is the escape character for special characters. Characters that may need to be escaped are the back slash (\) and the newline character (\n). The default is no escape character.
--fields-optionally-terminated-by=*char*	This option tells that the data may be enclosed by a special character. Otherwise it works just like the command of the same name.
--fields-terminated-by=*char*	This option specifies what character separates the values from one another. In a comma-delimited file, it would be the comma. The mysqlimport utility defaults to the tab character.
--lines-terminated-by=*string*	This option specifies what ends a line of data. By default, mysqlimport assumes the newline character. A string could be used instead of a single character, a new line and a carriage return, for example.

Suppose that you need to create a file for the accountants to use in a spreadsheet. Management wants to see all the orders for this year. They are bean counters and are not really interested in the DDL. They also need the file comma-delimited because it's easy to import into Excel that way. To complete this task, you could use the following statement:

INPUT
```
bin/mysqldump -p
-where "Order_Date >='2000-01-01'"
-tab = /home/mark -no-create-info -fields-terminated-by=, Meet_A_Geek
➥Orders
```

This will produce the wanted results.

SELECT INTO OUTFILE

If the mysqldump utility isn't cool enough, MySQL also has a counterpart to the LOAD DATA INFILE command. It is the SELECT INTO OUTFILE command. These commands have a lot in common. For starters, they pretty much share all the same options. The only major difference is that one command imports the data and one command exports the data.

To demonstrate how to use this command, you are going to perform the same operation you did previously with the mysqldump utility. To do that, perform the following steps:

1. Make sure the mysqld daemon is running and you are in the mysql directory.
    ```
    cd /usr/local/mysql
    bin/mysqladmin ping
    ```

2. Start the MySQL monitor program.
    ```
    bin/mysql -p Meet_A_Geek
    ```

    This command will start the Meet_A_Geek database as the active database. Of course, you will be prompted for the password.

3. From the command line, type the following command:
    ```
    SELECT * INTO OUTFILE '/home/mark/Orders.txt'
    FIELDS
    TERMINATED BY = ','
    FROM Orders
    WHERE Order_Date >= '2000-01-01'
    ```

After you press Return, your file will be created. This statement is just like a regular SELECT statement except that instead of the output going to the screen, it is redirected to the file that you have named. This means that you can do advanced queries using JOINs and multiple tables. This feature can also be used as a report generator. For example, you could combine some of the methods discussed in this chapter to produce some very interesting reports. Try one:

1. Create a text file called **Report_G.rpt** in the mysql directory and enter in the following lines:

8

```
USE Meet_A_Geek;
INSERT INTO Customers (Customer_ID, Last_Name, First_Name)
VALUES (NULL, "Kinnard", "Vicky");
INSERT INTO Customers (Customer_ID, Last_Name, First_Name)
VALUES (NULL, "Kinnard", "Steven");
INSERT INTO Customers (Customer_ID, Last_Name, First_Name)
VALUES (NULL, "Brown", "Sam");
SELECT Last_Name INTO OUTFILE '/home/mark/Report.rpt'
FROM Customers
WHERE Customer_ID > 1;
```

2. Next, make sure the mysql daemon is running and you are in the mysql directory.

3. Enter the following command:

    ```
    bin/mysql < Report_G.rpt
    ```

4. Check the file that you named as the out file. It should have all the last names of the customers you have entered in the Customers table.

As you can see, you can combine the import/export methods you learned today to help generate reports.

Summary

Today, you have learned why databases need to export and import data. Information is like a river, it is always moving, flowing from one source to the next. Along the way, it can carry important pieces of information that may need to be shared.

MySQL has many utilities to import as well as export data. You learned how to use the mysqlimport utility to bring in data in all different types of formats. You also learned how to use its MySQL monitor counterpart—the LOAD DATA INFILE statement. You learned that this statement can be used by the various APIs to programmatically LOAD DATA into the database, and you learned about the mysql command's ability to process a file with the redirection symbol.

You then applied your new-found knowledge by converting an Access table into a text file and importing that file into MySQL. You saw how sometimes the data needed to be massaged before it would be accepted by MySQL.

You also read about some of the various shareware utilities that exist to help make DBA's lives easier.

You learned about the many different ways MySQL can export data. You learned about the `mysqldump` command, and how this utility could reverse-engineer your database, from the schema to the actual stored records. Finally, you learned about the `SELECT.......INTO OUTFILE` statement. You saw how this statement can be used to generate some very complex reports that are formatted to various specifications.

Hopefully, you learned how data can be easily moved into and out of MySQL today.

Q&A

Q **What can I do with the contents of a `mysqldump` file?**

A This file is a complete replica of your database in SQL format. You can do a lot of things with this data. You could re-create your database in Microsoft SQL Server or Sybase by simply cutting and pasting the contents of the file. You could also restore your database by using the dump file and the batching ability of the `mysql` program. For example, to reload your database from the output of a `mysqldump` command, you would use the following syntax:

```
bin/mysql < file_name_of_dump_file
```

This would totally restore your database.

Q **Am I limited to exporting the data in text format?**

A Don't think of it as being limited; think of it as being limitless. The developers at TcX believe that parsing the data into various formats is a job that doesn't belong on the server level. They believe it should be up to the programmer and the application to format the data. They have provided a means to export the data in the simplest manner. After you get the data, it is up to you to do what you want with it. This is the same for importing the data. You write the front-end that gets the data—all you have to do is produce a text file for MySQL. Pretty easy stuff.

Exercises

1. Use the `mysqlimport` command, with the proper options, to complete the following task:

   You need to import a spreadsheet from the shipping department. The shipping department gives you its worksheet to import into the database that keeps track of all the orders that have been shipped. The fields are separated by forward slashes, and the data is enclosed by single quotes. Everything that is on the sheet is new data, no old data has been updated. Import the file.

8

2. Use the `mysqldump` command properly in the following scenario:

   The boss wants to give a report to the accountants based on the `Orders` table. The accountants need the quantity and price of every item that was ordered to figure out commissions. They do not need the DDL, but they do need the report comma-delimited. Create the report.

WEEK 2

DAY 9

Querying the Database

Defining the structure of a database is only the first part of a RDBMS. The real power and usefulness of a database is in the way it is manipulated. MySQL uses the Structured Query Language to do this.

Today, you will learn

- What Structured Query Language (SQL) is and its history.
- SQL basics—SELECT, UPDATE, INSERT, DELETE
- How to use joins
- Aggregate functions

What Is SQL and Where Did It Come From?

There have been many books written on SQL (Sams *SQL Unleashed, 2nd Edition*, is a great place to start). My goal here is to give you a working knowledge of the language and its syntax—enough to let you do most of the things you are going to do with a database. I have found that the SQL language is very easy to learn—it was built that way. The difficult part is actually using it in a productive manner. This can only be learned by experience.

The Structured Query Language or SQL—pronounced either as "Ess Que El" or "Sequel"—was developed by IBM in the mid 1970s. It was developed for the logical manipulation of data in a relational database. Until then, there was no easy way of manipulating data residing in databases. The goal of the language was to be easy to use and very English-like in its syntax. IBM envisioned businessmen and women using this language to "talk" to a database to retrieve the wanted information. The language did not take off as expected and wasn't really utilized until Oracle based its database access on this language. Since then, it has become the standard way data is accessed in a relational database.

As stated earlier, SQL is a language that allows the manipulation of relational databases. It is very English-like in its syntax. For example, if you wanted to know all of the names of the people who were born in January in your database, an SQL statement might look like the following:

```
SELECT First_Name, Last_Name FROM Customers WHERE DOB= "January"
```

This language is more like a communication tool than a programming language. Most programming languages are compiled and then executed. Generally, SQL is not compiled. Some forms of SQL, such as T-SQL, are compiled, but that's a different database and a different language. SQL is the language of databases, just as English is a language of people. To communicate with another person, you would ask a question and, if the person knew the answer, he or she would reply back to you. SQL works in much the same way.

To begin "talking" to your database, you must first open a line of communication with it. MySQL provides a very nice utility to accomplish this task—the MySQL monitor. If you have been following along from the start, you should already be very familiar with the MySQL monitor. In fact, the commands that you have used to manipulate and create the tables and columns of the sample databases were SQL statements. So you have already seen SQL in action.

SQL is a very powerful language. After you ask a question or issue a command, there is no pulling back. The command is completed without any hesitation or warning. Be very careful when issuing your commands, especially against a live production system. I can't begin to tell you the countless stories of lost data because of sloppiness in an SQL statement. Even I am guilty of this terrible sin. I was responsible for wiping out about 20,000 rows of production data because of a sloppy DELETE statement. So take heed and be very careful with all SQL statements you execute against a production system.

Components of SQL

SQL can be broken down into subcomponents. Because the language covers a broad spectrum, it has been segmented to help users understand it better. SQL can be broken down into two parts—the part that creates database objects and the part that manipulates them. The part that creates objects is often called *DCL* or *data creation language*. It is still SQL, but the statements apply only to creation, not manipulation. The other part that deals with manipulation of data is called *DML* or *data manipulation language*. You have already learned about the DCL part of SQL. You used this when you created your tables and columns.

As stated previously, SQL is a language that is used to talk to databases. Because SQL is a language, it has certain rules and grammar that must be followed. There is also a list vocabulary words used in SQL. These words can be thought of as *reserved* words because they have special meaning. SQL understands the following verbs: CREATE, DROP, ALTER, DELETE, INSERT, UPDATE, and SELECT. SQL also understands the following words: SET, FROM, INTO, WHERE, JOIN, LEFT JOIN, CROSS JOIN, RIGHT JOIN, FULL JOIN, INNER JOIN, ON, ORDER BY, and GROUP BY. See Table 9.1 for a full list of special words.

TABLE 9.1   Reserved Words

CREATE	DROP
ALTER	DELETE
INSERT	UPDATE
SELECT	SET
FROM	INTO
ON	WHERE
ORDER BY	GROUP BY
JOIN	LEFT JOIN
CROSS JOIN	FULL JOIN
RIGHT JOIN	AND

Basic SQL Syntax

To talk to the database, you use one or more of the special words that SQL understands, as well as the information you want to manipulate, in a statement that is issued to the database. Suppose you have a table named Customers in your database. This Customers table is made up of the following columns: First_Name, Last_Name, Address, and DOB (birth month). If you wanted to view all the Customers in the database who have a birthday in January, the SQL statement would look like the following:

```
SELECT First_Name, Last_Name FROM Customers WHERE DOB= "January"
```

The first word of any SQL statement is the verb. This verb tells the database what you want. You'll learn about what each verb does later in this chapter. In the example, you are using the SELECT verb. This tells the database that you want to choose or select the information requested in your statement.

The words following the verb are a list of parameters that you want to view. These parameters are the names of the columns that contain the information you want to see. Imagine that you need a report for your boss that shows all the customers who were born in January so the company can send birthday cards. You can generate this report using the previous SQL statement. Think of the parameter list as the column headings for your report. This is the list of information you want to see in your report. For the current example, you want to see the First_Name and the Last_Name of everyone who has a birthday in January.

After the column heading list, you have the reserved word FROM. This tells the database where to search for the information.

Following the FROM is the name of the table where the data you want is located. This can be a list of tables—it doesn't have to be just one. In this example, you only want to use the data that is available in the Customers table.

The next part of the SQL statement is the WHERE clause. This clause limits the information that you want to be displayed. In this example, the WHERE clause says that you only want the records where the DOB is equal to January. There can be multiple expressions in your WHERE clause. To limit the amount of information even further, you could add the following:

```
SELECT First_Name, Last_Name FROM Customers
WHERE DOB = "January" AND Last_Name LIKE "M%"
```

This statement would return all the first and last names of your customers whose birth month is January and whose last name begins with the letter M.

A word of caution about your WHERE clause. When issuing a WHERE clause, make sure you are specific and that your condition is logical. If you are not specific enough in your WHERE clause, or if your condition is not logical, you may not get the results for which you are looking. This can wreak havoc and cause serious bugs later when you start interfacing your database. The WHERE clause is where most people make their mistakes, so be certain to pay attention when designing a WHERE clause.

The only required fields in your SQL statement are the verb, column headers, and FROM fields. The WHERE clause is optional. So if you wanted to see all the records in your Customers table, you could issue the following statement:

```
SELECT * FROM Customers
```

This statement would show you all the columns and all the data. Quick, simple statements like this will show you what information your table contains. Be aware that these statements may also consume large amounts of processor time if the table is very large. Imagine performing this query on a table that contains half a million records. If you need to see just a sample of data that is contained in a table, use the LIMIT keyword. This keyword limits the number of rows of data that is returned from a query. If you wanted to see a sampling of data from the Customer table, you could perform the following query with little worry:

```
SELECT * FROM Customers LIMIT 10
```

This statement would just return the first 10 rows of data.

Another point worth mentioning is that the rows are returned in the order in which they were entered in the sample statement. So, if Mia Claymore was entered before Ana Akin, Mia would be displayed first. This can be troublesome, especially if you are creating a report for your boss and he likes things in alphabetical order. Thankfully, SQL has functions that do exactly that. They are called aggregate functions. These are the ORDER BY and GROUP BY clauses. These clauses will be explained in detail later in this chapter.

As you can see, SQL can be a very powerful and useful tool for retrieving the data that you need. You may be asking yourself, "How would I use this in a real-life situation?" The answer is simple; You would embed your SQL statements inside a programming language to retrieve the data that you want. This is covered in detail on Day 12, "How to Get to the

Data—Database Interfaces," Day 13, "How to Use MyODBC," and Day 14, "The Perl Database Interface." Today, you will learn the basics of SQL. In the coming days, you will learn how to manipulate your data. You will be able to easily view what is contained in your tables, delete unnecessary data, and even add new data to your database.

Manipulating Data with SQL

The data manipulation segment of the structured query language can be broken down into the following four commands: SELECT, INSERT, UPDATE, and DELETE. These commands cover the full range of what you can do to your data. Each command has its own nuances and will be further explained later in this chapter. I would like to take a moment and explain some of the things that are common to all the statements.

After each verb, there is a list of column headers. You can name each column that you want to receive or, if you need to, you can use the wildcard character to view them all. The asterisk (*) is the wildcard character for MySQL (as well as most other RDBMS). If you wanted to see all the columns from the Customer table, you could issue the following statement:

```
SELECT * FROM Customers
```

This statement would show all the columns.

There are some rules that are common to all statements. These are general syntax rules and must be followed for the database to understand what you are telling it.

The following are some of the rules that must be followed:

- If you are using more than one table in the FROM clause, all fields that are the same name must be prefixed by the table name wherever they are used. For example: The Orders table and the Customers table both have a Customer_ID field. If you were to perform a query on these tables, you would have to explicitly state the table name for the Customer_ID field whenever you use it:

```
SELECT Orders.Order_ID FROM Orders, Customers
WHERE Customer.Customer_ID = Orders.Customer_ID
```

- Multiple statements in a WHERE clause must be connected by either an AND or an OR keyword. Be careful of the order in which you use these commands. You can group statements using parentheses to get the desired query.

- All SQL statements must have a verb, a FROM or INTO clause, and usually a parameter list of column names that may be one or all of the columns in a given table.

Another thing that is common to all the verbs is the ability to alias a table. To *alias* a table is to give it another name to help save time and space when identifying the tables from which you want to get information. Aliasing looks like the following:

```
SELECT O.Order_ID from Orders AS O, Customers AS C
WHERE C.Customer_ID = O.Customer_ID
```

As you can see, aliasing allows you to use a kind of shorthand when referencing tables, instead of typing the following code. The keyword AS must be used when you alias with MySQL.

```
SELECT Orders.Order_ID FROM Orders, Customers
WHERE Customers.Customer_ID = Orders.Customer_ID
```

It can save you some time and is less cumbersome then typing the full table name out. You have to state the table name when using more than one table in the FROM clause so that the database knows which field you are talking about. If you have to do that, you might as well take this shortcut.

Be careful when using more than one table in a SELECT, UPDATE, or DELETE command. Make sure your joins are complete and succinct (joins are covered in the "Working with Joins" section later today). If not, you may cause a Cartesian join. A *Cartesian join* is when you join every row of one table to every row of another table. This is very CPU-intensive and is usually done by mistake. To avoid this, make sure you understand what you are joining and that the join is complete. If not, you will have the distinct pleasure of recreating data from a log because you wiped out a whole lot of needed data.

SELECT

The SELECT statement is probably the most used of all SQL statements. The SELECT statement will only return the data that is held in the database. MySQL probably performs this type of query faster than any other database on the market. The SELECT syntax is as follows:

```
SELECT column name FROM table name WHERE conditions
```

The column name can be one or more columns that are in a table in the FROM clause. You cannot select a column name that is not available in the FROM clause. For example, if you wanted to select the Last_Name field of the Customers table, but you did not have the Customers table defined in the FROM clause, MySQL would generate an error. As mentioned before, you can use aliasing as a shortcut. You only have to mention the table name if there is an ambiguity in the field names. This means that if one table has a field named Order_ID and another table has a field named Order_ID, you must identify which table/field name pair you want to use. If the field name is unique to all the tables in your table parameter list, you do not have to specify a table.

The order in which you specify the column names is the order in which they will be displayed. If you choose First_Name, Last_Name, the data will be displayed in that order. If you change them around to Last_Name, First_Name, the output will match the order specified.

The SELECT statement can also be used to show outcomes of equations. For example, the following statement

```
SELECT 1 + 1
```

would produce the following output:

OUTPUT   2

The following statement is also legal:

```
SELECT concat(First_Name, " ",Last_Name) AS Name FROM Customers
```

This statement would return a column named Name with the results of the concatenation function. The concat() function is an intrinsic function of MySQL and will be covered in more detail in tomorrow's lesson. So, if you wanted a resultset that contained the person's name and address, you could use the following SQL statement:

Note   The concat() function combines two strings into one. Intrinsic functions will be covered on Day 10, "Letting MySQL Do the Work—Intrinsic Functions."

```
SELECT concat(First_Name, " ", Last_Name)
AS Name, Address, City, State
FROM Customers;
```

The resulting output would look like Table 9.2.

TABLE 9.2   Results of Concatenation

Name	Address	City	State
Glen Brazil	133 Foxview Ln.	Hoptown	KY
Roxanne Tor	123 Center Ave.	Glen Burnie	MD

Notice that the columns have the names that you assigned them in the AS clause. This technique is highly useful, especially when using intrinsic functions. Another example is the MAX() function. The MAX function returns the maximum value of a numeric type column. This could be used instead of the auto_increment modifier. For example, to get the current maximum value of a numeric column, you could use the following statement:

```
SELECT MAX(Customer_ID) as Current_Num FROM Customers
```

The resultset would look like the following:

OUTPUT
```
Current_Num
78
```

In a MySQL SELECT statement, you can also set the priority in which the MySQL engine serves this query. If MySQL receives a request for an INSERT and a request for a SELECT at the same time, MySQL will process the INSERT before the SELECT. To force MySQL to perform the SELECT first, you can set the priority of the query by doing the following:

```
SELECT HIGH_PRIORITY Customer_ID FROM Customers
```

The HIGH_PRIORITY argument should only be used on small queries.

A feature that is not yet available in MySQL is the subselect. The subselect allows you to base a query on the results of another query. For example

```
SELECT * FROM Customers
WHERE Customer_ID
IN (SELECT Customer_ID FROM Orders AS O, Shippers As S
WHERE S.Shipper_ID=12
AND S.Shipper_ID = O.Shipper_ID)
```

This is not the greatest example, but it shows basically what a subselect is. There are certainly workarounds for this type of select. You could do more multiple joins inside a single query. Of course, this isn't the best answer, but until MySQL has subselects, that is all that you can do.

Another new feature that is available in version 3.23 is the ability to SELECT INTO a table. This is an extremely useful feature, especially in batch programming. The table that is created here can only be a temporary table and will be dropped when the current connection is dropped. To do this, enter the following command:

```
CREATE TEMPORARY TABLE temp_table SELECT * FROM Customers
```

This command creates a temporary table that holds an exact copy of the records contained in the Customers table. This feature is close to the SELECT INTO that is offered by other RDBMs of the same class. Another workaround for SELECT INTO is the INSERT INTO command. It basically does the same thing.

9

INSERT

The INSERT INTO command adds new rows of data to an existing table. The format is basically the same as a SELECT statement. In fact, you can use a combination of the INSERT INTO and SELECT syntax to insert rows of data from one table into a different one. The basic INSERT INTO command looks like the following:

```
INSERT INTO Customers VALUES(NULL, "Glen", "Brazil")
```

The name of the table into which you want to insert the new record is after the INTO keyword. Following the VALUES keyword is a list of values that you want to insert. If you insert a record this way, you must have a value for every column, and the order of the data must match the order in which your columns were declared in the database. In the example, you have a table that is defined by the following columns: Customer_ID, First_Name, Last_Name. When you insert a row of data into this table, the data must fall in this specified order—the Customer_ID value, the first name, and so on. The inserted values must match the column order precisely, or an error will occur. To avoid this hassle, SQL allows you to name the values you are going to insert. For example, your SQL INSERT statement could look like the following:

```
INSERT INTO Customers (Customer_ID, Last_Name, First_Name)
VALUES (NULL, "Brazil", "Glen")
```

Using this technique, the order or number of columns in the table do not have to match. This is the preferred way of inserting a row of data. In this way, you specify the order and the actual columns that you want to insert. You are not bound by the table's order but your own. This method also allows you to add the data you want to add—you don't have to add the values you don't have or don't want to add as you would have to with the previous method.

With MySQL version 3.23, you can use the INSERT INTO...SELECT statement. This statement allows you to add data to a table based on the criteria in the SELECT statement. For example, you could extract required data from a table and insert that information into another. Suppose that you needed to extract all the customers from the Customers table that are from Maryland and place them into a table that the shippers use so they can plan their trucking routes. To do this, you have to have an existing table that you'll call Shipper_Info. This table has the following schema:

```
CREATE TABLE Shipper_Info (
Shipper_Info_ID INT NOT NULL PRIMARY KEY AUTO_INCREMENT,
Customer_Name VARCHAR(50),
Address VARCHAR(30),
```

```
City VARCHAR(20),
Zip VARCHAR(15),
Truck_Number INT,
Driver_ID INT)
```

You could then issue an SQL statement that fulfills the shipper's needs. It would look like the following:

```
INSERT INTO Shipper_Info
    (Customer_Name, Address, City, Zip)
VALUES
     SELECT CAT(First_Name + " " + Last_Name)
AS Name, Address, City, Zip
FROM Customers
WHERE
    State = "MD"
```

This would add a row for every row of this resultset. If there were 100 rows of data that matched the criteria, 100 rows would be added to the `Shipper_Info` table. Another point worth mentioning is that you cannot insert data into the table from which you are selecting the data. Additionally, the number of columns, as well as the data in the column, must match the columns and data types of the columns into which you are going to insert the data. For example, you cannot insert rows of data that do not match the columns in the table. If you did so, MySQL would generate an error.

MySQL has another useful ability—the ability to delay an `INSERT` statement until the table is no longer in use. This would be beneficial when there are many long `SELECT` queries to the database that are of higher priority than the `INSERT`. Remember, MySQL performs any manipulation statements before it performs any `SELECT`s. So an `INSERT` statement naturally has higher priority than a `SELECT`. To take advantage of this capability, you must use the `INSERT DELAYED` syntax. That syntax looks like the following:

```
INSERT DELAYED INTO Customers (Last_Name) VALUES ("Newton")
```

The major advantage to doing this is that the new data will not be inserted until the table is free. If a long `SELECT` query and multiple `INSERT DELAYED` statements were issued at the same time, the `INSERT`s would be queued until the `SELECT` statement was completed. Then the `INSERT`s would be issued all at once. This is better performance-wise than issuing multiple `INSERT`s. The major disadvantage to using an `INSERT DELAYED` is that if the `mysqld` daemon were to shut down, all the statements that were queued would be deleted without being executed. Fortunately, the `mysqld` daemon is a very stable process and rarely, if ever, dies unexpectedly on its own. Generally, it would take a kill -9 or a reboot for this to happen.

UPDATE

The UPDATE command allows you to edit the values of existing data. This command is a lot like a SELECT statement, but the values you are selecting can be manipulated. The following is the syntax for an UPDATE statement:

```
UPDATE tablename SET columnname = value WHERE x=y
```

As with all SQL statements, the reserved verb come first. Immediately following the verb is the name of the table that you are going to manipulate. After the table name, the reserved word SET is used. What follows the SET command is a list of column names and values that you want to set. For example, if you wanted to change the City column to Dunkirk, your command would look like the following:

```
City = "Dunkirk"
```

Multiple values can exist after the SET command. Each column/value pair must be separated by a comma. You can update every column in the table if you want with one UPDATE command. The WHERE clause follows the column/value list. This clause designates which rows will be updated. This can be dangerous if you do not pay close attention to what you are doing. For example, if you wanted to update one of your customers because she got married and changed her name, you would issue the following statement:

```
UPDATE Customers SET Last_Name = "Smith" WHERE Customer_ID = 12
```

If a WHERE clause was not used in this statement, all the values in the Last_Name column would be set to Smith. You can see where this could be bad news. Remember that SQL does not issue any warnings—if you are going to change something, be sure that you are changing the right things.

It is common practice to perform a SELECT statement before you UPDATE or DELETE any data. Doing this ensures that you are going to remove or change only the data that you intend. Using the previous example, you would issue the following SELECT statement before you issued your UPDATE statement:

```
SELECT * FROM Customers WHERE Customer_ID = 12
```

This statement should only return one row of data containing the information you want to update. Because it only returned one row of data, you can be sure that only one row will be affected when you execute your UPDATE statement. This extra step can save you a lot of grief in the long run.

MySQL has also added an extra feature to the UPDATE statement. If you want to execute an UPDATE statement when no one else is using the table you are updating you can set the priority to low. This causes the UPDATE statement to execute only when the table is not being used. The syntax looks like this:

```
UPDATE LOW_PRIORITY Customers SET First_Name = "Judy"
WHERE Customer_ID =16
```

MySQL is also smart enough to know if you are trying to update a value with the value that the field already contains. If you were trying to update a customer's record that originally had Steve in the First_Name column with the value Steve, MySQL would be smart enough to recognize this and ignore the operation. This saves on CPU cycles and helps MySQL be more efficient overall.

With MySQL, you also can update a value based on the value it currently holds. For example, if you wanted to add one year to everyone's age in the database, you could use the following statement:

```
UPDATE Customers SET Age = Age + 1
```

It is important to remember that MySQL evaluates UPDATE statements from left to right.

Another safeguard you can implement when updating the database is to use the LIMIT function. Using this will control the number of rows that are affected by your UPDATE statement. If you wanted to limit the number of rows you updated in the last example, you could do the following:

```
UPDATE Customers SET Age = Age + 1 LIMIT 10
```

This statement would limit the update to the first 10 rows of the table. That way, you can check your work and make sure that your SQL statement did exactly what you wanted it to do.

DELETE

The DELETE statement is very similar to the SELECT statement. The only difference is that instead of selecting records to view, this statement deletes those records. Again, caution should be used when issuing this statement to avoid accidentally deleting rows in error. MySQL does not provide any warnings when you are deleting records. So be very careful. You can exercise the same precautions described previously—performing a SELECT statement first to ensure that you are deleting the records you want to delete and using the LIMIT keyword to ensure only the number of rows you specify are deleted.

The DELETE syntax looks like the following:

```
DELETE FROM Customers WHERE State = "KY"
```

Like all SQL statements, the verb comes first. Following the verb is the keyword FROM, followed by the name of the table from which you want to delete the records. Following the table name is the WHERE clause. The WHERE clause is very important in a DELETE statement. This limits the number of deletions based on the criteria that are set here. Without the WHERE clause, all records from the database are deleted by default. The following syntax would delete everything in the Customers table:

```
DELETE FROM Customers
```

Like all the previous statements, MySQL provides a priority level for the query. To have a DELETE statement execute while no one else is reading from the table from which you want to delete records, you could issue the following statement:

```
DELETE LOW_PRIORITY FROM Customer WHERE State = "KY"
```

A DELETE statement on a very large table can take some time. To free up the table for other queries, you can use multiple LIMIT statements. You can set the limit to 10 and execute the query multiple times. Each time, it will delete at most 10 rows. When the WHERE clause is no longer true, it will not return any rows. For example, your client wants you to delete all the customers from Kentucky because his or her store no longer supports that state. Perform your initial SELECT query:

```
SELECT * FROM Customers WHERE State = "KY"
```

This query returns 2756 records from your database. You now want to take advantage of the LIMIT key word to optimize the performance of your table:

```
DELETE FROM Customers WHERE State = "KY" LIMIT 100
```

This query would delete up to 100 rows of data that match the criteria in your WHERE clause. So, 2656 records would be left that matched your WHERE criteria. You would then perform the query again, and 100 more records would be deleted, leaving you with 2556. Every time this query is run, the number of records that match your WHERE clause criteria would be decremented by up to 100. This would continue until there are no records that match your criteria. By using this technique, you will be able to perform your database cleanup without sacrificing performance.

Another point to consider when deleting records is that when a record is deleted, it does not just disappear. It becomes part of an internal linked list. This means that even though the record is deleted, it is still taking up space on disk. To remove the remnants of these deleted records, you will have to perform an OPTIMIZE table query or use the myisamchk utility. Both of these tools will clean up the space taken by these dead records.

Working with Joins

Joins are an integral part of a relational database. Joins allow the database user to take advantage of the relationships that were developed in the design phase of the database. A *join* is the term used to describe the act when two or more tables are "joined" together to retrieve needed data based on the relationships that are shared between them. For example, in your Meet_A_Geek database, you have a relationship between the Customers and Orders tables. To select data out of the Customers table based on some criterion that is contained in the Orders table would require you to use a join of some kind. For example, to retrieve all the customers who have placed an order, you could use the following syntax:

```
SELECT First_Name, Last_Name
 FROM Customer AS C, Orders AS O
WHERE C.Customer_ID = O. Customer_ID
```

This would return only the records of customers who have placed orders, or where records exist in both tables. If a customer has placed multiple orders, you would see all his or her orders.

ANSI-92 Compliance

In 1992, the American National Standards Institute developed a set of standards for SQL. These standards are called ANSI-92. MySQL takes great pride in being truly ANSI-92-compliant. ANSI-92 standardizes the ways to create joins. Instead of putting the joining logic in the WHERE clause, it allows you to put it in the FROM clause. There are two schools of thought: those who have embraced the new way—the ANSI-92 way—and those who continue to use the WHERE clause for joins. The old way is easy to read and makes a lot of sense. Plus, the majority of DBAs and programmers grew up learning it the old way. The new way does offer some advantages. First, it is the ANSI standard. All new databases must use the ANSI-92 way of doing things if they want to be compliant. So you can be sure that the new way will be around in the future. Also, the new way is a little better when it comes to performance. Instead of MySQL parsing the WHERE clause and then developing its query plan, the join is stated well before the WHERE clause is parsed, making the queries a little better when it comes to performance.

The ANSI-92 way of implementing a join is a little different syntactically than the old way, but the concept is the same. You want to combine the information in two tables based on a relationship into one resultset. An ANSI-92 JOIN used to accomplish the same resultset as the previous example would look like the following:

```
SELECT First_Name, Last_Name
FROM Customers as C
JOIN Orders as O ON C.Customer_ID = O.Customer_ID
```

The following is the basic format of the ANSI-92 JOIN:

```
SELECT Column List
FROM table name
JOIN table name ON join criteria
WHERE condition criteria
```

The JOIN follows the basic SELECT syntax. The only addition is the JOIN clause. After the keyword JOIN, the name of the table that shares a relationship with the table after the FROM keyword is used. Following the table name is the JOIN criterion. This criterion is basically the definition of the relationship between the two tables. It is also the same logic that you would use in your WHERE clause. After the JOIN clause is the WHERE clause. The WHERE clause would add further limiting criteria to your SELECT statement. If you wanted to see all the orders for a customer, you could use the following syntax:

```
SELECT C.First_Name, C.Last_Name, O.Order_Date, O.Order_ID
FROM Customers as C
JOIN Orders as O ON C.Customer_ID = O.Customer_ID
WHERE Customer_ID = 12
```

The old way would look like the following:

```
SELECT C.First_Name, C.Last_Name, O.Order_Date, O.Order_ID
FROM Customers as C, Orders as O
WHERE C.Customer_ID = O.Customer_ID
AND C.Customer_ID=12
```

Again, whichever way you choose to use is entirely up to you. It is mostly a matter of preference. There can be a small gain in performance using the ANSI-92, but sometimes, for the sake of readability and clarity, the old way is preferred.

MySQL supports the following JOINs: CROSS JOIN, INNER JOIN, LEFT JOIN, and NATURAL LEFT JOIN. Don't let the names or style confuse you. Just remember that you can implement a JOIN by using logic in your WHERE clause. Both styles, the ANSI-92 and the old way, will be covered today. Use what feels comfortable and makes the most sense to you.

CROSS JOIN

The CROSS JOIN is not used very much at all. In fact, most of the time it is done by mistake. A CROSS JOIN returns all the records from all the tables mentioned in the JOIN. This is also referred to as a *Cartesian join*. These joins are very processor-intensive and should be avoided. The syntax for a CROSS JOIN would look like the following:

The old way:

```
SELECT C.First_Name, C.Last_Name, O.Order_ID
FROM Customers as C, Orders as O
```

The ANSI-92 way:

```
SELECT C.First_Name, C.Last_Name, O.Order_ID
FROM Customers as C
CROSS JOIN Orders as O
```

The resultset that is returned from this type of join is huge. It basically returns all the data in all the tables. There aren't too many uses for a join like this.

INNER JOIN

INNER JOINs are probably the most common of all joins.

An INNER JOIN simply means that all records that are unmatched are discarded. Only the matched rows are displayed in the resultset. This is the default type of join, so the word INNER is optional. This type of join is based on the criteria in the JOIN clause. Your first example was an example of an INNER JOIN:

```
SELECT C.First_Name, C.Last_Name, O.Order_ID
FROM Customer as C
(INNER) JOIN Orders as O ON C.Customer_ID = O.Customer_ID
```

Again, the word INNER appears in parentheses because it is optional. The old way to create an INNER JOIN would look like the following:

```
SELECT First_Name, Last_Name, O.Order_ID
FROM Customer as C, Order as O
WHERE C.Customer_ID = O.Customer_ID
```

This is probably the most frequently used of all joins—the primary reason why it's the ANSI-92 default.

LEFT JOIN

A LEFT JOIN returns all rows from the left table in a join. For example, if you were to continue using your Customers and Orders example, the following statement shows the syntax for a LEFT JOIN:

```
SELECT C.First_Name, C.Last_Name, O.Order_ID
FROM Customer as C
LEFT JOIN Order as O ON C.Customer_ID = O.Customer_ID
```

In this example, all the rows from the table on the left side of the equation will be returned, regardless of whether they have a match with the table on the right side. If there is no match, a NULL value will be returned.

In other database systems, the LEFT JOIN is implemented the "old way" using a symbol. The symbol is an asterisk (*) equal sign (=) combination. The placement of the asterisk (left or right of the equal sign) indicates the type of join. So, to implement a LEFT JOIN, the following would be the syntax:

```
SELECT C.First_Name, C.Last_Name, O.Order_ID
FROM Customers AS C, Orders as O
WHERE C.Customer_ID *= O.Orders_ID
```

The developers at TcX decided not to implement this feature in MySQL. They probably did it for several reasons. First, joins of this type are rarely used. If you need to do a join like this, you can use the ANSI-92 equivalent. Another reason why they probably chose not to implement this feature is that TcX works on a very low budget. This is an extra feature that is rarely used—their time is better spent developing the standards, not the extras.

The keyword USING can be used as a replacement for the ON keyword. The USING keyword allows you to use a list of columns that appear in both tables and is equivalent to saying C.Customer_ID = O.Customer_ID AND S.Shipper_ID = O.Shipper_ID. The syntax looks like the following:

```
SELECT C.First_Name, C.Last_Name, O.Orders_ID
FROM Customers AS C
LEFT JOIN Order as O USING Customer_ID
```

In this example, the USING keyword would be like using the ON keyword with C.Customer_ID = O.Customer_ID following it. This is another shortcut to save time.

NATURAL LEFT JOIN

The NATURAL LEFT JOIN is the same as a regular LEFT JOIN except that it automatically uses all the matching columns as part of the join. It is syntactically equivalent to a LEFT JOIN with a USING clause that names all the identical columns of the two tables. The syntax looks like the following:

```
SELECT C.First_Name, C.Last_Name, O.Orders_ID
FROM Customers as C
NATURAL LEFT JOIN Orders as O
```

This would return all the rows from the Customers table, regardless of whether they had a matching record in any of the same columns of the Orders table. The Orders table would return a NULL if it did not have a match.

Again, this join is rarely used. The only way to accomplish this type of join is to use the given syntax.

Joins are fairly straightforward, But don't let the syntax fool you. Joins allow you to take advantage of the relationships you defined earlier when you created the tables. Practice and experience will aid greatly when creating joins.

Aggregate Functions

Aggregate functions are functions that perform a mathematical operation on a column. MySQL implements the following aggregate functions: COUNT(), COUNT(DISTINCT), MAX(), MIN(), AVG(), SUM(), and STD().

COUNT( )

The COUNT() function is used to count the number of occurrences of all non-null values in a column. For example

```
SELECT COUNT(C.First_Name)
FROM Customers as C, Orders as O
WHERE C.Customer_ID = O.Customer_ID
```

This statement would return the number of rows that had a non-null value in the First_Name column of the Customers table that matched the WHERE clause criteria.

Another use of the COUNT() function is to use it in the following way:

```
SELECT COUNT(*) as Num
FROM Customers as C, Orders as O
WHERE C.Customer_ID = O.Customer_ID
```

This statement would return the total number of rows. This is especially useful when you need to find out how many rows you have in a table.

COUNT(DISTINCT)

The COUNT(DISTINCT) function is used to count the unique non-null occurrences of a column or columns. For example

```
SELECT COUNT(DISTINCT First_Name,)
FROM Customers
```

This statement would return the number of rows of different first names. For example, there are 10 rows of data in the Customers table. The first three rows have Taylor in the First_Name column. The next 2 rows have Sydney, the next has Jill, the last 4 rows have Trisha. The previous statement would return the number 4. That is the total number of unique names that are stored in the First_Name column.

The COUNT and COUNT(DISTINCT) functions can be used on any data type. The rest of the functions must be used on numeric data types.

MAX( )

The MAX( ) function returns the highest value in the column. This function is handy when you are creating your own sequence numbers. The syntax looks like the following:

```
SELECT MAX(Customer_ID)
FROM Customers
```

This statement would return the highest value in the table.

MIN( )

The MIN( ) function returns the lowest value in a column. The syntax for the MIN( ) function looks like the following:

```
SELECT MIN(Customer_ID)
FROM Customers
```

AVG( )

The AVG( ) function returns the average value of the designated column. The function would be used as follows:

```
SELECT AVG(Price)
FROM Orders
```

This statement would return the average price of all the prices in the Orders table. MySQL performs all the calculations for you.

 Note   Remember that a NULL value is really no value at all. So, when you SUM or AVG a column that contains NULL values, the NULL values will not affect your results in any way.

SUM( )

This function totals the values in a given column. The function is used as follows:

```
SELECT SUM(Price)
FROM Orders
```

This function adds all the values together and returns the sum.

STD()

The STD() function returns the standard deviation of a given column, as shown in the following:

```
SELECT STD(Price)
FROM Orders
```

9

 Note

> *Standard deviation* is a measure of dispersal. It is used to gauge how far from the average a value is. It can be expressed mathematically as follows:
>
> Sqrt $E[(X-E(X))2]$
>
> where E is a known point.

Aggregate Functions and the WHERE Clause

Remember that a WHERE clause could also be used in any of the previous examples. This could limit what values are calculated in the function. Using the WHERE clause with these functions gives you a powerful set of tools to perform most any financial or scientific calculation.

Aggregate Functions and the GROUP BY Clause

MySQL also supports the GROUP BY clause. The GROUP BY clause can only be used in conjunction with an aggregate function. The GROUP BY clause allows you to group a set of results together. For example, suppose you wanted to know the number of orders a person placed in a given day. You could use the following statement:

```
SELECT C.First_Name, C.Last_Name, O.Order_Date,
Count(C.Customer_ID)AS Orders
FROM Customer as C
JOIN Orders as O ON C.Customer_ID = O.Customer_ID
WHERE O.Order_Date = '2000-01-13'
GROUP BY C.First_Name
```

The resultset would look similar to Table 9.3.

TABLE 9.3 Aggregate Functions with GROUP BY

First_Name	Last_Name	Order_Date	Orders
Taylor	Smith	2000-01-13	3
Sydney	Sue	2000-01-13	1
Stan	Behm	2000-01-13	6

Notice that the results are grouped together based on the column name in the GROUP BY clause. The GROUP BY clause is an invaluable tool when generating reports.

Sorting

Most RDBMs provide a way for the user to sort results. MySQL is no different. To sort a resultset based on a given column, you can use the ORDER BY clause. The ORDER BY clause causes a resultset to be sorted by the column you name and the directions you specify. For example, if you wanted to sort the previous example by last name then by first name in descending order, you would issue the following statement:

```
SELECT C.First_Name, C.Last_Name, O.Order_Date
Count(C.Customer_ID) AS Orders
FROM Customer as C
JOIN Orders as O ON C.Customer_ID = O.Customer_ID
WHERE O.Order_Date = '2000-01-13'
GROUP BY C.First_Name
ORDER BY Last_Name, First_Name DESC
```

If you wanted to sort your data in ascending order, replace the DESC with ASC. That's all there is to it. To sort Text and BLOB type columns, you must ORDER BY a fixed length part of the data. To do this, you would use the SUBSTRING function. This is covered in tomorrow's lesson.

In the example, you have two column names in the ORDER BY clause. The ORDER BY will sort the column primarily by the first column and then by the second column. This follows the natural order of things—you generally would sort names by the last name and, if two people had the same last name, you would then use the first name to determine in what order the names should come. This is exactly how the ORDER BY clause treats multiple column names. It will sort by the first column and, if that column has identical values it, will then shift to the second column and compare those values to determine placement in the resultset.

Summary

SQL is a powerful tool that was originally developed by IBM for the average person to access relational databases. SQL is the language that databases understand. It has a syntax and a vocabulary that it can use to communicate. Each reserved word in SQL has a certain meaning and performs a particular function.

You have covered a lot of ground today. Remember that this is just a basic overview of the SQL language. It is not complete, nor was it intended to be. It is in this book to provide you with a means of manipulating your data and building a base on which you can build. Later lessons will explore the interface APIs that will use what you have learned today to build reports and support applications. The hardest part of SQL is not the language or syntax but the logic that is used to gather the data from the database. Take the time to learn how to create good WHERE clauses and how to use JOINs. It will help you in the future.

Q&A

Q   **In today's lesson LEFT JOINs were discussed. Is there such a thing as a RIGHT JOIN?**

A   There is such a thing as a **RIGHT JOIN**. Most major RDBMs support **RIGHT JOIN**s. However, MySQL does not, for good reason. If you take a minute and think what a **RIGHT JOIN** is—the reverse of a **LEFT JOIN**— then there is a simple workaround. Simply switch the table names in your query. For example, if the following was your **LEFT JOIN**:

```
        SELECT C.First_Name
    FROM Customer as C
    LEFT JOIN Orders as O ON C.Customer_ID = O.Customer_ID
```

Your RIGHT JOIN would look like the following:

```
        SELECT C.First_Name
    FROM Orders AS O
    LEFT JOIN Customers as C ON C.Customer_ID = O.Customer_ID
```

As you can see, there really is no reason to code and implement a RIGHT JOIN when simply reversing the order of your tables will accomplish the same thing.

Q   **I was looking through the MySQL manual and saw something about a REPLACE statement. What is it, and how do I use it?**

A   The REPLACE statement is the same as using an INSERT INTO command. The syntax
          is pretty much the same. The difference between an INSERT statement and a
          REPLACE statement is that MySQL will delete the old record and replace it with the
          new values in a REPLACE statement, hence the name REPLACE. The syntax for a
          REPLACE statement looks like the following:

```
REPLACE INTO Customers
(Customer_ID, First_Name, Last_Name)
VALUES(NULL, "Dina", "Newton")
```

The REPLACE statement shares the same rules and parameters as the INSERT statement to
include the REPLACE INTO...SELECT statements, as well as the LOW_PRIORITY modifier.

Exercises

1. Translate the following into SQL statements:
   - View all the records from the Customers table of the customers who have
     placed orders.
   - View all shippers that have been used in the past month.
   - View all customers.

2. Create an SQL statement that accomplishes the following:
   - Add the following information to the Customers table:
   - First Name: Jerry
   - Last Name: Maxon
   - Address: 123 N. Hampton Lane

3. Change the name of the last record you added from "Jerry" to "Sam."

4. Delete all records from the Customers table whose first name is Jerry.

5. Create an SQL statement that returns the number of customers whose names begin
   with M.

6. Create an SQL statement that returns the average number of products each customer
   purchases. (Hint: use the quantity column.)

7. Create an SQL statement that returns all the customers who have placed an order in
   the past month, sort it in ascending alphabetic order, and group the records by date.

DAY **10**

Letting MySQL Do the Work—Intrinsic Functions

Almost all databases provide the user with a series of common functions. These functions provide administrators or people querying the database a way of performing complex tasks within a query. Some of these tasks may be string manipulation or complex mathematical equations. This allows users to take advantage of the more powerful processing power of a database server.

MySQL provides a lot of intrinsic functions. Today, you will learn

- Programming at the server level and how MySQL can help
- Basic functions, such as numerical operations, string manipulations, and logical conditions

Programming at the Server Level

A lot of discussion goes on about where to put the programming logic. Do you let the application that is installed on the user's desktop do all the heavy processing, or do you let it take place on the database server? What about a third place—a middle tier? The answers to these questions are not easy. A lot depends on the application and the purposes for which it is used. A traditional Web-based application has different needs than a three-tier application. These needs vary from heavy database traffic, as in a Web-based store, to heavy data manipulation, as in a finance application. The remainder of this section takes a look at some scenarios and explains why and where the best place to put the logic is.

The first example is a Web-based application, such as the Meet-A-Geek Web site. The following are the general steps in a Web-based application:

1. A user types the URL of a Web site into his or her browser.
2. The browser then finds the server and requests a Web page.
3. The Web server answers the request and sends the page.
4. The browser receives the page.
5. The user navigates around the site repeating steps 1-4 until he or she gets to a page that requires some sort of database access (a form or dynamically generated page).
6. A program or script runs, getting the requested data from the database server.
7. The page is then returned to the user.

As you can see, there are a lot of trips back and forth to the database and Web servers. Now imagine a site that receives a lot of traffic—the trips and requests to and from the server could be astronomical.

To help ease the load on the servers, you could add the programming logic at the client. The client is the computer or application that is either receiving or sending the requests. The more logic you can place at the client level, such as error handling or string manipulation, the better off you are.

Now don't think you can't use any intrinsic functions on the database server—you can, just consider the size of your database and the amount of traffic you think that your site is going to have. If you have a small site with a relatively small amount of data, you are pretty free to do anything you want. But if your site is extremely busy and you need a lot of calculations done or a lot of string manipulation needs to be provided, think about placing this logic on the client.

In the Enterprise, things may be a little different. At the Enterprise level, you may have many client machines accessing your database via an application. This application could be written in Java, Visual Basic, C++, or any other programming language. The application talks to a middle tier. This middle tier handles all the business logic. It accesses the database and returns requests to the client. The middle tier is an application too. Its responsibility is to process the requests and send them to the appropriate places.

The following is the flow in a three-tier design:

1. A user uses a front-end application and issues a request.
2. The request is checked for any errors and sent to the middle tier.
3. The middle tier receives the request, performs any business logic, and passes it on to the database.
4. The database performs its function on the request—whether it is to return a query from a SELECT statement or update some rows. It then passes the data back to the middle tier.
5. The middle tier performs any other logic that is required and returns the request to the client.
6. The client receives the data and displays the results to the user.

The majority of the business logic is done at the middle tier, while simple parsing and error handling is done on the front-end application. Generally, the database server's only responsibility is to serve up the data that is requested or manipulate the data that it stores. In this type of architecture, the load is balanced between all tiers. Each is responsible for its own duties. The front-end application is pretty much a display tool—a way for the user to interact with the data. The middle tier is responsible for all the heavy logic and also handles the requests and connections to the database. The database does what it does best—serve up data.

In a straight client-server environment, both machines must perform their own duties. In the earlier days of client server technology, the majority of logical operations were performed at the server level. The servers were generally much more powerful then the client machines, so the processing had to be done on the server level or things came to a standstill. With the advent of the cheap, powerful PC, more logic could be performed at the client level more efficiently. Today, most large applications use a three- or n-tier design. However, for smaller applications, a middle tier may not be needed.

10

The general flow of data in a client-server application is as follows:

1. The user uses a graphical application. He or she issues a request. The application handles all the logic, parsing, and error handling and sends the finished request to the database server.

2. The database server receives the request. It performs any of the needed operations and sends the completed request back to the client.

3. The client performs any other operations and displays the information to the user.

This process doesn't have as many steps as the other applications, and it does have its limitations. However, for small to mid-size applications, there really isn't a need for the complexity that the other types of architectures possess.

The final type of architecture is the straight report. This is the simplest of them all. It can be performed from the command line of the MySQL monitor or contained in a simple shell or Perl script. All it does is generate a report. The report can be very complex, but it generally flows as follows:

1. The user connects to the database and runs a query or series of queries.

2. The result outputs to the screen or a file.

3. The user disconnects from the database.

This type of program is not worried about a graphical interface or a user keying in data. It is simply a report. The logic, depending on how complex the query, can be performed almost exclusively on the database server using the functions that MySQL provides.

Some examples are a batch job that prints out invoices after it finishes, and a report that is run every day that calculates the standard deviation of test results. The uses are countless, but these types of programs generally use the database instead of the client for their logic.

How Does MySQL Help?

MySQL provides a lot of functions that can help perform many tasks. These functions can be used in lieu of code at the application level, or they can be used in conjunction with the code in your application. Let the guidelines that were discussed earlier help you decide what to do.

Because of MySQL's speed, it is sometimes to your advantage to implement some of the functionality that you would need in your application at the server level. Cheat a little. Take advantage of what MySQL has to offer. If you need a full name to be displayed in your application and you store the last name and first name in two different columns, use a MySQL intrinsic function to tie them together before it is returned to your application. This can save some time and headaches.

The Basic MySQL Functions

The MySQL functions can be broken down into four types: numerical or mathematical functions, logic functions, string manipulation functions, and date and time functions. You will learn about the first three types today. Because of the complexity and number of the date and time functions, they will be covered on Day 16, "MySQL and Time." There is also an alphabetical listing of each function with a brief description and example listed in Appendix B, "Current MySQL Functions," for your convenience.

Today's lesson covers only a partial listing of the functions. The most frequently used functions are discussed, and there are some examples showing how to use them.

Numerical Functions

The numerical functions are composed of various mathematical operations. They range from the complex (standard deviation) to the simple (addition). In this section, the use and syntax of the more simple operations will be discussed. After you get the hang of how they're used, you can look at Appendix B and try it with the more complex functions.

The anatomy of a function is quite simple. You have the function name followed by its arguments, which are enclosed in parentheses (see Figure 10.1). There is no space between the name of the function and the opening parenthesis ("("). If you put in a space unintentionally, you will get an error because MySQL will think you are trying to name a column from your table instead of a function—that's the way the parser works. A function may take one, more than one, or no arguments. The numeric function can only use number data types, and the string functions can only use character or string data types. If you try to operate on something for which the function was not intended, an error is returned.

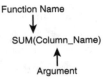

FIGURE 10.1

The anatomy of a function.

Function Name

SUM(Column_Name)

Argument

Addition

All of the MySQL functions operate pretty much the same way. To use the addition function, or any other function for that matter, you must call the function from inside an SQL statement. You would use the addition function as shown in the following:

```
SELECT (Column_1 + Column_2) as Total FROM Orders
```

This statement would return the total of the values in `Column_1` and `Column_2` for every row in the table. For example, suppose you have two rows in your table. The first column in the first row has a value of 3, and the second column in the same row has a value of 4. The second row of your table has the values 3 and 3. It would look something like the following:

```
Column 1      Column 2
   3             4
   3             3
```

Now, if you performed the query shown in the beginning of this section, your resultset would be

OUTPUT
```
Total
7
6
```

It added every row individually. To add the totals of both columns for every row, you would use the following statement:

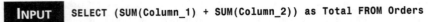

INPUT   `SELECT (SUM(Column_1) + SUM(Column_2)) as Total FROM Orders`

Your resultset would look like the following:

OUTPUT
```
Total
13
```

The `SUM()` function totals the values of the column that is given as the argument. It is covered here because it's addition—just on a larger scope.

A practical use of this function is when your application or Web page needs to have the total of one or more of the columns from your table. Financial applications and Web site shopping carts are two prime examples where something like this could be used. Remember, it is recommended that you give a name to the return value of your function. If you don't, you will have to refer to your column by its number rather than a name, which can be a little confusing when you try to use these operations in your applications.

Subtraction

Subtraction works a lot like addition. You would use this function to subtract column values from each other. A statement that uses subtraction would look like the following:

```
SELECT (Column_2 - Column 1) as Difference FROM Orders
```

This statement would return the difference of every row from the table individually. There is no function for subtraction that would give you the difference of two columns together as with the SUM() function. You could, however, total the two columns and then subtract them. Your statement would look like the following:

```
SELECT (SUM(Column_2) - SUM(Column_1)) as Difference FROM Orders
```

This would accomplish the same thing.

Again, practical uses for the subtraction function would be Web carts and finance applications.

Multiplication

The multiplication function works the same way as the previous functions. The operator that is used for multiplication is the asterisk (*), as in most programming languages. A multiplication function would look like the following:

```
SELECT (Column_1 * Column_2) as Product FROM Orders
```

This statement would return the product of the two values for every row that exists in the table. To get the product of the two columns, you would have toSUM() them, and then multiply them together as you did for subtraction. It would look like the following:

```
SELECT SUM(Column1 * Column2) AS Product FROM Orders;
```

Note

An important point to remember is that MySQL follows the normal mathematical order of statements. The operations in parenthesis will be performed first, followed by multiplication, division, addition, and then subtraction. Keep that in mind when performing your mathematical operations. For example, 2+3*5 = 17, not 25.

Division

MySQL also can perform division. It works the same way as the previous functions. A statement that uses division would look like the following:

```
SELECT (Column_1 / Column_2) as Result FROM Orders
```

A NULL value will be returned if you try to divide by zero. Fractional values will be returned as a decimal.

Modulo

The modulo function returns the remainder of two numbers. For example, if you were to divide 14 by 3, the remainder would be 2. This is what modulo or MOD() returns.

The MOD() function takes two arguments. The first argument is the numerator, and the second argument is the divisor. To express the previous example, the statement would look like the following:

 INPUT   `SELECT MOD(14, 3) as Result`

The output would be

OUTPUT
```
Result
2
```

As you can see, this function differs from the previously discussed functions. If you try to divide by 0, (MOD(4, 0)), MySQL will return a null value. To separate arguments inside a function, use a comma. This is much like any other programming language. In fact, MySQL uses C to perform these functions. If you wanted to create your own function, you could. Day 18, "How MySQL Compares," covers user-defined functions.

This covers the basic numeric functions. As you can see, they are relatively simple to use. Refer to Appendix B to see the additional numeric functions that MySQL has to offer.

Logical and Conditional Functions

The next few sections will cover logical and conditional functions as they are used by MySQL.

IF(), IFNULL(), and CASE

MySQL provides a way to perform conditional testing on expressions. It is a little crude, but it works. It is basically a function that takes three arguments. If the expression in the first argument is true, it will return the second argument. If expression one is false, it will return the third argument. Say you are comparing Column 1 to Column 2. If Column 1 is larger than `Column 2`, you want MySQL to return a 1 to your program. If `Column 2` is larger, you want a 0 returned to your program. The statement to use would look like the following:

```
SELECT IF(Column1 > Column2, 1, 0) FROM Orders
```

So, if `Column1` had a value of 12 and `Column2` had a value of 3, this statement would return 1 (the second argument). If `Column1` had a value of 3, and `Column2` had a value of 12, this statement would return 0 (the third argument). As you can see, this could take a little getting used to.

This function is quite useful when you need a straight comparison of columns. You may be wondering why you would want to use this instead of placing your conditions in the WHERE clause. Doing it this way is faster than using a WHERE clause. If you use a WHERE clause, MySQL will have to parse the entire statement, generate a query plan, choose the right keys, and then perform the statement. When a function is used, a query plan is not generated. The results are returned much faster. If you are going to do some straight comparisons, use this function instead of a WHERE clause.

If you need to compare more than one value, MySQL provides a CASE statement, which is pretty similar to the CASE statement in C. The syntax for the CASE statement is as follows:

```
SELECT CASE value WHEN comparison THEN result ELSE results
```

So, to use the previous example, you could have used a CASE statement as follows:

```
SELECT CASE 1 WHEN Column1 > Column2 THEN 0 ELSE 1
```

The CASE statement allows you to make multiple comparisons. Suppose you wanted to compare the value of three columns. You are looking to see if a column has a value of "Y". To do this, you could use the following statement:

```
SELECT CASE 1 WHEN Column1 = "Y" THEN 1 WHEN Column2 = "Y" THEN 2
WHEN Column3 = "Y" THEN 3 ELSE "NONE"
```

This would return the first number of the column that was equal to "Y". If none of the columns had a "Y" in them, this statement would return the word "NONE". This is a handy function when you need to perform multiple comparisons. As before, it is much faster to perform the comparison this way, because a query plan will not be generated.

The other comparison operation MySQL has is the IFNULL() function. This function will return the first argument if it is not NULL; it will return the second argument if it is NULL. For example, you want to make sure your division function worked and that you did not accidentally divide by zero. To do this, you could use the following statement:

```
SELECT IFNULL((Column1 / Column2), 0))
```

10

If the division of `Column1` by `Column2` was okay—meaning that `Column2` did not have a zero value—the result of that division was returned. If it turned out wrong and the value was `NULL`, the `0` would be returned. You can use numbers to clear things up:

INPUT   `SELECT IFNULL((12 / 2), 0) as Result`

Your resultset would be

OUTPUT   `Result`
             `6`

If things went wrong

`SELECT IFNULL((12 / 0), 0) as Result`

the output would be

OUTPUT   `Result`
             `0`

If you did not use the `IFNULL()` function and tried to divide by zero, a `NULL` would be returned. Instead, you wanted to catch the error before it caused any serious problems, so you used the `IFNULL()` function.

The `IFNULL()` function is a great way to check for any unexpected results. This can be a lifesaver when you have no control of the values that are being entered in a column.

AND, OR, NOT

MySQL also provides a set of logical operator functions. These functions will return a `1` if the values being compared are true and a `0` if they are not.

The `AND` function or operator (depending how you look at it) will return a true value if both the values are true and false if either of the values are false or `NULL`. Suppose you had the following statement:

INPUT   `SELECT 3 AND 4`

The return value would be

OUTPUT   `1 or TRUE - both values are true (not 0 or NULL)`

What would the following statement return?

`SELECT 0 AND 3`

If you guessed `0`, you are right. Both values have to be true for the expression to be true.

The AND operator can also be expressed as &&, as in many other programming languages.

The OR operator will return a true value if one of the values being compared is true. For example

INPUT   SELECT 1 OR NULL

returns a value of 1, and

SELECT NULL OR 0

returns a value of 0.

The OR operator can also be expressed as two pipe symbols. This is the symbol located right above the Enter key on the keyboard (| |). Again, most programming languages use this nomenclature.

The NOT operator negates the value of the argument. The exception is NULL. NOT NULL still returns NULL. For example

INPUT   SELECT NOT (1 + 1)

returns 0 and

SELECT NOT (1 - 1)

returns 1.

The NOT operator can also be expressed as the exclamation point (!).

These operator functions can be used to perform logical operations before a query gets to the WHERE clause. This speeds up queries and increases overall performance.

String and Character Functions

The string and character functions can manipulate text before it is returned to the client. This can save some time and processing power in your applications.

LTRIM, RTRIM, TRIM

These handy little functions trim excess spaces from either the beginning or the end of a string. These functions should be used when doing any kind of string comparisons. For example, the string "Hello" is different than "Hello". You could use the LTRIM function to get rid of any leading spaces, so that when you compared them again, LTRIM("Hello") now equals "Hello".

As explained earlier, the LTRIM function takes one argument. That argument is the string expression from which you want to trim all the leading spaces. For example

INPUT `SELECT LTRIM("     Mark")`

returns

OUTPUT `"Mark"`

and

INPUT `SELECT LTRIM("Mark    ")`

still returns

OUTPUT `"Mark    "`

To trim the trailing spaces, you would use the RTRIM function. It works exactly like its counterpart, except that it trims the trailing spaces instead of the leading ones. For example

INPUT `SELECT RTRIM("Mark      ")`

would return

OUTPUT `"Mark"`

The TRIM() function does a little bit more. With just one argument, it will trim both trailing and leading spaces. For example

INPUT `SELECT TRIM("    Mark    ")`

returns

OUTPUT `" Mark"`

The TRIM() function can trim spaces and characters or groups of characters. For example

INPUT `SELECT TRIM(TRAILING 'XXX' FROM "FileName.XXX")`

returns

OUTPUT `"FileName"`

You can also specify leading characters. If you wanted to trim leading and trailing characters, you would use the keyword BOTH. For example

INPUT `SELECT TRIM(LEADING 'XXX' FROM "XXXFileName")`

returns

OUTPUT `"FileName"`

and

INPUT `SELECT TRIM(BOTH 'XXX' FROM "XXXFileNameXXX")`

returns

OUTPUT `"FileName"`

10

SUBSTRING()

The SUBSTRING() function takes two arguments. The first argument is a string expression. The second argument is a number. The SUBSTRING() function returns a string from the position that is given as the second argument. For example, if you wanted to return everything after the word Hello in Hello World, you could use the SUBSTRING() function as follows:

```
SELECT SUBSTRING("Hello World", 7)
```

This statement would return the word World.

You could use this function in a variety of ways. It may not be as useful alone as when combined with other functions, such as the INSTR() function. See Appendix B for more details.

LOCATE()

The LOCATE() function takes three arguments. The first argument is the string expression you are trying to find. The second argument is the string that may contain the string for which you are looking. The final argument is the position from which you want to start looking. If you wanted to find the word "brown" in the string "The quick brown fox jumped over the lazy dog", you would use the following statement:

```
SELECT LOCATE("brown",
➡"The quick brown fox jumped over the lazy dog", 1)
```

This statement would return 10. This is the first position it found the string for which you were looking. You can combine functions to get more out of them. For example, you could combine the SUBSTRING() function with the LOCATE() function to return a string that may exist in a BLOB data type. It would look something like the following:

```
SELECT SUBSTRING(Column1, LOCATE("Doctor", Column1, 1))
```

The output from this function would be everything after the word Doctor in that column. For example, say that `Column1` had the value `"Dr. Ramirez"` and you only wanted his last name. Using the previous syntax, the statement would look like the following:

```
SELECT SUBSTRING("Dr. Ramirez", (LOCATE(".","Dr. Ramirez",1) + 2))
```

The `LOCATE` function would evaluate to 3. You know that there is a space between the name and the title. The function also starts counting at the position given as the second argument. To get just the last name, you have to add two to the result of the `LOCATE` function. That would be the start of the position for the last name.

Combining functions can be a powerful tool. It can also save time and logic in your applications.

REPLACE()

The `REPLACE()` function replaces a string expression with another string expression. This function takes three arguments. The first argument is the main string expression. The second argument is the string you want replaced, and the last argument is the string that is going to replace what is in argument two. For example, if you have a string `"FileName.xxx"`, and you want to replace the `"xxx"` with `"123"` Your function call would look like the following:

INPUT
```
SELECT REPLACE("FileName.xxx","xxx","123")
```

Your result would be

OUTPUT
```
"FileName.123"
```

REVERSE()

The `REVERSE()` function simply reverses the string expression that is given as its argument. For example, suppose you needed to reverse the string `"Hello"`. Your function call would be

INPUT
```
SELECT REPLACE("Hello")
```

The results of this function call would be

OUTPUT
```
"olleH"
```

UCASE(), LCASE()

The `UCASE()` and the `LCASE()` function takes whatever string expression that it has as its argument and either makes it all upper- or all lowercase. For example

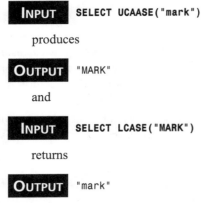

INPUT `SELECT UCAASE("mark")`

produces

OUTPUT `"MARK"`

and

INPUT `SELECT LCASE("MARK")`

returns

OUTPUT `"mark"`

10

As you can see, MySQL has a number of useful and not so useful string manipulation functions. These can save time on the client, or allow you to create robust reports without leaving the database server.

Summary

MySQL provides a number of internal functions that allow you, the database administrator or application programmer, to accomplish complex tasks within the database. Today, you learned about the advantages and disadvantages of including logic on the database server. You also learned some guidelines to determine where the best place is to put your application logic. You also learned about the various intrinsic functions MySQL has to offer.

Q&A

Q   **MySQL has a lot of neat functions. What if I need one that isn't there?**

A   MySQL is so flexible that it allows you to create your own functions. These user-defined functions act the same way that MySQL's own intrinsic functions operate. It is also possible to recompile your functions into the application so that you will always have them, no matter how many times you install. An overview of user-defined functions, as well as an example of how to do one, is covered on Day 18.

Q   Why are there so many functions?

A   The creators of MySQL included as many functions as they did for several reasons. The main reason is that MySQL should be able to provide a reporting mechanism for the data it contains. As you know, reporting can become quite complicated. For that reason, many functions are provided. Another reason is for compatibility. If you are changing database platforms, you may have some queries in your old database that contain some intrinsic functions. MySQL has tried to include many of the most common of these so that transferring your old database to a better one is easy.

Exercises

1. Use some of the functions you learned today in queries using the `Meet_A_Geek` database.

2. How would you get the total number of transactions that occurred on March 1, 2000?

WEEK 2

DAY 11

MySQL Table Locks and Assorted Keys

This chapter introduces you to two key concepts in the design of a database. Locks are important for protecting data integrity in a multithreaded environment. Keys are important both for designing the architecture of a database and for improving performance.

Today, you will learn

- What a lock is, and what kinds of locks are supported by MySQL
- How and when to use locks
- What keys are
- The concepts of primary, unique, and non-unique keys

- The importance of primary keys to database structure
- The performance advantages and disadvantages of using keys

What Is a lock?

Imagine the situation when your database gets rather busy, so busy that accesses are being made almost simultaneously. While some threads are trying to read data, others need to read, perform a calculation, and then write data back.

Note

What is a thread? Imagine a *thread* as a sub-process that goes on within the MySQL daemon. Every time a query is made to MySQL, it initiates a thread. When finished, the thread dies. This way, several things can be happening concurrently, even on the same table in a database, and yet each one is safely kept from interfering with another.

Although threads are similar in principle to processes in UNIX systems, they are not actually the same because the MySQL daemon is actually a single UNIX process, but it can have many threads within it.

For example, consider a scenario in which you have a table containing stock levels. For each product, the table contains a `qty_in_stock` field. If a customer orders an item, the server application would check the quantity in stock for this item and, provided the stock level is greater than the customer's order, you process the order. Finally, you reduce the stock level and update your table accordingly:

```
SELECT qty_in_stock FROM gadgets WHERE gadget_id=some_gadget_id;
 .
#some code here to check qty_in_stock against customer's requirement;
#if okay...
 .
UPDATE gadgets SET qty_in_stock=(qty_from_previous_statement-qty_purchased)
➥WHERE gadget_id=some_gadget_id;
```

While these lines of code are being executed, there's a slight chance that another customer is simultaneously purchasing the same product from the store. The same piece of code would be executed by a second thread, but the threads would confuse each other's calculations. The result would be erroneous data being written back into the table (see Figure 11.1).

FIGURE 11.1

Processing without locks.

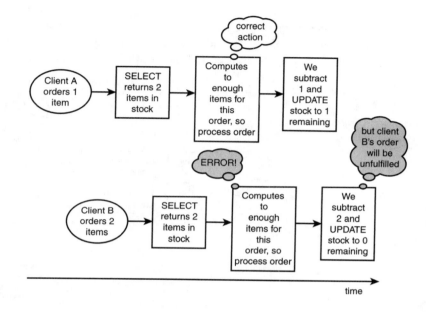

Clearly, you're going to upset the second customer. You'll promise him the goods, but when you try to fulfill, you'll find you've already emptied the store.

The answer to this is to use a lock. Locking allows a thread to have exclusive access to a number of tables, ensuring that it can go about its business without interference from other threads. When it's finished, it releases its lock and other threads can get to the data again.

Using locking, your code would look something like the following:

```
LOCK TABLES gadgets WRITE;
SELECT num_in_stock FROM gadgets WHERE gadget_id=some_gadget_id;
...
#some code here to check qty_in_stock against customer's requirement;
#if okay...
...
UPDATE gadgets SET num_in_stock=(num_from_previous_statement-num_purchased)
➥WHERE gadget_id=some_gadget_id;
UNLOCK TABLES;
```

Now your process is a little better managed, because the thread for the second customer has to wait until the thread for the first customer has finished, as shown in Figure 11.2.

In this simple example, you have used only one table. More commonly, a query will involve more than one table, and a sequence of related queries may involve several. In either situation, you would need to lock all of the tables you're going to use.

FIGURE **11.2**

Safer processing with locks.

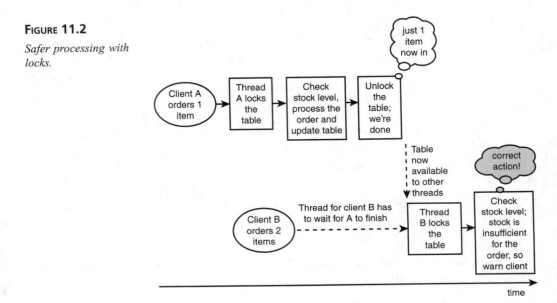

Imagine that your code gets a little more sophisticated, and you want to add this sale to a transactions table together with the customer's name and address.

Your code might look something like the following:

```
LOCK TABLES gadgets WRITE, transactions WRITE, customer READ;
SELECT num_in_stock, price FROM gadgets WHERE gadget_id=some_gadget_id;
.
#some code here to check qty_in_stock against customer's requirement;
#if okay...
.
UPDATE gadgets SET num_in_stock=(num_from_previous_statement-num_purchased)
➥WHERE gadget_id=some_gadget_id;
SELECT cust_name, address, zip, from customer
➥WHERE cust_id=this_customer_id;
INSERT INTO transactions VALUES (cust_name, address, zip, price, qty);
UNLOCK TABLES;
```

Notice here that you use WRITE locks on the gadgets and transactions tables, but you used a READ lock on the Customers table. This is because you have no need to write anything to the Customers table. In fact, other threads will still be able to read from the Customers table, even though you've locked it.

It is important to realize that all tables used need to be locked while you execute the code. This ensures that a deadlock situation cannot arise. Deadlock might occur if a thread locked just one of a set of tables it needed while another thread simultaneously locked another table in that set. Each thread would commence its processing. Suppose that thread A locks table 1, and thread B locks table 2. But if thread B also wanted to use table 1 (which it failed to lock), it would have to stop and wait until table 1 is released by thread A. This might never happen, because thread A may be paused, waiting for thread B to release table 2. This is a deadlock situation and would be the equivalent of gridlock on your database.

How MySQL Uses Locks

The syntax for LOCK TABLES is as follows:

```
LOCK TABLES table1_name (AS alias) {READ | [LOW_PRIORITY] WRITE}
➥[, table2_name  {READ | [LOW_PRIORITY] WRITE} ...]
```

As you can see, the LOCK TABLES command can be given a list of tables, some to READ lock and some to WRITE lock.

There are some simple rules about how MySQL handles READ and WRITE locks:

- If a thread obtains a READ lock, that thread and all other threads can only read from those tables.

- If a thread obtains a WRITE lock, it becomes the only thread with any access to those tables. It can read and write, but no other threads can access the tables until it has released the lock.

Issuing a LOCK TABLES command to request a lock isn't quite the same thing as obtaining one! There's an important queuing process first, which has to occur before a lock can be granted to a thread.

Queuing Lock Requests

A queuing mechanism exists so that, when a thread requests a LOCK, it may have to wait in line until any other locks on the tables concerned are released. There's a WRITE queue and a READ queue, which work in subtly different ways.

11

The following is the order of priorities:

When a WRITE lock is issued

- If there are no locks currently on the table, the WRITE lock is granted without queuing.
- Otherwise, the lock is put into the WRITE lock queue.

When a READ lock is issued

- If the table has no WRITE locks on it, the READ lock is granted without queuing.
- Otherwise, the lock request is put into the READ lock queue.

Whenever a lock is released, threads in the WRITE locks queue are given priority over those in the READ queue. Therefore, if a thread is requesting a WRITE lock, it will get it with minimal delay.

There's a good reason for this. By giving priority to threads wanting to perform a write operation, MySQL ensures that any updates to the database are processed as quickly as possible.

MySQL only grants a lock to a thread in the READ queue when there are no threads waiting in the WRITE queue. However, there are ways to override this default behavior.

LOW_PRIORITY WRITE

You may have an application for which it's more urgent for READ locks to be granted than WRITE locks.

Issuing a LOW_PRIORITY WRITE makes the queuing system behave the other way around: a WRITE lock will have to wait until all READ locks have cleared their queue before the WRITE lock is granted.

However, if you write such an application with a busy stream of READs, you should ensure that there is time in the system for the WRITEs to occur. Beware of performance risks because a WRITE may have to wait some time until the thread can proceed.

SELECT HIGH_PRIORITY

Another way to influence the queuing policy is to use a SELECT HIGH_PRIORITY. If this statement is issued, it allows the SELECT to read from the table, even if there is a WRITE lock in the queue.

It's wise to use this only for SELECT queries that must be done at once and are quick to complete.

Unlocking Tables

UNLOCK TABLES will unlock any tables held by the current thread. Tables will also be unlocked if the same thread issues another LOCK command, or if the connection to the server is closed. Locks will not be released because of any timeout.

Using LOCK TABLES

In MySQL, there are a couple of reasons you may need to use a LOCK.

Running Several Table Operations

As you've seen, a thread may issue a LOCK when it wants to ensure that nothing can access data in its chosen tables between a SELECT and an UPDATE. The more SQL statements processed in a sequence during which your thread needs exclusive access to the database, the more important it is to use LOCK TABLES. This is probably the most common reason for using locks.

However, note that individual UPDATE statements are *atomic*. This means that no other thread can interfere with the statement, no matter how complex it is. Therefore, if your query consists of a single UPDATE statement, you don't need to LOCK because a single statement cannot be interfered with. Even if your UPDATE affects 100,000 rows, no other thread can access these rows until the update is complete.

Performance

An application may need to perform several lines' worth of operations on a number of tables. In this case, the code may run fastest by locking the tables, thus guaranteeing exclusive and uninterrupted access to them.

The biggest impact may be if you have multiple INSERT statements in your code. Normally, the index buffer is flushed to disk once per INSERT statement; but when locking is in force, the flushing will be delayed until all INSERTs are completed.

Locking may help in the case of speed-critical parts of code. The downside is that other sections of code will suffer because they have to wait for it to finish before they continue.

Overcoming the Lack of Transactional Control

MySQL lacks transactional control, the ability to manage the various transactions occurring within the database management system.

11

With transactional control, changes to the database do not affect the target tables immediately, even though they may appear to do so. Instead, the changed data is held in a temporary buffer until you issue a command to commit the new data to the table.

Transactional commands (in ANSI SQL) include COMMIT, ROLLBACK, and SAVEPOINT, which can be used with INSERT, UPDATE, and DELETE. (More information about these commands, and how MySQL does without them, is presented in Day 17, "MySQL Database Security.")

For example, ROLLBACK can be used to drop any changes you've made to target tables before actually committing the changes to the tables. You might do a ROLLBACK if you suspected that another thread had interfered with some of the data you were trying to update.

Using locking, you can get around this limitation with a simple technique. After you have locked the required tables, you should test for any adverse conditions that might make you want to do a ROLLBACK. Then, if everything is okay, you do your updates. Finally, you unlock the tables.

Backing Up Your Database

You may want to back up your database and, in doing so, you want to make sure you get a consistent and complete snapshot.

Consistency is important. In other words, you want to ensure that no tables are partway through being modified by a thread at the moment you create your backup copy.

In this situation, you would perform a READ LOCK on the tables to ensure that no thread could be in the middle of modifying something.

What Is a Key?

A key on a database table provides a means to rapidly locate specific information. Although a key need not mean anything to the human user of the database, keys are a vital part of the database architecture, and can significantly influence performance.

Key Principles

Imagine that you have a very simple collection of data in which you hold just plain "useful" data. For example, you might create a Customers table similar to an old-fashioned card-index file, with one customer's name and details on each card. When you want to look up a customer, you flip through the file, reading each card in turn. When you see the card or cards you want, you read that useful information—such as the customer's name, address, and telephone number.

Conventionally, you might sort your card-index file in order of surname. This helps if you know the name of the person for whose data you're looking. But what if you want to find people by some other criterion?

Of course, you could set up your MySQL database in the same way. But you would soon run into difficulties. For example, imagine that you wanted to find all the customers in a given geographical area. Your database would have to read each customer's information in turn, a very inefficient operation.

You would call this operation a table scan. A *table scan*, the equivalent of flipping through that card-index file until you find the entries you want, is the most time-consuming of database operations.

That's where a key, or index, can help. A *key* is a field in the table that helps you locate entries in a table in a far more efficient way.

How Keys Work

A key exists like an extra table in the database, albeit belonging to its parent table. It takes up physical space on the hard disk (or other storage areas) of the database. It can be as big as the main table and, theoretically, even bigger.

You define your key to relate to one or a number of columns in a specific table. Because the data in a key is totally derived from the table, you can drop and re-create a key without any loss of data. As you will see, there may be good reasons for doing this.

Suppose that you wanted to select by the state line of each customer's address. You might create a key as shown in Figure 11.3. After you have the state key, you can easily locate all customers living in California, for example. You could just as easily sort customers by state rather than by name.

Benefits of Using a Key

Proper use of keys can significantly improve database performance. To use the analogy of a book index, consider how few pages it takes in the index of a book to give you a fast way of searching for the important themes. Compare that to how long it would take if you were scanning through the volume page-by-page.

11

Figure 11.3

Using a key to access the state *column of a* Customers *table.*

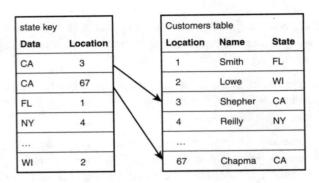

state key	
Data	**Location**
CA	3
CA	67
FL	1
NY	4
...	
WI	2

Customers table		
Location	**Name**	**State**
1	Smith	FL
2	Lowe	WI
3	Shepher	CA
4	Reilly	NY
...		
67	Chapma	CA

Keys in modern databases are designed to minimize the amount of disk accessing needed when reading from them. Even the method of scanning through the key and determining whether the data matches what you're looking for comprises sophisticated matching algorithms.

MySQL's Key Support

MySQL supports the following commands for creating keys on existing tables:

```
ALTER TABLE table_name ADD (KEY|INDEX) index_name (column_name[,...]);

ALTER TABLE table_name ADD UNIQUE index_name (column_name[,...]);

ALTER TABLE table_name ADD PRIMARY KEY index_name (column_name[,...]);
```

Note that in MySQL, key and index are synonymous.

These are the preferred formats for adding keys to existing tables. For compatibility with other implementations of SQL, MySQL also supports the following:

```
CREATE INDEX index_name ON table_name (column_name[,...]);

CREATE UNIQUE INDEX [index_name] ON table_name (column_name[,...]);

CREATE PRIMARY KEY ON table_name (column_name,...);
```

You can define keys when you create a table. The following is an example of defining a key:

```
CREATE TABLE table_name (column_namefield_type [NULL|NOT NULL],
➥KEY col_index(column_name));
```

For a primary key (with more options shown), you would use the following syntax:

```
CREATE TABLE table_name (column_name [NULL|NOT NULL] [DEFAULT default_value]
➥[AUTO_INCREMENT] [PRIMARY KEY] [reference definition]...);
```

You should look at the CREATE TABLE syntax for its full range of syntactical options, because you will concentrate on the ALTER TABLE syntax for your examples.

Now you'll look a little closer at MySQL's support for the various types of keys.

Single-Column Keys

The basic syntax to create a key on a single column is as follows:

```
ALTER TABLE table_name ADD KEY index_name (column_name[,...])
```

To create a key on the customer state column, as in Figure 11.3, the syntax would be

```
ALTER TABLE customers ADD KEY lastn_idx (lastname);
```

or

```
ALTER TABLE customers ADD INDEX lastn_idx (lastname);
```

If you now type

INPUT   `DESC customers;`

you can view the table description:

OUTPUT

```
mysql> DESC customers;
+-----------+--------------+------+-----+---------+-------+
| Field     | Type         | Null | Key | Default | Extra |
+-----------+--------------+------+-----+---------+-------+
| lastname  | varchar(30)  |      | MUL |         |       |
| firstname | varchar(30)  |      |     |         |       |
| address   | varchar(100) |      |     |         |       |
| state     | varchar(30)  |      |     |         |       |
| country   | varchar(30)  |      |     |         |       |
+-----------+--------------+------+-----+---------+-------+
5 rows in set (0.00 sec)
```

You can see that something has appeared in the Key entry for lastname. You have created a single-column index!

11

The MUL in the Key column tells you that it is a non-unique key. If you now want to check what keys exist, type the following:

INPUT   SHOW KEYS FROM *customers*;

or

SHOW INDEX FROM *customers*;

You will see that you have the following:

OUTPUT

```
+-----------+------------+----------+-------------+-------------+-----------+-----------+----------+
| Table     | Non_unique | Key_name | Seq_in_index | Column_name | Collation |Cardinality|Sub_part |
+-----------+------------+----------+-------------+-------------+-----------+-----------+----------+
| customers |          1 | lastn_idx |           1 | lastname    | A         |      NULL |     NULL |
+-----------+------------+----------+-------------+-------------+-----------+-----------+----------+
1 row in set (0.01 sec)
```

To drop the index, enter the following:

INPUT   ALTER TABLE *customers* DROP KEY *lastn_idx*;

which is the same as

ALTER TABLE *customers* DROP INDEX *lastn_idx*;

Multiple-Column Keys

You can create a multiple-column key, also called a *composite index*, on more than one column in the same table. For example

ALTER TABLE *customers* ADD KEY *comp_index* (*lastname, state, country*);

When constructing the key, MySQL works from the left across the columns specified, creating subsets of the column to include in the key. Thus, the following sets of columns would be indexed:

- (lastname, state, country)
- (lastname, state)
- (lastname)

You can ask MySQL to display the composite index:

INPUT `mysql> SHOW KEYS FROM customers;`

OUTPUT

```
+-----------+------------+-----------+--------------+-------------+-----------+-------------+----------+
| Table     | Non_unique | Key_name  | Seq_in_index | Column_name | Collation | Cardinality | Sub_part |
+-----------+------------+-----------+--------------+-------------+-----------+-------------+----------+
| customers |          1 | comp_index|            1 | lastname    | A         |        NULL |     NULL |
| customers |          1 | comp_index|            2 | state       | A         |        NULL |     NULL |
| customers |          1 | comp_index|            3 | country     | A         |        NULL |     NULL |
+-----------+------------+-----------+--------------+-------------+-----------+-------------+----------+
3 rows in set (0.00 sec)
```

When creating multiple-column keys, it's good practice to place the most restrictive column first (in the previous example, lastname is more restrictive than state, which is more restrictive than country). This will help database performance when doing a read operation.

Compiling a WHERE clause using the field or fields at the left side of the composite key is most efficient, because it will ensure that MySQL uses the key in its lookup.

To drop the composite key, the procedure is the same:

`ALTER TABLE customers DROP KEY comp_index;`

Multiple-column keys present a greater database overhead than single-column keys. Bear this in mind when deciding whether to use a multiple- or single-column key.

Partial Keys

When creating a key on a CHAR or VARCHAR type column, it is possible to index the first few characters of the column. You reference the first part, or *prefix*, of a column by appending (length) to the name of the column.

For example, you may want to create a key on the first 6 characters of a customer's name:

`ALTER TABLE customers ADD KEY lastn_idx (lastname(6))`

If you were doing this at the time of creating the table, you would specify (showing only syntax related to (lastname)):

```
CREATE TABLE customers (lastname VARCHAR(30) NOT NULL,
➥KEY lastname_idx (lastname(6)),...)
```

If you enter the following

INPUT   `mysql> SHOW KEYS FROM customers;`

you would get the following output:

OUTPUT

```
+-----------+-----------+------------+--------------+-------------+----------+------------+-----------+
| Table     |Non_unique |Key_name    |Seq_in_index  | Column_name |Collation|Cardinality |Sub_part   |
+-----------+-----------+------------+--------------+-------------+----------+------------+-----------+
| customers |         1 |lastn_index |            1 | lastname    | A        | NULL       |         6 |
+-----------+-----------+------------+--------------+-------------+----------+------------+-----------+
1 row in set (0.00 sec)
```

Note

> For columns of the TEXT and BLOB data type, you have no option but to make a partial index of the column.

Composite Partial Keys

You can create partial keys on multiple columns. For example

```
ALTER TABLE customers ADD KEY comp_index (lastname(6),state(2),country(3));
```

Now, suppose that the data in your table included the following:

INPUT   `mysql> SELECT * FROM customers;`

OUTPUT

```
+----------+-----------+-----------------------------+--------+---------+
| lastname | firstname | address                     | state  | country |
+----------+-----------+-----------------------------+--------+---------+
| Shepherd | Tom       | 33 Madison Drive, Oakland   | CA     | USA     |
| Chapman  | Frederick | 52 Ocean St, Sacramento     | CA     | USA     |
| Lowe     | Justin    | 3 Hill Walk, Twin Creeks    | WI     | USA     |
| Spokes   | Chris     | Red Fern House, Bradwell    | Oxford | UK      |
+----------+-----------+-----------------------------+--------+---------+
4 rows in set (0.00 sec)
```

You can imagine your key would then hold data looking like Table 11.1.

TABLE 11.1 Composite Partial Keys

lastname	state	country	comp_index
Shepherd	CA	USA	ShephCAUSA
Chapman	CA	USA	ChapmCAUSA
Lowe	WI	USA	Lowe WIUSA
Spokes	Oxford	UK	SpokeOxUK

11

When designing queries, you must remember that a query of the following form

```
SELECT * FROM customers WHERE lastname='Chapman';
```

would make use of the index when it is run. However, the following query

```
SELECT * FROM customers WHERE state='WI';
```

would not use the index. This is because indexes of (lastname, state, country), (lastname, state), and (lastname) exist, but the second query tries to use only state; MySQL must find a composite index with the required field leftmost to use it.

Much the same applies when using a partial key. If you have the following query

```
SELECT * FROM customers WHERE lastname LIKE 'Chap%';
```

it would use the key because it is looking for a lastname match by comparing the leftmost characters. However, the following query

```
SELECT * FROM customers WHERE lastname LIKE '%hap%';
```

would not because it is looking for matches both before and after the given text.

Performance-wise, holding partial indexes will usually take up less space in the key (and hence the disk) than having a key on the entire field. This saves space and may be just as effective; for example, most names are fairly unique after six characters.

Unique Keys

By definition, a unique index allows only unique values in the column. When you construct a WHERE clause to access one specific row, the unique key will take you to one—and only one—matching row.

Unique keys are not only used for performance, but also for ensuring data integrity. MySQL will not allow the creation of a second row with duplicate key data.

If you try to insert duplicate data into a table where a column is unique, MySQL will give you an error. The same will happen if you try to update an existing row to make a unique column the same as another existing row.

Additionally, if you try to alter a table and add a unique key to a column where data in that column is already non-unique, it will generate an error.

The following would be possible, in the hope of using customers' last names as a unique key:

```
ALTER TABLE customers ADD UNIQUE lastn_index (lastname);
```

However, it would be impractical.

You can create more than one unique key. For example, add a second unique index as follows:

```
ALTER TABLE customers ADD UNIQUE address_index (address);
```

If you ran the previous commands in that order, your table would look as follows:

INPUT
```
mysql> desc customers;
```

OUTPUT
```
+-----------+--------------+------+-----+---------+-------+
| Field     | Type         | Null | Key | Default | Extra |
+-----------+--------------+------+-----+---------+-------+
| lastname  | varchar(30)  |      | PRI |         |       |
| firstname | varchar(30)  |      |     |         |       |
| address   | varchar(100) |      | UNI |         |       |
| state     | varchar(30)  |      |     |         |       |
| country   | varchar(30)  |      |     |         |       |
+-----------+--------------+------+-----+---------+-------+
5 rows in set (0.00 sec)
```

Notice how MySQL has called lastnamePRI, and addressUNI. It has made lastname the primary key, a special kind of unique key, automatically.

MySQL encourages you to create a primary key, so much so, that if you DROP `lastn_index`, it will now make `address` the primary key.

Unique keys are an important concept—primary keys, in particular. These are covered in more detail a little later in this chapter.

Foreign Keys

Foreign keys are not currently supported in MySQL. Some syntax is included for completeness and to facilitate porting code from other database systems. However, the commands will not work in current implementations and allowance of all forms of syntax is not yet complete.

Primary Keys

A primary key is similar in principle to a unique key; its data must be unique, but the primary key of a table has a more privileged status. Only one primary key can exist for each table, and its field values can never be null.

A primary key is generally used as a structural link in the database, defining relationships between different tables. Wherever you want to join from one table to another table, you would like to have that table's primary key. In contrast, keys that are merely unique can be added purely for performance reasons.

MySQL requires you to specify NOT NULL when creating a table with a given column specified as PRIMARY KEY, even if it may allow a unique key to have null values (as in recent implementations).

The choice of a primary key is very important in the design of a database; a primary key is the fundamental piece of data that facilitates the joining of tables and the whole concept of a relational database. This is why you must be careful to base your primary key on information that will always be unique.

In the last example, you saw that *lastname* might not be a wise choice for a primary key. However, you might create a more elaborate primary key by combining a number of fields to concoct something that will be unique.

Multiple-Column Primary Keys

It is possible to create a primary key as a multiple-column key.

You cannot do this in your CREATE TABLE statement, but must use the ALTER TABLE syntax, as shown in the following:

11

`INPUT`   ALTER TABLE *customers* ADD PRIMARY KEY (*lastname,firstname*);

Similarly, you could use partial indexing:

`INPUT`   ALTER TABLE *customers* ADD PRIMARY KEY (*lastname*(6),*firstname*(6));

To remove a primary key, you can use

`INPUT`   ALTER TABLE *customers* DROP PRIMARY KEY;

Synthetic Keys

You have the choice of making your key out of some unique pieces of real data or creating it as a separate unique identifier, known as a *synthetic* or *surrogate key*.

You would make your key from the base data only if you were totally sure that it would never be null and that a duplicate would never arise. For example, you might hope to base a key on the precise time of someone's birth, or on their Social Security number, on the assumption that no two people would ever be identical in these respects.

However, these ideas are not perfect. People rarely know their time of birth precisely, and even if you could record it to the second, there's no guarantee that a duplicate wouldn't arise at some time. Not all countries in the world issue Social Security numbers, and in many areas it might be illegal to store them without good reason, not to mention that customers may prefer not to tell you their numbers.

It is not so difficult to find a unique key arising from the data in some scenarios. For example, if I were creating a database of my extensive photo collection, I probably could use time as a unique identifier, as long as I record the time I took each photo, and I never take photos more rapidly than the granularity of the key—perhaps one per second.

Consider again the `Customers` table with a composite unique key, comprising say, last name, first name, and address. This would be better, but still not ideal. It would fall down because people move and even change their names. If a customer did this, the next time you tried to access the data using your unique key, you might have problems finding him or her in the data. You are faced with the choice of maintaining the customer's previous name or address as the key to his or her data, or updating your key to contain the new data.

In trying to modify a key field, you would meet even worse problems. If you use the key to join a `Customers` table with an `Orders` table, you would find yourself having to update the references to customers in the `Orders` table too.

You would run the risk of losing referential integrity. This is a serious situation in a relational database in which important links between pieces of data become lost.

In this example, it would be better to create a unique customer identification number, what's known as a *synthetic key*. A synthetic key is one that can be totally meaningless outside the context of the database, and which we have "synthesized" purely for the purpose of finding a unique and convenient way to refer to each entry in the table. A synthetic key for each customer will never change, irrespective of what other changes happen to customers as individuals.

To create a synthetic `customer_number` field to be the primary key for your customers, you can define it as follows:

```
CREATE TABLE customers (customer_number INT(8) PRIMARY KEY NOT NULL,
➥last_name VARCHAR(30), ...)
```

This tells MySQL to create a primary key of type integer, with 8 digits (enough for 100,000,000 customers!).

Choosing keys is no trivial matter. After you decide you need a primary key in a table, it may be tempting to create synthetic keys all over the place. Should you do this?

Before deciding to create a synthetic key, you should be sure that you've looked hard enough for some other naturally unique identifier. Otherwise, you risk complicating the design and slowing down the performance of your database without reason.

11

Key Choices

When should you use a key? What kind of key should you use? Using keys appropriately in your database design can improve both design and performance. But making the wrong choices may work against you.

The following sections provide a brief guide to using and choosing keys.

When to Use Keys

Whether to use a key on a column will depend on the types of queries you intend to carry out.

When to use keys:

- WHERE *clauses*—If you are frequently using a column for selection criteria, a key on this column will generally improve performance. The lower the number of rows in a table that are likely to be returned by a SELECT...WHERE statement, the more a key will be beneficial. In particular, when a query is expected to return a unique result, a key should be created on the column or columns used by the WHERE clause.
- ORDER BY *and* GROUP BY *clauses*—Sorting data is a costly exercise. Because a key automatically renders results in alphabetical order, columns that you want to ORDER BY or GROUP BY are good candidates for keys.
- MIN() *and* MAX()—Keys are highly efficient at finding minimum and maximum values in a column.
- *Table joins*—The use of keys will always help performance where the indexed columns are being used to join tables. In general, most, if not all, columns that are at some stage used in a table join should be indexed.

When Not to Use Keys

Although keys can bring great benefits to SELECT operations, this can come at a price. Consider a few instances in which you should avoid using keys.

- *Tables used in frequent write operations*—Whenever you perform a write operation, such as an INSERT, UPDATE, or DELETE on a table, both the main table and the key have to be written to. A key thus presents an overhead. On a system where you are performing frequent write operations, you must consider this overhead carefully and try to balance it against the benefits you may get when you perform read operations.
- *Instances when a* SELECT *will return a high proportion of rows*—You would not bother to index the words he, she, or it in the index of a book. In the same way, you would not want a key on "customer salutation" because WHERE conditions selecting on Mr, Ms, and so on would return a high proportion of rows each time. Performance would be degraded because each time a successful match is made, the database has had to read both the index and the table data. A table scan would be faster than performing two reads for such a high proportion of rows.
- *Small tables*—There's little advantage to be gained creating keys on small tables; a table scan may be just as fast.
- *MySQL will not allow you to create a key on a column with NULL values.*
- *A table in MySQL cannot contain more than 16 keys.*

When to Use Primary and Unique Keys

In general, every table in the database in which you want to uniquely access a row should have a primary key.

The AUTO_INCREMENT Option

Imagine that you're going to use a customer number, a synthetic key, to uniquely identify each person in your database. You would write your CREATE TABLE statement as follows:

```
CREATE TABLE customers (
➡customer_number INT(8) AUTO_INCREMENT PRIMARY KEY NOT NULL,
➡last_name VARCHAR(30), ...
```

Notice that you have an AUTO_INCREMENT option specified for customer_number.

This is a convenient way of numbering your entries sequentially and ensuring that two identical entries can never arise.

AUTO_INCREMENT can be applied to any column in the table of type INTEGER. If you put a NULL or 0 value into a field of this type during an INSERT or UPDATE, MySQL will automatically set the new field value to 1 greater than the largest value for that column currently in the table.

When used with PRIMARY KEY or UNIQUE, MySQL gives you an easy way of ensuring the integrity of your key.

11

Dropping a Key

If your database spends a lot of its time handling queries with read operations, and at certain times gets updated with a large number of write operations, there may be a case for using keys that are dropped just before update time and reinstated afterward.

You would drop the key with the following syntax:

```
ALTER TABLE customers DROP INDEX lastn_idx;
...
(perform batch write operations)
...
CREATE INDEX lastn_idx ON customers (lastname);
```

You may also want to drop an index to experiment with database performance. When an index is dropped, performance may get worse or improve.

Dropping an index does not remove any data. Nevertheless, the DROP command should always be used with care because DROP TABLE can be disastrous.

Summary

This chapter has introduced you to the concept of locks. You have seen that in a multithreaded database environment, locks may be needed to allow one thread to process a multiline query without risk of another thread interfering with the data before it has finished. You've seen how READ locks prevent other threads from writing to the locked tables, while WRITE locks prevent other threads from accessing them at all.

You've examined the mechanism by which MySQL queues up lock requests, prioritizing the granting of locks according to a given policy.

You've also seen how performance can be affected by the use of locks, and how they can be used to overcome MySQL's lack of transactional control.

Keys, or indexes, are an even more fundamental concept that play a role not only in MySQL but in relational databases of all kinds. At their simplest, keys give you a way of looking up data in an efficient way. You've seen that the concept of primary keys is the cornerstone of relational database design.

Keys can exist in a variety of forms: unique or non-unique; single-column or multiple-column. You've seen how the whole or just part of a column can be indexed.

You've looked at how to apply keys and whether you should. You can use a key to make lookups more efficient, to help performance when you are selecting unique results, or when sorting or grouping data. However, you have also seen that the unnecessary use of keys in frequently updated tables may degrade performance.

Unique keys are used not only for performance but also to preserve the integrity of the data. Unique keys can be formed out of the data itself or created as synthetic keys, independent of the data content. MySQL gives you the AUTO_INCREMENT option when defining a numeric column, which can be conveniently used to create unique synthetic keys.

You've seen how primary keys are a special type of unique key, essential in relating all relevant tables. They must be unique and must never be null, thus guaranteeing that no row of data can ever fail to be referenced through its primary key.

Q&A

Q **When do I need to be concerned about locks?**

A Locks are important in a multithreaded environment, in which some threads have the job of updating, inserting to, or deleting from the database. If there are other threads concerned with reading from the database that may be doing so simultaneously, you should consider using locks.

Essentially, if a thread needs to use several lines of SQL to perform its task, you must consider using a lock to preserve data integrity. However, there may also be performance reasons why you would want to use locks.

Q **What's the point of creating a non-unique key?**

A Non-unique keys can improve database performance during read operations. Although the resultant rows may not be uniquely identified by the key, access to them and sorting and grouping of the result will be much faster.

Q **Do all unique keys have to be primary keys?**

A No. MySQL permits only one primary key per table, but there may be a number of unique keys. Both unique keys and primary keys can speed up the selecting of data with a WHERE clause, but a column should be chosen as the primary key if this is the column by which you want to join the table with other tables.

Q **Should every table have a primary key?**

A Not necessarily. In general, tables should have a primary key whenever you want to use them in a join with another table. However, you may not want to do this with every table, and there are circumstances when it's better not to use a key.

Q **I'm confused about when to use keys, and when not to. How do I decide?**

A Although the need for a primary key is easy to define, the use of other keys may not be. There may be factors both for and against the use of keys and, in some circumstances, they may be contradictory. In this case, the database should be run with the keys and its performance measured. The keys can then be dropped and the performance measured again. Then, re-create the keys, perhaps in a different way, and keep experimenting until performance is optimized. If need be, the database can be run with a view to regularly dropping certain keys and creating them again, such as around the time of a series of write operations.

11

Exercises

1. Imagine that you have a table called Orders, and you want to update it while no other threads can read from it. You also have a table called Products, which you want to read from but not update. Write the syntax for appropriate locking and unlocking of these tables.

2. Consider each of the following scenarios. In which would you consider applying a key to the table? Would you use a unique or non-unique key?

    a. A table containing the birthdays of all of the people you know. Your computer accesses it once a day to see if it's anyone's birthday today and, if so, emails him or her a greeting.

    b. A table of products available to order from your online shop. Duplicates are not allowed.

    c. A table that records the sales tax applied to products sold. It is written to each time a product is sold, but read from only once per quarter.

DAY 12

How to Get the Data—Database Interfaces

Up to this point, you have communicated with your database solely through the MySQL monitor. While this is a convenient and easy way to create your database and manipulate data, it may not always suit your needs. The MySQL monitor may not fill the needs of your users who must use the data day in and day out either. Don't worry, there is more than one way to skin a cat.

MySQL provides you with a number of programming interfaces. These interfaces or APIs allow you to build applications that use MySQL. Applications that are built to interface with databases are generally called "front-end" applications. They supply the user interface, while the database engine is usually called the "back end." MySQL makes for a very good "back-end" database.

Today, you will learn about interfacing MySQL. You will learn

- How interfacing works
- The basic steps that all interfaces share

Making the Connection

Nowadays, it is hard to create a business application that does not interface with a database at some point. Sure, there are utility programs, but, for the most part, if you create an application in the business world, it is going to talk to a database. To understand how applications can interface with databases, you need to know how database servers work and a little about client/server programming.

As you have learned, database servers are programs that run continuously in the background. They are known as services or daemons, depending on which operating system you use. To take advantage of the database, an application must first establish a connection to this server program. This connection is usually established through an interface of some sort.

An *interface* is a layer between your program and the database. It acts as a kind of middleman. Commands issued from your program go through this interpreter and are translated for the database. The interface is simply a collection of functions that are available to the programmer. The programmer can use these functions to accomplish certain database tasks, such as connecting to the database or issuing a query.

There are generally two parts to the interface today. One part is the actual code you use in your application. This part contains the actual function calls and variables. This part is also universal, meaning that no matter which database you're using, the functions and variables you use remain the same. The second piece is the actual interpreter, or as it's usually called, the driver. This piece of the interface handles the grunt work. It takes the function calls from the first part, translates them, and then interacts with the database to produce the requested results. These drivers are created by the database manufacturer and are specific to that database. So, if you were using Sybase and you switched to MySQL, you would need to get the MySQL driver for your code to work. See Figure 12.1.

One of the advantages of interfacing a database in this way is that you only have to learn one set of function calls. It doesn't matter what your back end is, your code will remain the same. For example, say that you developed an application that was using Sybase as its back-end database product. Because you are smart and know how the real world works, you used the Perl DBI/DBD in your application. After everything was completed, the code was tested, beta versions were sent out, customers seemed pretty happy, and then management decided to change database products. They heard about this absolutely incredible database called MySQL and opted to use it instead. Now the question is—how much code are you going to have to change? The answer—hardly any. A few changes might need to be made to accommodate discrepancies between database products, but that's about all. Before database-independent interfaces, the programmer had to code the functions that interfaced with the databases themselves. Changing a database product meant writing an entirely new interface from scratch. Not a lot of fun.

FIGURE 12.1

Process flow for interfaces and drivers.

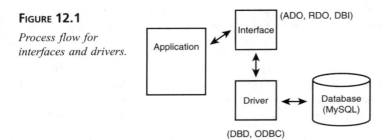

There are many interfaces/drivers available for MySQL. Perl, PHP, C++, Python, and ODBC are just a few of the programmable interfaces that have been written for MySQL. Of course, you do not have to use them if you do not want to. Sometimes, it makes more sense for you to do it the old way—creating an interface from scratch. If that is the case, MySQL includes the C++ source files. You can create your own interface or improve on the code that is made available to you.

Interfaces are a fast, clean way for a developer to build applications that communicate with databases. You might be asking yourself, "How do they communicate with the database?" You can think of an interface as a customer and the driver as a switchboard operator. A switchboard operator takes calls and routes them to the right person. The driver and the interface share the same relationship. When a customer makes a call to the switchboard and asks for a specific person, the operator knows the number that person can be reached at and connects the customer to that number. The interface and the driver do the same thing. The application tells the interface to connect to the database. The application provides some information, such as the address and the name of the database to which the application wants to talk. The interface take this information and makes a call to the driver. The driver

12

receives this information and makes the connection. It knows which port to talk on and how to talk to the database. The port is very much like the telephone number for the person you're trying to call. It is a line of communication. Now data can flow freely between the application and the database.

Connection Requirements

Now that you have a basic understanding of how interfaces and drivers work, you'll move on to the actual connection. You have already read about the events that lead up to a connection, but you haven't learned about the requirements to make a connection.

The first requirement for making a connection to a database server, other than some sort of physical connection, is the driver. The proper driver must be installed. If the driver is not present, there is no way for your application to communicate with the database. Make sure you are using the most current driver. A lot of manufacturers update their drivers periodically, especially when a new release for the database has been made available.

The next requirement is the name or address of the server where the database is located. How can you make a telephone call if you don't know the number, or pay a friend a visit if you don't know where he or she lives? A database connection is the same. How can a driver connect to a database if it doesn't know where to connect? Before you can connect to a database, you need to get the IP address of the database server or, if you are using dynamic addressing, the server name. This is vital information for your connection.

Another requirement for making a connection is the database name. This is another important piece of information the driver will need to access the database. As in the previous example, if you don't know where to connect, how can you connect? If you don't specify a database, the driver doesn't know where to get the data.

The final requirement that all database connections need is the username and password for the connection. It is all about security. The database server will not allow just anybody to connect to it. It looks at its grant tables to see who is allowed access to which databases. If the username and password do not match up, a connection will not be made.

Note

> You can learn more about security issues in Day 17, "MySQL Database Security."

These four requirements are the same for almost every database interface/driver. If you are a developer getting ready to create your first application, you need to know these requirements before you can go any further.

Getting to the Data

Every interface shares the same concept for accessing data. There are a series of steps that are the same for accessing your data, no matter which interface/driver you are using. They all basically use the same information. The following is the general cycle:

1. Connect to the database.
2. Issue a query or a command.
3. If a query was issued, then next step is to receive a recordset.
4. Manipulate the recordset.
5. Close the connection. (See Figure 12.2.)

FIGURE 12.2

The common interface cycle.

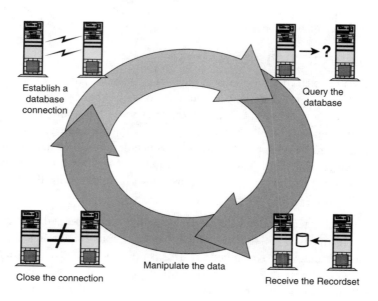

Establish a database connection

Query the database

Close the connection

Manipulate the data

Receive the Recordset

12

This cycle can be found in every interface, no matter what the programming language is or on what platform it is operating. You will hardly ever deviate from this natural, logical cycle. The following sections take a more in-depth look at what happens at every step.

Establishing the Connection

The first step of the process is to establish a connection with the database. This connection is what establishes a link between your application and the database. This link is used to transfer all your SQL commands from your application to the database and return all your resultsets from the database to your application.

The connection requires the parameters that were stated before. The database, the driver to use, the location of the database (either IP address or server name), and the username and password. A connection cannot be established if these parameters are not present. During the next three days, you will see this in action. You will see how each interface uses these same parameters to establish a connection and create a link between your program and the database.

This step only needs to occur once during a session. After you have established a connection, you can keep using the same connection for all your queries. You don't have to close the session and then reopen it to requery the database. After your application has created the link, that link remains in existence either until your application closes the link or the link is closed because it is not being used.

Querying the Database

The next step of the cycle is to query the database. This is where you will embed SQL commands into your application to pass to the database. These can be SQL commands that create data structures, such as tables, or they can be SELECT statements; It all depends on your program's requirements. Pretty much anything you can type in the MySQL monitor can be embedded in your program. This includes OPTIMIZE statements, as well as the FLUSH privileges statement. You can even use the LOAD DATA INFILE command statement. This allows you to create very flexible and powerful applications that use MySQL to its fullest extent.

Most interfaces differentiate between creating a recordset and issuing a command that does not return data. Most interfaces will have a simple execute function that will just execute the SQL that you have embedded. This is great for INSERT, UPDATE and DELETE queries, but not good for a SELECT query. How would you get the results back if you just executed a SELECT statement? There wouldn't be anywhere for the records to go. So the interfaces have supplied an object or an array to which these records can go. You will learn more about this in the upcoming days. You'll see how to pass variables from your application to the database to get the results you need.

Receiving the Recordset and Manipulating the Data

The next step in the cycle is receiving the recordset. A *resultset* or *recordset* is the result of a SELECT query. A recordset is the same information that is returned to the screen when you type a SELECT statement into the MySQL monitor program, but instead of these results being displayed onscreen, they are put into a variable of some sort to be used in your application. These variables are usually an array of some sort. The recordset is retrieved as a series of rows. Each row contains the columns that were used in the SELECT statements. This creates a grid-like structure, very much like the display in the MySQL monitor. To retrieve all records from a recordset, you have to pull the data out of the row, move to the next row and get the record, move to the next row, and so on. It's like walking—you are taking rows one step at a time. Hence, the term "walking a recordset."

The results are stored on a column name/value pair basis. For example, there is a First Name column in the Customers database. In your recordset, depending on the interface you were using, you could refer to the column by name. If you were using Perl, referring to the First_Name field in a resultset would look something like the following:

```
$ref->{'First_Name'}
```

This would return the value that was held in the First_Name column for that row. You can also refer to column names by their indexes. If the First_Name column was the first column named in your SELECT query, you could refer to it using an ADO Recordset object, as shown in the following:

```
RstCustomers.Fields(0)
```

You are not limited to the number of recordsets you have. You can create a new recordset for each query you issue. The choice is yours, just remember that these types of variables take up some memory. You may need to take performance into consideration before you create a hundred recordset objects.

Now that you have the recordset, you are free to do whatever you like with the data. You can display it to the user, use it in graphs and charts, or even create reports. The number of things you can do is endless.

Closing the Connection

Like your mother always said (at least mine did) you have to clean up all your toys when you are done playing. This same advice holds true in the programming world. When you are done creating objects and they no longer have a use, get rid of them—throw them away. The same holds true for connections. If you are no longer using a connection, get rid of it. Free it up for someone else to use. Each connection takes up resources both on the client and on the server. Cleaning up after yourself saves resources and prevents bugs.

12

Summary

This day provided you with a preview of things to come. It introduced you to the interface and driver concepts. You learned that these two layers work in conjunction with one another to provide access to your database. You saw that the interface provides you with the same functions and variables no matter which database you are using. The only thing that needs to be changed is the driver. You also learned the advantages of doing things this way.

Today, you also learned about the parameters that are required for every database connection. This information needs to be collected before any connections can take place.

You also learned about the common steps that all interfaces share when working with a database. You learned that this cycle is logical and provides a great deal of flexibility and power to the programmer. You saw how you can embed SQL commands in your application to accomplish any task from database administration to SELECT statements.

Interfacing your database is the most important part of any business. If you cannot access or manipulate your data, a database is useless. Interfaces provide a way for programmers, Web developers, and database administrators to manipulate their databases programmatically.

Q&A

Q   How are my queries executed?

A   The SQL statements that you embed in your program are passed to the driver. This driver contains all the database-specific functions. The driver calls the function that runs your query against the database. The result of this function is your resultset.

Q   Can I create databases using an interface?

A   You can do pretty much anything that you could do in the MySQL monitor. If you have the correct permissions, you can use CREATE, DROP, ORGANIZE, INSERT, DELETE, and UPDATE records and databases. You have the power to automate administrator tasks or manipulate the data through a program you can create.

Q   What interfaces are available for MySQL?

A   MySQL has many interfaces and drivers. Some were created by TcX and some are third-party creations. There are interfaces for Perl (DBD/DBI), ODBC (MyODBC), Java (JDBC), C/C++, Python, and PHP. Because MySQL is ODBC-compliant, you can use tools like VBScript, Visual Basic, Access, Crystal Reports or any other tool that can use an ODBC data source.

Exercises

1. List the advantages and disadvantages to using an interface as opposed to the MySQL Monitor program.

2. What are the basic requirements for a database connection?

12

DAY 13

How to Use MyODBC

The MyODBC interface is just one of the ways you can interact with your MySQL data on the Windows platform. Microsoft has created and embraced this technology and has made it an integral part of many of their applications.

Microsoft's Open Database Connectivity (ODBC) is a standard that allows a user to access any database using the same series of commands. It provides a layer of abstraction between the program and the database. Each database has its own ODBC driver that adheres to Microsoft's ODBC standard. This driver acts as the layer of abstraction. You can think of the ODBC driver as a translator. In your programs, you will issue a command that will be interpreted by the driver. This driver will forward this interpreted command to the database. The database will then send the resultset or message back to the driver, which, in turn, will send it back to the application.

This architecture allows the programmer to use the same code to interact with a database, regardless of what database to which it is talking. This works as long as the programmer sticks to the ANSI SQL standard when issuing commands. If the programmer uses database-specific commands, the ability to reuse is nullified.

If you create programs for a Windows platform (this includes Active Server Pages), more than likely you will use ODBC to talk to your database. ODBC is easy to use and follows the same steps you learned about yesterday.

In the examples and lessons today you will use ODBC to talk to a MySQL database. To do this, you will create an Active Server Page (ASP) using VBScript. Today you will also learn

- How to get and install the MyODBC driver
- How to set up a Data Source Name (DSN)
- How to connect to a MySQL using ADO (ActiveX Data Objects)
- Create an Active Server Page to access a MySQL database

Where Do I Get the Driver?

To begin using ODBC in your applications, you must first have the ODBC driver for your database. Microsoft automatically installs several of its drivers. Some databases install the ODBC driver during the initial application installation as well. If you perform the following steps, you can see what drivers are installed on your computer right now.

1. Click Start, Settings, Control Panel.
2. You should see an icon that is titled ODBC Data Sources (32 bit). Double-click it.
3. The Data Source Administrator will be displayed. This is where you can adjust or add new ODBC drivers, as well as create Data Source Names—you'll get to that in a little while.
4. Click the Drivers tab. A list of currently installed drivers will be displayed. If you haven't jumped ahead, you shouldn't see any MySQL drivers there, yet. You should see a bunch, mostly Microsoft products.

Now that you have seen what drivers are currently installed on your system, it's time to install one more.

On the CD-ROM, included with this book, you should see a folder containing all the downloadable products from the MySQL Web site. Look for the ODBC zip file. It should be named something like `myodbc-2.50-24-win95.zip`. Make sure you have WinZip installed (on the CD-ROM as well). Double-click the file and the self extraction program should begin. Perform the following steps to install the MyODBC driver onto your machine.

1. After the extraction process begins, the install program should run. The first screen you should see should be similar to Figure 13.1.

FIGURE 13.1

The MyODBC installation program.

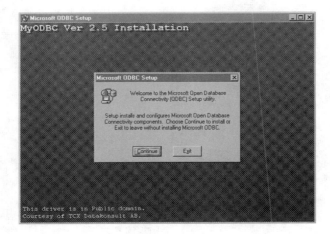

2. Click continue. The install drivers dialog box should appear, as shown in Figure 13.2. Click MySQL and then click OK.

3. The program files will then be copied to your hard drive. This will take a couple of seconds. You should then see the dialog box shown in Figure 13.3.

4. From here, click the Close button. You will add the Data Source Name later.

Congratulations, you have successfully installed the MyODBC driver.

13

FIGURE 13.2

The MySQL driver installation dialog box.

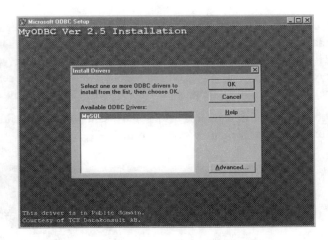

FIGURE 13.3

Data Sources dialog box.

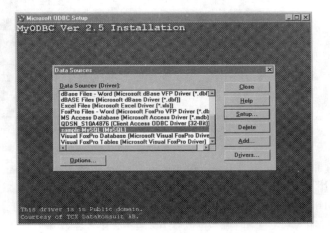

Setting Up the Data Source Name (DSN)

Now that the MyODBC driver is installed, you can create a Data Source Name for you applications to use. A Data Source Name is a file that contains all the specific information pertinent to your database. For example, a DSN will contain all the connection information, database names, and usernames for a particular database. In this way, an application only has to use the DSN to help configure the ODBC driver. You will learn how to get around using DSN to connect to your database later. Perform the following steps to add a DSN for the Meet_A_Geek database.

1. Click Start, Settings, Control Panel, as shown in Figure 13.4.
2. Double-click the ODBC Data Sources (32 bit) icon. It will open the ODBC Data Source Administrator (see Figure 13.5).

FIGURE 13.4

The Control Panel.

FIGURE 13.5

The Data Sources Administrator.

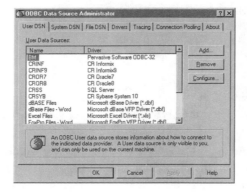

13

The Data Source Administrator consists of 7 panels. The first panel, User DSN, sets up DSNs specific to a user for the current machine. You would set up a User DSN for a specific person. The next tab, System DSN, creates a data source for everyone who can use the current machine. The next tab, File DSN, creates a DSN that is visibleto everyone and can be used by anyone who has the correct drivers installed. The next tab, Drivers, lists all the drivers that are currently installed on your machine. The fifth tab, Tracing, turns on logging for your ODBC driver; it will log all connections. Microsoft Visual Studio uses this feature to help debug programs. The next tab is the Connection Pooling tab. On this tab, you will find options that allow your ODBC driver to reuse open connection handles, which will save time and resources in your applications. The final tab is the About tab. On this tab, you will find the core ODBC Dynamically Linked Libraries (DLLs).

Because you are going to be creating an application that can be used by more than one person logging in to the current machine, you are going to create a System DSN for the Meet_A_Geek database.

1. Click the System tab. If you already have some System DSNs, you will see them here (see Figure 13.6). Click the Add button to create a new DSN.

FIGURE 13.6

The System DSN pane.

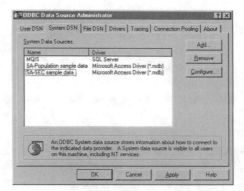

2. A dialog box, similar to the one in Figure 13.7, should appear. It displays a list of available drivers. Select the MySQL driver. After you have selected the driver, click Finish.

3. The next window to appear is the TcX mysql Driver Configuration window. This window contains all the information MyODBC needs to properly connect to the designated database. Enter the following information into the appropriate fields:

Windows DSN Name: **Meet-A-Geek**

MySQL Host (name or IP): The name or IP of your MySQL server

User: **root**

Password: your root password

Port and SQL command: leave blank

The completed window should look something like Figure 13.8.

FIGURE **13.7**

Creating a new Data Source.

FIGURE **13.8**

The configuration screen.

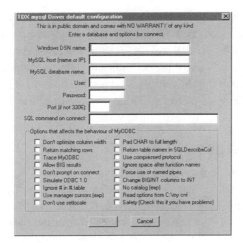

13

4.   Click OK to compete the DSN configuration. You will be returned to the ODBC
     Data Source Administrator. You should see your new DSN in the list box. Click OK
     to close the Administrator. You have now successfully created your first MySQL
     system DSN.

Remember that a DSN is simply a file that contains the data the driver needs to connect to a
database. It acts just like a configuration file.

Active Server Pages and VBScript

Microsoft, in its efforts to create a heterogeneous data environment, has included ODBC
connectivity in most of its popular programs. For example, every application in its Office
suite can connect to an ODBC data source. Because it is easy to use and makes a lot of
sense, other companies have jumped on the ODBC bandwagon and now offer ways to
connect to other data sources through ODBC.

The benefits ODBC can provide have not eluded the development community either.
Software developers realized right away what a heterogeneous data environment would
mean, and Microsoft responded. Microsoft has released many tools to aid a developer who
is using ODBC to connect to a database. They include ODBCDirect, Remote Data Objects
(RDO), Data Access Objects (DAO), and more recently ActiveX Data Objects (ADO).
They are all pretty much based on a object based approach to data.

These tools can be used in the applications that you develop. Because most of you reading
this book are probably using MySQL for some sort of database access through the Web, the
Microsoft technologies that you will use for examples will be Active Server Pages,
VBScript, and ADO. You will use these technologies because they are simple and easy to
use, and this is the direction that Microsoft is taking. ADO is going to be the premier way
to access data on the Windows platform. To do this, you need to first cover some of the
basics.

Active Server Pages

To take advantage of these technologies, you must be using a Web server with the
FrontPage extensions installed. Microsoft has these available on their Web site. They run
on all platforms, including Linux. Also, the MyODBC driver must be installed on the server
that is running these scripts. Optionally, a system DSN for the database should be created
on the Web server. This will allow you to create DSN connections.

An Active Server Page (ASP) is a Web page that contains code such as VBScript and standard HTML tags that is run in the space between the request for an ASP by the client (in this case a browser) and fulfillment of that request by the server. It takes the place of Common Gateway Interface (CGI) programs. CGI programs are actually programs that run and output HTML tags to the Web server. ASP pages are different in that they are very much like a Web page—the only difference is that they contain code that is run before they are displayed. For example, suppose that you are signing a guest book on the Web that utilizes ASPs. You fill out the guest book form and click Submit. The Submit calls an ASP that has code embedded in it that takes your information from the form and stores it in a database. It also contains code that displays a Thank You message. Take a look at the following examples to get a better understanding of the ASP process.

The first stage of the process is displaying a Web page. In the example, it is a normal form for a guest book see Figure 13.9). You simply add your comments and click Submit. When you click Submit, your browser passes the information contained in the guest book form as a variable to the Active Server Page. The Active Server Page takes that variable and inserts it into a database. It then sends out a Thank You message.

FIGURE 13.9

The Guest Book Form.

13

Take a look at Listing 13.1 for the GuestBook.asp.

LISTING 13.1   Code for Guestbook.asp

```
<%Language=VBScript%>
<HEAD>
</HEAD>
<%
    Dim Conn
    Dim Cmd

    Set Conn = Server.CreateObject("ADODB.Connection")
    Set Cmd  = Server.CreateObject("ADODB.Command")

    Conn.CommandTimeout = 40
    Conn.ConnectionString = "server=10.1.1.50;db=ThorGB;"&_
        "uid=root;pwd=tacobell;driver=MySQL"
    Conn.Open

    Cmd.ActiveConnection = Conn
    Cmd.CommandType = 1
    Cmd.CommandText = "INSERT INTO GuestBook (Comments)"&_
        " VALUES("& Request("Comments") & ")"
    Cmd.Execute

    Conn.Close
%>

<BODY>

<P align=center><FONT size=5><STRONG>Thank You For Signing
Our Guest Book. </STRONG></FONT></P>
<P align=center><FONT size=5><STRONG>Come Back Real
Soon!!</STRONG></FONT></P>

</BODY>
</HTML>
```

As you can see, the anatomy of an Active Server Page is not very different from a regular Web page. The only difference is the code that is between the <% %> tags. This code is executed on the server and not on the client. This means that this code actually happens before the page is ever sent to the browser. The actual output looks like Figure 13.10. If you were to view the source of the output of the final page, you would see the following:

```
<HEAD>
</HEAD>

<BODY>

<P align=center><FONT size=5><STRONG>Thank You For Signing
Our Guest Book. </STRONG></FONT></P>
```

```
<P align=center><FONT size=5><STRONG>Come Back Real
Soon!!</STRONG></FONT></P>

</BODY>
</HTML>
```

Notice that the code between the <% %> tags has disappeared. This is no error, the code was executed on the server and never sent to the client. You can do a lot of things here. You can actually generate a page dynamically from the contents of a database with Active Server Pages. This will be covered a little later today.

FIGURE **13.10**

The output of
GuestBook.asp.

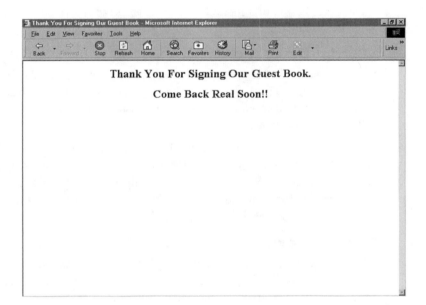

Working with VBScript

Now that you have a general idea of what an Active Server Page is and how it is used, look more closely at the code that appears between the <% %> tags. The code used in Active Server Pages is VBScript. VBScript is a subset of the Visual Basic programming language. VBScript is very easy to use because it uses the same syntax as Visual Basic. It also has the flexibility of Visual Basic. The Visual Basic language scripting edition retains the best of Visual Basic, such as error handling and string formatting. Also, like Visual Basic, VBScript is easy to use.

13

> **Note**
>
> VBScript in not the only scripting language used in Active Server Pages. Others include JScript, LotusScript, and PerlScript.

There are many books dedicated to VBScript and Active Server Pages, you should read one of those if you would like to learn more. This book will only cover the basics—enough to introduce you to the concepts and some of the syntax and how you can use it to connect to a MySQL database. For a more detailed account, read *Active Server Pages Unleashed* by Sams Publishing.

VBScript Declarations

Variables can be of only one type—variant. A variant is a variable that can hold any value—a string, number, object, you name it. VBScript also provides a number of built-in functions that it inherited from Visual Basic, such as the `MsgBox()`, `CreateObject()`, and `IsNumeric()` functions, to name a few.

You will see how you can use VBScript to manipulate a database via an Active Server Page. VBScript is not limited to ASPs. Microsoft has taken this scripting language to the next level. VBScript can now be used from the command line and can be used to handle non-interactive administration tasks. Let's take a look at some of the basic programming tasks you can accomplish with VBScript.

Program Flow

VBScript provides all the same conditional statements, flow control, and processing that its parent, Visual Basic possesses. For example, VBScript supports conditional statements like `If...Then ...Else`. The general syntax pattern is as follows:

```
If expression Then
    Do this
Else
    Do This
End If
```

Notice that in VBScript (as well as Visual Basic) you must include the word `Then`. Also, to end an `If...Then` statement you must use `End If`. Look at the following example:

```
Dim vCount
Dim vLastName
```

```
If vCount > 1 Then
    Response.Write("The name is "& vLastName)
Else
    Response.Write("<p></p>")
End If
```

In the first two lines of the example, variables are declared. The next block of code is the If...Then segment. Here, if the expression vCount>1 is a true statement, you will write the statement to the Web page. If it equates to false, nothing is written out. This is a simple example. Your conditional statements can be more complex but will follow the same structure.

Looping Control

VBScript also supports Do While, Do Until, While, and For...Next as general flow control statements. You would use a loop to walk through a recordset or complete a task a number of times before moving on. In VBScript, a typical loop can look like the following:

```
Do Until rstCustomers.EOF
    Response.Write("<P>"& rstCustomers("LastName") & "</P>")
    RstCustomers.MoveNext
Loop
```

In this example, whatever is in between the Do and Loop keywords will continue until the expression rstCustomers.EOF equates to TRUE. This type of statement is handy for walking through record sets.

VBScript also can perform calculations, such as addition and subtraction. It supports comparison operators as well. It is not recommended that you do complex computations in an Active Server Page. Remember that the code in an ASP is performed on the server prior to being downloaded to the client. If complex computations are being performed, this could delay the response to the client's request.

Commenting Your Code

You can also use comments in your server pages. A comment is denoted by a single quote ('). There are no block comments in VBScript. If your comment spans multiple lines, you must include a single quote at the front of every line.

```
' This is a single line comment.

' This
' is
' a
' multiple line
' comment
```

13

Another feature of VBScript that you can take advantage of is its built-in functions. VBScript supports many of the same functions in Visual Basic.

Generating a Web Page with VBScript

Now you'll look at a VBScript example that demonstrates what you have learned so far. The code segment in Listing 13.2 shows how VBScript, when used in an Active Server Page, can generate a Web page that takes values from a MySQL database and displays them in a Web page. The Web page is shown in Figure 13.11. Note that the line numbers appear only as a reference—they should not appear in your code.

LISTING 13.2   Generating a Web Page

```
10 <%@ Language=VBScript %>
20 <HTML>
30 <HEAD>
40 <META HTTP-EQUIV="Expires"CONTENT="0">
50 </HEAD>
60 <%
70     ' Variable Declaration
80     Dim rstCustomers 'ADO Recordset
90     Dim mConn        'ADO Connection
100    Dim mCmd         'ADO Command

110    Dim vRecordCount 'Counter
120    Dim vbgcolor     'Back Ground Color

130    'Creating the ADO Objects
140    Set mConn = Server.CreateObject("ADODB.Connection")
150    Set mCmd = Server.CreateObject("ADODB.Command")
160    Set rstCustomers = Server.CreateObject("ADODB.Recordset")

170    'Setting the connection parameteres
180    mConn.CommandTimeout = 40
190    mConn.CursorLocation = 1 'Client Side
200    mConn.ConnectionString = "server=10.1.1.50;driver=MySQL;"&_
       "db=Meet_A_Geek;uid=root;pwd=tacobell"
210    mConn.Open

220    mCmd.ActiveConnection = mConn
230    mCmd.CommandType = 1 'Text
240    mCmd.CommandText = "SELECT * FROM Customers"

250    'Opening the record set based on the Query from mCmd
260    rstCustomers.Open mCmd,,1,1

270%>
```

LISTING 13.2   continued

```
280<BODY>

290 <P align=center><STRONG>Here is a list of our
300 Customers</STRONG>          </P>
310 <P align=center>
320 <TABLE align=center border=1 cellPadding=1 cellSpacing=1 width="100%">

330  <TR>
340    <TD align=middle bgColor=silver><STRONG>First
350      Name</STRONG></TD>
360    <TD align=middle bgColor=silver><STRONG>Last
370      Name</STRONG></TD>
380    <TD align=middle bgColor=silver><STRONG>State</STRONG></TD>
390 </TR>

400<%
410    ' Set our counter to 0
420    vRecordCount = 0

430    ' Walk through the recordset
440    Do Until rstCustomers.EOF

450       ' This will alternate the row color, making it easier to read
460       If vRecordCount Mod 2 > 0 Then
470           vbgcolor = ''#C0C0C0"
480       Else
490           vbgcolor = ''#FFFFFF"
500       End If

510       'Output the results to the web page in a table520Response.Write "<TR>"
530Response.Write "<TD align=middle bgcolor ="& vbgcolor & ">"&
➥rstCustomers.Fields("First_Name") & "</TD>"
540Response.Write "<TD align=middle bgcolor ="& vbgcolor & ">"& rstCustomers.
➥Fields("Last_Name") & "</TD>
550Response.Write "<TD align=middle bgcolor ="& vbgcolor & ">"&  rstCustomers.
➥Fields("State") & "</TD>
560       Response.Write "</TR>"

570       'Move to the next record
580       rstCustomers.MoveNext

590       'Increase the record count
600       vRecordCount = vRecordCount + 1
610    Loop

620    rstCustomers.Close
630    mConn.Close
640 %>
650 </TABLE></P>
```

13

LISTING 13.2   continued

```
660  </BODY>
670  </HTML>
```

FIGURE 13.11

A Web page generated using VBScript with Active Server Pages.

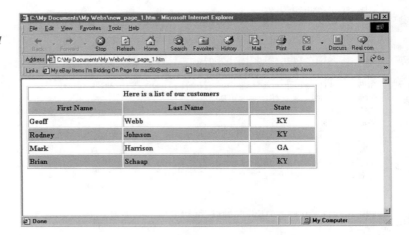

The very first line of text tells the server that this is an Active Server Page using VBScript. That's all it does. The next two lines are simple HTML tags. The first declares this is an HTML page and the second starts the page heading. The next line is a META tag. This tag tells the browser not to use the browser's cache for this file. This is an important line, especially when displaying data results. If the browser were to use its cache, it may be pulling old data. And as we all know, old data isn't always correct data. So to ensure that your users are getting the latest and greatest, use this META tag. The next line closes your header.

The next batch of code is executed on the server before it ever gets to the browser. This is designated by the <%. An important point to note is that the header is actually loaded to the client. The code you are creating takes place between the header and the body. This means the client will get all the head information before this code is executed. This space—between the header and body—is where most ASP programming is done. It allows some information to get to the client while the rest is being processed. This is a courtesy to the users so they know something is happening and are not lost in some cyber space void. The variables are declared in lines 70-120.

All variables declared in VBScript are a variant type by default. They will become whatever type is necessary when they get a value. The first three variables will eventually store objects, while `vRecordCount` will hold a number, and `vbgcolor` will hold a string.

Creating ADO Objects

Lines 130-160 are a little more interesting.

This is where you create ADO objects on the server. This is discussed in a little more depth later today. For now, examine the interesting event that is occurring here. You are setting your variables here equal to the results of the `CreateObject` method of the `Server` object. You may be asking yourself, "Where did this `Server` object come from?" This is a built-in object provided by the Internet Information Server (IIS). This is what makes an ASP an ASP and not some other Web page. In fact, there are seven built-in objects. They are the `Server` object, the `Application` object, the `Request` object, the `Response` object, the `Session` object, the `ObjectContext` object, and the `ASPErr` object. Each one has a bunch of useful methods and properties. This book will cover only those pertinent to our present goals.

The `Server` Object

The `Server` object, as you have seen, has a very important method—`CreateObject`. This method creates and instance of the named object on the server. An important point to remember is that the object that you are calling must be installed on the server and registered properly in the server's registry. If not, you will not be able to create this object. The `Server` object contains a few other rarely used methods and one property. These are not relevant to what you are doing, so they won't be discussed here.

The `Request` Object

The `Request` object is another built-in object provided by IIS. This object has a couple of often used methods and properties. The `Request` object retrieves the values passed from a browser to a server in a request. In the Guest Book example, a user submits his/her comments. These comments are passed along with a request to the Web server. You would use the `Request` object to get these comments. These are accessible via the `QueryString` property or the `Form` property. The values are stored as an associative array or collection, which means they are stored in a name=value pair. To access the value in a `Form` or `QueryString`, use the name that was used in the Web page to retrieve the value. In the Guest Book example, you passed the comments to the server via a form. The comments were stored in the `textarea` called `Comments`. To retrieve this value from the Active Server Page, you could use the `QueryString` property as follows:

```
Request.QueryString("Comments")
```

13

The value returned would be the contents of the textarea called Comments. The QueryString property contains all the requests passed between Web pages, regardless of their type. This means that the information that is passed via HTML Forms or parameters in a URL (?Last=Newton&First=Steve) will be held in the QueryString property. That is why it is the default property. Most often, you'll see a Request object such as the following:

```
Request("Comments")
```

instead of all spelled out

```
Request.QueryString("Comments")
```

The Response Object

The Response Object is the counterpart to the Request Object. The Response object sends data to the client. The most often used method of this object is the Write method. This method will send output directly to the browser. It is important to remember that because you are sending output to the browser, it must be in a language the browser can understand—HTML. So all your output must be properly formatted HTML tags. If it is not, it is likely that no one will ever see your output.

The next part of Listing 13.2 sets the properties of the ADO objects you created earlier. You'll get into ADO a lot deeper later today. For now, take a look at lines 280-670 of Listing 13.2.

The first thing to notice here is that you can place VBScript within an Active Server Page anywhere. Here, you have included some within the body of the Web page. This allows you to mix client-side and server-side code. Things that will always remain static can be normal HTML code, while things that are more dynamic can be created with VBScript.

Line 420, after the <% tag, resets your variable to 0. You then use a Do While...Loop block to walk through the recordset. What happens here is that the interpreter checks to see if it is at the end of the recordset; if it isn't, it processes the next line of code; if it is, it ends the loop.

Inside the loop (lines 460-500) is an If...Else statement code block. Here you are alternating the colors of the rows in the result table. This is a neat little trick that makes the results easier to view and the users happy. You divide your counter by 2. Using the modulus function, you check to see if there is a remainder. If there is a remainder, that means the row is odd, which you color silver. If there is no remainder, meaning the row is even, you make it white.

The next block of code, lines 530-550, outputs the values of your recordset to the browser, keeping the table format you started previously in the static code. It is necessary to do it this way because you do not know how much data you have. Data is in constant flux, so there is no way of knowing how many rows of data you have all the time. Think about the upkeep. If you had a static Web page that displayed all your customers, you would have to insert a new row manually every time you added a new one and delete a row every time someone went elsewhere. What a nightmare! This is one of the reasons why merging Web pages with data is so popular.

Next, you move to the next record and the increment the counter variable (line 580). If you do not move to the next record, the code will be stuck in an endless loop. The same contents will be displayed over and over again. This is very frustrating for an end user, so be careful when using loops on the Web.

The final pieces of code, after the loop, perform clean up duties. You close your recordset and then the connection. Then you end the server-side portion of the Web page and resume the static HTML again.

Hopefully, with these examples, you understand the Active Server Page concept and how it can be helpful. Again, this is only a cursory glance at VBScript and Active Server Page technology. If you are going to do any serious development, you may want to read more about it.

ActiveX Data Objects

The ActiveX Data Objects (ADO), as explained previously, are a group of objects that are used to communicate with a database. There is a hierarchy among the objects, but it is not enforced. That means that they can all be created independently of one another. This allows greater flexibility and ease of use. This section will explain some of the methods and properties that can be used to take advantage of the MySQL ODBC Application Programming Interface (API).

13

ADO consists of three main objects. These three objects embody everything you can do with a database. They are the Connection object, Recordset object, and the Command object. With these three objects you can connect, query, and view results from any database.

Connection Object Properties and Methods

The first step in any API is to make a connection. ADO is no different. ADO uses the Connection object to make its database connection. The Connection object has many properties and methods. These are outlined in Table 13.1:

TABLE 13.1 *Connection* OBJECT'S PROPERTIES AND METHODS

Method or Property	Description
Attributes	Indicates one or more properties of the connection object.
CommandTimeout	Indicates how long to wait for a command to execute before ending. The default is 30 seconds.
ConnectionString	The most important property of the Connection Object. Provides all the information necessary to connect to a database.
ConnectionTimeout	Indicates the amount of time to wait while trying to make a connection before ending in an error.
CursorLocation	Indicates where to use the cursor. It is better to use the cursor on the client for several reasons, one of which is to ensure the operations you are trying to perform are supported.
DefaultDatabase	If not provided in the connection string, this is where the connection will look for the name of the database to which to connect.
Open()	Opens a connection to a database using the parameters provided in the connection string.
Provider	Indicates the name of the provider used in the connection. With MySQL it will be the ODBC OLE DB provider.
State	Indicates the current status of the connection.
Version	Indicates the ADO version of the object being used.

Making an ADO Connection

To connect to a MySQL database using VBScript and ADO, several steps need to be taken. They are as follows:

1. The first step is to declare a variable that will become the Connection object.

    ```
    Dim mConn
    ```

2. The next step is to create the object and set your variable equal to it.

    ```
    Set mConn = Server.CreateObject("ADODB.Connection")
    ```

3. Set the properties of the Connection object.

    ```
    mConn.CommandTimeout = 40
    mConn.ConnectionTimeout = 40
    mConn.CursorLocation = 3
    ```

A little side note. There is a bug within IIS 4. The interpreter will not interpret the VBScript constants, so the number that is represented by that constant has to be used. Normally, you would use the `adUseClient` constant instead of the number 3. This will show up again when issuing the `Open` command of the `Recordset` object.

4. Create the connection string.

```
mConn.ConnectionString="server=10.1.1.50;db=Meet_A_Geek;"&_
driver=MySQL;uid=root;pwd=tacobell"
```

The connection string is made up of the following information:

Server—Can be a name or an IP

db—The name of the database

driver—The name of the ODBC driver to use

uid—The username of somebody who has permission to connect to this database

pwd—The password for the uid

The components of the connection string can appear in any order as long as they are all present. If you are going to use a DSN for a connection, the only thing you need in your connection string is the name of the DSN.

So if you had a DSN named "`MeetAGeek`", you could use the following connection string, as long as your DSN is configured correctly:

```
mConn.ConnectionString = "DSN=MeetAGeek"
```

5. The next step is to open the connection. This takes the connection string, applies it to the driver, and connects to the database. To do this, use the following syntax:

```
mConn.Open
```

That's all there is to it. If you follow these five simple steps, you can connect to any MySQL database, or any other database for that matter. That's the beauty of this technology. The same code you used here can be applied to any other database as long as you supply the correct information.

It is recommended that you use the DSN-less type of connection. By using this method, you avoid doing any extra work or relying on someone else to do it for you. With a DSN connection, someone must create a system DSN on the server. This isn't hard to do, if you are right there. When you are trying to do it remotely, you will have some problems. Plus, you are relying on a piece of information that is beyond your control. What if the server crashes and they have to reload NT? What happens to all your programs that rely on that DSN? What if they forget to redo your DSN? Now you're in real trouble. The best scenario is to create DSN-less connections. That way, everything is in your control.

13

Command Object Properties and Methods

The next important object in the ADO object list is the Command object. This object has many uses. It can execute SQL statements that do not return a resultset, be used to manipulate the structure of your database, and it can issue statements that are specific to a database, such as MySQL. The Command object, like the Connection object, has many methods and properties. These are listed with brief descriptions in Table 13.2.

TABLE 13.2 Command Object's Properties and Methods

Method or Property	Description
ActiveConnection	Sets the connection to use for any commands. Can be set to an open Connection object.
CommandText	A string that acts as the command. Can be an SQL command or, in some cases, just the name of a table. Pretty much anything you can type into the MySQL monitor program can be used here.
CommandTimeout	Indicates how long to wait for a command to execute before it times out.
CommandType	Indicates what type of command you will be issuing. The values can be a command string (1) or table (2). The other command types do not apply to MySQL because they deal with features that MySQL does not have (namely, stored procedures).
Execute()	This method will cause the execution of the commands in the command text.
Prepared	A Boolean value (True or False) that indicates whether the provider will save a copy of the command text in memory. This can improve the performance of a query. MySQL supports this option.
State	Indicates whether the Command object's connection is open or closed.

Working with the Command Object

As explained earlier, the Commandobject has many different uses. To use the Command object, perform the following steps:

1. You must first declare a variable to hold your Command object:

    ```
    Dim mCmd
    ```

2. Next, using the Server object's CreateObject method, create the Command object:

    ```
    Set mCmd = Server.CreateObject("ADODB.Command")
    ```

3. Tell the Command object which connection to use:

```
mCmd.ActiveConnection = mConn
```

4. Set some of the properties of the new Command object. This is where you tell what type of command you want to issue as well as set the timeout:

```
mCmd.CommandType = 1
mCmd.CommandTimeout = 40
mCmd.CommandText = ''SELECT * FROM Customers"
```

5. Depending on what your command is, you can use the Execute method to accomplish your task. For example, if you were to DELETE a record from the Customers table, you could use the following sequence of events (the following assumes you have already opened a connection to a database using the mConn object):

```
Dim mCmd
Set mCmd = Server.CreateObject("ADODB.Command")
mCmd.ActiveConnection = mConn
mCmd.CommandType = 1
mCmd.CommandText = "DELETE FROM Customers WHERE Customer_ID= 1345"
mCmd.Execute
```

As you can see, the Command object is how you convey your statements to the database. Now what if you wanted to see the results of a query? How would you go about getting that from a command? The answer is that you would use the Resultset object.

Resultset Object Properties and Methods

The Resultset object, like the other ADO objects, has many properties and methods. The methods and properties of the Resultset object deal with the data that is returned from the database. Table 13.3 is a listing of some of the properties and methods of the Resultset object.

TABLE 13.3 Resultset Object's Methods and Properties

Method or Property	Description
AddNew()	Adds a new record to an updateable recordset.
BOF, EOF	Returns either True or False, depending on whether you are at the beginning of the recordset or at the end (BOF = beginning of file, EOF = end of file).
Clone()	Creates a duplicate copy of the current recordset.
Close()	Closes the current recordset.
CursorType	Indicates the type of cursor used in the recordset. The types of cursors and what they can do are explained later today.

13

TABLE 13.3   continued

Method or Property	Description
Fields	Contains information about each individual record in the recordset.
Find(Criteria, Skip, Dir, Start)	Searches the recordset for the specified criteria.
LockType	Specifies what type of locking to use with this recordset. This will be covered in more detail later today.
Move()	Moves to the specified record.
MoveNext()	Moves to the next record in the record set.
MoveFirst()	Moves to the beginning of the recordset.
MoveLast()	Moves to the end of the recordset.
MovePrevious()	Moves to the previous record in the recordset.
MaxRecords	Indicates the maximum number of records that can be contained in the recordset. Provides the same function as using the LIMIT keyword in your SQL statement.
Open(Source, ActiveConnection, CursorType, LockType)	Opens the recordset based on the criteria that is provided.
RecordCount	Indicates how many records are contained in the current recordset.
Sort	Tells the recordsset which fields to sort and in what order, descending or ascending. Same as using the Order By clause in your query.
Source	Indicates the source from which the data will come. This can be a Command object, SQL statement, or a table name.
Format)	Saves the recordset in the destination that is provided in the format that is indicated. Can be XML.
State	Indicates whether a recordset is open or closed.
Status	Returns a number indicating the status of the current record operation.
Update	The counterpart to the AddNew method. After the Update command is given, all records that were given in the AddNew command will be added to the database.

Working with the `Resultset` Object

The best way to use a `Recordset` object is in conjunction with the `Command` and `Connection` objects. Perform the following steps to open a recordset:

1. Declare a variable that will contain the `Recordset` object.

   ```
   Dim rstCustomers
   ```

2. Set that variable equal to the results of a `Server` object's `CreateObject` method.

   ```
   Set rstCustomers = Server.CretaeObject("ADODB.Connection")
   ```

3. Open the `Recordset` object. There are many ways to open a recordset. They all require that you supply a source. This source can be a `Command` object, SQL query, or a table name. The best way is to use a `Command` object that already has a set active connection.

   ```
   RstCustomers.Open mCmd,,1,1
   ```

   This statement will open a recordset based on the Command object. An active connection does not need to be stated in the second argument of this method because you are using a `Command` object that already has an active connection. The next two arguments are the type of cursor and the type of locking to use. A number is used instead of the Microsoft constant because there is a bug within IIS that causes an error if you use the constant.

If everything was supplied correctly and the SQL string in your `Command` object is valid, a recordset will be opened containing the data you want. What you do after that is up to you. You can manipulate, display, edit, or add records to the recordset.

There are four parameters that can be used when opening a recordset. They are the `Source`, `ActiveConnection`, `CursorType`, and `LockType`. There is a fifth parameter, but it is never used. In fact, Microsoft says not to use this parameter because it can produce errors.

The first parameter is the `Source`. As explained earlier, there are basically three types of sources. The first, which is the recommended way, is to use a `Command` object as your `Source`. This provides the most flexible way to open a recordset. The second way is to use an SQL statement as a source. The final way is to use a table name as the source for your data in the recordset. What you use is up to you. The recommended way is definitely the best way to go, but if you use the other methods, don't forget to supply the `ActiveConnection`.

13

The `ActiveConnection`, the second optional parameter in the `Open` method of a `Recordset` object, is an open `Connection` object. If you are using a `Command` object whose active connection has already been set, you can leave this option blank. However, if you do not supply a `Command` object as your source, you must use a `Connection` object here.

The next parameter is the `CursorType`. This defines what actions are performed on the recordset and how the data is displayed in the recordset. The following are the choices for this parameter:

- *Keyset*—Data thathas been added since this type of cursor was opened will not be seen. This type of recordset will allow you to move forward and backward through the recordset. Data can also be added or deleted.

- *Dynamic*—This is the most flexible cursor available. You can freely move backwards and forwards through the recordset. Any records that were deleted or added since this type of recordset was opened will change the recordset. It is a mirror to the data in the database.

- *Static*—This type of recordset cannot be updated, nor will any changes made after this recordset is created be visible. This type of recordset is generally used in reporting or static displays. The default recordset is 0—Forward only. This is same as a static cursor, except that you can only move forward through the records. This recordset is good for quick, one time passes through your data.

- *Lock*—MySQL allows you to control locking via SQL statements; some databases do not. In an attempt to make a heterogeneous environment, Microsoft has added this option into the mix. You can specify what type of locking to use. The ODBC driver will take care of issuing the commands for you. The following are the choices for your locks:

  - *Read only*—This allows you to only read the data, you can not alter it.

  - *Pessimistic locking*—The ODBC driver issues whatever command necessary to ensure the proper editing of records. It will lock the table before any editing is done, and then will release the lock when the update has been completed.

  - *Optimistic locking*—The provider will only lock the table when the `Update` method is called. The best choice is to use Pessimistic locking. This will lock the tables when you use them. If you feel you need to add more locking, issue the commands in a `Command` object.

Using the Meet-A-Geek Database on the Web

Now that you have looked at the ADO objects and seen what they can do, take a look at how to use them in a typical real life situation. You are going to create a series of Active Server Pages that allow someone to post a personal ad via a Web page. The data from the Web page will be used to populate a MySQL database.

Setting Up the Web Page

The first step is to design the Web page. You'll use the same one that was used in your database design example back on Day 3, "Designing Your First Database." The following is a partial list of some of the HTML tags that were used to produce this page:

```
<form method="POST" action="PostAd.asp">
<p> To post your free ad, please answer the following questions. 
 We will not give your name or email address to
anyone without your consent.  Items with a
( <font color="#FF0000">*</font><font color="#000000">)</font>
 are required fields.</p>
<P>Please provide the following contact information:
 <font color="#FF0000" size="4" face="Arial">*</font></P>
<BLOCKQUOTE>
<TABLE>
<TR>
<TD ALIGN="right">
<EM>First Name</EM></TD>
<TD>
<INPUT NAME="Contact_FirstName" SIZE=25>
</TD>
</TR>
<TR>
<TD ALIGN="right">
<EM>Last Name</EM></TD>
<TD>
<INPUT NAME="Contact_LastName" SIZE=25>
</TD>
</TR>
<TR>
<TD ALIGN="right">
<EM>Middle Initial</EM></TD>
<TD>
<INPUT NAME="Contact_MiddleInitial" SIZE=4 MAXLENGTH=1>
</TD>
</TR>
<TR>
<TD ALIGN="right">
<EM>Home Phone <br>
</EM><font size="2" face="Arial">(no dashes or spaces, <br>
```

13

```
include area code)</font></TD>
<TD>
<INPUT NAME="Contact_HomePhone" SIZE=25 MAXLENGTH=10>
</TD>
</TR>
<TR>
<TD ALIGN="right">
<EM>E-mail</EM></TD>
<TD>
<INPUT NAME="Contact_Email" SIZE=25>
</TD>
</TR>
</TABLE>
</BLOCKQUOTE>
<P>
Please describe yourself:<font size="4" face="Arial">
<font color="#FF0000">*</font></font></P>
<BLOCKQUOTE>
<TABLE>
<TR>
<TD ALIGN="right">
<EM>Age</EM></TD>
<TD>

<INPUT NAME="Personal_Age"SIZE=3 MAXLENGTH=2>
</TD>
</TR>
←-------------- Code Continues ----------→
```

Most of the code from this page was left out because I wanted you to see how data from this form would be passed to the next. This is a regular HTML page. It contains a form and a series of elements within the form. The first line of the code listing is the form tag. Form tags have a GET and POST method. You are using the POST method here. The POST method will post all the elements of this form in name=value pairs with your request for the next page, which is noted in the ACTION section of the tag. You are requesting the PoatAd.asp page. After the Submit button is clicked, the browser will send the variable and request the PostAd.asp page.

The rest of the code segment shows an element of the form. Each element is designated the <INPUT> tag, and each element has a name. This name will be paired up with the value the user provides in the element. For example, the user enters his or her name in the first box on the form. In the HTML code, you see that the first element is called Contact_FirstName. This name will be paired up with whatever the user entered in this field. So, if the user entered Larry into the box, the name=value pair that would be passed to the server would be Contact_FirstName=Larry.

Posting an Ad

The more interesting code happens on the next page. First take a look at the entire code in Listing 13.3 for the PostAd.asp page. You will then walk through, line-by-line, and examine what is happening.

LISTING 13.3   Posting an Ad on a Web Page

```
10 <%@ Language=VBScript %>
20 <HTML>
30 <HEAD>
40 </HEAD>
50 <%
60      'Variable Declaration
70      Dim mCmd
80      Dim mConn
90      Dim strSQL

100     'Create the ADO objects
110     Set mCmd = Server.CreateObject("ADODB.Command")
120     Set mConn = Server.CreateObject("ADODB.Connection")

130     'Set up the Connection
140     mConn.CommandTimeout = 40
150     mConn.ConnectionTimeout = 40

160     mConn.ConnectionString = "server=10.1.1.50;driver=MySQL;" &_
"db=Meet_A_Geek;uid=root;pwd=tacobell""            ""

170     mConn.Open


180     'Build the SQL string
190     strSQL = "INSERT INTO Customers"
200     strSQL = strSQL & "(Customer_ID, First_Name, Last_Name, Address,"
210     strSQL = strSQL & " City, State, Zip, Email, Age, Gender, Race, "
220     strSQL = strSQL & "Eye_Color, Activity, Movie, Occupation. Smoker)"
230     strSQL = strSQL & " VALUES(NULL, " &_
240      Request("Contact_FirstName") & ", "
250     strSQL = strSQL & Request("Contact_LastName") & ", "
260     strSQL = strSQL & Request("Contact_MiddleInitial") & ", "
270     strSQL = strSQL & Request("Contact_Address") & ", "
280     strSQL = strSQL & Request("Contact_City") & ", "
290     strSQL = strSQL & Request("Contact_State") & ", "
300     strSQL = strSQL & Request("Contact_Zip") & ", "
310     strSQL = strSQL & Request("Contact_Email") & ", "
320     strSQL = strSQL & Request("Contact_Age") & ", "

330     'check gender
```

13

LISTING 13.3   continued

```
340     If Request("Contact_Gender") = "Male" Then
350         strSQL = strSQL & "M, "
360     Else
370         strSQL = strSQL & "F, "
380     End If

390     strSQL = strSQL & Request("Contact_EyeColor") & ", "
400     strSQL = strSQL & Request("Contact_Activity") & ", "
410     strSQL = strSQL & Request("Contact_Movie") & ", "
420     strSQL = strSQL & Request("Contact_Occupation") & ", "

430     'check smoker
440     If Request("Smoker") > 1 Then
450         strSQL = strSQL & "Y, "
460     Else
470         strSQL = strSQL & "N, "
480     End If

490     'Set up the command
500     mCmd.ActiveConnection = mConn
510     mCmd.CommandTimeout = 40
520     mCmd.CommandType =1

530     'Add the command to the command object
540     mCmd.CommandText = strSQL

550     'execute the command
560     mCmd.Execute

570 %>

580 <BODY>

590<P>Thank You, <%Response.Write Request("Contact_FirstName%> </P>

600 </BODY>
610 </HTML>
```

The first line, like most ASPs, tells the server to use VBScript as the language in this server page. Lines 10-40 tell the browser that this is an HTML document and are followed by the HEAD tags.

The next part of code actually starts the active part of the server page (line 50). Lines 70, 80, and 90 declare the variables. It is customary to name your variable in this manner. The m designates that it is a class variable. The rest is an abbreviation of the object's type.

The third variable is going to contain your SQL command. It is going to be quite large, so it is best to build it into a variable and then use that variable as the command text.

The objects are instantiated and set equal to your variables in lines 110 and 120.

The next segment of code sets the properties of the Connection object. Lines 140 and 150 set the Command and Connection timeouts to 40. These can be higher or lower, depending on your network's speed. For Internet use, they should be a little higher than for intranet use. The connection string is created in line 160. Notice that you are not using a DSN. Because this is an Internet page, you don't want to rely on your ISP to provide and maintain a DSN that affects your business. This is the reason you chose to use a DSN-less connection. As you can see, you provided the driver name, database, user identification, and password. Notice how the driver is spelled. This is one of the rare instances where Microsoft is case sensitive. This driver name must match (both in case and punctuation) with the name of the driver that was installed. This is an easy one—the access driver is Microsoft Access Driver {*.mdb}. Makes MySQL look easy. The final step is to open the connection (line 170).

If you were to try opening a connection without providing all the variables beforehand, an error would occur. These variables must be set prior to opening the connection. Order does matter.

The next segment of code, lines 180-480, creates the SQL command string. It is a normal INSERT command. The place it starts to get interesting is when you request the values for the columns (lines 250-420). To do this, you use the built-in Request object. Remember that the POST action in your form sent all the name=value pairs along with the page request. All you have to do is retrieve them. You provide two checks in the code—one for gender and one for whether the user smokes (lines 330-380 and line 430-480). You do this is because these are enumerated columns and accept only two fields. You need to massage the data to fit into the database.

You build the Command object starting on line 500. You set the command timeout (line 520) and command type properties (line 530). You also set the connection for the Command object (line 510). After all that is done, you set the command text equal to your SQL command (line 540) and then execute the command (line 560). If there are no errors, the record will be added to the database.

13

The last little bit of code, lines 580-610, demonstrate that you can place server-side code anywhere in your Web page. It is not recommended that you interchange server-side and client-side script very often. It can slow down the loading of the page to the client. But for small pages that do not have a lot of material to present, it is okay. You personalize your page here a little bit by offering a thank you to the person who submitted an ad using his or her first name.

This page and code demonstrated how you can add data to a MySQL database using ADO, VBScript, and Active Server Pages. What if you wanted to display some information? A different method is used to display a data. You will need to use a `Recordset` object in addition to the `Command` and `Connection` objects.

Displaying Data to the Web Page

Now you'll create a Web page that displays all your customers. This page could be called from a hyperlink in another page, or a person could go to it directly. As in the previous example, the code is shown in its entirety, and then broken down a segment at a time. The code in Listing 13.4 was used earlier in the chapter. We'll go over it again, now that you have a better understanding of ADO.

LISTING 13.4   Displaying Customer Data on the Web Page

```
10 <%@ Language=VBScript %>
20 <HTML>
30 <HEAD>
40 <META HTTP-EQUIV="Expires"CONTENT="0">
50 </HEAD>
60 <%
70     ' Variable Declaration
80    Dim rstCustomers 'ADO Recordset
90    Dim mConn         'ADO Connection
100     Dim mCmd          'ADO Command

110    Dim vRecordCount 'Counter
120    Dim vbgcolor      'Back Ground Color

130     'Creating the ADO Objects
140     Set mConn = Server.CreateObject("ADODB.Connection")
150     Set mCmd = Server.CreateObject("ADODB.Command")
160     Set rstCustomers = Server.CreateObject("ADODB.Recordset")

170     'Setting the connection parameters
180     mConn.CommandTimeout = 40
190     mConn.CursorLocation = 1 'Client Side
200     mConn.ConnectionString = "server=10.1.1.50;driver=MySQL;" &_
"db=Meet_A_Geek;uid=root;pwd=tacobell"
```

LISTING 13.4   continued

```
220    mConn.Open

230    mCmd.ActiveConnection = mConn
240    mCmd.CommandType = 1 'Text
250    mCmd.CommandText = "SELECT * FROM Customers ORDER  BY Last_Name"

260    'Opening the record set based on the Query from mCmd
270    rstCustomers.Open mCmd,,,1

280 %>

290 <BODY>

300 <P align=center><STRONG>Here is a list of our
310 Customers</STRONG>         </P>
320 <P align=center>
330 <TABLE align=center border=1 cellPadding=1 cellSpacing=1 width="100%">

340  <TR>
350    <TD align=middle bgColor=silver><STRONG>First
360      Name</STRONG></TD>
370    <TD align=middle bgColor=silver><STRONG>Last
380      Name</STRONG></TD>
390    <TD align=middle bgColor=silver><STRONG>State</STRONG></TD>
400 </TR>

410 <%
420    ' Set our counter to 0
430    vRecordCount = 0

440    ' Walk through the recordset
450    Do Until rstCustomers.EOF

460        ' This will alternate the row color, making it easier to read
470        If vRecordCount Mod 2 > 0 Then
480            vbgcolor = "#C0C0C0"
490        Else
500            vbgcolor = "#FFFFFF"
510        End If

520        'Output the results to the web page in a table
530        Response.Write "<TR>"
540        Response.Write "<TD align=middle bgcolor =" & vbgcolor & ">"&
rstCustomers.Fields("First_Name") & "</TD>"
550        Response.Write "<TD align=middle bgcolor =" & vbgcolor & ">" &
rstCustomers.Fields("Last_Name") & "</TD>
560        Response.Write "<TD align=middle bgcolor =" & vbgcolor & ">"
& rstCustomers.Fields("State") & "</TD>
570        Response.Write "</TR>"
```

13

LISTING 13.4   continued

```
580        'Move to the next record
590        rstCustomers.MoveNext

600        'Increase the record count
610        vRecordCount = vRecordCount + 1
620    Loop

630    rstCustomers.Close
640    mConn.Close
650 %>
660 </TABLE></P>
670 </BODY>
680 </HTML>
```

What the header and META tags are doing in lines 10-50 has been discussed earlier. Let's skip to the code that deals with the ADO objects.

As usual, you declare your variables and create the objects (lines 70-160).

Notice this time you are creating a Recordset object. It is good programming practice to name your recordset after the data it will contain. It makes it easier to remember what the purpose of the recordset is and to help identify it when you are using more than one recordset at a time.

Lines 170-220 set the variable of your Connection object. Because you've seen this a couple of times previously, move on to the Command object. This time, you are going to issue an SQL statement that will return a recordset with our Command object. Lines 230-270 of the code segment do just that. Remember, you can issue any command that you could issue in the MySQL Monitor in the command text. Here, you are issuing a SELECT statement, choosing to receive all the columns and all the rows from the table.

Another way to accomplish this task is to use the table type instead of the text type as the type used in the Command object's CommandType property. You could use a 3 instead of a 1 to indicate a table is going to be used. Then in the command text, all you would have to do is use the table's name. For example, to use a table type command, you would do the following:

1. Set the CommandType = 3
2. Change the CommandText = "Customers"

This would return the exact same results as the SELECT * statement. This shows you the flexibility ADO has to offer. You can do things a number of different ways. It's just a matter of preference.

The next part of the code opens the recordset (line 270). The first parameter of the `Open` method is the `Source`. You chose to use the `Command` object as your source. The next parameter is the `ActiveConnection`. Because you are using a `Command` object that already has an `ActiveConnection`, you don't need to state one here. The next parameter is the type of cursor the recordset will use. Because you are just going to display data and not alter it, you opt to use the default, which is `Forward Only`. The next parameter is the `LockType`. Because you are using a static recordset, you will use a `Read Only` type lock. This will free up the table for other people to use.

Lines 440-620 deal with walking through the recordset. This code is really straightforward. To walk through the recordset, which means stepping through each record one at a time, you use a `Do...Until` loop. This tests the condition first. If the condition proves `False`, it steps through the rest of the loop. If not, it goes on without going through the loop. The loop contains the code that will output the data in the recordset to the Web page. You use the `Fields` property of the recordset to do this. The `Fields` property is really a collection of name=value pairs. You can refer to a value in a column by using the name of the column, as you do in the code. Here, you display the current value of the customer's last name, first name, and state.

The last bit of code (lines 630 and 640) closes the recordset and then closes the connection.

As you can see, you can use Microsoft technology with MySQL in a multitude of ways. It is up to you and your imagination. This marries two very diverse, yet capable technologies. You can have a MySQL server running on a Linux platform and connect to it using ADO technology. This allows you to take advantage of the best of both worlds. You get a stable, reliable, fast database engine, as well as an application that can run on the world's most popular desktop operating system. Everything has its place; it's finding the best place that makes it all come together.

Summary

13

Today, you learned about ODBC—how it is Microsoft's answer to a heterogeneous data environment, where data access is the same no matter where or what database from which the data is coming. You learned that to take advantage of ODBC, you needed to use some other tools. The tools you used in the examples were ActiveX Data Objects, VBScript, and Active Server Pages.

You learned that there are three primary objects in ADO: the `Connection` object, `Command` Object, and the `Recordset` object. You learned how they interacted with each other and about their methods and properties.

You also learned about Active Server Page technology. You saw how an ASP could process data and create pages dynamically.

You learned that VBScript is an easy language to use—that it is a subset of Visual Basic. You learned how to use VBScript to manipulate and access the ADO objects.

Finally, you saw how everything comes together—how using VBScript in an ASP can manipulate a database using ADO.

Q&A

Q   Can I add a user with this technology?

A   With ADO, you can accomplish anything you can do at the MySQL monitor command line. You can add users, flush privileges, and even optimize your tables programmatically.

Q   It seems like you are adding a lot of interface layers. How does this affect performance?

A   Even with the added layers, ADO is extremely fast. This lesson has used a MySQL database and a Visual Basic application over a dial-up connection. The users didn't even know they were accessing their database remotely. That's how fast it is.

Q   Can I only use ADO in Active Server Pages?

A   No. ASPs are only one place where you can use ADO. Visual Basic, Java, and Visual C++ can all use ADO. The only requirement is that you have the myodbc driver installed. You cannot access any MySQL databases without it.

Q   Why should I even bother with a DSN?

A   A DSN provides you with a quick and easy way to access your database. It is great for the desktop. Also, other applications need a DSN to access ODBC data sources. For example, to import or export anything out of Microsoft Access you need a DSN. Additionally, you can change the database without having to rebuild your application.

Exercises

1. Using ADO, connect to the MySQL database and optimize your tables.
2. Create an ASP that allows a user to edit data from the Customers table.

DAY 14

The Perl Database Interface

The Perl language was developed in 1987 by Larry Wall. Since then, Perl has become one of the most popular programming languages used in the computer industry. It runs on nearly every computer platform (including Windows) and can be ported very easily, sometimes without changing a line of code. It is a very robust language with very strong string manipulation capabilities. This makes Perl an excellent choice for CGI programs, as well as many other business applications.

Because of Perl's popularity, it was only a matter of time before people started using Perl to interact with databases. The very first versions of these modules were a little cumbersome compared to what is available today. Back then, each database had its own module that was specific to that database. These modules were named after their database-producing names, such as Sybperl and Oriperl. These were good at the time, but did not fit the heterogeneous data model that was becoming a standard in the industry. Enter the Perl Database Interface, commonly referred to as DBI. DBI provided programmers with a standard set of functions and variables to use to access any database—much like ODBC provides access to databases on the Windows platform. The interface talked to a driver that was specific to the database. This part of the architecture is called the DBD or database driver. These two parts combined provide an architecture that is easy to learn and use. Fortunately, MySQL has a DBD. This allows you to use Perl to interface your MySQL database.

Today, you will learn

- How to install the DBI/DBD driver for MySQL
- How to use the MySQL DBI/DBD
- How to create a CGI program that interacts with a MySQL database

Installing the Perl DBI and the MySQL DBD

To take advantage of the Perl DBI, you need to install the necessary modules. This process is easy, but it can be a little intimidating for a beginner. The first step is to get the latest Perl DBI. You can find this in several locations. The Comprehensive Perl Archive Network (CPAN) has the latest available version of the interface, as well as the various database drivers. Another place to find the driver and interface is at the MySQL Web site. This may not be the latest version, but it will still work. You can also find the Perl DBI and the MySQL DBD on the CD-ROM that is included with this book. This will save you the hassle of downloading it from the Internet.

Perl is made up of a series of modules. Each module extends the capabilities of MySQL. There are a ton of modules that are available for Perl. There are modules for CGI, Tk, various math functions, and even modules that extend other programs like the Apache Web server.

Installing modules is really easy with Perl. You can do it one of two ways. The first way is to download it and install it as you would any other program, following the instructions in the README file. The other way is to let Perl do it for you.

Unfortunately, the way to do this is different depending on the platform you are using, though they work similarly. The next section covers Perl for the Windows platform.

Downloading and Installing Perl

You must have already installed the Windows version of Perl. This can be downloaded and installed from ActiveState's Web site at www.activestate.com. You can also find a very useful FAQ at www.perl.com. After you have installed Perl, go to the Perl directory. In it, you will find a subdirectory called bin. In this directory, you will see all the various utilities that come with Perl. Find the file named PPM. This utility is the Perl Package Manager. This neat little utility will find a Perl module on the Internet, download it, and install it automatically. You can't ask for better service.

To begin installing the DBI, double-click the PPM file. A DOS shell window will open. You will work with this window and the command line. It's pretty basic, but that's Perl—programs that perform one job well. To see a list of available commands, type **help**. A list of commands will scroll by, giving you several options. If you would like a more thorough explanation of a command, type the word **help** followed by the command. For example, if you wanted to learn more about the set command, you would type the following:

INPUT   `PPM> help set`

This command would display a list of options from which you can choose. You are going to use the install command. This will tell the PPM to install the specified package. Remember that this utility is case sensitive, so all your commands and packages must be typed correctly or it will not function in the expected manner. If you want to install the DBI from the Internet, make sure your Internet connection is active, and then type the following command:

INPUT   `PPM> install DBI`

The PPM will go out and search for the latest DBI module and begin downloading it. Unfortunately, the PPM provides no indicators on where it stands in the process, so be patient. It may not look like PPM is doing anything—rest assured that it is.

After the PPM has downloaded the package successfully, it will begin to install it. A lot of data will flash across the screen, indicating that PPM is hard at work. After it has completed the process, it will tell you if it was successful or not. More likely than not, you will have a successful install. If you don't, repeat the process or try to install the module manually.

As you can see, PPM is a great tool to use to add modules to your Perl for Windows. All other platforms can use a similar utility available as an option with the Perl command. You can accomplish the same goal as PPM by typing the following from the command line (this assumes that you have Perl installed and that it is part of your path):

14

INPUT `%> perl -MCPAN -e shell`

After typing this command, you will enter an interactive session, just like PPM. You will be asked a few questions, mostly about where to find key files and so on. The defaults are generally correct. After you have answered all the questions, type the following from the command line:

INPUT `%> install DBI`

This will install the DBI in the correct place.

Installing from the CD-ROM

Note The following instructions are specific to Linux.

If you choose to use the distribution that is available on the CD-ROM, you will have to do a manual install. To do that, perform the following steps:

1. First, you will need to mount the CD-ROM. Refer to your operating system's user manual to do this.

2. After you have the CD-ROM mounted, you will need to copy the file to a directory on your system. From the command line, type the following:

INPUT `%> cp DBI-1.11.tar.gz /home/mark/DBI-1.11.tar.gz`

Use a directory to which you have access. Generally, your home directory is a good choice.

3. After you have copied the file, change directories to that directory if you are not there already.

INPUT `%> cd /home/mark`

4. The next step is to unzip the file. To do this, type the following from the command line:

INPUT
```
%> gunzip DBI-1.11.tar.gz
%> tar -xvf DBI-1.11.tar
```

5. After the files have been extracted properly, you are ready to compile them. To do this, change to the newly created DBI-1.11 directory by typing the following:

INPUT   `%> cd DBI-1.11`

6. The next step is to create the make file. To do this, type the following:

INPUT   `%> perl Makefile.pl`

A lot of data will flash across the screen, providing you with progress notes. Upon completion, you will be notified if the file was successfully created. If it was, you can continue with the installation.

7. The next step is to actually add the module to the correct directories. To do this, type the following:

INPUT   `%> make`

A lot of data will again fly across the screen. When this is done, type the following command:

INPUT   `%> make test`

Again you will see a lot of flying data. After it finishes, type the following command:

INPUT   `%> make install`

After this successfully finishes, you will have installed the Perl DBI.

Installing the MySQL DBD

The next step is to install the MySQL DBD. This driver can be found at CPAN or the MySQL Web site. For your convenience, it has been added to the CD-ROM as well. To install the DBD, perform the following steps:

1. Mount the CD-ROM drive if you haven't already. Follow your operating system's user guide to accomplish this.

2. Copy the MySQL driver to a directory you can access. The filename for the driver is `Msql-Mysql-modules-1.2209.tar.gz`.

3. After you have copied the file, unzip it as you did the DBI using the same commands—just change the filename.

4. After you have unzipped your file, enter the following command at the command line:

14

INPUT   `%> perl Makefile.PL`

You should be prompted with the following choices:

OUTPUT
```
1. MySQL only
2. mSQL only (either of mSQL 1 or mSQL 2)
3. MySQL and mSQL (either of mSQL 1 or mSQL 2)
4. mSQL 1 and mSQL 2
5. MySQL, mSQL 1 and mSQL 2
```

The default choice is 3. This is probably the easiest choice to make. mSQL is an earlier predecessor to MySQL. You will not harm anything by adding this driver to your system.

After you make your selection, the installation program prompts you with some more questions. The first of these questions ask if you want to keep any previous modules. If you have installed other modules on your system and are still using them, select Yes; if not, select No. You will then be prompted for the directory where you installed MySQL. If you installed MySQL into the default directory (/usr/local/mysql), you can just press Enter. The next few questions pertain to a database that this driver can test itself against. If you still have the test database in your MySQL installation, you can press Enter for these questions, taking the default. If not, you must enter a database for the driver to test against. You will also have to give a username and password to use, as well as a host name.

After you have completed this step, and no errors are generated, then you have installed the driver successfully and are ready to begin writing Perl scripts to access your database.

You have now installed the tools you need to take advantage of this powerful technology. A word of caution, a lot of books do not mention how to install the various drivers and so on onto a machine because they fear that by doing so they are locked into that version. This is partly true. Most installation techniques do not change often. If they do, it is generally to help the ease the process. The best advice is to view the README documents before you install anything to make sure that you are using the latest guidelines.

You can also use the PPM to install the driver. To do this, start the PPM by double-clicking it. When the window is open, type the following at the command line:

INPUT   `PPM> install DBD-Mysql`

If the driver cannot be found under this name, you can do a search for it. To do this, type the following from the command line:

`PPM> search mysql`

This will return the most current driver name. From there, you can just type **install** *drivername* and let the PPM do the rest for you.

Creating Your First Perl DBI/DBD Script

This chapter assumes that you have a basic knowledge of Perl. If you do not, you may want to read some books that provide you with more detail about the language. Even if you don't know Perl, you can still read on to see how useful and powerful this language is.

As discussed in previous chapters, there is a common thread with all interfaces. The Perl DBI is no different. A connection has to be made, queries have to be passed to the database, results are returned, and then the connection is closed—these are the general steps that all database interfaces share.

The Perl DBI Object

The Perl DBI is made up of one object—the DBI object. From this object, you can find out what drivers are available with the data_sources() method, or you can create a database handle with the connect() method. The connect() method returns a database handle through which you can enter statements. A database handle can be thought of as a type of connection. For example, when you make a phone call, you dial the numbers on the phone to make a call. Someone on the other end answers and you can begin a conversation. The connection you have with the other person is similar to a handle, and the telephone company is like the DBI. You make a connection through the phone company much like you make a connection through the DBI. If all your data is correct, you have a good connection. You can have a conversation and then hang up. These same things occur with the DBI. The DBI can generate many handles to different databases, much like the telephone company can connect you to a lot of people with your phone.

The DBI is a very powerful interface because it can generate as many handles as needed, and they all don't have to be from the same database. For example, if you need to swap data between databases, you could easily generate two handles with the DBI—one handle pointing to the one database and the other handle pointing to the other database. This allows you to make very powerful programs that allow data transfer. This type of an application would be very useful in a data warehouse.

14

Connecting with the DBI

Several pieces of information are needed to make a connection with the DBI. You need the driver name, the database you are going to use, and the username and a password of the person who can connect to this database. Nothing new here; you've seen these requirements before. The syntax for the connection statement is as follows:

```
$dbh = DBI->connect(DBI:driver name:database=database name,
username, password);
```

The very first item is the variable that will hold the database handle. The current style is to name it $dbh or database handle, although it can be whatever name you want it to be. It's just an ordinary Perl variable. The item after the equal sign is the DBI object. Using the arrow syntax from the DBI object to denote that you are calling a method of this object, you call the connect method with the following parameters:

1. DBI:*driver name*:database=*database name*   The first half of this statement is the driver you'll be using to connect. For MySQL, it is mysql. The second part—separated by a colon—is the name of the database you'll be using. A proper argument here for a MySQL database would be

    ```
    DBI:mysql:database=Meet_A_Geek
    ```

2. The next argument is the username. This has to be a valid name that can be used to connect to the MySQL server.

3. The third argument is the password for the user mentioned in the second argument. If the user does not have a password (a very big security risk), this argument would be empty. You would still pass it as empty quotation marks (" ").

To connect to the Meet_A_Geek database, you would issue the following connect statement:

INPUT   `$dbh = DBI->(DBI:mysql:database=Meet_A_Geek, "root", "tacobell");`

The database handle, commonly referred to as $dbh, has many methods associated with it. While they are not all covered here, the ones that are the most commonly used are listed. If you would like to learn more about the rest of the database handle methods, please refer to the man pages by typing in **man DBI** at the command line. The following are some of the database handle methods:

1. `$dbh->do(SQL statement)`   This statement executes the SQL statement contained in the parentheses immediately. This is used if you are issuing commands that do not return a resultset, such as an `INSERT` or `UPDATE` statement. You can also use DCL statements here as well, such as the `CREATE` and `DROP` commands.

2. `$dbh->prepare(SQL Statement)`   This statement will generate a statement handle. A statement handle is a record set object. It has methods and properties that can be used to manipulate or describe the data it contains. The resultset that is returned is the result of the query that is contained in the parentheses.

3. `$dbh->disconnect`   This statement destroys your database handle and closes the database connection.

The database handle also contains more methods, such as the `table_info()` and `ping` methods. Because this is a book about MySQL and not about the Perl DBI, these methods are beyond the scope of this book. Please refer to the man pages mentioned earlier for more information.

Writing Perl Script

Now you can create your first Perl script. The following is a simple script that will connect to the `Meet_A_Geek` database and `INSERT` three rows of data:

```perl
#!/usr/bin/perl -w

use DBI;

$database = "Meet_A_Geek";
$driver = "DBI:mysql";
my $dbh = DBI->connect($driver:database=$database, "root", "tacobell")
    or die "Can't connect";

# Insert the values
$dbh->do("INSERT INTO Customers (First_Name, Last_Name)
 VALUES ('Renee', 'Robertson')");
$dbh->do("INSERT INTO Customers (First_Name, Last_Name)
VALUES ('Larry', 'Isacson')");
$dbh->do("INSERT INTO Customers (First_Name, Last_Name)
VALUES ('Mark', 'Harrison')");
```

14

```
# Disconnect from the database
$dbh->disconnect;

exit;
```

Take a line-by-line look at the anatomy of this script. The first line tells where the Perl interpreter is found. This allows you to execute this program without explicitly calling the Perl interpreter. The next line tells the interpreter to use the DBI module. If you forget this line, the rest of your code will not work. You start to build the connection string in the next two lines. You will see this technique used a lot. It allows you to change things quickly in the future or let you build your connection string based on command-line arguments. The next line is where you actually connect to the database. The or die statement is the minimum amount of error checking you can provide. There is more you can use, and they are available in the man pages. The next few lines add the records to the Customers table in the database. The next line disconnects you from the database and destroys your handle. The final line tells the interpreter that it has reached the end of the script.

As you can see, the process is very simple and straightforward. In the previous code sample, you saw how two of the three functions of the database handle object were used. Now take a look at the third function.

The prepare() method of the database handle object is different from the other two methods in the database handle. This method returns a statement handle. The statement handle has its own set of methods and properties. The following are some of these methods:

- execute()   This method carries out the SQL statement that was issued in the prepare() method of the database handle object.

- fetchrow_hashref()   This method returns an associative array containing the values of the resultset in a name=value pair relationship.

- finish()   This method destroys the statement handle and frees resources.

- rows()   This method returns the number of rows the statement contains.

Listing 14.1 is an example of how to use the prepare() method to generate a statement handle.

LISTING 14.1 The Prepare Statement and the Statement Handle

```perl
10 #!/usr/bin/perl -w

20 use DBI;

30 $DSN = "DBI:mysql:database=Meet_A_Geek";
40 my $dbh = DBI->connect($DSN, "root", "tacobell")
50 or die "Can't connect";

60 $my $sth = $dbh->prepare("SELECT * FROM Customers WHERE State = "KY");
70 $sth->execute();

80 while(my $ref = $sth->fetchrow_hashref()){
90    print "$ref->{'First_Name'} $ref->{'Last_Name'}";
}

100 $sth->finish();
110 $dbh->disconnect;
120 exit;
```

Now examine the code down line by line. You've seen lines 10−50 before. These lines just enable the script to run using the DBI module, set up the connection string, and then connect to the database. Line 60 is where it starts to get a little interesting. Here you set a variable $sth equal to the results of the prepare() method of the database handle. The prepare() statement parses the SQL statement and makes sure it is correct. Then a statement handle is created. The SQL statement is held until the execute() method is called. This is done on line 70 of the code.

When the execute() method is called, the query is actually passed to the database and a resultset is returned. All the information regarding this resultset is contained within the statement handle, such as the number of rows it contains and information about the data itself.

After the execute()statement, you use one of the statement handle's methods to work with the data. Using a while loop in line 80, you walk through every row of the data, printing the data that is contained in the column mentioned in the print statement (line 90). The data is retrieved in the same way it is stored in the database.

Line 100 destroys the statement handle object, freeing up the resources. The next line destroys the database handle, closing the connection. The script ends with the exit statement.

14

In this example, you saw how you could connect to a database, issue a query, and manipulate the results returned from the database. Remember that every time you interface with a database you will follow these same steps:

1. Build a connection string and use it to connect to a database. With Perl, this is done using the DBI object.

    ```
    $dbh = DBI->connect(DBI:mysql:database=Meet_A_Geek, "root", "tacobell");
    ```

2. After you establish a connection, use the database handle ($dbh) to issue queries. For queries that do not return a resultset, use the do() method. For queries that will return a resultset, use the prepare() statement.

    ```
    $dbh->do("DELETE FROM Customers WHERE State = 'KY'");
    ```

3. If you need a resultset, use the prepare() statement.

    ```
    $sth = $dbh->prepare("SELECT * FROM Customers");
    ```

4. Before you can use the results of the query, you need to run the query on the database. To do this, use the statement handle's ($sth) execute() method.

    ```
    $sth->execute();
    ```

5. After you have executed the query, you can manipulate the resultset by using the fetchrow_hashref() method to return a row's worth of data. You will need to use some sort of looping statement to retrieve all the data in the resultset.

    ```
    While($ref = $sth->fetchrow_hashref()){
        # Code that manipulates your data in some way
        print "ref->{'Last_name'}";
    }
    ```

6. After you have finished with your resultset, get rid of it so that you can free up system resources. You do this by using the finish() method.

    ```
    $sth->finish();
    ```

7. You can continue issuing queries with your current handle. You can even generate multiple statement handles with one database handle. When you are completely finished using the database contained in the handle, close your connection. You do this by calling the disconnect() method.

    ```
    $dbh->disconnect();
    ```

That's all there is to it. If you take it step by step, it's an easy process. Now that you've got this part down, look at how you can use this knowledge in the real world.

CGI, Perl, DBI, and MySQL: How They All Fit Together

Perl, because of its great string manipulation capabilities has, found itself a natural home on the Internet and with Common Gateway Interface (CGI) programming. CGI is the environment where programs that send, receive, and translate data from the Internet to your server operate. These programs tend to be an interface to much larger applications and databases that need data from a Web site to perform their duties. Examples of CGI applications are online stores, catalogs, and any other Web sites that need to dynamically generate Web pages based on criteria presented by a user.

You may be asking yourself, "How does this all tie together?" Well, Perl is probably the best language to use for CGI type programming. It's extremely fast and has strong string manipulating features—two definite strong points when dealing with the Internet and HTML. The DBI is Perl's database interface. It is easy to use and very powerful. And when it comes to databases that are suited for the Internet, no other database comes even close to MySQL's speed and ease of use. With this great combination, there is nothing you can't accomplish.

The best way to show you how this all works is to start with a sample and explain as you go along.

Handling Data on a Web Page

You are going to create a Web page that takes data from a form on a Web page and adds that data to the Vendors table in the Meet_A_Geek database. To start, take a look at the Figure 14.1 to see what the HTML form you will be using looks like. The form has all the fields you need to collect for the database. In a CGI type program, the fields from this form will be passed to the Web server, along with the request for the next page. The HTML <FORM> tag has two properties that need to be set. The first is the action method that tells the browser what program to run. The other property to set is the Method property. This property tells the browser how to send the information in the form. There are two choices, GET and POST. In all the examples, you will use the POST method. This is the most frequently used method of sending the information.

Listing 14.2 show the code for the vendor.html page.

14

FIGURE 14.1

Handling data using a Web form.

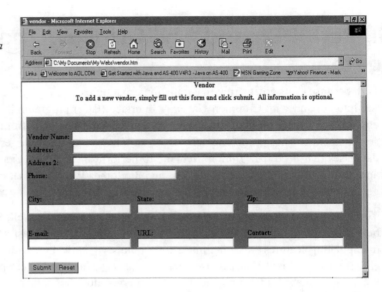

LISTING 14.2 Capturing Vendor Data with a Web Form

```html
<html>

<head>

<title>Vendor</title>
</head>

<body>
<form method=post action= "/cgi-bin/AddVendor.pl">
<div align="left">
  <table border="0" width="824" height="27" cellspacing="0"
      cellpadding="2">
    <tr>
      <td width="824" height="27" colspan="3">
        <p align="center"><b>Vendor</b></td>
    </tr>
    <tr>
      <td width="824" height="27" colspan="3">
        <p align="center"><b>To add a new vendor,
        simply fill out this form and
        click submit.  All information is optional.</b></td>
    </tr>
    <t
r>
      <td width="824" height="27" colspan="3"><b>
<font color="#FFFFFF">f</font></b></td>
    </tr>
```

LISTING **14.2**   continued

```
    <tr>
      <td width="824" height="27" colspan="3"
bgcolor="#9C9C4E"> </td>
    </tr>
    <tr>
      <td width="824"height="27"colspan="3"
bgcolor="#9C9C4E"><b>Vendor Name: </b>
<input type="text" name="Vendor_Name" size="91"></td>
    </tr>
    <tr>
      <td width="824" height="27" colspan="3" bgcolor="#9C9C4E"><b>
Address:          
        </b><input type="text" name="Address" size="91"></td>
    </tr>
    <tr>
      <td width="824" height="27" colspan="3"
bgcolor="#9C9C4E"><b>Address
        2:         </b>
<input type="text" name="Address2" size="91"></td>
    </tr>
    <tr>
      <td width="824" height="27" colspan="3" bgcolor="#9C9C4E">
<b>Phone:    </b>
          
        <input type="text" name="City" size="32"></td>
    </tr>
    <tr>
      <td width="824" height="27" colspan="3"
bgcolor="#9C9C4E"> </td>
    </tr>
    <tr>
      <td width="245" height="27" bgcolor="#9C9C4E">
<b>City:    </b>
<input type="text" name="City" size="32"></td>
      <td width="247" height="27" bgcolor="#9C9C4E"><b>State:</b>
<input type="text" name="State" size="30"></td>
      <td width="309" height="27" bgcolor="#9C9C4E">
<b>Zip:      
       
    
        </b><input type="text" name="Zip" size="30"></td>
    </tr>
    <tr>
      <td width="245" height="27" bgcolor="#9C9C4E"> </td>
      <td width="247" height="27" bgcolor="#9C9C4E"> </td>
      <td width="309" height="27" bgcolor="#9C9C4E"> </td>
    </tr>
    <tr>
      <td width="245" height="27" bgcolor="#9C9C4E"><b>E-mail:</b>
```

14

LISTING **14.2** continued

```
<input type="text" name="E_Mail" size="32"></td>
      <td width="247" height="27" bgcolor="#9C9C4E"><b>URL: </b>
<input type="text" name="URL" size="30"></td>
      <td width="309" height="27" bgcolor="#9C9C4E">
<b>Contact:    
    
      </b><input type="text" name="Contact" size="30"></td>
   </tr>
   <tr>
      <td width="801" height="27" colspan="3"></td>
   </tr>
   <tr>
      <td width="801" height="27" colspan="3">
<input type="submit" value="Submit" name="B1">
<input type="reset" value="Reset" name="B2"></td>
   </tr>
  </table>
</form>
</div>

</body>

</html>
```

There are a number of text boxes inside the form. These boxes can take input from the user and pass it to your CGI program. Notice that each box is given a name. This name will be passed to the server in a name/value pair that you can parse and use.

Modifying the Database with Perl Script

Now take a look at a Perl Script that will take the data from this Web page and add it to your database. Listing 14.3 adds vendor data to the database.

LISTING **14.3** Perl Script for Adding Vendor Data

```
#!/usr/bin/perl

use DBI;

#####################################Connect to the Meet_A_Geek database#
#####################################

$database = "Meet_A_Geek";
$driver ="mysql";

$dsn = "DBI:$driver:database=$database;$options";
```

Listing 14.3 continued

```perl
$dbh = DBI->connect($dsn,"root",'tacobell')
        or die "Error connecting to database";

%postInputs = readPostInput();

$Vendor_Name = $postInputs{'Vendor_Name'};
$Address = $postInputs{'Address'};
$Address2 = $postInputs{'Address2'};
$State = $postInputs{'State'};
$City = $postInputs{'City'};
$Zip = $postInputs{'Zip'};
$Phone = $postInputs{'Phone'};
$E_Mail = $postInputs{'E_Mail'};
$URL = $postInputs{'URL'};
$Contact = $postInputs{'Contact'};

$dbh->do(''INSERT INTO Vendors
        VALUES(NULL, '$Vendor_Name', '$Address',
        '$Address2', '$City','$State', '$Zip', '$Phone', '$E_Mail',
        '$URL', '$Contact')");

$dbh->disconect;


####################################################
# Subroutine that gets the post from the previous#
#form and puts the values                       #
# into an associative array
####################################################

sub readPostInput{
    my (%searchField, $buf, $pair, @pairs);

    if ($ENV{'REQUEST_METHOD'} eq 'POST'){
        read(STDIN, $buf, $ENV{'CONTENT_LENGTH'});
        @pairs = split(/&/, $buf);

        foreach $pair(@pairs){
            ($name, $val) = split(/=/,$pair);
            $val =~ tr/+/ /;
            $val =~ s/%([a-fA-f0-9][a-fA-F0-9])/pack("C", hex($1))/eg;
            $name =~ tr/+/ /;
            $name =~ s/%([a-fA-f0-9][a-fA-F0-9])/pack("C", hex($1))/eg;
            $searchField{$name} = $val;
        }
    }

    return (%searchField);
}
```

14

LISTING 14.3   continued

```
print "Content-Type:  text/html\n\n";



print "<html><head><title>Record Added</title></head>";
print "<body>The Vendor has been added</body>";
print "</html>";
```

The first line of this listing tells where to find the Perl interpreter. The next line tells the
interpreter to use the DBI module. There is also a CGI module that does a lot of neat things.
You can find this out on CPAN as well.

```
$database = "Meet_A_Geek";
$driver ="mysql";

$dsn = "DBI:$driver:database=$database;$options";
$dbh = DBI->connect($dsn,"root",'tacobell')
        or die "Error connecting to database";
```

This piece of code builds the connection string. Notice that a third variable ($DSN) is used to
store the driver and database information. It was done this way to make the code easier to
read.

```
%postInputs = readPostInput();
```

This line of code calls the readPostInput() function. This function parses the name/value
pairs and creates a hash that contains these values.

> **Note**   A hash or an associative array is an array that stores items in a name=value
> pair.

```
$Vendor_Name = $postInputs{'Vendor_Name'};
$Address = $postInputs{'Address'};
$Address2 = $postInputs{'Address2'};
$State = $postInputs{'State'};
$City = $postInputs{'City'};
$Zip = $postInputs{'Zip'};
$Phone = $postInputs{'Phone'};
$E_Mail = $postInputs{'E_Mail'};
$URL = $postInputs{'URL'};
$Contact = $postInputs{'Contact'};
```

This segment of code takes the associative array that was returned from `readPostInput()` and assigns the values to variables. This is done to make the code easier to read and understand. You could have easily skipped this step and used the array. The only problem is that your SQL statement would be incredibly long and hard to read. This step saves you a lot of eyestrain later. Notice that the names in the array are the names that were used on the Web page. This is important to remember because Perl is case sensitive. A misspelling here could mean hours of debugging later. So take your time and be cautious.

```
$dbh->do("INSERT INTO Vendors VALUES(NULL, '$Vendor_Name', '$Address',
       '$Address2', '$City','$State', '$Zip', '$Phone', '$E_Mail',
       '$URL', '$Contact')");
```

This code segment creates the SQL statement and executes it on the database. The values that were in the text boxes on your form are now being added to the database. Seems a little too easy, doesn't it?

```
$dbh->disconnect;
```

Because you are all done with the database handle, you need to clean up. Disconnect from the database to free up system resources and the connection to the database.

```
sub readPostInput{
    my (%searchField, $buf, $pair, @pairs);

    if ($ENV{'REQUEST_METHOD'} eq 'POST'){
        read(STDIN, $buf, $ENV{'CONTENT_LENGTH'});
        @pairs = split(/&/, $buf);

        foreach $pair(@pairs){
            ($name, $val) = split(/=/, $pair);
            $val =~ tr/+/ /;
            $val =~ s/%([a-fA-f0-9][a-fA-F0-9])/pack("C", hex($1))/eg;
            $name =~ tr/+/ /;
            $name =~ s/%([a-fA-f0-9][a-fA-F0-9])/pack("C", hex($1))/eg;
            $searchField{$name} = $val;
        }
    }

    return (%searchField);
}
```

This is the function that performs the parsing routine that splits out your name value pairs, creating an associative array. This is a very handy function, feel free to use it with any CGI application you create. This work is already done for you in the CGI module that is available from CPAN.

14

```
print "Content-Type:  text/html\n\n";
```

```
print "<html><head><title>Record Added</title></head>";
print "<body>The Vendor has been added</body>";
print "</html>";
exit;
```

The final segment of code sends a response back to the browser. In it, you tell the user that the vendor has been added. You can get very creative here. What you are doing in this step is passing a Web page back to the browser. See Figure 14.2 for the result. Whatever you can do in a Web page, you can do here. JavaScript, DHTML, and Flash animations are some examples. You are not limited because you are embedding the HTML in a Perl script. You can be as creative as you want to be. There is one point to mention—the first line in the code segment is mandatory. Your page will not be displayed if you do not include it exactly as it appears. The two new lines are required for the content to be displayed in the browser.

That's it. That's all you need to do to include database access with your Web pages.

FIGURE 14.2

Sending confirmation
back to the browser.

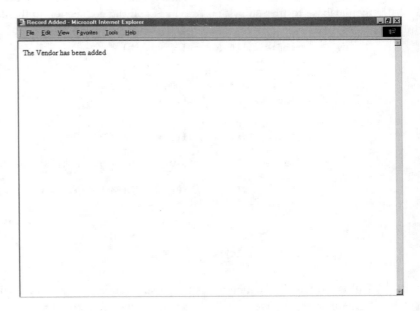

Take a look at the CGI process one more time. A user fills a form or clicks a link that passes values along with a request to a Perl Script. The script processes the values that were passed. It also performs any database interactions and then sends a response back to the browser in the form of HTML.

Summary

Today, you learned the basics of the Perl Database Interface as it applies to MySQL. You have just touched the tip of the iceberg. There is a lot you can do with Perl and MySQL. You can use Perl to help automate MySQL administrative tasks, as well as help perform duties, such as reporting and maintaining your data. The sky's the limit.

You also learned about the three objects that Perl gives you to help accomplish your database interface. They are the DBI object, the database handle, and the statement handle. You learned how these objects interact to provide you with a powerful and flexible interface for your database.

Another thing you learned today was how to create simple Perl CGI programs to accomplish Web/database integration. You saw how you could use the DBI object to perform these tasks.

There is a whole world to discover when it comes to Perl/CGI/Database programming. Only the basics were touched on today. If you would like to pursue this type of programming even more, Sams Publishing offers a large selection of books to get you on your way, such as *Sams Teach Yourself Perl in 21 Days*, by Laura Lemay or *Sams Teach Yourself CGI in 24 Hours*, by Rafe Colburn.

Q&A

Q   Why is the Perl DBI so powerful?

A   One of the main reasons it is considered so powerful is because of its simple yet elegant design. For example, you could create a database handle to an Oracle database with one line of code. You could create a database handle to a MySQL database in the next line of code. From there, you could create two more statements that exchange data between two database. You can do all that with maybe six lines of code. It doesn't get any easier than that.

14

Q   **Am I limited to just simple SQL statements with the Perl DBI?**

A   No. You can issue any command with the Perl DBI that you could issue from the MySQL Monitor. So statements, such as the OPTIMIZE and LOAD DATA INFILE, are fair game. In fact, the database handle has a func() method that allows you to pass statements such as CREATE database all in one line. The syntax looks like the following:

```
$retVal = $dbh->func('createdb', database name, 'admin')
```

Other statements include the dropdb, shutdown, and reload functions. These all follow pretty much the same syntax. The shutdown and reload functions do not have the database name argument that the createdb and dropdb have. They need to be typed exactly as they appear in the previous code.

Exercises

1. Create a Perl script that takes a request from the user and displays values from the database based on the given value. For example, with the Meet_A_Geek database, create a Web page that allows a person to see a list of customers based on the states in which the customers live. Pass this value to a Perl script that uses that parameter in an SQL SELECT query.

2. Create a Perl script that adds a user to the database. (Hint: use the GRANT statement).

WEEK 2

In Review

You've finished your second week of learning about MySQL. You have learned about populating your database and using MySQL's intrinsic functions. You have also learned about programmatic interfaces and what they can do for you.

8

9

10

11

12

13

14

WEEK 3

At a Glance

You've finished your second week of MySQL. You should know how to work with data that is stored in a MySQL database. Now that you know how to manipulate the data, you will learn how to maintain the database.

Where You're Going

In the third week, you'll complete your study of MySQL. You'll learn about the administrator tasks of a MySQL database. Again, this week builds on your existing knowledge, taking you further down the road to becoming a true MySQL DBA.

After you complete this week's training, you should have a thorough understanding of MySQL. Day 15 starts off the week by finishing up the last of the interfaces with "MySQL and PHP." On Day 16, you'll learn how MySQL supports time. Day 17, "MySQL Database Security," covers all the aspects of securing your database. On Day 18, you'll learn how MySQL compares to other relational database in the market. Day 19 covers MySQL's administrative tasks. You'll learn what you can do to get the most out of your MySQL database server on Day 20, "Optimizing MySQL." Finally, on Day 21, "Putting it All Together," you'll cover the entire development process of a Web site that uses MySQL to create pages dynamically and store information from the user.

15

16

17

18

19

20

21

DAY 15

MySQL and PHP

This chapter will introduce you to PHP, a server-side scripting language that can be embedded into HTML files.

Today, you will learn

- PHP's principles of operation
- How to embed PHP within HTML files on a Web server
- How to use PHP as a front-end to a MySQL database

What Is PHP?

PHP stands for PHP: Hypertext Preprocessor. It is a language that has come out of the open source stable. Fast growing in popularity, it is a competitor to Perl, ASP, JSP, and numerous other server-side scripting solutions.

Server-Side Scripting

A Web server that contains nothing but HTML and graphics files might run a cosmetically good Web site. The site might hold files with client-side scripts, such as JavaScript, DHTML, and Java to make the Web site more dynamic. Nevertheless, an important interactive component will still be missing.

No matter how clever you get designing your HTML pages and writing your client-side code, there will always be some aspects of interactivity that cannot be achieved. Communication with the user will still be primarily one way: from server to client.

With a truly dynamic Web site, you overcome this limitation; you can allow users to interact with a vast database, let them browse online stores, book a plane ticket online, and so on. For such scenarios, you need code that is server-side executable.

That's where *CGIs* (*Common Gateway Interfaces*) come in. These are server-side executable programs, in which the lines of program code are being run on the server rather than the client.

This has a number of advantages. CGIs allow interaction with large, online databases. They allow for the two-way passing of information between client and server.

Another advantage is that the code is usually client-independent. While client-side code often needs to be modified—even written twice—to cope with the differences between Netscape and Internet Explorer and the different versions of these browsers, CGIs run on a single machine—the server. Being independent of the client platform, you minimize development costs and ensure that the maximum number of clients can use your site.

Enter PHP

CGIs can be written in a number of languages. On typical UNIX-based systems, they are written in Perl, but C, C++, and other languages can be used. Newer languages include Microsoft's ASP, Sun's JSP, and NetObjects, a fourth-generation solution to server-side programming. PHP has emerged from the open source camp.

PHP scripts are embedded within HTML files. When a PHP-enabled Web server receives a request for an HTML file containing PHP, it does not simply give the file to the user—it first executes the PHP scripts contained within the file.

The script may result in HTML, which is generated on-the-fly. But, at a more complex level, it may include instructions to update files and data stored on the server, even send email and generate graphics on-the-fly.

15

The result is totally transparent to users; they need not know that the page has been generated especially for them! They never get to see the PHP script and may not even realize it is there.

PHP, unlike other traditional CGIs, such as Perl, has the convenience of being contained within HTML pages; it does not have to reside in a `cgi-bin` directory. It also has a well-developed library of functions and APIs that enable it to interface with all manner of server functionality.

As of this writing, PHP is at version 3, but version 4 is in beta and will be released soon. This introductory chapter intentionally avoids going into a close examination of the language, so differences between PHP3 and PHP4 should not be relevant for learning the basic principles.

Installing and Running PHP

Here's the good news: there are versions of PHP that will run on the various versions of Microsoft Windows, on UNIX and Linux, and for the most popular Web servers, including Apache and IIS. It's also free, whether it's used for personal, educational, or commercial use.

Space in this book does not permit a complete guide to installing and setting up PHP. However, it is freely downloadable from the official PHP Web site (`http://www.php.net/`) where you will find a full guide to installation on your particular platform.

Another useful site is `http://www.phpbuilder.com/`, with lots of resources and discussion archives for PHP developers.

PHP Basics

Consider a simple example of a Web page containing some PHP code:

```
<HTML>
<HEAD>
<TITLE>My first PHP page</TITLE>
</HEAD>
<BODY>
<?php
echo "The time is now ".time();
?>
</BODY>
 </HTML>
```

You would save this file on your Web server as `showtime.php3`. (Note that you have used a `.php3` extension. Depending on the PHP setup in the Web server's configuration file on your system, you may be able to use `.php` or even `.html`.)

When you visit the page with a Web browser, you should get an output along the lines of

OUTPUT   The time is now 951164380

>
>
> If your browser displays the HTML and PHP code at this point, you may have a configuration problem on the server. It may be as simple as the filename extension needing to be changed. Try changing the extension to .php. This setup, which defines when PHP can be invoked, is held in your Web server's configuration file (srm.conf on Apache). Failing that, you will need to study the PHP documentation.

What happened here? It's a plain HTML page, except for two important things: one is the filename extension (.php3) and the other is the lines between the <?php and ?> tags. These are special tags denoting a section of PHP script. You'll look a little more into invoking PHP in a moment.

The *echo* command is PHP-speak for print to screen. In the example, it displays the text in quotes, together with the system time since 1970 in seconds. Rudimentary stuff this may be, but you've just built your first PHP-enabled dynamic Web page.

How PHP Works

When a request comes into a PHP-enabled Web server from a client's browser, the Web server does a number of things:

- It receives and reads the request from the client browser.
- It locates the requested page on the server.
- It executes any instructions given by the embedded PHP code, unlike a normal HTML page.
- It sends the resultant page to the client.

Now that you have a grasp of the basic principles of PHP, you'll take a look at the language in more detail. After that, you'll learn how PHP can help you make the users of your Web site interact with a MySQL database.

A Quick-Start Guide to PHP

Here's a guide to the PHP language, designed to get you started quickly. To keep it lightweight, it's assumed that you're comfortable with the basic principles of coding, and that you're comfortable writing simple HTML pages. Included is a useful but non-exhaustive set of PHP syntax. It's designed more to whet your appetite than to be a reference manual but, nevertheless, you should be able to compile quite sophisticated dynamic Web pages after digesting it.

Basic Syntax

PHP requires escape codes to indicate where your HTML file flips into PHP mode. You can use any of the following tags around your code (an echo statement is given as example):

```
<?php
echo "PHP mode now";
?>
```

or

```
<? echo "PHP mode now with short tags"; ?>
```

or

```
<script language="php"> echo "PHP mode now"; </script>
```

You can use multiline or single-line forms, no matter which tag style you choose.

The second option is the easiest (using just <? and ?>, it's shortest!) but requires you to enable "short tags" (these may already be enabled, depending on your installation). The third may make life easier with certain WYSIWYG HTML editors, which don't like unusual tags.

An important thing to notice here is that there is a semicolon (;) after every PHP statement. This is the end-of-statement character. This is essential. However, PHP doesn't mind if you put several statements on one line or spread one statement across several.

Types

PHP supports integers, floating-point numbers, strings, arrays, and objects. When PHP accesses a variable, it decides which type to use it as, according to the context in which it is used. It can even use the same variable as different types—this is known as *type juggling*. Variable types are usually not set by the programmer (there's often no need, although it can be done).

The following are some simple assignments:

```
$num = 20;  # integer
$price = 14.95;  # floating-point
$size = 'large';  # string
$myarray[0] = "red";  # scalar array, first element (0)
$myarray["qty"] = 6;  # associative array, element "qty"
```

Note that either single (') or double quotes (") can be used for string values, but yield different results. With double quotes, any variable contained within will be evaluated. With single quotes, they will not. Thus,

```
$var = "red $price";
echo $var;
```

produces an output as follows:

OUTPUT   red 14.95

However,

```
$var = 'green $price';
echo $var;
```

produces a more literal output:

OUTPUT   green $price

If you want to use objects, use the new statement to create an instance of an object and relate it to a variable, as shown in the following:

```
class myobj {
    function do_myobj ($p) {
        echo "Doing myobj with parameter $p.";
    }
}
$var = new myobj;
$var->do_myobj(5);
```

This produces output:

OUTPUT   Doing myobj with parameter 5.

You are advised to study a more thorough text on object-oriented techniques if you are not familiar with them already.

PHP variables can also be equated to Boolean types (TRUE and FALSE). If a variable is undefined, null, or zero, it equates to FALSE, and if it contains some value, it will equate to TRUE. Comparing a variable with TRUE or FALSE is useful in conditional expressions and loops, as you will see later today in the "Control Structures" sections.

Variables

Variables of all types are preceded with a dollar sign ($) and are case-sensitive.

By default, variables are available to the script in which they are used and in any scripts that are included in that one (you'll look at incorporating one script into another script soon, using the INCLUDE statement). In this sense, they are global.

However, when you use user-defined functions, variables are local to that function and are not available outside it by default.

You've already seen some examples of manipulating user-defined variables, but there are also a large number of pre-defined variables.

The easiest way to view the pre-defined variable for your system is to run phpinfo:

```
phpinfo();
```

This one line of code will produce substantial output. In the output you'll find a number of variables relating to your Web server. You can isolate some of these variables, for example:

```
echo "$HTTP_USER_AGENT\n";
```

may produce something like the following:

OUTPUT   Mozilla/4.7 (Macintosh; I; PPC)

Such information can be useful in knowing what kind of client you've got, where he or she just came from (HTTP_REFERER), what script you're running (SCRIPT_FILENAME), what request method was used (REQUEST_METHOD), what query was sent (QUERY_STRING), if any, and so on. In HTML form processing in particular, these variables can become very useful.

Variables from HTML Forms

PHP makes life fairly easy when you solicit user input in an HTML form. Forms use the common name=value structure, and anything declared using name= in HTML, creates a variable of that same name in PHP with the corresponding value.

For example, look at the following HTML form:

```
<form action="form_example.php3"method="post">
Enter your name: <input type="text"name="username">
What size do you wish to order? <select name="size">
<option value="S">small
<option value="M">medium
<option value="L">large
</select>
<input type="submit"name="SUBMIT"value="Submit">
</form>
```

When the PHP script is called in form_example.php3, it will have the variables $username and $size already assigned, according to the user's input. For example, you can use these values to create a dynamically-generated output, as in the following:

```
<?php
echo "You entered your name as $username and size as $size.";
?>
```

You can even receive a whole array of data from a form. You do this with your HTML SELECT tag, which you declare as SELECT MULTIPLE, and add brackets ([ ]) after the name of the variable:

```
What colors do you want? <select multiple name="color[]">
<option value="R">red
<option value="G">green
<option value="B">blue
<option value="Y">yellow
</select>
```

Here, you made color[] into an array by the way you declared it in the HTML form, and you now have the $color array ready for use in PHP.

Expressions

You set equality in PHP by using a single equals sign (=):

```
$size = 10;
```

sets the $size variable to the integer 10.

You can do multiple assignments, such as

```
$leftcolor = $rightcolor = 'brown';
```

which sets both variables to the same string.

Apart from assigning values, you can also compare. You can use

- == for testing equality
- != for not equal to
- < for smaller than
- <= for smaller than or equal to
- > for greater than
- >= for greater than or equal to

Note

Don't confuse = with ==. If you write something like the following:

`if ($name = 'John') { echo "Hello John"; }`

you will always get "Hello John" output. Why? Because = does an assignment, not a comparison. Once assigned, $name evaluates to TRUE (because it is not blank), and the if statement executes the echo statement.

What you probably meant was

`if ($name == 'John') { echo "Hello John"; }`

which will compare $name with the given string and then decide on the action to take. If the comparison evaluates to TRUE, the echo statement is executed.

PHP gives you a few shortcuts for assigning variables in a quite compact way. The following are a few examples:

- $n++ and ++$n increment $n by 1.
- $n-- and --$n decrement $n by 1.
- $n += 6 increments $n by 6.
- $n -= 2.5 decrements $n by 2.5.
- $n /= 10 divides $n by 10.
- $text .= "yours sincerely" appends text to the end of a string called $text.

Note

$n++ is a little different from ++$n. If the ++ (or --) is put before the variable, the incrementing (or decrementing) is done before anything else, such as returning the value of the expression. If the ++ is put after the variable, the incrementing is done after returning the value.

Thus

```
$n = 5; echo $n++;
```

returns '5' and then sets $n to 6, while

```
$n = 5; echo ++$n;
```

sets $n to 6 and then returns '6'.

Operators

PHP has the usual arithmetic operators, including

- + for addition (*$x* + *$y*)
- - for subtraction (*$subtotal* *$discount*)
- * for multiplication (*$annual* = *$monthly* * 12)
- / for division (*$x* / 10)
- % for modulo arithmetic (*$x* % *$y* gives remainder of *$x* / *$y*)

Control Structures: `if`

PHP offers a number of means of controlling the flow of your script. Look first at conditional control using `if` that takes the following form:

```
if (expression) {
        # do this
} elseif (expression) {
        # do another thing
} else {
        # do something else
}
```

`elseif` tests and actions, and `else` actions are optional. At it's very simplest, you just need `if` and the parentheses surrounding the first expression:

```
if ($price > 100) echo "This is expensive";
```

is correct syntax and will print the message only if $price is greater than 100.

When there's more than one statement to execute, you must surround them with braces:

```
if ($price > 100) {
echo "This is expensive";
echo "Another time";
}
```

You can make a construct with `if () { } else { }`, such that if the first condition is not met (evaluates to `FALSE`), the statements contained within the braces of the `else { }` clause will be executed. (Note that the braces can be omitted if there is only one statement to execute.)

The most complex form of `if` is to use `if () { } elseif () { } else { }`. There can be any number of `elseif ()` conditions. If the first `if ()` condition is not met, it will try to match the `elseif ()`, and the next, and so on until the last `elseif ()`.

When one of the conditions is met (evaluates to `TRUE`), it will execute the given statements and then finish. If none of the conditions is met, it will execute the `else` statements. If there is no `else`, it will finish without doing anything.

Control Structures: `while`

PHP offers a simple loop structure in the form of `while`. A `while` loop takes the following basic form:

```
while (expression) {
        # do some statements;
}
```

Upon entering the loop, the expression is evaluated and, if it is `TRUE`, execution proceeds to the statements within the loop. Braces around the statements are only required when there is more than one statement.

`while` is actually quite similar to `if` without the `elseif` and `else` options. Like `if`, it only executes the statements if the expression evaluates to `TRUE`, but, having done the statements once, `while` will go back to the beginning and evaluate *expression* again, and keep doing so until it evaluates to `FALSE`, whereupon it will finish the loop and continue with the rest of the code.

Consider a simple example of HTML and PHP for counting down from 3 to 0:

```
Countdown with while<br>
<?php
$n = 4;
```

```
while (--$n)
        echo "$n...";
?>
```

which will produce

OUTPUT   Countdown with while
             3...2...1...

What happens here? Each time execution enters the while loop, the $n variable decrements by one and is then evaluated as TRUE or FALSE. The first time into the loop, it evaluates to 3, which is TRUE as far as the while logic is concerned, so it executes the echo statement.

The fourth time through into the loop, $n is 1 and decrementing again makes it zero. This means FALSE, and execution therefore skips the echo statement and finishes.

A second form of the while loop is do...while. This takes the following form:

```
do {
        # some statements
} while (expression)
```

Unlike the first form of while, this form guarantees that the statements within the braces will be executed at least once. The expression will not be evaluated until the end of the loop; if TRUE at that point, the loop will be repeated. The looping will continue until *expression* evaluates to FALSE.

Control Structures: for

A more complex form of looping is available in the form of the for loop. This takes the following form:

```
for (expression1; expression2; expression3) {
        # some loop statements
}
```

The choice of expressions is important; these work as follows:

- *expression1* is evaluated only once, unconditionally, because execution starts at for the first time.
- *expression2* is evaluated each time execution starts at for. If TRUE, the loop statements are executed; if FALSE, you exit the loop.
- *expression3* is evaluated each time execution finishes the statements in the loop. If TRUE, you execute the loop statements again; if FALSE, you exit the loop.

For example, consider how you could rewrite your `countdown` loop with `for`:

```
Countdown with for<br>
<?php
for ($n=4; --$n; $n)
        echo ''$n...'';
?>
```

It really does just about the same as before. You start the loop by setting $n to 4; the second expression decrements $n by 1 to 3, which evaluates to TRUE, so execution of the loop statements begins.

(As before, when there's only one loop statement, you can omit the braces.)

At the end of the loop, you use the third expression to simply test if $n is still TRUE (non-zero). On the fourth time through, the `for` will be zero (FALSE), at which point you finish looping.

Incidentally, you could equally have written the `for` loop as

```
for ($n=3; $n; $n--)
```

This sets $n to 3 the first time, and then checks that it's non-zero each time into the loop. At the end of the loop each time, it decrements it. When it tries to start the loop the fourth time, $n will have been set to zero, and it exits because the second expression is then FALSE.

Optional Commands for Loops: break and continue

You can use `break` anywhere within a `for` or `while` loop to break out of it immediately:

```
do {
        # repeatable statements
        if (expression) {
                # some exceptional statements
                break;
        }
} while (expression)
# continue executing here
```

`break` is a way of leaving a loop "inelegantly." It lets you exit at any point during the loop and makes execution skip to the code beyond the end of the loop.

The `continue` command is similar but less drastic; `continue` will force execution of the loop statements to be curtailed, but not the loop itself. Execution skips to the end of the loop but not necessarily out of it. It will try to keep executing the loop as normal, providing conditions are met.

FIGURE **15.1**

Exiting a loop using break and continue.

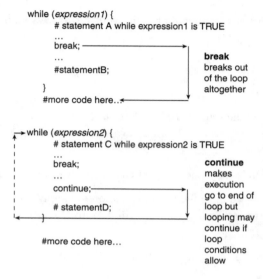

Control Structures: `include()` and `require()`

PHP gives you the `include()` and `require()` statements, allows you to include a second file into the first. For example, in your first PHP, you may have

```
include ("file2.php3");
```

or

```
require ("file2.php3");
```

The two commands do the same essential thing but work a little differently. `require` causes the contents of the required file to completely replace the `require` statement. However, `require` cannot be used conditionally. In other words, if you want to run the statement more than once and load in a different file each time, it won't. This is where you need the `include` statement. `include` is more flexible, and you need it if you want to get more clever with specifying what you are including.

`include` and `require` can be immensely helpful when building a Web site, even if you use no other PHP. You might want to put a common header, navigation bar, and footer on every page of your site. Each Web page would include something like the following:

```
<HTML>
<HEAD>
<TITLE>My web site, page one</TITLE>
<?php
include ("some_javascript.html");
include ("my_bodytag.html");
```

15

```
include ("my_header.html");
include ("standard_navbar.php3");
?>
<P>Some HTML content here</P>
<?php
include ("standard_footer.html");
?>
```

That's your page! Each such page would just have the "central" bits customized. You only need to create a single file for each of the included bits—more importantly, these components are reusable across your entire Web site.

Functions

PHP gives you the ability to create user-defined functions. These are blocks of code that can be defined once and invoked from many different places in your code—even from another PHP file.

Apart from user-defined functions, PHP has a vast library of built-in functions. These cover a wide range of applications, and the limited set covered later in this chapter will give an explanation of those that relate to the MySQL API.

When you define a user-defined function, you specify how it should execute and what values (if any) it should return. You can optionally give it parameters and tell it what to do with them.

The way to define a function in PHP is as follows:

```
function function_name (parameters) {
        # function statements here
        return variables  # optional
}
```

Then you can invoke the function using the following:

```
function_name (parameters);
```

For example, imagine that you want a function to add a percentage to a number (such as adding sales tax). You want to pass it two values: one the raw price and one the percentage.

INPUT
```
function add_percent ($price, $percent) {
        $newprice = $price * (1 + ($percent/100));
        return $newprice;
}
```

Then you want to invoke it:

INPUT
```
echo "The new price is ".add_percent (150, 25);
```

This would print

`The new price is 187.5`

Arrays

Understanding how arrays work in PHP is an essential step in learning how to access MySQL databases.

In PHP, sequentially indexed arrays contain elements starting at the "zeroth" element (*$myarray[0]*). Arrays can also be string-indexed, as you'll see in a moment. You can get the number of elements in an array by using the count() function (count(*$myarray*)).

A sequentially indexed array can be populated in a number of ways. For example, you can write the following:

```
$myarray[] = 'red';
$myarray[] = 'green';
$myarray[] = 'blue';
```

which is the same as

```
$myarray[0] = 'red';
$myarray[1] = 'green';
$myarray[2] = 'blue';
```

Then you can view the contents of the entire array by looping through it with a for loop:

```
for ($i=0; $i<count($myarray); $i++) {
        echo "Element $i is ".$myarray[$i]."<br>\n";
}
```

This would produce the following output:

```
Element 0 is red
Element 1 is green
Element 2 is blue
```

You can also index arrays using strings:

```
$myarray["R"] = 'red';
$myarray["G"] = 'green';
$myarray["B"] = 'blue';
```

Now, to pass through the array, you would do something like the following:

```
while (list ($abbrev, $color) = each ($myarray)) {
    echo "Element $abbrev is $color<br>\n";
}
```

There's a couple of new things here: there's `list`, which is a language construct that assigns elements of an array across a list of variables (in this case the array consists of a pair of keys and values, not the entire example array); and there's each, which is a function for single-stepping through an array.

> **Note**
>
> In PHP, arrays have an internal pointer. You can use this pointer to keep a note of where you are in an array.
>
> This is handy because it means that you're not forced to use a separate variable in simple cases.
>
> There are corresponding functions—`each()`, `next()`, `prev()`, and `array_walk()`—that give you ways of single-stepping through the array, invisibly moving the internal pointer each time.

each takes the name of an array as argument, returns the key and value of the current element (according to the internal pointer), and then moves the pointer on by one. `list($key, $value)`, or something similar to what you used previously, is a convenient way to get at the `key=value` pair result.

You've only covered single-dimension arrays in this introductory guide. However, it's worth noting that PHP has the ability to handle multidimensional arrays. It also has a good range of functions for array processing, such as for sorting. It's worth exploring other PHP resources for more details on the possibilities available.

PHP Meets MySQL

PHP has a range of sophisticated functions for interfacing with MySQL. Look at what happens when a client makes a request to a PHP-enabled Web server where some interaction will occur with a MySQL database:

- The server receives and reads the request from the client browser.
- The server locates the requested page on the Web server.
- The server executes any instructions given by the embedded PHP code.
- PHP queries the MySQL database server via an API and compiles the result.
- The Web server sends the resulting page to the client.

PHP comprises a considerable suite of functions for interfacing with MySQL database servers. You can create powerful applications using just a small subset of them (as you'll see in a moment). For reference, the following is a summary of the full function list.

TABLE 15.1 MySQL Functions

Function name	Action
Connecting and Disconnecting	
mysql_connect	Opens a connection to a MySQL server
mysql_pconnect	Opens a persistent connection to a MySQL server
mysql_select_db	Selects a MySQL database
mysql_close	Closes a MySQL connection
mysql_change_user	Changes the identity of the logged-in user with an active connection
Creating and Dropping Databases	
mysql_create_db	Creates a MySQL database
mysql_drop_db	Drops (deletes) a MySQL database
Performing Queries	
mysql_db_query	Sends a MySQL query to a named MySQL server
mysql_query	Sends an SQL query to the already selected MySQL server
Handling Results from Queries	
mysql_fetch_array	Fetches a result row as an associative array
mysql_result	Returns result data from a query
mysql_fetch_row	Returns a result row as an enumerated array
mysql_affected_rows	Returns the number of affected rows in the previous MySQL INSERT/UPDATE/DELETE operation
mysql_num_rows	Returns the number of rows in result
mysql_fetch_field	Returns column information from a result and returns it as an object
mysql_fetch_lengths	Returns the length of each output in a result
mysql_fetch_object	Returns a result row as an object
mysql_field_name	Gets the name of the specified field in a result
mysql_list_fields	Returns a list of MySQL result fields
mysql_num_fields	Returns the number of fields in result
mysql_field_seek	Sets result pointer to a specified field offset
mysql_field_type	Returns the type of the specified field in a result
mysql_field_flags	Returns the flags associated with the specified field in a result
mysql_insert_id	Returns the ID generated from the previous INSERT operation

TABLE 15.1   continued

Function name	Action
	Connecting and Disconnecting
mysql_data_seek	Moves the internal result pointer
mysql_free_result	Frees result memory
	Error Handling
mysql_errno	Returns the error message number from the previous MySQL operation
mysql_error	Returns the error message text from the previous MySQL operation
	Other Information About the Database
mysql_list_dbs	Returns a list of databases available on the MySQL server
mysql_list_tables	Returns a list of tables in a MySQL database
mysql_field_len	Returns the length of the specified field
mysql_field_table	Gets the name of the table containing the specified field
mysql_tablename	Returns the table name of field

Connecting to the MySQL Database Server

You use mysql_connect to connect to the specified database server. The following is the full syntax for mysql_connect:

```
mysql_connect ([hostname[:port][:/path/to/socket]], username, password);
```

This function returns a positive integer when successful, denoting the link identifier, or zero for failure. To connect to a MySQL database, you might do the following:

```
$link_id = mysql_connect ("localhost", $dbuser, $userpass);
echo "Link ID is ".$link_id;
```

Provided your variables are correctly set, this statement produces the following:

OUTPUT   Link ID is 1

Success! The returned link identifier of 1 indicates that you have connected to your database on the Web server (localhost) using the database name given by $database, the username given by $dbuser, and password given by $userpass.

Creating a Database

You can create a database by using the following:

```
mysql_create_db(database_name[, link_identifier]);
```

The *link identifier* is optional; if omitted, the last opened link will be used. This function returns an integer result—positive (TRUE) if successful. In the example, you might write

INPUT
```
$create_id = mysql_create_db("mydb");
echo "Creation ID is ".$create_id."<br>\n";
```

When you run this script, you should get

OUTPUT   `Creation ID is 1`

You have now successfully created a database called mydb on your server.

Basics of PHP Database Queries

Now, imagine that you want to create a table in the database. You have mysql_db_query and mysql_query to send just about any query to MySQL. These commands work as follows:

```
mysql_db_query(database, query[, link_identifier]);
mysql_query(query[, link_identifier]);
```

When you use these functions, they return an integer that is a result identifier to point you to the query result. If an error occurs, they return 0 or FALSE.

The *link identifier* is optional; if omitted, the last opened link will be used.

mysql_db_queryallows you to specify a database to query, while mysql_query runs the query on the currently selected database. You select a database using the following syntax:

```
mysql_select_db(database_name[, link_identifier] );
```

Look at an example of selecting a database and then running a create table query.

INPUT
```
$select = mysql_select_db ("mydb");
$sql = "CREATE TABLE photos (
     num INTEGER NOT NULL PRIMARY KEY,
     date_taken DATE,
     description VARCHAR(200))";
$result = mysql_query ("$sql");
echo "Result of table creation is $result<br>\n";
```

If everything goes to plan, you should get the following output:

OUTPUT   `Result of table creation is 1`

Handling Query Errors

How would you know if the query failed? To report an error and handle it appropriately, you could improve the last two lines of your code as follows:

INPUT
```
if ($result = mysql_query ("$sql")) {
    echo "Result of table creation is $result<br>\n";
} else {
    echo "Error: ".mysql_errno()."; error description: ".mysql_error();
}
```

If you run this now (with the *photos* table already in existence), you will get the following output, as returned by `mysql_errno()` and `mysql_error()`:

OUTPUT   `Error: 1050; error description: Table 'photos' already exists`

You may want to make your error handling a little more slick, such as by creating a small function at the beginning of your code:

```
function error_report () {
    echo "Error: ".mysql_errno()."; error description: "
➥   .mysql_error()."<br>\n";
}
```

Then, whenever you want to handle an error, you just call

```
error_report ();
```

Queries to Insert Data

Now, look at how you would enter some data into a table. You can use the same `mysql_query` function you used previously:

```
$sql = "INSERT INTO photos VALUES
➥   (10000, '99-07-15', 'At the beach, Tobago')";
if ($result = mysql_query ("$sql")) {
    echo "Data added\n";
} else error_report ();
```

With an `INSERT`, `UPDATE`, or `DELETE` query, the integer result of the `mysql_query` function will be an integer—positive for success, `FALSE` for failure.

Running SELECT Queries and Handling the Result

Imagine that you've now added a few more rows of data into your photos table (you can do this yourself now!). Now comes the time to start interrogating your table to get some data out of it.

Imagine that you want to run a query that searches for all photos for a description that includes the word "beach". You would write a query like the following:

INPUT

```
$sql = "SELECT num, date_taken, description FROM
    photos WHERE description LIKE '%beach%'
if ($result = mysql_query ("$sql")) {
    while ($row = mlysql_fetch_array ($result)) {
        echo "Date: ".$row[date_taken].""".$row[description]."<br>\n";
    }
} else error_report ();
```

If all's well, the output should be

OUTPUT

```
Date: 1999-07-15 At the beach, Tobago
Date: 2000-02-01 The beach in Mauritius
```

Now things are warming up! Examine what happened here.

First, you set the $sql variable to hold your SELECT query. Then you called mysql_query with $sql as a parameter. This executed the query and captured the result in $result. This result is an integer that is a pointer to the resultset.

If the MySQL server returns an error, $result will be FALSE, so you handle the error. (Note that if the query returns no rows, this is not an error!)

Provided there's no error, the if statement would resolve to be TRUE, and you would go on to call mysql_fetch_array.

This introduces you to another function, whose syntax is the following:

```
mysql_fetch_array (result[, result_type]);
```

This function returns an array containing the data for the row that was "fetched," or FALSE if no rows were returned. It stores two lots of the returned data in the array: one lot that can be referenced numerically ($row[2]), and one lot that can be referenced by using the field names as string keys ($row["description"]).

The optional result_type argument can take the values MYSQL_ASSOC, MYSQL_NUM, or MYSQL_BOTH. (You probably won't need this in simple scripts like the present example.)

Remember that in PHP every array has an internal pointer. Now it comes in really handy. Each time you invoke `mysql_fetch_array`, the pointer helpfully moves itself on by one row, starting the first time with row zero.

In this way, you can embed the pointer in your `while` loop without referencing it explicitly. Each time you invoke `mysql_fetch_array` and make the $row array equal to its result, the pointer moves forward one row through the array that resulted from the query. This happens until the pointer reaches the end of the resultset, whereupon it can't be moved on any more, and you get a FALSE result. $row thus becomes FALSE, you exit the `while` loop, and you're done.

This basic functionality is fairly straightforward but should be sufficient to perform almost any query on a MySQL database. Just a small set of PHP instructions can be sufficient to create a truly dynamic experience for people visiting your database-driven Web site.

Summary

Today, you paid a brief visit to the world of PHP. You learned how PHP scripts can be embedded in HTML Web pages, and looked at how to write basic PHP code.

You learned how to use a range of PHP's control structures, such as `includes`, `ifs`, `while`, and `for` loops. Although you have by no means explored the PHP vocabulary to any great extent, you have learned a basic toolkit with which you can write powerful scripts.

You went on to examine the MySQL API, with its basket of functions for accessing a MySQL server. You learned how to connect to a MySQL server, create databases and tables, insert data, and handle errors.

Finally, you looked at running MySQL SELECT commands via PHP. Results are returned in array form, and you learned some commands for handling and processing the results so that they can be retrieved and presented to the client in a useful form.

Q&A

Q   How do I learn more about PHP?

A   You should visit `http://www.php.net/` and read other Sams titles on the subject. You will also need a Web server onto which you can install PHP, although you should find it free to download and easy to set up.

Q   **Why should I use PHP rather than another language?**

A   There's a good choice of server-side languages and tools on the market. PHP has the advantage that it's free, fast, and can be installed on the most popular platforms.

PHP is also easy to write; you merely have to insert some PHP code into a Web page to create a PHP script.

Exercises

1. Write the PHP syntax doing a SELECT on a table called products. The table includes the fields name and price. Your query should retrieve all products whose price is less than $50. You should allow for an error condition and, if need be, call the user-defined error_report function.

2. Write the PHP function for connecting to a MySQL database on localhost and returning the link identifier to the calling program.

DAY 16

MySQL and Time

Today, you will look at how MySQL handles time. You will understand the formats that MySQL uses to represent dates and time, and learn how to use the special functions MySQL has that help you handle date and time formatting and arithmetic.

How Dates Are Treated in MySQL

MySQL has a range of data types for handling date and time information. In general, MySQL will accept several formats when being given data to put into a field. However, date and time output will always be standardized and appear in a predictable format.

All date and time data types have a range of legal values and a "zero" value to which a field will be set if you attempt to put an illegal value into it.

Time formats have an intuitive order that you're used to in daily life: hours at the left of the field, minutes, and then seconds.

Dates, on the other hand, are always output with year at the left, month, and then day (never day/month/year).

When outputting date and time, you usually have the option to ask MySQL to give you the data as either string or numeric data, even though it is the same information. The format used will depend on the context in which it is used in your SQL.

MySQL is quite flexible when accepting date and time data: for example, the date 2001-05-12 means the same to MySQL as 2001/05/12, 1+5+12, or even 20010512. You can use a wide range of separators between the components of the field or none at all, and you can omit the leading zero for numbers less than 10.

MySQL does partial checking of date and time information. For example, it expects days to be in the range 1 to 31 and months in the range 1 to 12. However, it does not rigorously check whether a specific date can really exist. It will not reject 30 February, for example. This makes it more efficient when accepting data, putting the responsibility on your application to ensure valid dates are being entered.

Date-related Data Types

MySQL has a range of date-related data types to make your life a little easier when handling date and time information. It offers DATETIME, DATE, TIME, YEAR, and TIMESTAMP types. Take a quick look at the field formats shown in Table 16.1.

TABLE 16.1 Date and Time Data Types

Data Type	Standard Format	Zero Value
DATETIME	YYYY-MM-DD HH:MM:SS	0000-00-00 00:00:00
DATE	YYYY-MM-DD	0000-00-00
TIME	HH:MM:SS	00:00:00
YEAR	YYYY	0000
TIMESTAMP	varies (see "TIMESTAMP" section later in this chapter)	00000000000000 (at longest)

DATETIME

The DATETIME format holds the entire date and time of an event, to the nearest second.

DATETIME values can range from 1000-01-01 00:00:00 to 9999-12-31 23:59:59.

DATE

DATE records the date of an event to the day, without storing time information. MySQL is Y2K compliant in its date storage.

DATE values can range from 1000-01-01 to 9999-12-31.

TIME

16

The TIME data type stores the time of an event independent of a particular date.

TIME values can range not just from 00:00:00 to 23:59:59, but, in fact, from -838:59:59 to 838:59:59. This allows you to represent not just time of day but the elapsed time or difference between two events.

As with DATE and other date and time types, MySQL has a relaxed approach to accepting data, and you can use any punctuation marks as delimiters to separate the hours, minutes, and seconds. Thus 08:32:20 is the same as 08-32-20, or you can do without leading zeros, as in 8.32.20.

You can specify time without delimiters, as in 083220 or 83220. However, be careful before getting too minimalist: MySQL reads times from the right, expecting seconds to be declared but not necessarily hours! Therefore 8:32 or 0832 will be understood as 00:08:32 (eight minutes and 32 seconds past midnight) rather than 8:32 a.m.

Caution

> Valid time values outside the allowable time range will be clipped at the -838:59:59 and 838:59:59 ceilings, but not set to 00:00:00. However, invalid times, such as with minutes or seconds greater than 59, will be set to 00:00:00. This means that if you see a time of 00:00:00, which is itself a valid time, you have no way of knowing if the data is correct or if there has been an attempt to store an illegal time.

YEAR

YEAR records the year of an event and occupies just 1 byte of data.

YEAR values can range from 1901 to 2155. You can specify a year in either string or numeric notation.

YEAR values can be specified in either two- or four-digit form, but two-digit years are converted to four digits. Thus, years can be given by numbers (in the range 1 to 99) or by strings (in the range '0' or '00' to '99').

Two-digit years specified in the range 1 to 69 (or a 0' to '69') will be taken as meaning years from 2001 through 2069 (or 2000 through 2069). Years in the range 70 to 99 will be interpreted as being in the range 1970 through 1999.

TIMESTAMP

TIMESTAMP is a useful field format whereby that column will be set to the current date and time whenever that row is updated or inserted in the table. It conveniently gives you a "last updated" stamp without having to set it each time you change some data in that row.

TIMESTAMP can only handle dates in the range 1970 through 2037, with the data being held with the maximum resolution of one second.

Although a TIMESTAMP field is always held in the same way internally, it can have a number of external formats. These can be made up of any even number of digits from 2 to 14. Table 16.2 shows a list of the formats that TIMESTAMP offers.

TABLE 16.2   TIMESTAMP Display Formats

Data Type	Display Format
TIMESTAMP(14)	YYYYMMDDHHMMSS
TIMESTAMP(12)	YYMMDDHHMMSS
TIMESTAMP(10)	YYMMDDHHMM
TIMESTAMP(8)	YYYYMMDD
TIMESTAMP(6)	YYMMDD
TIMESTAMP(4)	YYMM
TIMESTAMP(2)	YY

Look briefly at what this table means. If an update is made at 9:30 on 12 May 2000, a TIMESTAMP(14) would be set to 20000512093000, while a TIMESTAMP(8) would be set to 20000512 because it contains no time information.

Note

> TIMESTAMP fields are set to the current time if you do *not* write anything to them. In other words, you must either not specify the column name in an INSERT or UPDATE statement, or you must write NULL to it. Either of these will set the TIMESTAMP field to the current time. The same will be achieved if you write NOW() to the field, a function for retrieving the current time and date that you will look at later.

16

You can write new data to a TIMESTAMP field just by specifying the new data explicitly. You can set it to whatever date and time you want within its legal range. (You might consider this is faking its true purpose!) Illegal values will be discarded and replaced with the "zero" value for this field type.

As in DATETIME, DATE, and TIME data types, MySQL is flexible in the formats it will accept for the TIMESTAMP. For example, it will accept 2000-05-12, 2000+05+12, and so on, allowing you to use whatever separator you want, or none at all, as in 20000512.

Note

> When setting a TIMESTAMP field, values specified as numbers, rather than strings, should be 14, 12, 8, or 6 digits long.
>
> When specifying a date as a string, you should always use at least 6 characters. This is because dates, such as 98-12 or 98, which you might assume mean December 98 or just the year 1998, will be taken as having zero values for day, month, and day, respectively. This would result in your date being treated as illegal and assigned a zero value. Therefore, always remember to specify year, month, and day, even if you are only interested in the year or the year and the month.

All TIMESTAMP fields occupy the same amount of storage—4 bytes. You can alter a TIMESTAMP field using ALTER TABLE without losing data. By widening a field, you will find that new data is revealed in the previously hidden parts of the field. Likewise, if you narrow the field, you will not actually lose data; your field will just display less information the next time you use it.

MySQL will always set a TIMESTAMP column to the current time if NULL (or NOW()) is written to it. However, if the field is left out of the list of fields when doing an insert or update, it will only update the first TIMESTAMP field in the table. Subsequent TIMESTAMP fields will contain the zero value (which itself is a valid time value) if not set explicitly.

Transferring Data Between Data Types

MySQL enables you to transfer data from one type to another. For example, you may have a DATETIME field that has recorded the precise time a customer made a transaction. After a while, you may want to transfer the data to another table but are only interested in the date of the purchase.

If you have data from a DATETIME or TIMESTAMP column and want to assign it to a DATE column, the time information will simply be lost because the DATE type has no capacity to store time information.

Conversely, if you have a DATE value and want to write it to a DATETIME or TIMESTAMP column, MySQL will insert 00:00:00 for the time portion because this data was not previously available.

Remember that the various field types have different ranges for legal values, and the accepting column must be able to represent the given data or it will be lost. For example, attempting to place DATE information, where the year is not between 1970 and 2037, into a TIMESTAMP field will cause the data to be "zeroed."

Internal MySQL Date Functions

MySQL gives you a nice range of date and time-related functions that you can use in SELECT and WHERE clauses.

For example, there is a MONTHNAME() function that returns the name of the month in a date field. You can use this in a SELECT; for example, SELECT monthname(20000105) returns January. Similarly, you can do something like the following:

INPUT   `mysql> SELECT mod_date FROM orders WHERE MONTHNAME(mod_date)='January';`

which results in

OUTPUT
```
+-----------+
| mod_date  |
+-----------+
| 20000104  |
| 20000117  |
| 20000117  |
+-----------+
3 rows in set (0.06 sec)
```

It's worth remembering that where MySQL expects you to pass a DATE to a function, this should be in the form YYYYMMDD (where given as a number) or in the form YYYY-MM-DD (ideally using "-" as delimiters, or using any other punctuation) when passed as a string.

Look now at each of the functions available in a little more detail.

Getting Day Information

There are four functions for converting a date to a day number:

- DAYOFYEAR(*date*)
- DAYOFMONTH(*date*)
- DAYOFWEEK(*date*)
- WEEKDAY(*date*)

DAYOFYEAR(*date*) returns the day of the year for a given date (in numeric format); in other words, how many days since January 1 of that year.

For example, the 1st February 2000

INPUT   `mysql> SELECT DAYOFYEAR(20000201);`

Produces:

OUTPUT
```
+---------------------+
| DAYOFYEAR(20000201) |
+---------------------+
|                  32 |
+---------------------+
```

Similarly, you can pass DAYOFYEAR a *date* as a string parameter:

INPUT   `mysql> SELECT DAYOFYEAR('2000/02/01');`

OUTPUT
```
+-----------------------+
| DAYOFYEAR('2000/02/01') |
+-----------------------+
|                    32 |
+-----------------------+
```

DAYOFMONTH(*date*) returns the day of the month for a given date.

Not surprisingly, 1st February 2000 gives us

INPUT   `mysql> SELECT DAYOFMONTH(20000201);`

OUTPUT
```
+----------------------+
| DAYOFMONTH(20000201) |
+----------------------+
|                    1 |
+----------------------+
```

Or, put another way

INPUT   `mysql> SELECT DAYOFMONTH('00-02-01');`

returns the following:

OUTPUT
```
+----------------------+
| DAYOFMONTH('00-02-01') |
+----------------------+
|                    1 |
+----------------------+
```

DAYOFWEEK(*date*) returns the day of the week for a given date, starting with 1=Sunday, 2=Monday, 3=Tuesday, and so on.

For example, examining the same date

INPUT   `mysql> SELECT DAYOFWEEK('0-2-1');`

results in the following:

OUTPUT
```
+--------------------+
| DAYOFWEEK('0-2-1') |
+--------------------+
|                  3 |
+--------------------+
```

WEEKDAY(*date*) is a little different and returns the weekday index for the given date (0=Monday, 1=Tuesday, 2=Wednesday, and so on).

INPUT   `mysql> SELECT DAYOFWEEK('0-2-1');`

OUTPUT
```
+-------------------+
| DAYOFWEEK('0-2-1') |
+-------------------+
|                 3 |
+-------------------+
```

16

Getting Names for Months and Days

There are two functions that can be used to look up month and day names for a given date:

- MONTHNAME(*date*)
- DAYNAME(*date*)

MONTHNAME(*date*) can be used to obtain the name of the month in which *date* occurs as a string:

INPUT   `mysql> SELECT MONTHNAME('0-2-1');`

results in the following:

OUTPUT
```
+-------------------+
| MONTHNAME('0-2-1') |
+-------------------+
| February          |
+-------------------+
```

DAYNAME(*date*) is similar:

INPUT   `mysql> SELECT DAYNAME('2000-01-01');`

results in the following:

OUTPUT
```
+--------------------+
| DAYNAME('2000-01-01') |
+--------------------+
| Saturday           |
+--------------------+
```

But remember, *date* must be a valid date, or the function will fail. Thus, an illegal date returns a NULL result:

INPUT   `mysql> SELECT MONTHNAME('9');`

produces the following:

OUTPUT
```
+----------------+
| MONTHNAME('9') |
+----------------+
| NULL           |
+----------------+
```

Extracting Years, Quarters, Months, and Weeks

MySQL has a range of function for extracting numerical data from a date:

- YEAR(*date*)
- QUARTER(*date*)
- MONTH(*date*)
- WEEK(*date*[,*firstday*])
- YEARWEEK(*date*[,*firstday*])

YEAR(*date*) returns the 4-digit numeric year of a given *date*:

INPUT   `mysql> SELECT YEAR('01/12/25 11:00:00');`

results in the following:

OUTPUT
```
+---------------------------+
| YEAR('2001/12/25 11:00:00') |
+---------------------------+
|                      2001 |
+---------------------------+
```

QUARTER(*date*) gives us the quarter in the range 1 to 4:

INPUT   `mysql> SELECT QUARTER('01/12/25 11:00:00');`

results in the following:

OUTPUT
```
+------------------------------+
| QUARTER('01/12/25 11:00:00') |
+------------------------------+
|                            4 |
+------------------------------+
```

MONTH(*date*) returns the month in the range 1 to 12:

INPUT   mysql> SELECT MONTH('01/12/25 11:00:00');

results in the following:

OUTPUT
```
+---------------------------+
| MONTH('01/12/25 11:00:00') |
+---------------------------+
|                        12 |
+---------------------------+
```

WEEK(*date*), when used with a single parameter, returns the week of the year in the range 0 to 53:

INPUT   mysql> SELECT WEEK('2001-12-26');

results in the following:

OUTPUT
```
+-------------------+
| WEEK('2001-12-26') |
+-------------------+
|                52 |
+-------------------+
```

Without a second parameter, WEEK(*date*) assumes that Sunday is the first day of the week, and, at the beginning of the year, any days before the 'first day' come in week 0. For example, WEEK('2000-01-01') returns 0 because it was a Saturday.

You can override the default behavior by adding the *firstday* parameter. Instead of 0 representing Sunday, 1=Monday, and so on, you can set the first day to be a different day of the week.

Without the second argument, you have WEEK('2000-01-09'), a Sunday, returning 2 (week 2 of the year).

But with a *firstday* of 1, WEEK('2000-01-09',1) returns 1 because you told MySQL to start counting from the Monday.

YEARWEEK(*date*[,*firstday*]) works in much the same way, but prepends the week with the year. In the previous example, YEARWEEK('2000-01-09',1) returns 200001.

This may sound a little academic, but internationally, not all diaries use the same convention!

Current Date and Time

There are several methods for obtaining the current date and time:

- `NOW()`/`SYSDATE()`/`CURRENT_TIMESTAMP`
- `CURDATE()`/`CURRENT_DATE`
- `CURTIME()`/`CURRENT_TIME`

To get the full date and time in one of the standard `DATETIME` formats, it's easiest to use `NOW()`.

The answer can be returned as a string

INPUT   `mysql> SELECT NOW();`

results in the following:

OUTPUT
```
+---------------------+
| NOW()               |
+---------------------+
| 2000-02-05 18:05:11 |
+---------------------+
```

or as a number:

INPUT   `mysql> SELECT NOW()+0;`

results in the following:

OUTPUT
```
+----------------+
| NOW()+0        |
+----------------+
| 20000205181027 |
+----------------+
```

`SYSDATE()`and `CURRENT_TIMESTAMP` return exactly the same thing as `NOW()`.

If you just want the date portion, you can use `CURDATE()` or `CURRENT_DATE`, which are identical. They would return `2000-02-05` (or `20000205` if used in a numeric context).

If you're interested in the current time but not the date, you can use `CURTIME()` or `CURRENT_TIME`. These are also equivalent and would return a time looking like `18:14:57` (or `181457` if used in a numeric context).

Formatting Dates and Times

- DATE_FORMAT(*date*,*format*)
- TIME_FORMAT(*time*,*format*)

The DATE_FORMAT and TIME_FORMAT pair of functions are useful in allowing you to display a date or time in almost any format you choose. As well as passing a *date* or *time* parameter, you supply a *format* made up of the specifiers given in Table 16.3.

16

TABLE 16.3 DATE_FORMAT and TIME_FORMAT Output Formats

format Parameter	Output Format
%r	12-hour time (hh:mm:ss (AM | PM))
%T	24-hour time (hh:mm:ss)
%Y	Numeric year, 4 digits
%y	Numeric year, 2 digits
%m	Month with leading 0 (01, 02...12)
%c	Month without leading 0 (1, 2...12)
%M	Month name (January, February, and so on)
%b	Month name, abbreviated (Jan, Feb, and so on)
%D	Day of the month with an English suffix (1st, 2nd, and so on)
%d	Day of the month with leading 0 (00, 01, 02...31)
%e	Day of the month without leading 0 (0, 1, 2...31)
%W	Weekday name (Sunday, Monday, and so on)
%a	Weekday name, abbreviated (Sun, Mon, and so on)
%H	Hour (00, 01...23)
%k	Hour (0, 1...23)
%h	Hour (01, 02...12)
%I	Hour (01, 02...12)
%l	Hour (1, 2...12)
%i	Minutes (00, 01...59)
%S	Seconds (00, 01...59)
%s	Seconds (00, 01...59)
%P	AM or PM

TABLE **16.3**   continued

format Parameter	Output Format
%U	Week number in the year, in which Sunday is the first day of the week
$u	Week number in the year, in which Monday is the first day of the week
%X & %V	Year and week number, respectively, in which Sunday is the first day of the week
%x & %v	Year and week number, respectively, in which Monday is the first day of the week
%j	Day of year with leading 0's (001, 002...366)
%w	Weekday number (0=Sunday, 1=Monday, and so on)
%%	Literal %

The following are a few examples:

- `SELECT DATE_FORMAT('1999-12-31 23:00:00', '%r on %W')` would produce `11:00:00 PM on Friday`.
- `SELECT DATE_FORMAT('2001-11-05', '%D %M')` would produce `5th November`.
- `SELECT TIME_FORMAT(NOW(), '%H:%i:%s')` might produce `19:17:38`.

Note   DATE_FORMAT() is the most flexible of the two functions and can be passed either date, time, or date and time information together. TIME_FORMAT() can only be passed time information, or it will return a NULL result.

Extracting Hours, Minutes, and Seconds

- `HOUR(time)`
- `MINUTE(time)`
- `SECOND(time)`

These functions can be used to easily extract the hour, minute, and second elements of a given time.

HOUR returns a number in the range 0 to 23. For example, `HOUR(18:10:27)` returns 18. You can also do the following:

INPUT `mysql> SELECT HOUR(NOW());`

produces the following:

OUTPUT
```
+-------------+
| HOUR(NOW()) |
+-------------+
|          18 |
+-------------+
```

MINUTE and SECOND work in the same way, and both return a number in the range 0 to 59.

Days Since 1 A.D.

- TO_DAYS(*date*)
- FROM_DAYS(*number*)

TO_DAYS(*date*) takes a date as parameter and returns the number of days since the first day in the year 1 A.D. (there was no year 0). Thus, TO_DAYS('2000-01-01') returns the number 730485.

The opposite effect is obtained by using FROM_DAYS(*number*). SELECT FROM_-DAYS(1000000) would return 2737-11-28 as the millionth day after that original time.

These functions are only intended to be used on dates after 1582, when the Gregorian Calendar was introduced.

Seconds Since the Beginning of the Day

- TIME_TO_SEC(*time*)
- SEC_TO_TIME(*seconds*)

TIME_TO_SEC(*time*) returns the time in seconds (the number of seconds since the beginning of that day).

For example, TIME_TO_SEC('01.00.00') returns 3600, and you can also do the following:

INPUT `mysql> SELECT TIME_TO_SEC(110);`

which results in

OUTPUT
```
+------------------+
| TIME_TO_SEC(110) |
+------------------+
|               70 |
+------------------+
```

because 110 (numeric) is interpreted by MySQL as 1 minute, 10 seconds.

SEC_TO_TIME(*seconds*) does the opposite, converting the number of seconds from the beginning of the day into HH:MM:SS or HHMMSS format. You can do the following:

INPUT   mysql> SELECT SEC_TO_TIME(70);

which results in

OUTPUT
```
+-----------------+
| SEC_TO_TIME(70) |
+-----------------+
| 00:01:10        |
+-----------------+
```

or, when used in a numeric context

INPUT   mysql> SELECT SEC_TO_TIME(1000)+0;

which results in

OUTPUT
```
+---------------------+
| SEC_TO_TIME(1000)+0 |
+---------------------+
|                1640 |
+---------------------+
```

Handling UNIX Time

- UNIX_TIMESTAMP([*date*])
- FROM_UNIXTIME(*UNIX_timestamp*[,*format*])

The *UNIX timestamp* is the number of seconds since 1 January 1970. UNIX_TIMESTAMP(), without the optional *date* parameter, returns the UNIX time of the present moment (UNIX_TIMESTAMP() will return something like 949872354).

With the date specified in DATE, DATETIME, TIMESTAMP format, or a number in the form YYMMDD or YYYYMMDD, it returns the UNIX time of that date:

INPUT   mysql> SELECT UNIX_TIMESTAMP('2020-10-04 22:23:00');

would result in

OUTPUT
```
+---------------------------------------+
| UNIX_TIMESTAMP('2020-10-04 22:23:00') |
+---------------------------------------+
|                            1601864580 |
+---------------------------------------+
```

FROM_UNIXTIME() has the opposite effect. When used with *UNIX_timestamp* as the sole parameter, it returns the date and time in YYYY-MM-DD HH:MM:SS or YYYYMMDDHHMMSS format, depending on whether it is used in a string or numeric context. For example

INPUT   `mysql> SELECT FROM_UNIXTIME(949872354)*1;`

would result in date and time information in numeric format:

OUTPUT
```
+--------------------------------+
| FROM_UNIXTIME(949872354)*1     |
+--------------------------------+
|                 20000206212554 |
+--------------------------------+
```

You can optionally give this function a *format* parameter, which will cause the output to be formatted according to the rules of the FORMAT_DATE() function. For example, you can work out the day on which the billionth second of UNIX time will fall:

```
mysql> SELECT FROM_UNIXTIME(1000000000, '%W, %M');
+------------------------------------+
| FROM_UNIXTIME(1000000000, '%W, %M') |
+------------------------------------+
| Saturday, September                |
+------------------------------------+
```

Adding and Subtracting Time

MySQL offers a number of ways of adding and subtracting time. You have the following functions available:

- DATE_ADD(*date*,INTERVAL *expressiontype*) the same as
- ADDDATE(*date*,INTERVAL *expressiontype*)
- DATE_SUB(*date*,INTERVAL *expressiontype*) the same as
- SUBDATE(*date*,INTERVAL *expressiontype*)
- PERIOD_ADD(*period*,*months*)
- PERIOD_DIFF(*period1*,*period2*)

DATE_ADD takes a *date*, adds an INTERVAL of time given by *expression*, which in a format given by *type*, and returns the resulting date and time.

16

Note

> These functions are new for MySQL 3.22. MySQL 3.23 adds the ability to use + and - instead of DATE_ADD() and DATE_SUB() respectively. It also adds the EXTRACT(*type* FROM *date*) function. This can be used to extract date and time information and takes the same parameters for type as shown in Table 16.4.

Table 16.4 lists the supported types.

TABLE 16.4   Values for expression and type When Adding and Subtracting Time

type Value	Expected Format for expression
SECOND	SECONDS
MINUTE	MINUTES
HOUR	HOURS
DAY	DAYS
MONTH	MONTHS
YEAR	YEARS
MINUTE_SECOND	"MINUTES:SECONDS"
HOUR_MINUTE	"HOURS:MINUTES"
DAY_HOUR	"DAYS HOURS"
YEAR_MONTH	"YEARS-MONTHS"
HOUR_SECOND	"HOURS:MINUTES:SECONDS"
DAY_MINUTE	"DAYS HOURS:MINUTES"
DAY_SECOND	"DAYS HOURS:MINUTES:SECONDS"

Look at a few examples. First, take 4 July 1980 and add 15 years:

INPUT   `mysql> SELECT DATE_ADD('1980-07-04',INTERVAL 15 YEAR);`

results in

OUTPUT
```
+-------------------------------------------+
| DATE_ADD('1980-07-04',INTERVAL 15 YEAR)   |
+-------------------------------------------+
| 1995-07-04                                |
+-------------------------------------------+
```

Next, add 6 months from last Christmas:

INPUT   ```
mysql> SELECT DATE_ADD('1999-12-25',INTERVAL 6 MONTH);
```

results in

**OUTPUT**
```
+--+
| DATE_ADD('1999-12-25',INTERVAL 6 MONTH) |
+--+
| 2000-06-25 |
+--+
```

16

Experiment with a little time manipulation, say adding 72 hours to 9 a.m. Monday morning:

**INPUT**      ```
mysql> SELECT DATE_ADD('00-02-07 09:00:00',INTERVAL 36 HOUR);
```

results in

OUTPUT
```
+-----------------------------------------------+
| DATE_ADD('00-02-07 09:00:00',INTERVAL 36 HOUR) |
+-----------------------------------------------+
| 2000-02-08 21:00:00                           |
+-----------------------------------------------+
```

How about finding out what time it was two days ago? Now you'll use DATE_SUB():

INPUT   ```
mysql> SELECT DATE_SUB(NOW(),INTERVAL 2 DAY);
```

results in

**OUTPUT**
```
+-------------------------------+
| DATE_SUB(NOW(),INTERVAL 2 DAY) |
+-------------------------------+
| 2000-02-05 18:02:06 |
+-------------------------------+
```

You can also deal with composite intervals; for example, subtract 10 years and 4 months from next December 1st:

**INPUT**      ```
mysql> SELECT DATE_SUB(20001201,INTERVAL "10 4"YEAR_MONTH);
```

produces

```
+----------------------------------------------------+
¦ DATE_SUB(20001201,INTERVAL "10 4"YEAR_MONTH) ¦
+----------------------------------------------------+
¦ 1990-08-01                                         ¦
+----------------------------------------------------+
```

> **Note**
>
> If you fail to specify the full field length required of an interval, MySQL assumes you have left out the leftmost part of the field. So DATE_SUB(20001201,INTERVAL "10"YEAR_MONTH) would return 2000-02-01, subtracting 10 months but no years.

PERIOD_ADD(*period*,*months*) will take a *period* in the format YYMM or YYYYMM and add a certain number of *months* to it. (A period in the format YYMM will be assumed to contain an abbreviated 4-digit year and converted accordingly.) For example, you can add 12 months to June '08:

INPUT   mysql> **SELECT PERIOD_ADD(0806,12);**

results in

OUTPUT
```
+---------------------+
¦ PERIOD_ADD(0806,12) ¦
+---------------------+
¦              200906 ¦
+---------------------+
```

You can use the same function to subtract; take 2 months away from April 2000:

INPUT   mysql> SELECT PERIOD_ADD(200004,-2);

results in

OUTPUT
```
+-----------------------+
¦ PERIOD_ADD(200004,-2) ¦
+-----------------------+
¦                200002 ¦
+-----------------------+
```

Note

> PERIOD_ADD() deals with years and months but does not take a date parameter. If you try to pass it a date formatted in DATE format, or NOW(), you will get an invalid result.

For finding the difference between two time periods, you can use PERIOD_DIFF(*period1*,*period2*). Try to calculate how many months between January 1980 and June 2000:

INPUT   `mysql> SELECT PERIOD_DIFF(200006,198001);`

results in

OUTPUT
```
+---------------------------+
| PERIOD_DIFF(200006,198001) |
+---------------------------+
|                       245 |
+---------------------------+
```

As with PERIOD_ADD(), PERIOD_DIFF() expects YYYYMM or YYMM and not the normal date format.

Summary

In this chapter, you've examined the formats that MySQL uses for formatting dates and times. It is relaxed in accepting date and time information with a range of punctuation and field lengths, and interprets what you give it according to a set of rules. However, it outputs the same data in more predictable formats and accommodates both string and numeric formats according to how you're using the result.

You've looked at several formats:

- DATETIME   For combined date and time information
- DATE   For date information only
- TIME   For time information only
- YEAR   For year information only
- TIMESTAMP   Records date and time and, by default, will automatically set itself to the creation or last modification date of a row

You've also covered a number of functions for extracting both numerical and textual information on times and dates. You've seen how you can do date arithmetic using MySQL's tools for adding and subtracting time intervals, and even for finding the difference in time between two given months.

Q&A

Q   **What is the best way to get the present system time and insert it into my data?**

A   The present system time can easily be obtained using the NOW() function, which will return the date and time. You can insert this into any of the date and time fields in your table. However, you can also declare a column to be of the TIMESTAMP type, which will cause this column to be updated each time you write data to that row, provided you don't write anything to that field explicitly, since doing this will put specific data into the field.

Q   **How can I display times and dates in a user-friendly format?**

A   Use the DATE_FORMAT() and TIME_FORMAT() functions. These offer great flexibility in formatting date and time information according to the needs of the user.

Q   **What's the best format for specifying dates and times to MySQL?**

A   MySQL is very relaxed in that it can accept date and time data in a wide range of styles, delimited with punctuation marks or not delimited at all. For the sake of clarity, it may be best practice to submit your data in the same form as MySQL outputs it (YYYY-MM-DD for dates and HH:MM:SS for times) if data in these formats is available.

Exercises

1.   Write a SELECT statement to output the current time in the format "hour:minute am/pm weekday nth month year."

2.   Write a SELECT statement to find which weekday the 4th of July will fall on in 2010.

3.   Write a SELECT statement to add 1,000 days to 1 April 2000 and return the date. On what weekday will the subsequent day fall?

DAY 17

MySQL Database Security

Database security is an essential component to any database system. It is the security that protects your data, safeguarding it from would-be crackers. Security also protects your data from users. Sometimes users, in their ignorance, will delete records they don't want to delete. To help guard against these types of accidents, you can enforce a level of security to prevent users from deleting, updating, or adding records to your database.

Security plays a major role in any application that many users can access at once. MySQL handles security very well and is one of the most secure databases on the market today. Today, you will learn

- How security in MySQL is implemented
- Stages of control and control points
- Adding and editing users and their privileges

How Security Is Implemented in MySQL

The MySQL security system is very flexible. With it, you can give potential users various levels of access ranging from the ability to log in from a specific machine as a specific user to full administrator access from anywhere. It is up to you to decide how tight you want your security to be. Hopefully, this chapter will provide you with some guidelines and ideas about how to run your database security.

MySQL holds all permissions and privileges in the `mysql` database. This database is one of two databases that are created automatically when you install MySQL. (The other one is the `test` database). The only people who should have access to this table are the database administrators. This database is just like any other MySQL database. The data files are stored in data a directory under the `mysql` parent directory, where all other data files are stored. The tables in this database are

- `user`
- `db`
- `host`
- `func`
- `columns_priv`
- `tables_priv`

You can run queries on these tables, just as you can on any other table. These tables are collectively referred to as the *Grant* tables. Each column in these Grant tables reflect what permissions a person has by either a Y (meaning they can perform the operation) or an N (meaning they cannot). For instance, a person who has `DELETE` privileges in the `user` table would have a Y in the `Delete_priv` column.

The `user` Table

The `user` table contains the permission data for all the users that have access to MySQL. You can set all the permissions for users here. This table consists of the following columns:

- `Host`   This is the name of the user's computer. With MySQL, you can limit a person's access based on the location from which he or she is connecting.
- `User`   This is the user's name that he or she will use to access MySQL.

- password   The user's password.
- Select_priv   Grants the user the ability to perform SQL SELECT queries.
- Insert_priv   Allows the user to add data to databases by using the SQL INSERT statement.
- Update_priv   Gives the user the ability to edit table data by using the UPDATE statement.
- Delete_priv   Grants the user the ability to remove data from the database by using the DELETE statement.
- Create_priv   Grants the user the ability to add tables and databases to the MySQL server.
- Drop_priv   Gives the user the ability to delete tables and databases from the MySQL server. This ability can be very dangerous in the hands of a user, so take care when granting this privilege.
- Reload_priv   Allows the user to refresh the Grant tables by using the FLUSH statement.
- Shutdown_priv   Allows the user to shut down the server.
- Process_priv   Grants the user the ability to look at the MySQL processes by using the mysqladmin processlist command or with the SHOW PROCESSLIST statement. Also gives the user the ability to kill these processes.
- File_priv   Allows the user to read and write files that reside on the MySQL server. You should take special care when granting this permission. If it is not used properly, a malicious person could overwrite system files on the server machine. This is one of the reasons why MySQL should never run under the system's root user.
- Grant_priv   Allows the user to grant privileges to other users. This privilege should be restricted to database administrators for obvious reasons.
- References_priv   This is not used for anything right now.
- Index_priv   Grants the user the ability to create indexes on tables. It also allows the user to drop indexes. Create_priv and Drop_priv do not affect this privilege in any way. If a user has DROP and CREATE privileges already, he or she must have the Index_priv to create and drop indexes.

17

- `Alter_priv` Grants the user the ability to change a table's structure. Granting this privilege does not allow the user to add indexes to tables. The user must have those permissions as well to change the table.

By giving a user permissions at this level, you are giving him or her global access to the database. This means that a user who has DELETE privileges granted in the user table can delete records in any database that is in the MySQL server. There are times when you may not want to do this. For example, suppose that you are the administrator for a MySQL server that has two databases: one for Accounting and one for Human Resources. The Accounting database contains all the tables and data that are tracked by the business, such as AR (accounts receivable), AP (accounts payable), and Payroll. The Human Resources database contains all employee information. In a situation like this, you would want to give the users in Accounting the ability to delete their own records, but you wouldn't want them to have the ability to delete records from the Human Resources database. However, you would want the users in Accounting to have the ability to view records from the HR database. If you were to give the Accounting users the DELETE privilege in the user table, they would have the ability to delete records from the HR database. So how do you prevent this? Read on.

The db Table

The db table contains the permissions for all the databases that are contained in your MySQL server. Permissions granted here are given only for the named database. So, in the previous example, you could give DELETE permissions to the users at the database level instead of the user level.

The db table has most of the same columns as the user table with a few exceptions. Because this table governs permissions at the database level, there are no administrator-level privileges, such as Reload_priv, Shutdown_priv, Process_priv, and File_priv. These permissions do not relate to databases operations that can be performed on databases, so they are only found in the user table. The only new column in the db table is Db. This is the database for which to apply these privileges.

The host Table

The host table, along with the db table, controls access by limiting the hosts that can connect to the database. This table has the same columns as the db table.

The `columns_priv` and `tables_priv` Tables

The `columns_priv` and `tables_priv` tables govern the permissions for a database's tables and columns. With MySQL, you can limit what a user can do down to the column in a table. These tables share the following columns:

- `Host`   The host from which the user is connecting.
- `Db`   The database that contains the tables to which you're applying privileges.
- `User`   The username of the person to whom you are granting permissions.
- `Table_name`   The table name of the database on which you're setting permissions. This column is case sensitive.
- `Column_priv`   This column of either table controls the access a user has. It can contain the following values: SELECT, INSERT, UPDATE, and REFERENCES. If more than one privilege is granted, the fields must be separated by a comma.
- `Timestamp`   This column contains the timestamp indicating when changes were made.

The `Grantor` and `Table_priv` columns are the only ones in the `tables_priv` table that do not appear in the `columns_priv` table. The `Grantor` column holds the name of the person granting the permissions. The `Table_priv` column maintains the permissions for the given table. The values it can contain are: SELECT, INSERT, UPDATE, DELETE, CREATE, DROP, GRANT, REFERENCES, INDEX, and ALTER.

The `columns_priv` table has only one column that does not appear in both tables; it is the `Column_name` column. This column contains the name of the column that is affected by the permissions granted in the `Column_priv` column.

You may be wondering how this works—it works very similarly to the `user` and `db` tables. If you want to grant a user SELECT privileges for all the columns in a table, you can grant those privileges in the `tables_priv` table. However, if do not want a user to have certain rights, you have to limit his or her privileges in the column level.

Applying Security Controls

Now take a look at the big picture to help give you a better understanding. This section will expand on the previous Accounting and Human Resources example a little more. The scenario: You are the database administrator for all the databases in your company. In each division of the company, you have appointed superusers. These people help you with day-to-day administration tasks. And, of course, each division has its own set of workers who have varying access needs to their particular databases. To keep everything as secure as possible, you only grant people the privileges they need to do their jobs.

Bill is the superuser in Accounting, and Julie is the superuser in HR. Keeping with company policy, you want to give Bill and Julie administrator rights to their databases only, so these two people would have entries in the user table that would reflect their status. Because you are going to limit their access to their respective databases, you would not grant them any privileges in this table. They would only have their name, password, and Hostname. The db table is where you would grant all their privileges. By doing it this way, you limit their access. You, on the other hand, are the database administrator and would have global access. You would be the only person with full privileges in the user table. By limiting who can do what, you are ensuring a more secure environment.

Because you have limited their access, you are the only one who can add new users and give them permissions. Julie has a new person in HR. She wants that person to be able to update only a few columns in the Employee_Benefits table, but she still wants that person to be able to view all the records in the database. To do this, you give this person, Sheila, an entry in the user table. This is so she can at least connect to the database. The next step is to grant SELECT privileges on all the tables in the HR database. To limit Sheila's update capability, you must enter her privileges in the tables_priv and columns_priv tables.

Stages of Control

You will learn how to add users and their permissions shortly. For now, just understand that there is a hierarchy of security in the MySQL database system. When a user connects to the MySQL database, MySQL first looks in the user table to see if it can find a match for the hostname, username, and password. If it can, the user is given access to the system. When he or she issues a query against the database, MySQL first looks at the user table to see what privileges the user has. If the user has no privileges in that table, it looks to the db table. Again, it searches the table for a match with the hostname, username, and database. If it finds a match, it will look at the privileges the person has. If that person doesn't have the privileges needed to issue the query, MySQL will then search the tables_priv table and then the columns_priv table for the permissions necessary to execute the query. If it cannot find any permissions, an error will be generated. This all happens every time a query is performed in MySQL.

As you can see, there are two control points. One point is the connection verification, and the second control point is the request verification. These control points offer a more secure environment for your database. A person who can connect to the database may not be able to do anything once he or she is in the database. This provides a very secure wall against would-be crackers disrupting your business and protects the database from users who may do harm unintentionally.

Connection Verification

Connection verification occurs the moment you try to connect to MySQL. Any connection to MySQL requires a username, password, and hostname. The username is the name of the person who is trying to connect. The password is an additional verification tool to ensure the person who is connecting is really who he or she claims to be. The hostname is the name of the computer from which the user is connecting. MySQL cannot only limit a person from connecting, it can restrict a machine from connecting as well. You can allow or disallow connections from entire domains if you want. This provides a very secure place for your data.

The connection verification process is pretty simple. MySQL checks the incoming request against the information in the user grant table for a username, password, and hostname match. If it finds a match, the user is allowed to make a connection. If MySQL fails to find a match within the user table, it denies access (see Figure 17.1).

17

FIGURE 17.1

The connection verification stage.

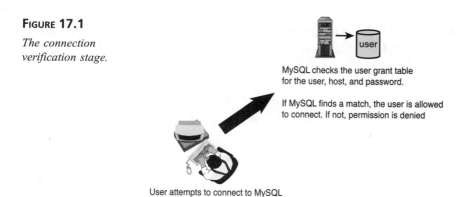

MySQL checks the user grant table for the user, host, and password.

If MySQL finds a match, the user is allowed to connect. If not, permission is denied

User attempts to connect to MySQL

Request Verification

Request verification occurs every time a user issues a query to the database. Every command that is issued after a connection is made goes through the same process. This ensures that users work under the restrictions that have been placed for them. This provides an extra blanket of security by preventing malicious people from doing any harm to your data even if they get into the database.

The process again is pretty simple. Whenever a request is issued, MySQL first checks the permissions given to the user at the user level. If the person has permissions here, he or she is allowed to do whatever he or she wants to any database that is contained in the MySQL RDBMS, so permissions at this level should be given out sparingly. If MySQL doesn't find the necessary privileges to carry out the command, it looks at the db table.

The db table is the next line of security. Permissions granted here apply only to the specified database. A SELECT privilege given at this level allows the person to view all the data in all the tables in the specified database. This is generally okay, but if you want to restrict access even further, you can hold off permissions here and give them in the tables_priv grant table.

The tables_priv table is the next table MySQL looks at to see if a user has privileges to carry out the command he or she is requesting. If the necessary privileges are found here, MySQL executes the query. If not, MySQL looks in one more place—the columns_priv table.

The columns_priv table is the last place MySQL looks to see if a person has the right to carry out the command. If the user does not have the permission here, MySQL returns an error, saying that the request is denied. All of this happens very quickly—so quickly that performance is hardly affected, so it behooves you to maintain a high level of security within your database. See Figure 17.2 for a diagram of the request verification process.

FIGURE 17.2

The request verification process.

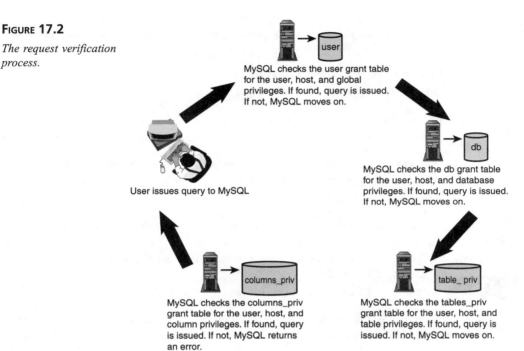

MySQL checks the user grant table for the user, host, and global privileges. If found, query is issued. If not, MySQL moves on.

MySQL checks the db grant table for the user, host, and database privileges. If found, query is issued. If not, MySQL moves on.

User issues query to MySQL

MySQL checks the columns_priv grant table for the user, host, and column privileges. If found, query is issued. If not, MySQL returns an error.

MySQL checks the tables_priv grant table for the user, host, and table privileges. If found, query is issued. If not, MySQL moves on.

Modifying User Privileges

You may be wondering if you have to worry about the way MySQL implements security. The simple answer is no. MySQL has tools that take care of this for you. But you really won't be a good DBA if you dodn't know how MySQL implements security. It will also help you find security holes if you ever have any.

As with most things, there is more than one way to protect your database. MySQL provides you with many tools to help you control security in your database. The following sections will start with the hardest way and work backwards.

Altering the grant Table

The hardest way, relatively speaking, is to alter the grant tables yourself. By first understanding how the grant tables are organized, you will gain a greater appreciation of the other methods that are used later in this chapter. It also may be necessary at times to alter the grant tables directly. This section will show you how. Because these are just ordinary MySQL tables, INSERT, DELETE, UPDATE, and SELECT queries work the way with which you are already familiar. Begin by adding a user.

To add a user, you must first log in to the MySQL database as root and use the mysql database. To do this, perform the following steps:

1. Change to the mysql installation directory.

    ```
    cd /usr/local/mysql
    ```

2. Ensure that the mysqld is up and running.

    ```
    bin/mysqladmin -p ping
    ```

3. You will be prompted for your root password. After you have entered it correctly, you be able to access the mysql database by typing in the following:

    ```
    use mysql;
    ```

The mysql database should now be the active database. The next step is to insert a row into the user table. Remember that this is the table MySQL checks to see if a person has access privileges. To insert a person without any permissions, enter the following:

INPUT
```
INSERT INTO user (Host, User, password)
VALUES("localhost", "Scott", PASSWORD("dinosaur"));
```

This statement adds a record to the user grant table. It adds Scott, who can only connect from the database server itself. Scott will not be allowed to connect remotely. It also gives Scott the password "dinosaur." Passwords in MySQL are case sensitive. The password function encrypts the password and stores it in its encrypted form in the table. This stops prying eyes from seeing everybody's password. Scott can now connect to the MySQL server. Once connected, Scott will not be able to do anything because haven't given him any global or database privileges yet.

Providing Remote Access

If you wanted to allow Scott to connect from a remote machine, you would have to change the hostname in the table to reflect this. Hostnames can be either IP addresses or domain names. For instance, a hostname could be 10.1.1.50, or it could be staff.jsmc.org. This would allow Scott to connect remotely if he wwere using the machine with the specified IP address or a computer in the staff.jsmc.org domain. If you do not want to limit the computers from which Scott can connect, you can allow him to connect from anywhere using the wildcard character (%). You could also leave the hostname column blank, which is in effect the same thing as the wild card. Another option you have here is to allow Scott to connect from anywhere within the jsmc.org domain. To do this you could use the wild card character in the following way:

INPUT
```
INSERT INTO user (Host, User, password)
VALUES("%.jsmc.org", "Scott",
PASSWORD("dinosaur"));
```

This allows Scott to connect from anywhere within the jsmc.org domain. One important point to remember is that even though the % means from any host, it really means from any remote host. For a user to log in to the local machine, meaning the machine on which the MySQL server is running, the user must have a localhost entry. If the user does not, he or she cannot log on to the machine locally.

Adding Privileges

Now that you have added a user, it's time to give him some privileges. To allow Scott access to any of the databases that are available within the MySQL RDBMS, you must give him an entry in the db table. Remember that this table holds all the permissions that are relevant to each individual database. If you want Scott to have SELECT access to the Meet_A_Geek database, you would make the following entry:

INPUT
```
INSERT INTO db (Host, User, Db, Select_priv)
VALUES
("localhost","Scott","Meet_A_Geek","Y");
```

This statement would give Scott SELECT privileges to the Meet_A_Geek database only if he connected to it from the local machine. He couldn't access this database if he were to connect from another computer or domain. This is an example of how MySQL can add security that no other database on the market can give. The same rules about the wildcard character apply here as well.

If Scott needed to access more than one database in your RDBMS, he would have to have more than one entry in this table, giving him explicit permissions to each database.

Removing Privileges

If you want to take away privileges from a user, you can use the UPDATE statement to carry out your plans. For example, if you want to take away Scott's SELECT privileges and give him UPDATE privileges instead, you would issue the following command:

INPUT
```
UPDATE db
  SET Select_priv = "N", Update_priv="Y"
WHERE User = "Scott"
AND Host="localhost"
AND Db ="Meet_A_GeeK";
```

17

This takes Scott's SELECT privilege away and gives him UPDATE privileges. Now that you have given Scott's permissions to the database, you're done—right? Not exactly. When MySQL starts, it loads the grant tables into memory to help speed things up. The only problem is that when you make changes to the grant tables, you are not updating the tables that are stored in memory. So a user that you just entered will not be able to connect to the database until the tables in memory are updated. To update those tables you need to flush them. This is done with the FLUSH privileges statement. Of course, you must have FLUSH or RELOAD privileges to issue this command. The other way to flush the grant tables is to use the RELOAD option with the mysqladmin command. This takes about a second to do, and then all the changes you have made are updated.

Using the GRANT Command

If you are not comfortable with directly updating the grant tables, there is another way to administer user privileges—with the GRANT command. The GRANT command has the following syntax:

```
GRANT [privileges] (column names)
ON databasename.tablename
TO username@hostname
IDENTIFIED BY "password"
[WITH GRANT OPTIONS]
```

This may seem a little intimidating at first, but it is quite easy. After the keyword GRANT, you would list all the privileges you want to grant the new user. The following are the privileges you can grant:

- ALL   Gives the user all the available privileges.
- ALTER   Allows the user to alter tables, columns, and indexes.
- CREATE   Allows the user to create tables or databases.
- DELETE   Allows the user to delete records from tables.
- DROP   Allows the user to delete tables or databases.
- FILE   Allows the user to read and write files on the server.
- INDEX   Allows the user to add or delete indexes.
- INSERT   Allows the user to add records to the database.
- PROCESS   Allows the user to view and kill MySQL system processes.
- REFERENCES   Not currently used in MySQL.

- RELOAD   Allows the user to use the FLUSH statement.
- SELECT   Allows the user to perform SELECT queries.
- SHUTDOWN   Allows the user to shut down the MySQL server.
- UPDATE   Allows the user to edit existing records in the database.
- USAGE   Allows the user to connect to the server. This type of user has no privileges at all.

The next part of the command is optional. It allows you to specify what columns of a table to which to apply the privileges. The column names are case sensitive, so be careful when entering them.

After the keyword ON, you list the database and table or tables to which to apply these privileges. To specify all the tables in the database, you would use an asterisk:

INPUT   `Meet_A_Geek.*`

If you wanted to apply these permissions globally, you would use two asterisks:

INPUT   `*.*`

The next part of the GRANT command is the TO clause. This is where you state the user and his or her hostname. Again, wildcard characters can be used here. If you want to give privileges to Scott, you can use any of the following:

INPUT   `"Scott@localhost"`

`"Scott@%jsmc.org"`

`"Scott@%"`

The next part of the statement is the password. You do not need to use the password function in the GRANT statement. MySQL does it for you automatically.

The final part of the command is entirely optional. It gives the specified user the ability to issue the GRANT statement as well.

Now look at some examples. You'll use your friend Scott again. To begin, give him the ability to connect to the MySQL server with absolutely no permission at all. To do this, use the following command:

INPUT   `GRANT USAGE ON *.* TO Scott@% IDENTIFIED BY "dinosaur";`

This statement allows Scott to connect from anywhere using the password "dinosaur." If you look at the grant tables, you'll see that Scott only has an entry in the user table. You'll also see that the password is encrypted. Pretty easy.

Now give Scott SELECT privileges on all tables in the Meet_A_Geek database. To do this, issue the following statement:

INPUT
```
GRANT SELECT ON Meet_A_Geek.* TO Scott@% IDENTIFIED BY "dinosaur";
```

This gives Scott the ability to connect from any computer and issue SELECT statements to any of the tables in the Meet_A_Geek database. Next, you'll get a little more strict with Scott. Give him SELECT privileges only to the Customers table in the Meet_A_Geek database. To do this, use the following command:

INPUT
```
GRANT SELECT ON Meet_A_Geek.Customers
TO Scott@% IDENTIFIED BY "dinosaur";
```

Notice how the dot (.) notation is used. The first part is the database name, and the second part is the table name. This is pretty much standard for all database systems.

Now give Scott UPDATE privileges only on the First_Name and Last_Name columns of the Customers table. To do this, issue the following command:

INPUT
```
GRANT UPDATE (First_Name, Last_Name) ON Meet_A_Geek.Customers
TO Scott@localhost IDENTIFIED BY "dinosaur";
```

This command limits Scott to updating the First_Name and Last_Name columns in the Customers table in the Meet_A_Geek database. As you can see, using this command is an easy way to maintain your user's accounts.

There is yet another way to grant permissions to users in MySQL. This command takes you out of the MySQL Monitor and into the mysql directory. In the bin subdirectory (where all the MySQL utilities are stored) you will find the mysql_setpermission utility. This is a script written in Perl that will walk you through setting permissions for your database.

To begin using this utility, you must be in the mysql installation directory and the mysqld daemon must be up and running. The first step is to start the utility. To do this, type the following from the command line:

INPUT
```
/usr/local/mysql> bin/mysql_setpermission
```

You should see the following output:

OUTPUT
```
>Password for user to connect to MySQL:
```

After you have entered your root password successfully, you should see a welcome screen followed by the following menu options:

```
1.     Set password for user.
2.     Add a database + user privilege for that database—User can do
all except all admin functions.
3.     Add user privilege for an existing database—User can do all
except admin functions.
4.     Add user privilege for an existing database—User can do all
except admin functions + no create/drop.
5.     Add user privilege for an existing database—User can do only
selects (no update, delete, insert, and so on).
Exit this program.
```

As you can see, this utility is fairly limited in what it can do for you. But if you need something that is quick and easy, you can use this. Using Scott again, add him to an existing database by choosing option 3.

When you choose option 3, you will be shown a list of databases from which to choose. Select the Meet_A_Geek database. The program will then prompt you for a username. Type in **Scott**. The program will then ask if you would like to create a password for Scott. Type **Y**. It is not recommended that you have users without passwords. This could potentially compromise your database. After you type **Y**, you are prompted for the password. Enter the word **dinosaur** or whatever you want. After you have entered the password, you will prompted to re-enter it. After you have completed that step, you will be asked for a hostname. You can supply a hostname, a wildcard, or any combination. Enter **%**. The utility will then ask you if you want to enter another hostname under this username. For now, answer **NO**. The program will then review what you have selected and prompt you before it makes any changes. If everything looks correct, accept your entries by typing **Y**. You have now created a user named Scott, with all the privileges except administrative privileges for the Meet_A_Geek database, who can connect from anywhere. This utility can save you a lot of time and thinking when you need to add somebody quickly.

Now that you know how to add a user, what happens if you want to get rid of him or her?

Removing Users and Revoking Privileges

You have read extensively about adding users and privileges. Now it's time to talk about removing users and revoking privileges. MySQL offers you only one way to remove a user. You must edit the grant tables manually. You issue a DELETE statement against every table in the MySQL database. To do this correctly and safely, you must specify the user and hostname in the WHERE clause. For example, you would use the following commands to remove Scott from the grant tables:

17

INPUT
```
DELETE FROM user WHERE User = "Scott"AND Host = "%";
DELETE FROM db WHERE User = "Scott"AND Host = "%";
```

These commands will delete Scott's records from the user and db tables where the hostname is the wildcard. Scott's other records might still exist, so you will have to perform some manual cleanup. To see if Scott has any other records, you could use the following statements:

INPUT
```
SELECT FROM user WHERE User = "Scott"AND Host = "%";
SELECT FROM db WHERE User = "Scott"AND Host = "%";
```

You can revoke a user's privileges in one of two ways. The first way is to edit the grant tables with SQL statements. The other way is to use the REVOKE statement. The REVOKE statement is the recommended way for removing someone's privileges because there is less chance of error.

The REVOKE statement's syntax is very similar to the GRANT statement's syntax. The REVOKE statement's syntax is as follows:

```
REVOKE [privileges](columns)
ON databasename.tablename FROM username@hostname
```

The privileges that can be revoked are the same set of privileges that were discussed during the GRANT statement. With the REVOKE statement, you can revoke some or all of the privileges a user has. Everything else in the REVOKE statement must match the corresponding GRANT statement exactly. In going over the parts of the REVOKE statement, everything should seem pretty familiar.

After the keyword REVOKE, you will list the privileges you are removing from the user. After the privilege list are the optional column names that have privileges. After the column names is the keyword ON. Following the keyword are the database and table from which you are removing the privileges. You can also specify all databases and all tables with the *.* syntax. Following the database/table name is the keyword FROM, followed by the user and his or her hostname. Look next at some examples.

To remove Scott's privileges entirely, you could use the following statement:

INPUT   `REVOKE ALL ON *.* FROM Scott@%;`

This removes all the privileges Scott had in all databases that had the wildcard as the hostname. If Scott were ever granted permission to log on to the local server, you would have to issue the following REVOKE statement to remove those privileges:

OUTPUT   `REVOKE ALL ON *.* FROM Scott@localhost;`

To remove specific privileges, you would use the REVOKE statement much like you would the GRANT statement. For example, revoke Scott's UPDATE privileges on the First_Name and Last_Name columns in the Customers table. To do this, use the following command:

INPUT
```
REVOKE UPDATE (First_Name, Last_Name)
ON Meet_A_Geek.Customers
FROM Scott@%.jsmc.org;
```

As you can see, the REVOKE statement is similar to the GRANT statement in syntax and use. The major difference is that in one you are granting privileges and in the other you are taking them away.

Taking Proper Security Measures

As the database administrator for the MySQL database, the security and integrity of the data is your responsibility. This means that it is up to you to maintain an accurate database. The information contained in the database is solely your responsibility. Everything rests in your hands. So when the data becomes corrupted because some disgruntled employee broke in and deleted rows and rows of data, everyone is going to be looking at you. Maybe the data you are in charge of is highly classified or confidential. It is your responsibility that it remains that way. This is a lot of responsibility, but if you are using MySQL, rest assured that you are taking the right steps to a very secure environment.

There are some additional steps you can take to provide a more secure environment. One of the first steps is to never run the mysqld as the operating system root. The main reason is that anybody who has FILE privileges in MySQL can access any file if the server is running as root. Instead of running MySQL as root, run it as another user, such as mysqladmin or mysqlgroup. In this way, you are assured that malicious users who are given root access will not overwrite system files.

The next step is to secure the data subdirectory in the mysql directory. All the files in this directory should be owned by the user who runs the mysqld daemon. They should only be readable and writeable by this user as well. This guarantees that no other user can access these files.

Another step you can take is to limit the % when defining hostnames. Specify an IP address whenever possible. This helps tighten up security.

When dealing with security, it is always best to start off as strict as possible, and then loosen up the security as you go. When granting permissions, give new users as few as possible—just enough to let them accomplish their jobs. With stringent security policies, you can help guard your database against malicious attacks.

17

Summary

Today you have learned a lot about security. You learned how MySQL implements security in a hierarchy, and that there are several stages of control and two verification points—the access verification and the request verification. You learned how this two-pronged attack can help prevent security breeches.

You also learned how to add users to a MySQL database. You learned that MySQL provides many ways of doing it. You can add users by directly editing the grant tables with SQL statements or by using the GRANT command from the MySQL monitor. You also read about the mysql_setpermission utility that offers a simple and quick way of adding new users and granting privileges.

Another topic that was covered today was the process by which users are removed from the database. You learned that the only way to remove users entirely from the database is to delete them from the grant tables directly by using an SQL DELETE statement. You also learned that you could remove some or all of a user's privileges with the REVOKE statement.

Finally, you learned some additional steps to take to help guard your database against malicious attacks. Ultimately, the responsibility of the data falls upon your shoulders as the DBA. You are in charge of the database, as well as all the data it holds. It behooves you and your business to implement very strict security policies, regardless of what data you are maintaining.

Q&A

Q   **Are there any other precautions that I can take to ensure the security of my database?**

A   There are a ton of things you can do to help you secure your database. This chapter discussed what you can do internally with MySQL. What wasn't covered is what you can do to make your server more secure. Adding firewalls and proxy servers are two ways to help deter crackers. Locking down services and installing security patches as they are available is another way to maintain the overall security of your machine. Unfortunately, this is beyond the scope of this book. You may want to look around and find some good books dealing with security for the operating system you are using.

Q   **I removed a user from my database entirely, but he still can get in. Why is this?**

A   There can be several explanations for this. The most likely one is that you have an anonymous user in your user database. An anonymous user is a user who has a blank entry in the User column of the user table. This allows anyone to connect to your database. To see if this is your problem, run the following query:

INPUT   `SELECT * FROM user WHERE User = "";`

This could cause a huge security breech without you ever knowing it.

Q   **I have written an Internet application that interacts with the MySQL database. I want the user to log in to my system, but I do not want to create a thousand user accounts. What should I do?**

A   It is common practice to create another user table inside your own database. You can add users to this database instead of to MySQL proper. You could verify their ability to use the database by performing a query on this table, in much the same way MySQL does.

Exercises

1. Add several users to the Meet_A_Geek database using the techniques that were discussed in this chapter. Add one using the GRANT statement, one using the mysql_setpermission utility, and one by manipulating the grant tables manually.

2. Revoke the privileges you granted the users you created in exercise 1 by using the REVOKE statement.

3. Delete the users from the database.

WEEK 3

DAY 18

How MySQL Compares

There has been a lot of discussion about open source software. A lot of people do not place value on a product because it is freely distributed. They do not feel that something that is open source can compete with the established companies. Most people are more comfortable with a well-known name, even if that company produces poor software. Linux has started to change that attitude. It has legitimized open source software and has opened the door for products like MySQL. In this chapter, MySQL will be compared with other databases in the same class. The strengths and weakness of MySQL will be discussed.

Today you will learn about

- The speed factor
- MySQL and stored procedures and workarounds

- MySQL and transaction-based databases
- MySQL and constraints

The Need For Speed

As the need to store and access larger amounts of data grew, so did the need for databases engines to retrieve and process requests quickly and efficiently. The race for the fastest database engine was on. At the same time, the need for more functionality grew. DBAs needed more tools and more efficient ways to manage the large amounts of data that they were storing. The problem was that the more functionality or features that were added to a database, the slower the database became. MySQL has taken great measures to ensure it provides the maximum number of features without sacrificing speed.

How fast is MySQL? TcX has set up a Web site (www.tcx.com) that displays the differences between MySQL and other databases in its class. The Web site uses the results from a program called crashme. This program lists and compares the functionality of all the major relational database systems. TcX also has a link that displays the speed results of MySQL and other databases on several different platforms using a common interface.

In almost every category, MySQL is the fastest. In a comparison of MySQL with DB2, Informix, Sybase Enterprise 11.5, and Microsoft SQL Server all running on Windows NT and using ODBC as the common interface, MySQL outperforms all the other databases in nearly every test. For example, in a test using 20,000 SELECT statements of various complexity, MySQL accomplished these tasks nearly 50% faster than Microsoft SQL Server and nearly five times faster than Informix. According to the statistics provided, MySQL outperforms all database engines in it class by an average of 40%.

As you know, statistics can be manipulated in many ways to illustrate a point. The best way to judge MySQL is to use it. If you have ever used one of the big-name databases, you will be thoroughly impressed by what MySQL can do. If you haven't had the opportunity, you will be spoiled by the speed MySQL provides.

This is the reason why MySQL excels on the Internet. MySQL exceeds the speed requirements for the Web. Queries are executed faster and results are returned quicker. Because it works so well across the Internet, it makes a lot of sense to include MySQL in Enterprise applications as well. Imagine the flexibility MySQL could provide with its large table size and unprecedented speed.

As explained earlier, with an increase in speed comes a decrease in functionality. The developers of MySQL have done an excellent job of keeping the features-to-speed ratio relatively high. Of course they couldn't include all the features that are available in other database engines in its class. So they have selectively kept the essential features and let the optional features go by the wayside. In the near future, MySQL will include many of the features that other databases have and still retain most of its speed. Developers will let database administrators decide whether they want to use the more advanced feature set and sacrifice speed. Giving the administrator the option is a huge benefit; it will put the decision in the hands of the administrator instead of the manufacturer. That way, the people who really know what they need can make the decision, instead of people who think they know what their users need.

Transaction-Based Databases

Some databases use a form of SQL called Transact-SQL or T-SQL (Microsoft SQL Server and Sybase Adaptive Server). This form of SQL extends regular SQL by adding the ability to create programs. These are not programs in the sense that they are compiled or can stand alone, but they contain the same sets of controls that most programming languages have, such as loops and IF statements. For example, a T-SQL command set may look something like the following:

```
BEGIN TRAN update_orders
UPDATE Orders
SET Order_Shipped = 'Y'
WHERE  Order_ID = 1454
IF @@ERROR = 0
BEGIN
    COMMIT TRAN update_orders
END
ELSE
BEGIN
    ROLLBACK TRAN update_orders
    PRINT "Error encountered. Transaction failed"
END
```

As you can see, these statements are a little more complex than the SQL commands you have seen so far. The ability to perform complex routines and include logic on the database server opens the doors for numerous opportunities.

These opportunities have been added as a feature set for these databases. They include stored procedures, the ability to roll back transactions, and cursors. These features are not found in the current version of MySQL. The reasons why they are not included, as well as workarounds for you die hards, will be discussed next.

BEGIN TRAN and ROLLBACK TRAN

These databases are built on transactions. A *transaction* is considered to be any action that can be performed on a database. For example, every INSERT, UPDATE, or DELETE is considered a transaction, as well as any CREATE or DROP statements.

Every T-SQL command is processed by the database system before it is executed. This allows the engine to read all the commands and develop a good query plan. It will then execute the commands based on its query plan. Because the engine sees all the commands before it actually executes them, it allows for a very handy pair of features—the BEGIN TRAN and ROLLBACK TRAN.

The ROLLBACK TRAN is like a "Do Over." Remember when you were a kid and were playing kickball or baseball and somebody did something with which somebody else didn't agree? Usually a shouting match ensued. Then somebody would yell, "Do Over!!", and you replayed the last series of events as if nothing ever happened. Transactional databases allow a "Do Over." You can state a series of commands, and if something doesn't work out as expected, you can roll everything back and the transaction will not be committed. Take a look at the following example:

```
BEGIN TRAN
DELETE FROM Customers
WHERE Customer_ID = 13
ROLLBACK TRAN
```

The database engine would create a query plan for this series of commands, but because a ROLLBACK was issued instead of a COMMIT, the DELETE will never happen. The server would tell you how many rows would have been affected had you committed this transaction, but that's all it would do. As you can see, this is a pretty handy feature. You could safely try out your SQL commands with little fear of any repercussions. You could see how long a large query would take without affecting any of the data in your database. These are all really great things, but there is a price, and that price is speed. Because the server must process every command that is issued, it is spending time looking and checking the request instead of actually processing it, so a big performance hit is taken.

MySQL is not a transactional database system. It does not use T-SQL. You cannot issue a statement like the one in the previous example and expect it to work. This may seem like a disadvantage. You may be asking why MySQL doesn't have this feature. Well, here's why. MySQL is primed for speed and ease of use. It takes time for the transactional database server to process every command. This is time that could be spent executing your commands. This is one reason why MySQL doesn't use something like T-SQL.

Another reason MySQL doesn't have the COMMIT/ROLLBACK TRAN feature is that it would take away from the ease-of-use and low maintenance aspects of MySQL. In a transactional system, every transaction is written to a special log called the *transaction log*. That is why it can roll back a transaction if needed. The size of this log is set by the administrator. If he or she sets the size too small for the number of transactions that occur, the log will become full and no more transactions will take place. That means that nobody will be able to insert, update, or delete any records on a production database—talk about disasters. This is a huge concern for most DBAs on transactional databases. They are very concerned about this log—for good reason—so they watch it carefully. MySQL has a logging feature, but it will not cause the sort of problems that the transaction log in a transactional database will cause.

Hopefully, you can see why the people at TcX chose not to include this feature. It would take away from the speed of MySQL, as well as increase the amount of administration that needs to be performed. This feature probably will not show up in future releases of MySQL.

Stored Procedures

Stored procedures are another feature that takes advantage of T-SQL. A stored procedure is a series of T-SQL commands that have been compiled and stored within the database. The query plan for the series of commands is saved, so future calls will execute quickly because a plan does not need to be created. It is treated internally the same way a table or any other database object is treated.

Stored procedures have many advantages. One advantage is that stored procedures fit the modular programming model in that they are created to serve a specific purpose. They also lend themselves to reusability. Another benefit they provide is that they can take and pass parameters. This allows a programmer to link several stored procedures together, creating a kind of batch program. Yet another benefit is displaced security. A user, who may not have explicit permissions to a table, may be able to use that table through a stored procedure. This is handy if you want to limit the user's access but still provide him or her a way to manipulate data safely through a controlled environment that you provide.

Stored procedures can become very complex. T-SQL provides most of the tools that programming languages have to offer. In a stored procedure, a programmer can declare variables, create loops, and execute conditional statements—not to mention any of the intrinsic functions the database server has to offer. This can let a programmer accomplish a lot of the programming logic on the database server.

18

One of the major benefits of stored procedures is that they execute faster than regular statements. This is because the stored procedure saves the query plan. It has already thought out the best way to do something. It's kind of like having your whole day planned for you; you just follow the plan. This is a lot quicker than planning it as you go. It is also a lot cleaner in the application code to call one stored procedure than it is to have a series of SQL statements.

There are no real disadvantages to stored procedures. In fact, they are the preferred means of executing T-SQL on a transaction-based database system. The only drawback is that you need them beforehand. If a database was extremely fast—so fast that a series of statements executed from a remote system returned results faster then a stored procedure—why would you need them anyway? Understandably, it is nice to have code execute on the server and return just the results. But is it enough to sacrifice the overwhelming speed MySQL possesses?

The next version of MySQL may have a stored procedure option. Remember, the more fluff that is added, the more speed is decreased. MySQL is fast enough without stored procedures, but sometimes stored procedures make a lot of sense. For this, there is a workaround.

Stored Procedure Workarounds

The only available workaround right now for stored procedures is using user-defined functions (UDF). UDFs are functions written in C or C++. They are quite similar to the intrinsic functions of MySQL, and they are called the same way within MySQL.

Creating a UDF is quite an involved procedure. Each UDF should appear as a function in your C++ program. Each UDF can have an optional init and deinit function. These functions act like constructors and destructors. You can check your arguments in the init function and perform cleanup in the deinit function.

Listing 18.1 is an sample UDF that doubles a number that is passed as an argument. Your UDF will probably be a little more complex. This example was kept simple so you could see how a UDF is formatted.

LISTING 18.1   User-Defined Functions in C

```
#ifdef STANDARD
#include <stdio.h>
#include <string.h>
#else
#include <global.h>
#include <my_sys.h>
#endif
```

LISTING 18.1 continued

```c
#include <mysql.h>
#include <m_ctype.h>
#include <m_string.h>


extern "C"{
my_bool Double_Proc_init(UDF_INIT *initid,
UDF_ARGS *args, char *message);
void Double_Proc_deinit(UDF_INIT *initid);
long long Double_Proc(UDF_INIT *initid, UDF_ARGS *args,
            char *is_null, char *error);

}

my_bool Double_Proc_init(UDF_INIT *initid, UDF_ARGS *args, char *message)
{
  if (args->arg_count != 1 || args->arg_type[0] != INT_RESULT)
  {
    strcpy(message,"Wrong arguments to Double_Proc");
    return 1;
  }
  return 0;
}

void Double_Proc_deinit(UDF_INIT *initid)
{
}

long long Double_Proc(UDF_INIT *initid, UDF_ARGS *args,
            char *is_null, char *error)
{
 int ResultSet;
 ResultSet = args * 2;

 Return ResultSet;
}
```

All UDFs must include the libraries that are shown in the example. After the `include` statements, you will see the function prototypes. There can be only three types of return arguments for your function. They are REAL, INTEGER, and STRING. These types are equivalent to a C++ `double`, `long`, and `char *`, respectively. If you needed an SQL STRING returned, you would declare your prototype as a `char *`. If your return was an SQL INTEGER, it would be declared as a `long`, and if it were an SQL REAL, it would be declared as a double.

18

It is important to remember that your UDF must conform to the layout that is shown in Listing 18.1. The `init` and `deinit` must be named as shown also. If your naming convention does not match the one shown in the listing, the UDF will not work. For example, in Listing 18.1, the function that will be called in MySQL is `Double_Proc`. The `init` function must be called `Double_Proc_init`. If it were called something else, you could replace the `Double_Proc` with your name but still keep the `_init`. The same naming convention applies to the `deinit` function.

The declarations for the function arguments must match Listing 18.1. The argument types and number must match. Examine the previous code carefully.

The best technique is to download the MySQL source code from the MySQL Web site. After you have it downloaded, un-tar and gunzip it. Browse the directories until you find the `sql` directory. In this directory, there is a UDF example called `udf_example.cc`. You can edit this file to create your own UDFs. That way you are certain of the format and declarations.

It is also worth mentioning that you can have more than one UDF in a file; You could create as many UDFs in one file as you wanted. The sample that is provided in the MySQL source is an example of this.

After you have finished creating your UDF, you must compile it as a shareable object. (This means that the platform you are using must support this.) To compile your example, you would enter the following command:

INPUT   `gcc -shared -o Double_Proc.o Double_Proc.cc`

After you have compiled your procedure successfully, you need to move the object to the directory where the system looks for shared files. On Red Hat, it should be the `/usr/lib` directory. Copy that file to this directory. You then need to shut down and restart the MySQL server daemon.

After you have done that, you need to tell MySQL about these new functions. You do this by using the `CREATE FUNCTION` command. The `CREATE FUNCTION` command uses the following syntax:

```
CREATE FUNCTION function name
RETURNS return type
SONAME shared object name
```

After the CREATE FUNCTION keyword, use the function name that you have given your UDF. In this example, it would be Double_Proc. After the function name is the return type of the function. It could be REAL, INTEGER, or STRING. This should match the return type of your UDF. The final parameter of the command is the name of the compiled shared object. This is the object that you moved to the /usr/lib directory. Using the sample function, you would create an entry in the func table of the mysql database as follows:

INPUT
```
CREATE FUNCTION Double_Proc
RETURNS INTEGER
SONAME Double_Proc.so
```

If you need to delete a function, you must use the DROP FUNCTION command. This command uses the following syntax:

```
DROP FUNCTION function name
```

The keywords are followed by the name of the function that you want to delete. Using the previous example, you could delete the Double_Proc function by using the following statement:

INPUT
```
DROP FUNCTION Double_Proc
```

18

The CREATE and DROP functions add and remove entries from the mysql grant tables, namely the func table. Every time MySQL is started, it will load the functions from this table.

These functions are also available across any of the databases. They do not serve just one particular database. They can be used by anyone who has SELECT privileges to the database.

As you can see, UDFs are close to a stored procedure but do not provide all the functionality that stored procedures do. The nice thing about a UDF is that it does not affect the speed of MySQL. A major problem is that you cannot really embed any SQL commands as you can in a true stored procedure. But if you needed to verify data, perform complex calculations, or do some very specific manipulation, you could accomplish all of that with a MySQL user-defined function.

Future versions of MySQL will contain a PROCEDURE statement that will accomplish nearly the same tasks as a stored procedure. It will allow the manipulation of data before the resultset is released to the client.

Because MySQL is so fast, the need for stored procedures is relatively slight. Using the various APIs, you could create functions within those APIs that could produce the same effects as a stored procedure. For example, using Visual Basic and the ODBC interface, you could create a function that performs a table-wide update. Take a look at the following code:

```
Option Explicit
Dim mConn As New ADODB.Connection
Dim mCmd as New ADODB.Command

Public Sub UpdateCustomers(DateOrdered)
With mConn
        .ConnectionString = "Driver=MySQL;Server=10.1.2.23;"& _
        db=Meet_A_Geek;uid=sa;pwd=taco"
        .Open
End With

With mCmd
        .ActiveConnection = mConn
        .CommandType = adCmdText
        .CommandText = "UPDATE Customers SET Active = 'N' "&_
                        WHERE Last_Order < ''& DateOrdered
        .Execute
End With
End Sub
```

This code will update the Customers table, setting the active flag to N if the last order was placed before the date that was passed in the argument—DateOrdered. This code could be used again. The person executing this code from an application doesn't need UPDATE rights because you could use another user who had UPDATE rights in the connection string. Also, because this is a programming language, you could use the logic and functions that are available within the language. You could even create a COM object that contained this code and run it on the server. You would have all the benefits of a stored procedure at your fingertips, without sacrificing any speed.

Cursors

Cursors allow you to manipulate a row of data from a resultset one record at a time. It is quite similar to the way you walk through a recordset using an API. A cursor enables a programmer or DBA to perform complex processing on the server within the database. This is a handy little feature, but cursors are a little involved. There are usually several steps—declaring, opening, fetching a row, and closing the cursor are the most common.

The following is an example of what a cursor generally looks like and how it could be used:

```
DECLARE @Cust_ID VARCHAR(20)
DECLARE customers_c CURSOR
FOR SELECT Customer_ID FROM Customers WHERE State= "KY"
OPEN customers_c
FETCH customers_c INTO @Cust_ID
WHILE @@FETCH_STATUS=0
BEGIN
    UPDATE Orders SET Sales_Tax = .06 WHERE Customer_ID = @Cust_ID
    FETCH customers_c INTO @Cust_ID
END
CLOSE customers_c
DEALLOCATE customers_c
```

This isn't the best use for a cursor, but it shows you what one is and for what it could be used. The first line declares a variable called @Cust_ID that will hold the value of a row of data from the cursor. The next line declares the cursor. The third line is the query from which the cursor will be made. The cursor will hold the resultset of this query. The next line opens the cursor—basically it performs the query. The following line puts the first row of data from the resultset contained in the cursor into the variable @Cust_ID. The next few statements form a loop that basically walks through the resultset contained in the cursor, updating the Orders table based on the value contained in the cursor. It does this until the whole resultset is processed. Then the cursor is closed and deallocated.

The major disadvantage to using a cursor is the performance hit. Cursors take quite a few resources to accomplish their tasks. They generally are used as a last resort.

MySQL does not contain cursors for the simple reason that they are slow. The only way to accomplish cursor-type tasks is to create the algorithm in an API. This is faster and easier to read and follow. The MySQL developers did a good job of weeding out the features that are not necessary and would take away from what MySQL is good at—being fast.

Triggers

A trigger is a stored procedure that is executed when a specified action is taken on a table, usually on an UPDATE, INSERT, or DELETE. For example, every time a user deletes a record from the Customers table, you want to archive that record in the Customer_Archive table. Instead of adding code to the application that deletes the record, or calling a stored procedure manually from the application, you could use a trigger that would do this. The trigger would fire and insert a record into the Customer_Archive table whenever a record was deleted from the Customers table.

18

Triggers have many benefits. They can help ensure database integrity by maintaining table relationships. Because they are fired on a particular action, they can perform cleanup automatically—helping the DBA keep things in order. In a one-to-one relationship, for example, if a record was deleted from one table, a trigger could be set to delete it from the corresponding table. In a one-to-many relationship, a trigger could be set to fire when a record is deleted from the parent table and all the children in the corresponding table would be deleted as well. This could save a lot of work and extra code.

Another neat feature of triggers is their cascading effect. This occurs when a trigger that is fired on one table causes another trigger to be fired on another table, and so on. This can be very helpful and very dangerous. Suppose that you wanted to delete everything in the Meet_A_Geek database relating to a customer when that customer terminates his or her membership. Instead of writing a lot of code to perform cleanup, you could use triggers to do the job. You could create a trigger that deletes all that customer's orders from the Orders table when that customer is deleted from the Customers table. You can also have a trigger on the Orders table to delete any transactions with that order number whenever an order is deleted. Now, when you delete a customer, two triggers are fired. One deletes all the corresponding orders from the Orders table, which in turn fires the second trigger that deletes all the orders from the transaction table. This saves time and performs some valuable functions.

The downside to using triggers is that they slow down the system. Every time an action is taken, the database must first determine if there is a trigger for that action, and then it must perform that action. This can take away from the processing time for other actions. That is the primary reason why MySQL doesn't have triggers; They add a bunch of overhead to the database system. By keeping that overhead low, MySQL can outperform any database in its class.

There are really no workarounds for using triggers in MySQL. If your application code is good and your database design is good, the need for triggers is really minimal. The best advice—handle your integrity in your code. Clean up after yourself, and things will be okay.

Constraints

NEW TERM   A lot of databases use constraints to help ensure data integrity. A *constraint* is a way to enforce relationships and limit or ensure that data is in the expected format. There are several types of constraints—CHECK, FOREIGN KEY, and UNIQUE, just to name a few. They all pretty much share a common goal—ensuring data integrity.

There are many benefits to using constraints. One benefit is that there is no way you can break the rules of a relationship between tables. If a record in a one-to-one relationship is deleted, the corresponding record must also be deleted. If a record is added in one table, a new record must be added in the other table as well. This is a great way to take the code out of the client and keep it on the server—it's already built in.

Another benefit is to ensure data integrity. If an alphanumeric column is supposed to contain only alpha characters, you could use a check constraint to make sure that numbers are never entered in your column. Again, this allows you to remove the code from your client application and place it on the server.

The biggest detriment of using constraints is that they add a lot of overhead, especially when inserting and updating records. The system has to slow down, check the constraints, and then perform them.

The next biggest detriment is the hassle and frustration that constraints can cause. Working around constraints, especially when deleting records, is a headache. This headache is multiplied tenfold when the database is poorly designed.

MySQL does not support constraints. Constraints only add to the overhead and slow things down, which goes against the primary reason for using MySQL. The power is in the hands of the developer and the DBA. It is their responsibility to ensure data integrity and that table relationships are enforced. If you write good, database-aware applications and the schema is clear and easy to understand (good design), the need for constraints, much like triggers or any other extra feature, is minimal.

18

Summary

There are a lot of nice features that are available for databases. Stored procedures, triggers, and cursors provide more options for DBAs and developers. These options come at an expense. The price you pay is speed and complexity. MySQL can accomplish everything that can be done with these options, maybe not in the same way, but you can get the same results because of the flexibility and speed that MySQL provides.

When choosing options for your database, think about the reason why those features are there. Stored procedures are used because of the increased speed they provide compared to embedded SQL statements. If you already have the speed, why would you need a stored procedure?

Another thing to remember is that sometimes features tend to make people more lazy and sloppy. Generally speaking, programmers as a whole are lazy people (or what they like to think of as being efficiency minded)—always trying to make things easier. These features give a programmer an excuse not to produce sloppy code and not spend a lot of time in the design phase of the database. This doesn't mean that programmers who use constraints and stored procedures are sloppy and lazy—it just means that they now have an excuse to throw in a constraint or create a trigger that does the job that good design or good coding techniques could do.

MySQL puts the power in the developer's hands. Come up with a good design and code your application well, and you will not have any reason for stored procedures or any of the other features discussed today, because MySQL provides you with the speed that caused the other databases to invent those features.

Q&A

Q   Why would I need to create a user-defined function?

A   As explained today, UDFs can help fill the need for stored procedures. You can accomplish predefined routines in a UDF. A UDF can also accomplish very complex math and string manipulation functions—you have access to all C++ libraries—before the results are returned to the user. UDFs are very fast; They are compiled programs—not interpreted or parsed like SQL or Perl.

Q   If MySQL is missing so many of these features, why would I want to use it?

A   You are focusing on the negatives. MySQL may be missing some of the features other databases have, but look at what MySQL has that other databases lack:

- MySQL can be used from the command line. This means that you can control, access, and manipulate a MySQL database remotely from anywhere—no need for third-party tools, such as PC Anywhere or VNC.

- MySQL is extremely fast—almost twice as fast as all its competitors. Who needs extra features when your database is as fast as MySQL?

- MySQL comes with the source code. What other database can say that?

Exercises

1. Go to the crashme Web site and compare MySQL to your favorite database.
2. Create a user-defined function similar to the one in this day.

WEEK 3

DAY 19

Administrating MySQL

In this chapter, you will look at how to administrate MySQL. This covers a broad range of situations, including backing-up and restoring data and recovering a corrupted database.

You will learn how to use the `mysqladmin` utility for general MySQL administration, and you will also look at MySQL's internal functions for accessing administrative data from within SQL statements.

Backing up Your Data

Backing up is a vital part of the administration of any database system. Reasons for using a backup can range from fire and theft to accidental user corruption, but whatever the perceived risk, the backup addresses a business risk. Just as important as the backup files is the means of restoring data, if disaster strikes, in a way that is fast and safe and gets business back to normal operation with a minimum of downtime.

MySQL includes two useful utilities for backing up and restoring databases: `mysqldump` and `mysqlimport`.

Between these two utilities, you can save a part or the whole database and restore it into the same or a new location.

Saving Files

`mysqldump` is a useful utility for saving a MySQL database. It can be used both for backup and for saving a database so that it can be relocated. `mysqldump` can be run by typing it at a command line, or it can be invoked by a scheduler such as `cron` under UNIX or Linux or the `At` command in Windows NT/2000.

The syntax for `mysqldump` is as follows:

```
mysqldump [options] database [tables]
```

If run without any options or tables specified, `mysqldump` will dump (save) the entire specified database.

When you run `mysqldump`, it actually creates a file full of CREATE and INSERT statements that can be used as instructions to recreate the table specifications and data.

After you have the dump file, you can keep it for backup purposes or send it to the destination where you want the database moved. In a moment, you'll see how to use `mysqlimport` to go through this file and import the database. But first, look at a few of `mysqldump`'s most useful options:

- `--add-locks`   Adds LOCK TABLES commands before and UNLOCK TABLES commands after table dumps. These cause table locking at the `mysqlimport` destination, which will speed up the restore process.

- --add-drop-table Adds a DROP TABLE command before each CREATE TABLE statement. If a copy of the database already exists at the destination, this will ensure that no duplication occurs, and that the table specification completely replaces anything that was there before.

- -e, --extended-insert Causes mysqldump to use multiline INSERT syntax, which should give INSERT statements that are more compact and faster.

- -q, --quick Dumps the result directly to stdout rather than buffering. You may need to use this if you are short on system memory.

- --opt The same as --add-locks, --add-drop-table, --eextended-insert, and --quick and is a convenient way to get the fastest possible dump and import.

- -F, --flush-logs Flushes the MySQL server's logs file before starting the dump.

- -h=hostname, --host=hostname Causes the dump to be created on hostname rather than on localhost, which is the default.

- -l, --lock-tables Causes tables to be locked before beginning the dump. If you have complex updates occurring on your system, this will ensure that you get a complete set of data that is not partially updated.

- -t, --no-create-info Omits CREATE TABLE statements (saves the data only).

- -d, --no-data Omits the actual data and saves only the table definitions; useful if you just want to save your design but not the contents.

- --tab=path, -T=path Sends the dump to files at the destination in your file system given by path. For each table, mysqldump creates a file called table_name.sql that contains the CREATE TABLE statements and a table_name.txt file that contains the data. The data will be saved in tab-separated format (if --tab is specified); otherwise, the data is saved as specified by the --fields-terminated-by option. (Note that this will only work when mysqldump is run on the same machine as the mysqld daemon.)

- --fields-terminated-by='delimeter' Specifies the delimiter to use as a separator after each field. If unspecified, the default being '\t' (tab); used with -T.

- --fields-enclosed-by='delimeter' Specifies the delimiter to use to enclose each field; used with -T.

- --fields-optionally-enclosed-by='delimeter' Specifies the delimiter to enclose each CHAR or VARCHAR type field; used with -T.

- --fields-escaped-by='escape_char' Specifies the escape_char to place before any special character, the default being '\\' (amounting to one backslash); used with -T.

19

- `--lines-terminated-by='`*`delimeter`*`'`   Specifies the line *delimiter*, the default being `'\n'` (newline). See also LOAD DATA INFILE in Day 8, "Populating the Database," whose specification of delimiters corresponds to these options.
- `-F, --flush-logs`   Makes MySQL flush the logs file (see "Logging Transactions" later today, for more on logs) before starting the dump. This option can help synchronize full and incremental backups.
- `-u user_name, --user=`*`user_name`*   Allows you to specify a MySQL username when connecting to the server. Your UNIX login name will be used by default.
- `-p[`*`your_password`*`, -password[=`*`your_password`*`]`   Sends your password when connecting to the server. Remember not to type a space between `-p` and *your_password*. If you only enter `-p` or `-password`, MySQL prompts you for your password from the terminal (thus avoiding it being visible onscreen).
- `-w='`*`condition`*`',--where='`*`condition`*`'`   Dumps only records selected by the where condition.
- `-?, --help`   Displays the full `mysqldump` list of options and exits.

> **Note**
>
> `mysqldump` offers a few more options, including ones for debugging and compressing. We have listed just the most useful ones here. Run `mysqldump --help` for the full list of possibilities in your particular version.

> **Note**
>
> If you encounter permissions problems when trying to run `mysqldump` with either Errcode: 13 or Errcode: 2, this is probably due to an incorrectly set UMASK when `mysqld` starts up.
>
> The default UMASK value is usually 0660 (octal). However, you can correct this by restarting `mysqld` with the correct UMASK:
>
> ```
> shellprompt> mysqladmin shutdown
> shellprompt> UMASK=384  # this is 0600 octal
> shellprompt> export UMASK
> shellprompt> safe_mysqld &
> ```
>
> You should then be able to run `mysqldump` normally.

The following is an example of running `mysqldump`. Imagine that you want to make a backup of an entire database named book. You would type:

INPUT
```
mysqldump --opt book > /path/to/book.sql
```

This would produce a file containing something like the following (recalling your Customers table from Day 11):

OUTPUT
```
# MySQL dump 6.4
#
# Host: localhost    Database: book
#-------------------------------------------------------------
# Server version          3.22.27

#
# Table structure for table 'customers'
#
DROP TABLE IF EXISTS customers;
CREATE TABLE customers (
  lastname varchar(30) DEFAULT '' NOT NULL,
  firstname varchar(30) DEFAULT '' NOT NULL,
  address varchar(100) DEFAULT '' NOT NULL,
  state varchar(30) DEFAULT '' NOT NULL,
  country varchar(30) DEFAULT '' NOT NULL,
  KEY lastn_index (lastname(6),state(2),country(3))
);

#
# Dumping data for table 'customers'
#

LOCK TABLES customers WRITE;
INSERT INTO customers VALUES ('Shepherd','Tom','33 Madison Drive,
➡Oakland','CA','USA'),('Chapman','Frederick','52 Ocean St,
➡Sacramento','CA','USA'),('Lowe','Justin','3 Hill Walk, Twin Creeks',
➡'WI','USA'),('Spokes','Chris','Red Fern House, Bradwell','Oxford','UK');
UNLOCK TABLES;
```

19

Note the DROP TABLE, LOCK TABLES, and UNLOCK TABLES statements and the fact that the INSERT is an extended line; these are the effects of using the `--opt` option with `mysqldump`.

Alternatively, you may want to save your database as separate files for SQL statements and tab-delimited data files. You might type the following:

INPUT
```
mysqldump --tab=/root book
```

This produces two files per table, one with the SQL CREATE statements (`customers.sql`):

```
# MySQL dump 6.4
#
# Host: localhost    Database: book
#--------------------------------------------------------
# Server version       3.22.27

#
# Table structure for table 'customers'
#
CREATE TABLE customers (
  lastname varchar(30) DEFAULT '' NOT NULL,
  firstname varchar(30) DEFAULT '' NOT NULL,
  address varchar(100) DEFAULT '' NOT NULL,
  state varchar(30) DEFAULT '' NOT NULL,
  country varchar(30) DEFAULT '' NOT NULL,
  KEY lastn_index (lastname(6),state(2),country(3))
);
```

and one with the data, tab-delimited, in `customers.txt`:

```
Shepherd        Tom      33 Madison Drive, Oakland      CA      USA
Chapman Frederick        52 Ocean St, Sacramento CA     USA
Lowe    Justin 3 Hill Walk, Twin Creeks        WI      USA
Spokes  Chris   Red Fern House, Bradwell        Oxford  UK
```

Which Files Are Important

Your overall database design and its business application will dictate which parts of the database are most important and how to deal with backing up or otherwise saving information.

For example, on a system that is largely read-only, it might be sufficient to do a backup once every few weeks. You would probably do a `mysqldump --opt`, which saves all information (tables and data) ready for a total restore if you ever need it.

On the other hand, you may have a "master-slave" database split across two locations. The "master" location may be where all data-entry occurs, while the "slave" (perhaps on a Web server) may be the system that users can query (to search a product catalog, for example). Here, there is not just a need for a backup but also for copying the system on a regular basis from one location to the other.

In this second case, you may want to run `mysqldump` far more frequently, perhaps using the following, which will populate another MySQL server:

```
mysqldump --opt database_name --hostname=other_host new_database_name
```

These example have both discussed full table and data backups. While a full backup is sufficient to restore your database to full working order, these procedures for handling backups may not be the most practical.

Full backups are often stored to tape, CD-ROM, or other media that can be taken off-site. Storing such a large quantity of data each time can take up necessary storage space, and recovery from a mild accident can be unnecessarily complicated. This is where an incremental backup can be useful.

An incremental backup stores all the changes made in the database since the last full backup. If it is appropriate to make a full backup once a week, incremental backups can be done once a day, with each incremental backup being stored locally on hard disk.

In a moment, you'll take a more detailed look at creating incremental backups by logging transaction updates to the database.

Importing and Restoring Data

The `mysqlimport` utility reads a range of data formats, including tab-delimited, and inserts the data into the given database. Its syntax is as follows:

```
mysqlimport [options] databasefilename1filename2 ...
```

This can be used to restore a data dump created by using `mysqldump --tab`.

Like `mysqladmin`, it is invoked from the command line. It is really the same as the SQL statement LOAD DATA INFILE.

The specified filenames (any number of them) must correspond with the tables that they will be used to create. `mysqlimport` strips off any extension from each filename and applies the updates to the table with that name.

You can run `mysqlimport` with the following *options*:

- `-d, --delete`   Empties the table before performing INSERTs as specified by the text file.
- `-h host_name, --host host_name`   Imports data onto the specified host rather than the default localhost.
- `-l, --lock-tables`   Locks all tables before importing the text files.
- `-u user_name, --user user_name`   Passes the MySQL username to use when connecting to the server.

19

- -p[*your_password*], -password[=*your_password*]   Usually used in association with u; passes the password to use when connecting to the server. Note that there should be no space between -p and *your_password*. If you omit the password, you will be prompted for it.

- -r, --replace and -i, --ignore   Allows you to control the import of rows that may have unique key values. -r or --replace will cause imported rows to overwrite existing rows if they have the same unique key value. -i or --ignore will cause such rows to be skipped. If neither option is given and such a duplicate is found, an error occurs and the rest of the file is skipped. (Note that if you drop the table before importing, this situation is unlikely to arise).

- -s, --silent   Silences mysqlimport's commentary, and it will write messages to the screen only when errors occur.

- --fields-terminated-by='*delimeter*'   Specifies the *delimiter* used as a separator after each field, the default being '\t' (tab).

- --fields-enclosed-by='*delimeter*'   Specifies the *delimiter* used to enclose each field.

- --fields-optionally-enclosed-by='*delimeter*'   Specifies the *delimiter* enclosing each CHAR or VARCHAR type field.

- --fields-escaped-by='*escape_char*'   Specifies the *escape_char* placed before any special character, the default being '\\' (amounting to one backslash).

- --lines-terminated-by='*delimeter*'   Specifies the line *delimiter*, the default being '\n' (newline).

- -?, --help   Shows the full list of options for mysqlimport and exits.

> **Note**
>
> Note that this is not an exhaustive list of mysqlimport options. Type **mysqlimport --help** for a full list of options.

For example, suppose that you're importing the data from the Customers table in the example book database:

INPUT   `mysqlimport -u root book customers.txt`

This would import the data from the file into the table and produce a short output to confirm what has been done:

OUTPUT   book.customers: Records: 4   Deleted: 0   Skipped: 0   Warnings: 0

Logging Transactions

MySQL gives you some handy ways of logging transactions on your database. Look at why you might want to do this and how.

Using Update Logging to Assist a Backup Strategy

As outlined earlier, you may want to have a backup strategy that involves a combination of full and incremental backups.

Each of the incremental (daily) backups might be kept on the server's hard disk, and only the full (weekly) backups would be transferred to some other media. You would keep each day's incremental backup (rather than overwriting the one from the previous day). Then, if a full restore of the database is ever needed, the administrator would first restore from the most recent full backup, and then apply the updates from the most recent incremental backup.

Such a strategy means that incremental backups are never more than a day old and keeps storage requirements to a minimum, in addition to giving you a full off-system backup once a week.

Although you would use `mysqldump` to create your full backup, you would use another tool for creating the incremental backups. By starting the `mysqld` daemon with the `--log-update` option, you can tell MySQL to keep a log of every change to the database. This creates an update log in the form of SQL queries that can be re-run to replicate the updates that occurred.

Logs are named *hostname.n* where *n* is a number that is incremented each time a new log is started. A new log will be started whenever you issue any of the following:

- `mysqladmin refresh`
- `mysqladmin flush-logs`
- `mysqldump --flush-logs` with option
- `FLUSH LOGS`
- a server start-up or restart

19

With the update log file looking like a list of SQL statements (similar to a dump), the administrator can also selectively restore only certain updates, if need be.

Thus, the following would be the sequence of events:

1. Run the MySQL server with logging by starting it with
   `safe_mysqld --log-update &`.

2. Perform a `mysqldump` to create the full backup (weekly). Specifying the `--flush-logs` option will automatically flush logs each time you do a dump.

3. The log files will record all changes to the database and its data. At any given time, there will be one complete log file (or more) since the last full dump. For extra security, you may choose to save these off-system on a daily basis.

Other MySQL Logs

You have already seen how to make MySQL log all changes to a database, such as INSERTs, UPDATEs, and DELETEs, by running `mysqld` with the `--log-update` option. It creates a text log with each of the SQL queries within it.

You can also start `mysqld` (or `safe_mysqld`) with the `--log` option, which will cause MySQL to generate its main activity log. This records almost everything—SELECT queries as well as updates. The log will usually be stored in `/var/lib/mysql/hostname.log` where *hostname* is the name of the machine. (It may be in `/usr/local/var/` on older systems.)

The `--log` option to `mysqld` can be useful in diagnosing application bugs. If you suspect that incorrect queries are being made on the database, you can study the log to see exactly what query an application performed and when.

If you really want detailed information about what MySQL is doing, perhaps for debugging system problems at a deeper level, you can start `mysqld` with the `--debug` option. There are numerous sub-options for this debugging mode that can track MySQL's activities in detail.

To turn off logging, shut down `mysqld` and start it up again (or `safe_mysqld`) without the logging options.

Relocating a MySQL Database

There are several reasons why you may want to relocate a MySQL database. You may be upgrading your system, or you may want to transfer the database to another machine. You may even have a "master" copy of a database, held in a secure location, that you periodically want to take a copy of and have it available from a Web server or other system.

Whatever the reason, the process has basically three steps: saving, transferring, and restoring.

You already learned one method for saving your database, using mysqldump. This is the preferred method. It is possible to save a database directly from the file system by backing up the .frm, .ISD, and .ISM files. However, this will not ensure data consistency, and is not recommended.

Your database can then be *tape archived*, using a utility such as tar, and compressed, using ZIP, for speedier transfer.

When you are at the target machine, unzip and untar, and then you're ready to restore.

If you did a mysqldump --tab or something similar, you will have sets of SQL and data files. Alternatively, if you did mysqldump -opt, you will have a single large file containing both SQL CREATE commands and the data in the form of INSERT statements. To restore your database under UNIX or Linux, a command such as the following should do the job:

```
cat /home/mydata/dump.txt | /usr/local/mysql/bin/mysql
➥-u username -ppassworddatabase_name
```

The cat command combined with | (pipe) is immensely powerful. In a one-line instruction, you make cat read through the file and send it into mysql, as referenced in the example by its full pathname on the target system. You will usually need to add -u and -p parameters and the name of the target database.

MySQL System Functions   19

MySQL has a number of system functions, which provide access to administrative aspects of your database, that can be called from within your MySQL database.

The commands are quite broad in scope, ranging from database and user-related information to encoding and encryption methods.

DATABASE()

DATABASE() returns the name of the current database to which you are connected. For example, if your database is called "mydb"

INPUT   mysql> SELECT DATABASE();

would produce

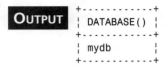

```
+------------+
| DATABASE() |
+------------+
| mydb       |
+------------+
```

USER(), SYSTEM_USER(), SESSION_USER()

These functions return the name of the current database user, including hostname. It will normally return something such as

tony@localhost

VERSION()

VERSION() returns the version of MySQL in use.

PASSWORD(*string*)

The PASSWORD(string) function will encrypt a given string and return the encrypted result, such as is stored in the password column of the MySQL Users table.

For example

```
mysql> SELECT PASSWORD("mypass");
```

would produce

```
+--------------------+
| PASSWORD("mypass") |
+--------------------+
| 6f8c114b58f2ce9e   |
+--------------------+
```

Note that PASSWORD() does not necessarily work in the same way as ENCRYPT(), which uses the UNIX crypt() function. An encrypted string created by PASSWORD() may bedifferent from the same string encrypted using ENCRYPT().

ENCRYPT(*string*[,*salt*])

ENCRYPT() will encrypt a given *string* with an optional two-character *salt* (later versions of MySQL will accept longer salt).

Encryption converts a text into a form that is unreadable by a human, thus converting private information to a form that cannot be read by others. There is no way to "decrypt" the data.

The *salt* "flavors" the encryption algorithm. If not specified, a random *salt* is used and the encrypted result is not predictable. But if specified, the *salt* will cause the result to be the same each time a given *string* is encrypted.

MySQL uses the UNIX crypt() system call, but if crypt() is not present on your system, the function will return a null result.

Have a look at how ENCRYPT behaves with *salt* omitted:

INPUT
```
mysql> SELECT ENCRYPT('something secret');
```

OUTPUT
```
+----------------------------+
| ENCRYPT('something secret') |
+----------------------------+
| rRtXXJPIhWwyc               |
+----------------------------+
```

Now you can run exactly the same thing again:

INPUT
```
mysql> SELECT ENCRYPT('something secret');
```

This time the result is different:

OUTPUT
```
+----------------------------+
| ENCRYPT('something secret') |
+----------------------------+
| tRCUBHu2/nW9g               |
+----------------------------+
```

19

By specifying the *salt*, you get a predictable result. There is no method of "decrypting," but you can check whether an encrypted string corresponds with an unencrypted string which is tested against it. For example, if you have an encrypted version of a password stored in your database but no "plain text" version, you can still establish whether a test password matches the one stored.

Using the second example, you'll use the salt—the first two characters—from the encrypted string, and once again encrypt your string (which might be the new test password):

INPUT
```
mysql> SELECT ENCRYPT('something secret','tR');
```

You have taken "tR" from the encrypted text, and the output is as follows:

```
OUTPUT
+--------------------------------------+
| ENCRYPT('something secret','tR') |
+--------------------------------------+
| tRCUBHu2/nW9g                        |
+--------------------------------------+
```

Carefully comparing the encrypted results, you see that they are the same.

ENCODE(*string*,*password*), DECODE(*encoded_string*, *password*)

The ENCODE() function encodes a given *string* with *password* as the access password and returns a binary string.

DECODE() does the opposite, taking the binary *encoded_string* and decoding it with *password*.

For example, to encode

```
INPUT    mysql> SELECT ENCODE('my string','mypass');
```

```
OUTPUT
+------------------------------+
| ENCODE('my string','mypass') |
+------------------------------+
| =,+?TSz9                     |
+------------------------------+
1 row in set (0.07 sec)
```

To decode

```
INPUT    mysql> SELECT DECODE(ENCODE('my string','mypass'),'mypass');
```

```
OUTPUT
+-----------------------------------------------+
| DECODE(ENCODE('my string','mypass'),'mypass') |
+-----------------------------------------------+
| my string                                     |
+-----------------------------------------------+
```

Decoding with the wrong password will give a spurious result, not an error. For example

```
INPUT    mysql> SELECT DECODE(ENCODE('my string','mypass'),'badpass');
```

results in

OUTPUT
```
+------------------------------------------------+
| DECODE(ENCODE('my string','mypass'),'badpass') |
+------------------------------------------------+
| aZ^                                            |
|     @}¿?                                       |
+------------------------------------------------+
```

Remember that the result of an ENCODE(), being binary, needs to be stored as a BLOB data type.

MD5(string)

MD5() returns an MD5 checksum for a given string. This is a 32-character hexadecimal number.

LAST_INSERT_ID([expr])

This function returns the last value that was inserted into an AUTO_INCREMENT column after having been generated automatically. It refers only to values handled by the current connection to the database.

Managing a Database with mysqladmin

The mysqladmin utility is used to perform a wide range of administrative operations on a MySQL database. It is usually run from a command line prompt.

When invoked, you should pass mysqladmin a number of options and commands that tell it how to run and what to do.

How to Use mysqladmin

The following is the basic syntax for mysqladmin:

```
mysqladmin [options] command1 [cmd1_opt] command2 [cmd2_opt]
```

Remember that you may need to prefix mysqladmin with the path to the mysql/bin directory where it resides.

Also, after you assign usernames and privileges to a database, you will need to use the -p and/or -u options when invoking mysqladmin if your MySQL username is different from your UNIX username. This tells MySQL that you are offering to provide it a username and password; if you do not and MySQL requires them, you will receive an error message.

19

To summarize, the following commands can be used with mysqladmin:

- create *databasename*   Creates a new database with the specified name
- drop *databasename*   Drops (deletes) the database with the specified name
- *status*   Gives a brief status message from the server
- *version*   Displays server version information
- *extended-status*   Creates an extended status message from the server
- *variables*   Displays available variables
- *processlist*   Displays a list of active threads in the server, useful to see how busy the server is
- *flush-hosts*   Flushes all cached hosts
- *flush-logs*   Flushes all logs
- *flush-tables*   Flushes all tables
- *flush-privileges*   Reloads the grant tables
- kill *id1*, *id2*   Kills mysql threads
- password *new_password*   Changes the old password to a new password
- ping   Sends a "ping" signal to mysqld to check that it is functioning
- reload   Makes mysql reload its grant tables
- refresh   Flushes all grant tables and closes and opens logfiles
- shutdown   Shuts down the MySQL server

As well as the commands, mysqladmin can be given the following options to tell it how to run the commands:

- -#, --debug=   To output to a debug log; often this is 'd:t:o,filename'.
- -f, --force   Dropping a database will give a warning, as will some other commands; --*force* will continue even if you get such a warning.
- -C, --compress   Use compression in server/client protocol.
- -h, --host=*hostname*   Connect to specified host.
- -p, --password[=*password*]   Specify password to use when connecting to server. If the password is not given, you will be prompted for one at the console.
- -P, --port[=*portnumber*]   Port number to use for connection

- -i, --sleep=*num*   Will cause mysqladmin to execute commands again and again, with a sleep between them of *num* seconds.
- -s, --silent   Will cause mysqladmin to silently exit if it can't connect to the server.
- -S, --socket=*socket*   The socket file to use for connection.
- -t, --timeout=*num*   Specifies timeout, in seconds, for connection to the mysqld server.
- -u, --user=*username*   Specify username for login if not current system user.
- -V, --version   Prints version information and exits.
- -w, --wait[=*retries*]   Waits and retries specified number of times if database connection is down.
- -?, --help   Displays commands and options and exits.

Because a number of these options are quite sophisticated, you'll look at some of them in more detail.

mysqladmin create *databasename*

If you have just installed MySQL, or if you want to create a new database, you will need to create a database, which you can you with mysqladmin create.

Look at a sample session in which I want to log on to MySQL as root and create a database for my photographs:

```
[tonyb@tigger tonyb]$ mysqladmin -u root -p create photo_db
Enter password:
Database "photo_db" created.
```

At this stage, the MySQL database is not much more than an empty directory—mysqladmin has simply created the photo_db directory on the server.

mysqladmin drop *databasename*

Should you ever want to drop (or delete) a database, the mysqladmin drop command will do just that.

Suppose that I want to get rid of the database I just created:

19

```
[tonyb@tigger tonyb]$ mysqladmin -u root -p drop photo_db
Enter password:
Dropping the database is potentially a very bad thing to do.
Any data stored in the database will be destroyed.

Do you really want to drop the 'photo_db' database [y/N]
y
Database "photo_db" dropped
```

The opposite of create, mysqladmin now deletes the directory containing the photo_db database and all its contents.

Status and Version Information

mysqladmin has a number of ways of providing status and version information about the MySQL server:

- mysqladmin status
- mysqladmin version
- mysqladmin extended-status
- mysqladmin variables

The first of these, status, provides a single-line status display on the MySQL server:

```
[tonyb@tigger tonyb]$ mysqladmin status
```

```
Uptime: 80000  Threads: 1  Questions: 168  Slow queries: 0 Opens: 30
    Flush tables: 1
    Open tables: 26
```

Examine what these status reports mean:

- *Uptime*—The number of seconds since the mysqld daemon was started.
- *Threads*—The number of threads, or clients, that are currently active. This will always be at least 1 because it includes the thread running the mysqladmin command.
- *Questions*—The number of queries that mysqld has received since it was started.
- *Slow queries*—The number of queries that have taken longer than a specified time to execute. This time is specified by *long_query_time*, which can be inspected by running mysqladmin extended-status.
- *Opens*—The number of tables that have been opened since the MySQL server was started.

- *Flush tables*—The number of `flush`, `reload`, and `refresh` commands that have been issued since the server was started.

- *Open tables*—The number of tables that are currently open.

Now look at a slightly more user-friendly option, `mysqladmin version`:

INPUT
```
[tonyb@tigger tonyb]$ mysqladmin version
```

OUTPUT
```
mysqladmin  Ver 7.11 Distrib 3.22.27, for pc-linux-gnu on i686
TCX Datakonsult AB, by Monty

Server version          3.22.27-log
Protocol version        10
Connection              Localhost via UNIX socket
UNIX socket             /var/lib/mysql/mysql.sock
Uptime:                 23 hours 54 min 19 sec

Threads: 1  Questions: 300  Slow queries: 0  Opens: 30
Flush tables: 1  Open tables: 26
```

Much of the information, in fact the last two lines, is the same as for `status`, except that Uptime is now in hours, minutes, and seconds. However, there is a useful display of other information.

It tells the version of MySQL I am running and the communications protocol version. You may need this information for debugging if you arerunning software that uses the MySQL communications protocol directly.

It tells how I am connected to MySQL—in this case, via a UNIX socket because I am logged on to the server using Telnet.

Because I am logged on in this way, I also get the UNIX socket specified. If I were connecting to MySQL via TCP/IP, you would see the TCP port number instead.

There are two more commands, `mysqladmin extended-variables` and `variables`, that provide more detailed information about current server status.

Thread Information

You can look at what MySQL is doing currently by running the `mysqladmin processlist` command, as follows:

INPUT
```
[tonyb@tigger tonyb]$ mysqladmin -u root -p processlist
Enter password:
```

19

OUTPUT

```
+----+------+-------------+----------+----------+------+-------+------+
| Id | User | Host      _ | db _____ | Command  | Time | State | Info |
+----+------+-------------+----------+----------+------+-------+------+
| 36 | dave | domain.com  | phone_db | Sleep___ | 0    |       |      |
| 37 | root | localhost _ | _____   | Processes| 0    |       |      |
+----+------+-------------+----------+----------+------+-------+------+
```

Note that a MySQL process, as shown on this process list, is different from a UNIX process. Although there may only appear to be a single MySQL process if you run ps under a UNIX shell, MySQL may be running many threads, as listed in the mysqladmin processlist command.

The list includes an Id for each thread, the User who initiated that thread, and the Host from which the user is connected. db is the name of the database to which the user is connected.

Command gives information about the type of command being executed by the thread. It may be any one of the following:

- *Sleep*—Thread is waiting for user input, as most processes will normally be.
- *Processes*—Thread is currently looking at the other threads that are running (as in the second entry, which represents the mysqladmin processlist command running).
- *Connect*—Thread is currently receiving an incoming connection from a client.
- *Init DB*—The thread is initializing the given database and preparing it for use. (Note that a thread can switch between databases.)
- *Query*—A query is currently being executed by the thread. You seldom see this because queries typically take a very short time to run.
- *Field list*—Thread is generating a list of fields in a table.
- *Create DB*—Thread is currently creating a new database.
- *Drop DB*—Thread is currently dropping a database.
- *Reload*—Thread is currently reloading MySQL access tables.
- *Refresh*—Thread is currently resetting log files and flushing caches.
- *Statistics*—Thread is currently generating statistics.
- *Kill*—Thread is currently terminating another thread.
- *Shutdown*—Thread is in the process of terminating all other live threads and is about to shut down the MySQL server.
- *Quit*—Thread is in the process of quitting.

Fixing a Corrupted Database

A suspected database corruption needn't mean disaster. MySQL has anticipated this moment of terror that comes to many a database administrator, and provided some tools for repairing damaged tables.

These tools come in the form of two utilities: isamchk and myasamchk.

Before looking at what these utilities do and how to invoke them, familiarize yourself with how MySQL stores its data.

MySQL Data Structure

First, cd into the data directory for the small database called book, and then list what's there:

INPUT

```
[root@tiger book]# ls -la
```

OUTPUT

```
total 28
drwx------   2 mysql    mysql        4096 Feb 14 13:15 .
drwxr-xr-x  11 mysql    root         4096 Feb 15 13:24 ..
-rw-rw----   1 mysql    mysql        1015 Feb 14 15:16 customers.ISD
-rw-rw----   1 mysql    mysql        2048 Feb 14 15:16 customers.ISM
-rw-rw----   1 mysql    mysql        8682 Jan 31 19:13 customers.frm
```

There's just one table in the book database, called Customers. However, Customers has three files.

The .FRM file is the format file that contains the data structure itself. Don't try to view this file, it's not a readable format.

The .ISD file holds the actual data, while the .ISM file contains information on keys and other internal cross-references. This is the file that the isamchk and myasamchk utilities are most concerned about repairing.

Try running isamchk -d to display information about the customers table:

INPUT

```
[root@tiger book]# isamchk -d customers
```

OUTPUT

```
ISAM file:      customers
Data records:                15  Deleted blocks:             5
Recordlength:               220
Record format: Packed
```

19

```
table description:
Key Start Len Index    Type
1   1     6   multip.  text
    161   2            text
    191   3            text
```

> **Note**
>
> Note that you will need to be in the correct directory, such as /var/lib/mysql/databasename/, or explicitly specify the path to the tables. Also note that you can use the * wildcard to check all the tables in a database directory.

This output tells you that the table has 15 records and 5 deleted blocks. The latter is wasted space on the hard disk.

Reclaiming Wasted Space

You can recover the wasted space shown in the previous example by running isamchk -r:

INPUT

```
[root@tiger book]# isamchk -r customers
```

OUTPUT

```
- recovering ISAM-table 'customers.ISM'
Data records: 15
- Fixing index 1
```

This command looks at the table and recreates it without using unnecessary space. In this particular example, running ls -l under Linux reveals that customers.ISD now occupies just 756 bytes compared with 1015 before isamchk -r was run.

It's a good idea to run isamchk -d on a regular basis on a growing database to keep an eye on what spare space is being left in the tables. This is especially important if your application performs a lot of DELETEs, which will most likely result in gaps among the data on your hard disk. Whenever the deleted blocks count appears to be getting high, or a significant proportion of the data records, run isamchk -r to clear out the wasted space.

> **Caution**
>
> If any clients are accessing your database via mysqld at the time you run isamchk, isamchk may be fooled into thinking the tables are corrupted when they're not. Any updates currently in progress may appear as corruptions to isamchk. Thus, carrying out an isamchk repair at this point could therefore be very harmful.

To avoid this, shut down mysqld before running isamchk. Alternatively, provided you're quite sure that nobody is accessing the tables, just run mysqladmin flush-tables before isamchk.

If you're going to do table repairs or optimization, it is essential that you shut down mysqld before letting isamchk loose. If you can't shut down mysqld for a while, at least run mysqladmin flush-tables and prevent clients from accessing the database until repairs are complete.

Repairing Damaged Tables with isamchk

The general syntax for using isamchk is as follows:

```
isamchk [options] table_name
```

While isamchk works on .ISM/.ISD table types, myisamchk does the same thing on the newer MyISAM table types with .MYI and .MYD extensions, respectively.

Options can be specified as follows:

- -a, --analyze   Analyzes the distribution of keys; useful to speed up some join operations.
- -#=debug_options, --debug=debug_options   Creates a log for debugging, often used in the form 'd:t:o,filename' to save to filename.
- -d, --description   Gets some descriptive information about the state of the table.
- -e, --extend-check   Checks a file very thoroughly. Not normally required because isamchk should find most errors without this option.
- -f, --force   Overwrites temporary files.
- -i, --information   Shows statistical information about the table.
- -k=num, --keys-used=num   Used with -r, tells isamchk to drop the first num keys before repairing.
- -l, --no-symlinks   Tells isamchk not to follow symbolic file links (it will follow them by default).
- -q, --quick   Used with -r for a faster repair. Only repairs .ISD files but not data files, unless an optional second -q is specified, in which case data files are repaired too.

19

- -r, --recover Performs recovery. This will fix most problems with the exception of unique key violations.
- -o, --safe_recover Uses the old recovery method. This is slower than -r.
- -s, --silent Prints errors only. Specify -ss for very silent.
- -v, --verbose Prints more information. Specify -vv for very verbose.
- -S, --sort-index Sorts index blocks for some speed improvement in applications doing a lot of "read next" operations.
- -R=*index*, --sort-records=*index* Sorts actual data records according to a given *index*. This may give speed improvements with some queries.
- -u, --unpack Unpacks a file packed with pack_isam.
- -V, --version Displays the version number and exits.
- -W, --wait Waits before processing if table is locked.
- -?, --help Shows full list of isamchk options.

Now you'll look at just a few of these options in a little more detail.

Quick Repairs

For a quick repair on a table or tables, use the following syntax:

```
isamchk -rq table_name
```

A sample quick repair might look like the following:

```
[root@tigger book]# isamchk -rq customers
```

```
- check delete-chain
- recovering ISAM-table 'customers.ISM'
Data records: 15
- Fixing index 1
```

This will perform a check and effect repairs if need be. It is a "quick" check because it only looks at the .ISM file, not the .ISD (data) file.

However, you can supply a second -q to force isamchk to alter its behavior and fix the data file too.

For a more extensive check on the data, use the following:

```
isamchk -e table_name
```

This checks the both `.ISM` and `.ISD` files. It takes a much closer look for any possible corruption. It will fix most problems, but it will exit if it finds a severe error.

```
isamchk -ev table_name
```

is a verbose form of the previous command and differs in that it will keep going if it finds a severe error, deleting any offending data if necessary. For this reason, it's wise to make a backup of your data before starting `isamchk` repairs. It's also a good idea to run the commands one at a time in the order shown previously, progressively burrowing into the data, to get a feel for the extent of corruption before going for an extended fix.

Fixing Problems with Keys

Although keys (or indexes) are usually intended to improve database performance, there are times when they impede performance, such as in `INSERT` or `UPDATE` operations.

If you run `isamchk` while there are corrupted keys, `isamchk` may assume that the data itself is corrupted and delete some of it.

Thus, you need to remove the keys temporarily, repair the table, and then reinstate the keys. The following command

```
isamchk -rqk=0
```

will do just this, setting keys-used to zero (removing keys) and doing a quick check and repair. For example

INPUT   `[root@tigger book]# isamchk -rqk=0 *.ISM`

OUTPUT
```
- check delete-chain
- recovering ISAM-table 'customers.ISM'
  Data records: 15
```

After this is done and you're happy with the repair job, run

```
isamchk -rq
```

to rebuild the keys.

Note

After you have run an `isamchk` repair, it may appear that your application appears not to be using the repaired tables. This is most likely to occur if you are unable to shut down the MySQL server before doing reparations. Just run `mysqladmin reload` if this happens.

19

Summary

Today, you have learned several aspects of MySQL administration:

- How to back-up your database, using `mysqldump` to create backups in a range of formats.
- How to restore your database, using `mysqlimport` to read data-only text files and the UNIX `cat` command to pipe both SQL and data directly into MySQL.
- How to make use of MySQL's various types of logs: update logs for changes to the database and full activity logs for watching MySQL at a greater level of detail. Update logs are useful for making incremental backups, while full logs may help in diagnosing application and system problems.
- How to use the system functions for accessing administrative information about your MySQL database
- How to use the `mysqladmin` utility, with its range of options for creating and dropping databases, getting server status and thread information, and for flushing logs and other administrative functions.
- What the underlying file structure looks like, how to get rid of wasted space, and how to check and recover a corrupted table.

With this knowledge in hand, you should be on the way to a properly backed-up database. You now have the ability to reach system information and to fix most problems, should they occur.

Q&A

Q **I just want to do a simple backup of my entire database. How should I do it?**

A Use the following command:

```
mysqldump --opt database_name > /path/to/mydump.sql
```

This will create a relatively compact and fast backup of the whole database with SQL statements for table CREATEs and data INSERT. It will save it as a single file called *mydump*.sql that you can store in a secure location.

Q   **How do I do a full restore from this file?**

A   At a UNIX or Linux command prompt, type the following:

```
cat /home/mydata/mydump.sql | /path/to/mysql -u username -p database_name
```

This will parse the entire file, drop the existing tables, and restore the whole file at the target machine.

Q   **What is `mysqladmin`?**

A   `mysqladmin` is a useful utility for creating or dropping a database, shutting down the server, watching client (thread) activity, and so on. It can flush logs, hosts, change access passwords, as well as perform other functions.

Exercises

1. Write the syntax for checking a table called "my_table" for deleted blocks.

2. Give the syntax for showing the current list of active threads on a MySQL server.

3. Write the function call for encrypting the string `"my string"` with the `salt` in `"ht1QbxA2IJPhU"`.

19

DAY 20

Optimizing MySQL

Now that you have your database up and running and it's been in production for a couple of weeks, everything is just beautiful. But wait, here comes an angry programmer telling you that your database is slow. He has a whole bunch of users yelling at him because the application is taking forever to run a simple query. You tell him that it is his code. He vehemently argues that it is your database and not his code that is causing the problems. You argue back saying that you are using MySQL and that there is nothing else faster. After a couple of minutes, the pain of a bruised ego fades and you both decide to sit down and look at the problem. You find that it is a combination of both problems, bad SQL statements on the programmers end and some design and performance problems on the administrator's end.

If this sounds familiar or if it may still be something on the horizon for you, this day will explain what and where to look for performance problems. MySQL is fast, very fast, but there are things that you can do to help tweak the out-of-the-box defaults. They may be design issues. They may be bad queries. This day will help you locate and solve your performance problems.

Today, you will learn

- Performance tuning
- Making better SQL statements
- Getting rid of dead space—cleaning up the database

Performance Tuning

One of the first places to look when you are having performance problems is the system itself. On what type of computer is your database server running? How much memory does it have? What is its processor speed? These are the types of question you should be asking yourself before you start using your database in production.

The ideal situation for a database server is a top-of-the-line system that has a ton of memory and is only used for the database server. This is ideal, but you don't always get what you want. MySQL is a different breed of database. It runs on almost any platform, and it performs better on some than it does on others.

MySQL was developed primarily on Intel machines running Linux. This is why Linux is probably the best platform on which to run MySQL. And because the machines are running Linux, the hardware does not need to be as high-end as it would if you were running Windows NT. This adds to the attractiveness of MySQL—a high-performance database that can run on older machines. What a deal! MySQL does not perform as well on the Windows platform as it does on other platforms. This can be attributed to many reasons—memory allocation at the operating-system level being the primary one.

MySQL is multithreaded. This means that every time a connection is made to MySQL, MySQL creates a thread. Each thread takes up memory. Caching results of queries also takes up memory. So the more memory the better. This generally helps performance.

Another area to look at for performance gains is the disk drive. A faster disk provides faster results. If you have a table that is accessed a lot, you may want to put that table on its own disk. This will speed things up immensely. Setting up a multiple-disk environment is beyond the scope of this book. The MySQL online documentation contains all the information that is needed to accomplish this task.

Setting System Variable

After you have the best hardware, the next easiest spot is to start tweaking the actual database system. There are a bunch of variables that control how MySQL operates. To check your current configuration, follow these steps:

1. Make sure you are in the `mysql` directory and that the server is currently running (the `mysqld` daemon).

2. Enter the following command:

INPUT   `bin/mysqladmin -p variables`

3. You will be prompted for the `root` password. Enter the password. You should see output similar to Table 20.1.

TABLE 20.1   MySQL System Variables

Variable Name	Value
back_log	5
connect_timeout	5
basedir	/usr/local/mysql/
datadir	/usr/local/mysql/data
delayed_insert_limit	100
delayed_insert_timeout	300
delayed_queue_size	1000
join_buffer	131072
flush_time	0
key_buffer	8388600
language	/usr/local/mysql/share/ mysql/english/
log	OFF
log_update	OFF
long_query_time	10
low_priority_updates	OFF
max_allowed_packet	1048576
max_connections	100
max_connect_errors	10
max_delayed_insert_threads	20
max_join_size	4294967295

20

TABLE 20.1 continued

Variable Name	Value
max_sort_length	1024
net_buffer_length	16384
pid_file	/usr/local/mysql/data/ CorelLinux.pid
port	3306
protocol_version	10
record_buffer	131072
skip_locking	ON
skip_networking	OFF
socket	/tmp/mysql.sock
sort_buffer	2097144
table_cache	64
thread_stack	65536
tmp_table_size	1048576
tmpdir	/tmp/
version	3.22.23b
wait_timeout	28800

To change any of these values, use the following syntax:

```
safe_mysqld -O variable = value
```

Where *variable* is one of the system variables and *value* is a logical value for that variable. Changes are not persistent. So if you end your session and start MySQL without any options, MySQL automatically uses the defaults. None of your previous changes will be present. To use your options every time, you must change your startup script to reflect your variable changes.

Most of the variables are self explanatory. The following are the most important variables for optimizing your system:

- back_log Set this to a higher value if you expect a lot of connections to occur at the same time. This option controls how many connections MySQL will hold while it is making new threads.

- delayed_queue_size This option controls the number of rows that will be queued when using an INSERT DELAYED command. Increase this if you expect a lot of inserts that will need to be queued.

- `flush_time` This option controls the amount of time, in seconds, before MySQL writes what is in cache to disk. The more I/O operations to disk, the slower a database becomes. Set this number higher to delay writing the cache to disk.
- `table_cache` This option controls the number of open tables for all threads. Increasing this size will increase the number of tables that can be open at the same time. This decreases the amount of overhead and could speed things up. However, the operating system may have limits that might affect how many files can be open at the same time.
- `wait_timeout` Controls the amount of time before a connection is closed due to inactivity. A lower number may increase speed.
- `buffers` Increasing any of the buffers will help speed up your database. Setting these buffers too high can be detrimental. These settings should be based on the amount of available memory.

> **Tip**
>
> If you have a lot of tables and a lot of memory, you can speed MySQL up by setting the buffer size equal to the amount of memory you have; for example, buffer = 32M.

`mysqld` and Its Parameters

`mysqld` is the heart of MySQL; It is the actual server program. In effect, when you think of MySQL, this is what it is. The database server can be started with some options that may help with optimization. The following is a list of some of the more important parameters that `mysqld` can take:

- `-b or -basedir=full path` This parameter points the MySQL server to the `mysql` installation directory. This tells the server where everything is located.
- `--big-tables` When MySQL is started with this option, it will allow large resultsets. This will eliminate table-full errors.
- `-h or -datadir=full path` This option points the MySQL server to the data directory. Set this option if you have moved your data do another place.
- `--enable-locking` This argument allows system locking. MySQL no longer defaults to system locking.
- `-l -log=[filename]]` Causes MySQL to log system messages to this file. If no file name is given, messages are written to `mysql-log-file`.

20

- `--log-update=filename`   Causes MySQL to log all transactions that affect the database. This is a great tool for creating backups of your database. This option has been covered in detail in Day 19, "Administrating MySQL."

- `--log-long-format=filename`   This feature causes MySQL to log more information than the `-update` option. Again, refer to Day 19 for more details.

- `--low-priority-insert`   This option causes MySQL to execute SELECT statements before INSERT statements.

- `--skip-grant-tables`   A handy feature for when you forget the root password. This option skips the grant tables when starting up, so all passwords and user-defined functions will not be enforced.

- `--skip-name-resolve`   This option may speed things up a little bit. It causes MySQL to use IP addresses instead of resolving the IP to a name.

- `-V` or `-version`   This outputs the version information of your current MySQL installation.

One way to speed up MySQL is to turn off logging, but this is not recommended. If your database were to crash, there would be no way to get the data back. However, turning off logging does improve performance. You just have to weigh the benefits.

Another minor performance improvement would be to use the `-skip-name-resolve` option. This saves a little bit of time and should have no adverse effects on your database operation.

Building a Better SQL Statement

The next place to look is at your database design and the SQL statements you are using to access your data. A whole book could be written on the best techniques to do these things, but that is beyond the scope of this book. This book will cover some of the basic steps you can take to help make your database faster.

The structure of your database plays a huge role in the overall performance of your database. If your tables are not constructed properly, bad things tend to happen. The following are some general guidelines for faster tables:

- *Use the smallest data type possible*—The smaller the data type the less disk space and memory it uses. The less memory, the quicker it can be retrieved and used. Keep things small.

- *Force values into columns by using* NOTNULL—*This saves a little space and speeds things up.*

- *Try to avoid using variable length columns*—If you have to, you have to. But if you can get away without using variable length columns, do it. This can vastly improve performance.

- *Avoid using too many indexes*—Indexes speed up SELECT statements but slow down INSERT and UPDATE statements. If you have too many indexes, it will slow down everything. Review Day 6, "Adding Tables, Columns, and Indexes to Your Database," for more information on indexes.

- *Choose your table type(s) with an eye to performance*—There are four table types in MySQL (non-paying members only have three). They are static (default), dynamic, heap, and compressed. The static table is created by default. It is the fastest of all normal tables. It can only contain non-variable length columns. If it has even one variable-length column, MySQL automatically changes it to a dynamic table. These tables are slower—they contain more information in them (each row has to contain information stating how big they are). The heap table is super fast for small- to medium-sized tables because it exists in memory only. This type of table is great for joins and the like. The compressed table is read-only. It takes up less disk space and is very fast. Again this is only available for paying MySQL customers with extended email support.

- *Use defaults in columns*—This decreases parsing time on INSERT statements and increases performance.

The next place to look for performance problems are the SQL statements that are used to manipulate the data in your database. The following are some general guidelines to follow to help improve overall performance:

- Write your queries so they make use of indexes whenever possible. This is what indexes are for, and they can greatly increase your database's performance.

- Use the LIMIT keyword in your queries. This can sometimes force MySQL to use an index when it normally would not.

- Do not use any extraneous punctuation whenever possible, such as extra parenthesis. MySQL will have to parse extraneous punctuation marks out before it can perform the query. If they aren't there to begin with, MySQL can execute the query much faster.

20

- Security is directly proportional to the amount of overhead that is created when executing queries. The more security that is used, the more overhead that is created. Do not sacrifice security for the sake of performance. Use security wisely and appropriately. Some suggestions would be to create a single user for a high-traffic database. Control security through the application and not at the server level. For example, you could create a table that stores usernames and passwords. Have the application check this table to see if a user has the necessary permissions to access the database. If the user passes this test, use the user in the grant table for the rest of the access to the database.
- Counting all rows in a database using SELECTCOUNT(*), is very fast—it uses the number contained in the table's header.

These are just some general tips to make a quicker query. The best gains are from the statements themselves.

Building a Better WHERE Clause

The best way to start building your WHERE clause is to look at the available indexes you have for the tables you are going to query. If a table has an index, use it; this will speed things up considerably. If you can not rewrite the WHERE clause, create an index.

Remember that conditional statements execute faster with numerical values than they do with string or character values. Compare numbers whenever possible.

The LIKE statement can slow things down as well. You may use an index with a LIKE comparison if the constant that is being compared does not have a wildcard character in the first position. For example, the following statement will use the index if the Last_Name column has one:

```
SELECT State FROM Customers WHERE Last_Name LIKE "Rober%"
```

However, an index will not be used for the following statement:

```
SELECT State FROM Customers WHERE Last_Name LIKE "%obert%"
```

Getting Rid of Dead Space

When a record is deleted from a file, or a column that contains variable length fields changes, a dead spot is created in the file that stores this data. See Figure 20.1.

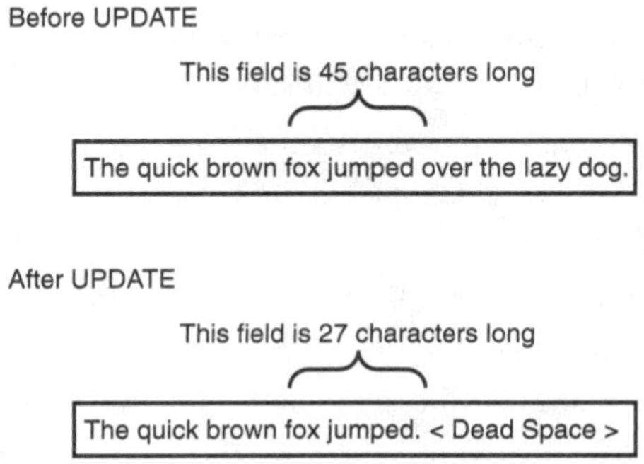

FIGURE 20.1

*A variable-length col-
umn before and after an*
UPDATE.

Before UPDATE

This field is 45 characters long

| The quick brown fox jumped over the lazy dog. |

After UPDATE

This field is 27 characters long

| The quick brown fox jumped. < Dead Space > |

This dead space can accumulate, taking up disk space and slowing things down. There is no way to avoid this completely. (Not using variable length fields helps).

Another problem that can affect database performance is the key order. Suppose you have an index on a unique AUTO_INCREMENT column. You have done many inserts and a few deletes, and the numbers may have fallen out of order. This can affect your index's performance—think what it would be like to find someone's file if the files were no longer in alphabetical order.

Fortunately, the developers at MySQL saw these potential problems and have provided a tool to fix them. This little tool is called myisamchk. It resides in the bin directory of a normal mysql installation directory.

The myisamchk tool can be used to help optimize tables and keys, much like the OPTIMIZE command, only quicker. This utility can also help repair damaged tables as well. The command is as follows:

INPUT   `myisamchk options table_name`

Where `table_name` is the name of a table or a group of tables designated by a wildcard. To perform this check on all your tables in the data directory, you could issue the following command:

```
bin/myisamchk /usr/local/mysql/data/*/*.myi
```

This will check all data files in the data directory. The myisamchk utility can take the following options:

- -a or -analyze   Analyzes the paths from tables to see how it can make joins faster.

20

- -d or -description   Outputs some information about the table, such as the record length, record format, number of records, deleted blocks, and key information.
- -f or -force   Automatically overwrites any temporary files.
- -i or -information   Provides detailed information about the table. Information that is provided includes record length, the space used, and the lost space. Some nice detailed information to see if you need to run the repair part of this utility.
- -q or -quick   Causes the utility to make a faster repair. The original file is not touched. To use the original file, add another -q (myisamchk -qq).
- -r or -recover   This makes the utility repair any damaged files. It will also clean up files and reclaim lost space.
- -o or -safe-recovery   This is the slower version of -r, and can sometimes repair things that -r cannot.
- -S or -sort-index   This option causes myisamchk to sort the index from high to low. This will result in faster queries when an index is used.
- -u or -unpack   Will uncompress a file that was compressed with myisampack.
- -v   This will give a more detailed explanation (verbose).
- -w   Causes the utility to wait until the table is unlocked before it performs any repair or sorting operations.

You can also set the memory that can be allocated for these tasks. The more memory, the quicker the task can be accomplished.

Maintaining your database tables is a must for good performance. A routine should be established so that your tables are in good order. A shell script in a cron job will do for UNIX based systems or a batch job or Perl script that is scheduled for a Windows platform. Most problems can be caught before they grow to the point where they would affect production.

To free up space and check your table for errors enter the following command:

INPUT   `>bin/myisamchk -r /usr/local/mysql/data/*/*.myi`

This will clear up the dead space and check and fix your table. If you want to reorder your indexes on a table, perform the following command:

INPUT   `>bin.myisamchk -S /usr/local/mysql/data/*/*.myi`

All your indexes will be reindexed. This can take some time, so you may want to raise the memory that would be used for this operation. You can do this by closing any other applications that are running and using the -o switch on the myisamchk utility.

The myisamchk utility can be used to help speed up your database. By clearing dead space, it allows for smaller records, which is the main focus of performance. Smaller is better.

Compiling and Compression

If everything you have done so far does not work, it is time to take more drastic measures. The first measure you may want to consider is recompiling the source for your platform using a different compiler. The RPM versions of MySQL are compiled using the fastest compiler with all the optimizations turned on. You may want to move to a different platform, such as a Sun system, to gain some more performance power and the use of more processors. You can also increase the speed of your executable by using a compiler that creates faster executables for that system. Some people have claimed that this alone increases their database's performance by 20-30%.

If you do not want to compile MySQL, the next option is to buy the email support so you can get the myisampack utility. When used on tables that are read-only, a significant improvement of performance is realized. This may make the difference.

Summary

Optimization is a black art. It takes a lot of practice and experience to know what works. And even then, it can be a trial-and-error ordeal. The points that were made today, as well as the guidelines that were provided, should give you a starting point to begin your quest for peak performance.

The following is a brief overview of the steps that can be taken to optimize your database:

20

1. Look at the hardware that is going to run your database server. Is it good enough to handle the volume of traffic that is going to be produced?

2. Look at the operating system. Some are better than others. Sun's OS, as well as Linux, is great for multiple processors. On the other hand, NT is easier to use. Weigh the pros and cons, and decide which is the best platform.

3. Look at your table design. Is it solid? Is it in third normal form? Are the column types the smallest they can be? Are there any variable length columns, if so, do you need them?

4. Look at the queries that are accessing your database. Are they using indexes? Are the WHERE clauses succinct?

5. Are your tables being maintained. When was the last time myisamchk was used? Do you have a cron job automatically checking your tables?

6. If everything else fails, look at compiling the source with a better compiler. This may help. Also look at purchasing the myisampack tool—this could also help increase performance.

There are many ways to increase performance. Unfortunately, it may take some time before you finally figure out what does the trick. Hopefully, this day has provided you with some insights into the black art of database optimization.

Q&A

Q   **How can I set up a cron job to automatically maintain my tables?**

A   Normally, to use a cron job, an entry must be made in the crontab file. This file tells the cron job what to do. The following entry should appear in a crontab file to check and repair your database tables every week:

```
45 0 * * 0 /usr/local/mysql/bin/myisamchk -r /usr/local/mysql/data/*/*.myi
```

Consult your operating systems documentation to see exactly what is required for a crontab entry.

Q   **What does the OPTIMIZE statement do?**

A   The OPTIMIZE statement is a lot like the myisamchk utility, but it is slower and does not have as much functionality as the myisamchk utility. However, it can be performed using an ODBC interface or any other interface for that matter because MySQL uses it the same way as an SQL statement. The syntax for the OPTIMIZE statement is as follows:

```
OPTIMIZE table_name
```

Where table_name is the name of the table you want to optimize. Optimizing reclaims dead space. It does not repair damaged tables.

Exercises

1. Perform the recovery option of the `myisamchk` utility on all of the `Meet-A-Geek` tables.

2. Gather the specifications for a server to use for the `Meet_A_Geek` database, knowing that this database will be accessed around 10,000 times a day via the Internet. Keep in mind that MySQL runs best on UNIX-based systems.

20

DAY 21

Putting It All Together

You have learned a lot in these past three weeks. Today, you are going to review the steps you took to arrive at your current location. Every application or project can be broken down into a series of steps that need to be performed to accomplish the task at hand. That task could be creating a new database application to a Web site. The series of steps that need to be taken to help ensure success are

1. Problem definition
2. Requirements analysis
3. Structure/Architecture design
4. Building/Coding
5. Testing
6. Implementation

This lesson is going to take each step of the creation process and apply it to the Meet_A_Geek database. Hopefully, you will see how everything comes together by day's end.

Creating the Meet_A_Geek Database

Before you begin any project, it is a good idea to spend some time defining the project and gathering all the requirements before you dive right in and begin coding the application. To understand what needs to be done in a project, you must first define the project. You can define a project by asking some simple questions, such as: What is this system going to accomplish? What system are you going to be replacing? A well-defined project is the first step towards a successful project. If the project is never defined, how do you know if you have succeeded or failed? For the Meet-A-Geek project, the definition is pretty simple: Create a Web site where customers can place ads and respond to ads over the Internet quickly and easily. When the customer responds to ads placed by other members, he or she is given an option to send a gift from your Web-based store front.

It is during this first step of the process where you determine what you will be doing and what tasks need to be accomplished. This step should also define the success and failure of the project. If you are the project leader, this is your responsibility. After you have acquired this knowledge, you are ready to start working on the second step, which is gathering the requirements.

In the second step of the creation process, you begin gathering the requirements of the project. You will talk to the people who will be using the system to find out what this application needs to do. You need to find out what information they need to track and store, what rules must be applied to the data to see if it acceptable or not, and what kinds of reports need to be generated. It is in this phase when you will define the business process, business rules, and business objects. This is the first step in the database design process that you learned about on Day 3, "Designing Your First Database." It is in this phase of the creation process when you should start looking for potential business objects that will become tables in the database.

Requirements Phase

The requirements phase requires that you interview the various levels of management to gain a full understanding of what needs to be done and what the application must accomplish to meet the goals of the business. From here, you should start to get an idea of what you need to capture, what kind of equipment you are going to need, what platform you will be using, and what the database is going to look like.

From this part of the process, you discovered the following about the Meet-A-Geek project:

1. A potential customer can either respond to an ad or create an ad themselves.
2. Customers are required to be members before they can respond to ads.
3. After searching the database for potential dates, customers can send emails as well as gifts as a response to the ad.
4. All transactions must be tracked.
5. Members must log in before they can perform a search.
6. The products available as gifts must be maintained in the same database.

Design Phase

Now that the requirements have been gathered, you can start the architecture and design phase. This is the most important phase of the process. It is here that the foundation is created for the entire project. It is also in this phase when the database for the Meet-A-Geek project will be designed and a flow chart for the Web site will be created.

Based on the requirements that were gathered, the layout seen in Figure 21.1 was determined for the Web site.

Notice how the flow of the Web site helps influence the business rules that were gathered in the requirements phase. Specifically, the rule that states a user cannot post or search an ad unless he or she is a member. This rule is enforced by the site's design.

Database Design

Now that the basic flow of the site is designed, you can focus on the database. Remember that a database is the engine that runs the application. If the database is not designed well, it will not perform well. A poorly designed database is not flexible and cannot change with the business. Time spent here is time well spent.

From the requirements gathering stage, you determined the following business objects:

1. Customers
2. Ads
3. Orders
4. Products

21

Figure 21.1

The Meet-A-Geek Web site flowchart.

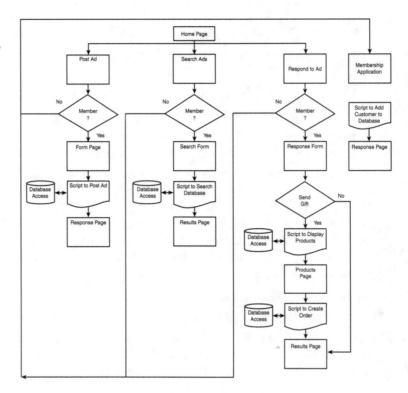

In this stage of the process, you will describe the business objects. This will help you determine the columns that will make up the database. You read about this process in detail on Day 3. By asking questions about the object's characteristics, you determined the descriptions of the business objects (see Tables 21.1 – 21.4). Also, it is a good idea to establish the data type of this characteristic at this point. It helps save time later. Remember that the column type can help enforce business rules as well.

TABLE 21.1 The Customers Table

Characteristic	Data Type
First_Name	VARCHAR(15), Not NULL
Last_Name	VARCHAR (20), Not NULL
Middle_Initial	CHAR(1)
Address	VARCHAR (50), Not NULL

TABLE 21.1 continued

Characteristic	Data Type
City	VARCHAR (30), Not NULL
State	CHAR(2), Not NULL
Zip	VARCHAR (15), Not NULL
Email	VARCHAR (30), Not NULL
Age	INTEGER
Gender	Male, Female, Unk
Race	VARCHAR(10)
Eye_Color	VARCHAR(15)
Hair_Color	VARCHAR(15)
Fav_Activity	VARCHAR(30)
Fav_Movie	VARCHAR(30)
Occupation	VARCHAR(50)
Smoker	Yes, No, Unk

TABLE 21.2 The Ads Table

Characteristic	Data Type
Ad_Text	TEXT, Not NULL
Date_Posted	DATETIME, Not NULL

TABLE 21.3 The Products Table

Characteristic	Data Type
Name	VARCHAR(30), Not NULL
Description	VARCHAR(255), Not NULL
Price	FLOAT(10,2), Not NULL
Manufacturer	VARCHAR(50), Not NULL
Picture	VARCHAR(50), Not NULL

21

TABLE 21.4   The `Orders` Table

Characteristic	Data Type
Order_Date	DATETIME, Not NULL
Quantity	INTEGER, Not NULL
Product	VARCHAR(30), Not NULL
Customer	VARCHAR(30), Not NULL
Amount_Due	FLOAT(10,2), NOT NULL
Payment_Received	Yes or No

Now that the objects are described and the business rules have been established, it's time to turn your objects into tables by adding a key to each table and performing some normalization.

Normalizing the Database

You decide to create a unique key in the `Customers` table and name it `Customer_ID`. A person can only have one membership, so the key must be unique. You add unique keys to all the tables and name them after the table they identify—`Ad_ID`, `Order_ID`, and `Product_ID`.

The next thing you normally would do is perform some normalization on the tables. Because these tables are pretty normalized, you'll leave them alone. The only changes you'll make is to change the `Products` and `Customer` columns in the `Orders` table to `Customer_ID` and `Product_ID`.

Note

> For the sake of simplicity, these tables are not truly normalized. They could be broken down further, that is, a `Manufacturers` table and probably an `OrderMasters` and `OrderDetails` table as well.

After that process is finished, the next step is to define the relationships that exist between the tables. You can establish a one-to-many relationship between the `Customers` table and the `Ads` table right away. Add a `Customer_ID` column to the `Ads` table. There is also a one-to-many relationship between the `Customers` and `Orders` tables and the `Products` and `Orders` tables. Because you already have those columns in the `Orders` table, you don't need to add them.

Well, it looks like you have ironed out all the wrinkles, so now you can create a model of the database. To do this, you use a modeling tool. Figure 21.2 shows a Microsoft Access representation of the database and the relationships.

FIGURE 21.2

The Meet_A_Geek *database model.*

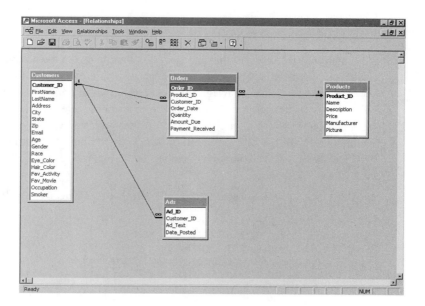

If you are working in a team environment, it's always a good idea to have the team look at your model. Sometimes someone else can spot something you may have missed. Share your design, let other people critique your work. It can only make your design better. After you are happy with your design, it is time to create the database.

Building the Database

To create your database, you need to have the mysqld daemon up and running, and you also need to have the CREATE privilege. If these two things are good to go, you can create your database in one of two ways. You can do this by using the mysqladmin command or the SQL CREATE DATABASE statement. It's your choice.

21

To create a database with the `mysqladmin` command, type the following from the command line:

```
%> bin/mysqladmin -p CREATE DATABASE Meet_A_Geek
```

To create the database in the MySQL monitor using an SQL statement, use the following command:

```
mysql> CREATE DATABASE Meet_A_Geek;
```

Now that you have created the database, it is time to create the columns. There are several ways you can do this. The recommended way is to create a text file containing the DDL statements and run them through the `mysql` program in batch. That way, you will always have a copy of the schema, just in case your database ever crashes and you need to start from scratch. If you do not choose to do it this way, you can type the SQL statements interactively with the MySQL monitor. You learned about this on Day 4, "Creating Your First Database." To refresh your memory, the command to create the `Orders` table would look like the following:

```
CREATE TABLE Orders (Order_ID INT NOT NULL AUTO_INCREMENT PRIMARY KEY,
            Customer_ID INT NOT NULL,
            Product_ID INT NOT NULL,
            Order_Date DATETIME NOT NULL,
            Quantity INT, NOT NULL,
            Amount_Due FLOAT(10,2) NOT NULL
            Payment_Received ENUM(''Y'',''N''));
```

As was explained earlier, you could put all these statements in a file and issue them in batch. This allows you to create a copy of your schema to use in case of a system failure or if you wanted to duplicate your work on another machine.

Remember that you can also create indexes at this time. Remember that an index can help boost your database's performance during `SELECT` statements. Take a look at the tables you have and choose some possible candidates to receive an index. MySQL automatically indexes the primary key in each table. So the table that would probably need the index—the `Ads` table—already has one. The `Ads` table is a good choice because people will be searching this table quite frequently. You could place an index on the `TEXT` field to improve performance if you needed to. For now, you'll wait and see how your database performs.

Import Existing Data

Now that the schema is in place, you can begin populating your database. Your client may have data in an Access or other type of database that he or she may want to port over into the new database. Populating databases was extensively discussed on Day 8, "Populating the Database." Today, you'll briefly go over importing data.

If you are currently using Access as your database and are making the move to MySQL, you are in luck. Because MySQL is ODBC-compliant, you may be able to move your data quite easily if you have the same exact structure in the MySQL database. You simply use the Export menu choice from the main toolbar. It will walk you through exporting the data.

Another way to import data from an existing database is to use the Perl DBI. Write a simple script that simply SELECTs all the data from one database and INSERTs it into the other.

One other way to bring data into your new database is with the LOAD DATA INFILE command. This command is available through the MySQL monitor and allows you to bring formatted data in a file into your database. To bring data from a comma-delimited text file, you would issue the following command:

```
LOAD DATA INFILE ''/home/olddata.txt''
INTO TABLE Customers IGNORE
FIELDS
TERMINATED BY '',''; 
```

This command would import the file named olddata.txt that resides in the home directory of the MySQL server computer. It would load the data into the Customers table, ignoring any duplicate data. The last part of the command describes how the file is delimited.

Sometimes you may need to massage the data to fit into your new schema. This can be done with a custom script or one of the tools available on the CD-ROM. Remember that MySQL stores dates differently than most database. Take care when importing date information.

Implementing Security

Before you can begin designing scripts that can access the database, you need to take a look at security. How are you going to handle access to the database? To keep things simple, you will use MySQL's grant tables to handle all your database access.

21

The New Customer script will access the database using a user_id that has only INSERT privileges on the Customers table. After a customer has been added to the database, he or she will get a username and password that will allow him or her to search the database, create ads, and edit his or her existing record. The username will be his or her full name separated by an underscore, and his or her password will be his or her email address. All our customers will have INSERT privileges on the Ads table, UPDATE privileges for some of the columns in the Customers table, and SELECT privileges on all of the tables. They will also have INSERT privileges on the Orders table so they can send gifts. Table 21.5 shows a summary of the privileges.

TABLE 21.5 Summary of the Meet_A_Geek User Privileges

User	Table	Privilege
New Customer	Customers	INSERT Only
All Customers	Customers	UPDATE, SELECT
	Orders	INSERT
	Ads	INSERT, UPDATE, DELETE
Staff	All tables	FULL

Create the Web Pages and Scripts

You have now entered the fourth phase of the creation process—the actual building of the database. This is the longest phase of the process but also the most rewarding. You get to actually build what you have designed. By looking at the flow chart, it can be determined that there are five scripts that need to be written that access the database for one reason or another. When creating a Web site like this, you normally would pick one kind of technology and stick with it. For example, you wouldn't decide to use Perl CGI scripts for some things and Active Server Pages for others. The technologies overlap each other. It just wouldn't make sense. Perl Scripts are chosen using the DBI to demonstrate how easy it is to use with MySQL.

Building the Web Page

The first step is to create a Web page that will send the data you need to your Perl Script. You will then create the script that adds a new customer to the database. You'll be using a Perl Script to accomplish this task. Other members of your team are responsible for that part of the project. They have been hard at work and have come up with the Web page shown in Figure 21.3.

FIGURE 21.3

The Meet-A-Geek New Customer Application form.

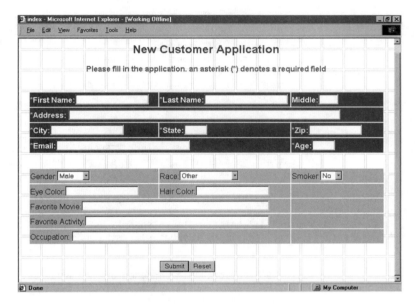

Listing 21.1 shows the code behind the NewCustomer.html Web page.

LISTING 21.1 Adding New Customers to the Database

```html
<html>

<head>
<meta http-equiv="Content-Type" content="text/html;
charset=windows-1252">
<meta http-equiv="Content-Language" content="en-us">
<title>Home Page</title>
<meta name="GENERATOR" content="Microsoft FrontPage 4.0">
<meta name="ProgId" content="FrontPage.Editor.Document">
<meta name="Microsoft Theme" content="blank 011, default">
</head>

<body background="_themes/blank/blbkgnd.gif"
bgcolor="#FFFFFF" text="#000000" link="#999999"
vlink="#990000" alink="#666666"><!--mstheme-->
<font face="Arial, Arial, Helvetica">
<div align="center">
  <center>
  <!--mstheme--></font><table border="0" width="741" height="31">
    <tr>
      <td width="741" height="51" colspan="3"><!--mstheme-->
```

21

LISTING 21.1 continued

```
<font face="Arial, Arial, Helvetica">
        <p align="center"><b><font color="#990033"
size="5">New Customer
        Application</font></b><!--mstheme--></font></td>
    </tr>
    <tr>
        <td width="741" height="31" colspan="3"><!--mstheme-->
<font face="Arial, Arial, Helvetica">
        <p align="center"><b><font color="#666666">Please fill in the
        application. an asterisk (*) denotes a required field</font>
</b><!--mstheme--></font></td>
    </tr>
<form action="../cgi-bin/AddCustomer.pl" method = POST>
    <tr>
        <td width="741" height="31" colspan="3"><!--mstheme-->
<font face="Arial, Arial, Helvetica"><!--mstheme--></font></td>
    </tr>
    <tr>
        <td width="262" height="31" bordercolor="#990033"
bgcolor="#990033">
<!--mstheme--><font face="Arial, Arial, Helvetica">
<font color="#FFFFFF"><b>*First
        Name:</b><input type="text" name="FirstName" size="20"></font>
<!--mstheme--></font></td>
        <td width="268" height="31" bordercolor="#990033" bgcolor="#990033">
<!--mstheme--><font face="Arial, Arial, Helvetica"><font color="#FFFFFF">
<b>*Last
        Name:</b>
<input type="text" name="LastName" size="23"></font>
<!--mstheme--></font></td>
        <td width="188" height="31" bordercolor="#990033"
bgcolor="#990033"><!--mstheme-->
<font face="Arial, Arial, Helvetica"><font color="#FFFFFF">
<b>Middle:</b><input type="text" name="Middle" size="4"></font>
<!--mstheme--></font></td>
    </tr>
    <tr>
        <td width="741" height="31" colspan="3" bordercolor="#990033"
 bgcolor="#990033"><!--mstheme--><font face="Arial, Arial, Helvetica">
<font color="#FFFFFF"><b>*Address:
        </b><input type="text" name="Address" size="79"></font>
<!--mstheme--></font></td>
    </tr>
    <tr>
        <td width="264" height="31" bordercolor="#990033" bgcolor="#990033">
<!--mstheme--><font face="Arial, Arial, Helvetica"><font color="#FFFFFF">
```

LISTING 21.1   continued

```
<b>*City:</b><input type="text" name="City" size="20"></font>
<!--mstheme--></font></td>
      <td width="267" height="31" bordercolor="#990033"
bgcolor="#990033"><!--mstheme--><font face="Arial, Arial, Helvetica">
<font color="#FFFFFF"><b>*State:</b>
<input type="text" name="State" size="5"></font><!--mstheme--></font></td>
      <td width="187" height="31" bordercolor="#990033"
bgcolor="#990033"><!--mstheme--><font face="Arial, Arial, Helvetica">
<font color="#FFFFFF"><b>*Zip:</b>
<input type="text" name="Zip" size="14"></font>
<!--mstheme--></font></td>
    </tr>
    <tr>
      <td width="538" height="31" colspan="2"
bordercolor="#990033" bgcolor="#990033"><!--mstheme-->
<font face="Arial, Arial, Helvetica"><font color="#FFFFFF">
<b>*Email:</b>
<input type="text" name="Email" size="38"></font>
<!--mstheme--></font></td>
      <td width="187" height="31" bordercolor="#990033"
bgcolor="#990033"><!--mstheme--><font face="Arial, Arial, Helvetica">
<font color="#FFFFFF"><b>*Age:</b>
<input type="text" name="Age" size="5"></font><!--mstheme--></font></td>
    </tr>
    <tr>
      <td width="725" height="31" colspan="3"><!--mstheme-->
<font face="Arial, Arial, Helvetica"><!--mstheme--></font></td>
    </tr>
    <tr>
      <td width="265" height="31" bgcolor="#C0C0C0">
<!--mstheme--><font face="Arial, Arial, Helvetica">Gender:
<select size="1" name="Gender">
        <option value="Male" selected>Male</option>
        <option value="Female">Female</option>
      </select><!--mstheme--></font></td>
      <td width="267" height="31" bgcolor="#C0C0C0">
<!--mstheme--><font face="Arial, Arial, Helvetica">Race:
<select size="1" name="Race">
        <option value="Caucasian">Caucasian</option>
        <option value="African American">African American</option>
        <option value="American Indian">American Indian</option>
        <option value="Hispanic">Hispanic</option>
        <option value="Asian">Asian</option>
        <option value="Other" selected>Other</option>
      </select><!--mstheme--></font></td>
      <td width="187" height="31" bgcolor="#C0C0C0">
<!--mstheme--><font face="Arial, Arial,  Helvetica">Smoker:
```

21

LISTING 21.1 continued

```html
<select size="1" name="Smoker">
        <option value="Yes">Yes</option>
        <option value="No" selected>No</option>
      </select><!--mstheme--></font></td>
   </tr>
   <tr>
      <td width="265" height="31" bgcolor="#C0C0C0">
<!--mstheme--><font face="Arial, Arial, Helvetica">Eye Color:
<font color="#FFFFFF">
<input type="text" name="EyeColor" size="20"></font>
<!--mstheme--></font></td>
      <td width="267" height="31" bgcolor="#C0C0C0">
<!--mstheme--><font face="Arial, Arial, Helvetica">Hair Color:
<font color="#FFFFFF">
<input type="text" name="HairColor" size="20"></font>
<!--mstheme--></font></td>
      <td width="187" height="31" bgcolor="#C0C0C0">
<!--mstheme--><font face="Arial, Arial, Helvetica"> 
<!--mstheme--></font></td>
   </tr>
   <tr>
      <td width="532" height="31" colspan="2" bgcolor="#C0C0C0">
<!--mstheme--><font face="Arial, Arial, Helvetica">Favorite Movie:
<font color="#FFFFFF">
<input type="text" name="FavMovie" size="54"></font>
<!--mstheme--></font></td>
      <td width="187" height="31" bgcolor="#C0C0C0">
<!--mstheme--><font face="Arial, Arial, Helvetica"> 
<!--mstheme--></font></td>
   </tr>
   <tr>
      <td width="532" height="31" colspan="2" bgcolor="#C0C0C0">
<!--mstheme--><font face="Arial, Arial, Helvetica">Favorite
        Activity:<font color="#FFFFFF">
<input type="text" name="FavActivity" size="53"></font>
<!--mstheme--></font></td>
      <td width="187" height="31" bgcolor="#C0C0C0">
<!--mstheme--><font face="Arial, Arial, Helvetica"> 
<!--mstheme--></font></td>
   </tr>
   <tr>
      <td width="532" height="31" colspan="2" bgcolor="#C0C0C0">
<!--mstheme--><font face="Arial, Arial, Helvetica">Occupation:
<font color="#FFFFFF">
<input type="text" name="Occupation" size="30"></font>
<!--mstheme--></font></td>
      <td width="187" height="31" bgcolor="#C0C0C0">
```

LISTING 21.1   continued

```
<!--mstheme--><font face="Arial, Arial, Helvetica"> 
<!--mstheme--></font></td>
    </tr>
    <tr>
      <td width="532" height="31" colspan="2">
<!--mstheme--><font face="Arial, Arial,  Helvetica">
<!--mstheme--></font></td>
      <td width="187" height="31">
<!--mstheme--><font face="Arial, Arial, Helvetica">
<!--mstheme--></font></td>
    </tr>
    <tr>
      <td width="265" height="31">
<!--mstheme--><font face="Arial, Arial, Helvetica">
<!--mstheme--></font></td>
      <td width="267" height="31">
<!--mstheme--><font face="Arial, Arial, Helvetica">
<input type="submit" value="Submit" name="cmdSubmit">
<input type="reset" value="Reset" name="cmdReset">
<!--mstheme--></font></td>
      <td width="187" height="31">
<!--mstheme--><font face="Arial, Arial, Helvetica">
<!--mstheme--></font></td>
    </tr>
</form>
  </table><!--mstheme--><font face="Arial, Arial,  Helvetica">
  </center>
</div>
<!--mstheme--></font></body>

</html>
```

After you receive this page, the first thing to notice is the names of the `<input>` fields. These are the names you will need to access the values that are passed from this page to your CGI script and then added to the database. Another thing to look at is the `<form>` tag. Make sure that it is pointing to the right script and that the method property is set to POST.

Creating the Script

Now it is time to create the Perl Script. Because this is a production application, you want to make sure that the data you are putting into your database is correct. Therefore, you will validate the data in your script. This could also be accomplished on the client side with JavaScript but, because you are doing a script, you'll see how you can check your data there.

21

Listing 21.2 shows the `AddCustomer.pl` script.

LISTING 21.2   Script for Adding Customers

```perl
#!/usr/local/bin/perl


use DBI;

&GetFormInput;

# The intermediate variables below make your
#script more readable
#but somewhat less efficient
#since they are not really necessary.

$FirstName = $field{'FirstName'} ;
$LastName = $field{'LastName'} ;
$Middle = $field{'Middle'} ;
$Address = $field{'Address'} ;
$City = $field{'City'} ;
$State = $field{'State'} ;
$Zip = $field{'Zip'} ;
$Email = $field{'Email'} ;
$Age = $field{'Age'} ;
$Gender = $field{'Gender'} ;
$Race = $field{'Race'} ;
$Smoker = $field{'Smoker'} ;
$EyeColor = $field{'EyeColor'} ;
$HairColor = $field{'HairColor'} ;
$FavMovie = $field{'FavMovie'} ;
$FavActivity = $field{'FavActivity'} ;
$Occupation = $field{'Occupation'} ;


$message = "" ;
$found_err = "" ;

## Checks the values for errors

$errmsg = "<p>Field 'First Name' must be filled in.</p>\n" ;

if ($FirstName eq "") {
    $message = $message.$errmsg ;
    $found_err = 1 ; }


$errmsg = "<p>Field 'Last Name' must be filled in.</p>\n" ;

if ($LastName eq "") {
```

LISTING 21.2 continued

```
    $message = $message.$errmsg ;
    $found_err = 1 ; }


$errmsg = "<p>Field 'Address' must be filled in.</p>\n" ;

if ($Address eq "") {
    $message = $message.$errmsg ;
    $found_err = 1 ; }


$errmsg = "<p>Field 'City' must be filled in.</p>\n" ;

if ($City eq "") {
    $message = $message.$errmsg ;
    $found_err = 1 ; }


$errmsg = "<p>Field 'State' must be filled in.</p>\n" ;

if ($State eq "") {
    $message = $message.$errmsg ;
    $found_err = 1 ; }


$errmsg = "<p>Field 'Zip' must be filled in.</p>\n" ;

if ($Zip eq "") {
    $message = $message.$errmsg ;
    $found_err = 1 ; }


$errmsg = "<p>Please enter a valid email address</p>\n" ;

if ($Email !~ /.+\@.+\..+/) {
    $message = $message.$errmsg ;
    $found_err = 1 ; }


$errmsg = "<p>The value in field 'Age' is not valid</p>\n" ;

if ($Age =~ /\D/) {
    $message = $message.$errmsg ;
    $found_err = 1 ; }

elsif ($Age < 0) {
    $message = $message.$errmsg ;
    $found_err = 1 ; }
```

21

LISTING 21.2   continued

```
if ($found_err) {
    &PrintError;
     }

# Only add these records to the database after they pass all
# the tests

$DSN = "DBI:mysql:database=Meet_A_Geek";

my $dbh = DBI->connect($DSN,"NewCustomer","mdew34")
or die "Error conneting to database";

$dbh->do("INSERT INTO Customers
(First_Name, Last_Name, Middle_Initial,
                Address, City, State, Zip, Email, Age,
                Gender, Race, Eye_Color,
                Hair_Color, Fav_Activity, Fav_Movie,
                Occupation, Smoker)
        VALUES('$FirstName', '$LastName', '$Middle',
                '$Address','$City', '$State', '$Zip', '$Email', $Age,
                '$Gender','$Race', '$EyeColor', '$HairColor',
'$FavActivity',
                '$FavMovie', '$Occupation', '$Smoker')");

## Create the user in the MySQL database

$UserName = $FirstName."_".$LastName."@%";

$dbh->do("GRANT INSERT, DELETE, SELECT ON Meet_A_Geek.Ads
        TO $UserName IDENTIFIED BY '$Email'");

$dbh->do("GRANT INSERT ON Meet_A_Geek.Orders
        TO $UserName IDENTIFIED BY '$Email'");

$dbi->do("GRANT
        UPDATE (Fav_Movie, Fav_Activity, Occupation, Smoker)
        ON Meet_A_Geek.Customers
        TO $UserName IDENTIFIED BY '$Email'");

$dbi->do("GRANT SELECT ON Meet_A_Geek.Customers
        TO $UserName IDENTIFIED BY '$Email'");

$dbi->do("FLUSH PRIVILEGES");

$dbh->disconnect;

## if everything checks out re-direct the user here
```

LISTING 21.2   continued

```
print "Location: http://CustomerAdd.html\nURI:";
print "http://CustomerAdd.html\n\n" ;


## If there is an error with the submission this
## sends a message to the user
sub PrintError {
print "Content-type: text/html\n\n";
print $message ;

exit 0 ;
return 1 ;
}


## Routine that parses out the name/value pairs of the form
sub GetFormInput {

    (*fval) = @_ if @_ ;

    local ($buf);
    if ($ENV{'REQUEST_METHOD'} eq 'POST') {
        read(STDIN,$buf,$ENV{'CONTENT_LENGTH'});
    }
    else {
        $buf=$ENV{'QUERY_STRING'};
    }
    if ($buf eq "") {
            return 0 ;
        }
    else {
        @fval=split(/&/,$buf);
        foreach $i (0 .. $#fval){
            ($name,$val)=split (/=/,$fval[$i],2);
            $val=~tr/+/ /;
            $val=~ s/%(..)/pack("c",hex($1))/ge;
            $name=~tr/+/ /;
            $name=~ s/%(..)/pack("c",hex($1))/ge;

            if (!defined($field{$name})) {
                $field{$name}=$val;
            }
            else {
                $field{$name} .= ",$val";


            }


        }
```

21

LISTING 21.2   continued

```
        }
return 1;
}
```

This script shows you how you can check the input values before inserting them into your database. It is important to remember that if you want good data to come out, you need to put in good data. You are also creating the users and giving them privileges in the MySQL database in this code. You can see that this is accomplished with the GRANT statement. You also FLUSH the grant tables before you disconnect from the server. This is done so that the user can log in immediately. You have seen everything in this code before, with the exception of the error checking and adding users and privileges.

Logging in a User

The next part you're going to tackle is how to handle a user logging in. The task here is to get the username and password and somehow retain this identity throughout a user's session. There are several ways you could handle this. You could use a cookie to pass this value on to each page that needs the log in variables. There are a couple of gotchas here. What if the user has cookies turned off? Then you're stuck. The best way to handle this is to pass these values along using a <hidden> field in a Web page. Because users have to log in to get to a certain page, you could dynamically create that page, passing along their information in <hidden> fields. For example, a valid customer clicks the Post Ad link. This link takes him or her to the login Web page. A Perl Script runs that validates his or her username and password against the MySQL database and then creates the PostAd Web page. In the HTML of this Web page, you could have two <hidden> fields—one for the username and one for the password. These fields are just like any of the other fields in a form. When the customer is done creating his or her ad, he or she submits the form to the Web server. You use the hidden fields to gain access to the MySQL database. This may seem a little confusing, so look at the code to help clear things up.

A person wants to post an ad. According to your business rules, this person must be a member. To check his or her ID, he or she must log in. Your Web page people created the LogIn.html page shown in Figure 21.4.

FIGURE 21.4

The login form.

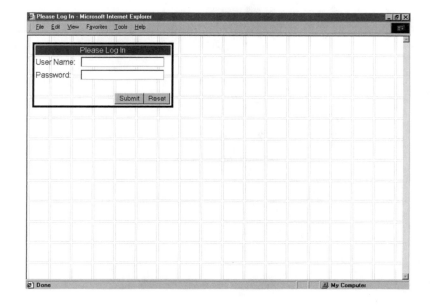

Listing 21.3 shows code that created the LogIn.html Web page.

LISTING 21.3   Logging in a User

```html
<html>
<head>
<title>Please Log In</title>
<meta name="Microsoft Theme" content="blank 011, default">
</head>

<body>

<div align="left">
<form action="../cgi-bin/login.pl" method=post>
  <table border="0" width="294" height="21"
style="border-style: solid; border-color:  #000000">
    <tr>
      <td width="294" height="21" bgcolor="#990033" colspan="2">
        <p align="center"><font color="#FFFFFF">
Please Log In</font></td>
    </tr>
    <tr>
      <td width="91" height="21">User Name: </td>
      <td width="187" height="21">
```

21

LISTING 21.3   continued

```
<input type="text" name="Username" size="23"></td>
    </tr>
    <tr>
      <td width="91" height="21">Password:   </td>
      <td width="187" height="21">
<input type="text" name="Password" size="23"></td>
    </tr>
    <tr>
      <td width="91" height="21"></td>
      <td width="187" height="21"></td>
    </tr>
    <tr>
      <td width="91" height="21"></td>
      <td width="187" height="21">
        <p align="right">
<input type="submit" value="Submit" name="B1">
<input type="reset" value="Reset" name="B2"></td>
    </tr>
  </table>
</form>
</div>

</body>

</html>
```

The script that is called when a user clicks the Submit button is Login.pl. This script will take the values in the Username and Password box and validate that they match against the database. If a match is found, the requested Web page will be generated; if not, the user will be asked to log in again.

Listing 21.4 is the complete listing of Login.pl.

LISTING 21.4   Script for User Log In

```
#!/usr/local/bin/perl

&GetFormInput;

# The intermediate variables below
#make your script more readable
# but somewhat less efficient
#since they are not really necessary.
```

LISTING 21.4   continued

```perl
$Username = $field{'Username'} ;
$Password = $field{'Password'} ;


$message = "" ;
$found_err = "" ;

$errmsg = "<p>Field 'Username' must be filled in.</p>\n" ;

if ($Username eq "") {
    $message = $message.$errmsg ;
    $found_err = 1 ; }


$errmsg = "<p>Field 'Password' must be filled in.</p>\n" ;

if ($Password eq "") {
    $message = $message.$errmsg ;
    $found_err = 1 ; }

if ($found_err) {
    &PrintError; }

$DSN = "DBI:mysql:database=Meet_A_Geek";

$message = "Invalid Log In - Try Again";

my $dbh = DBI->connect($DSN, $Username, $Password)
or &PrintError);

$dbh->disconnect;

print "Content-type: text/html\n\n";
print "<html>\n" ;
print "\n" ;
print "<head>\n" ;
print "<title>Post Ad</title>\n" ;
print "<meta name="Microsoft Theme";
print "content="blank 011, default">'."\n" ;
print "</head>\n" ;
print "\n" ;
print '<body background="_themes/blank/blbkgnd.gif"';
print 'bgcolor="#FFFFFF" text="#000000" link="#999999" vlink="#990000"';
print 'alink="#666666"><!--mstheme-->';
print '<font face="Arial, Arial, Helvetica">'."\n" ;
print '<form action="../cgi-bin/PostAd" method=post>'."\n" ;
```

21

LISTING 21.4   continued

```
print '<div align="left">'."\n" ;
print '<input type="hidden" name="Username" value="$Username">'."\n" ;
print '<input type="hidden" name="Password" value="$Password">'."\n" ;
print '   <!--mstheme--></font>';
print '<table border="0" width="498" height="30" ';
print 'style="border-style: solid; border-color: #000000">'."\n" ;
print "    <tr>\n" ;
print '        <td width="498" height="20"><!--mstheme-->';
print '<font face="Arial, Arial, Helvetica">'."\n" ;
print '<p align="center">';
print '<b>Enter the following information to Post an Ad</b>';
print '<!--mstheme--></font></td>'."\n" ;
print "    </tr>\n" ;
print "    <tr>\n" ;
print '        <td width="498" height="20">'
print '<!--mstheme--><font face="Arial, Arial, Helvetica">';
print '<!--mstheme--></font></td>'."\n" ;
print "    </tr>\n" ;
print "    <tr>\n" ;
print '        <td width="498" height="20">'
print '<!--mstheme--><font face="Arial, Arial, Helvetica">';
print '<b><font size="2">Use this box to form a'."\n" ;
print 'message for you ad. You can say anything you like. ';
print '</font></b><!--mstheme--></font></td>\n" ;
print "    </tr>\n" ;
print "    <tr>\n" ;
print '        <td width="498" height="132" valign="top">';
print '<!--mstheme--><font face="Arial, Arial, Helvetica">';
print '<textarea rows="6" name="S1" cols="61"></textarea>';
print '<!--mstheme--></font></td>'."\n" ;
print "    </tr>\n" ;
print "    <tr>\n" ;
print '        <td width="498" height="30" valign="top">';
print '<!--mstheme--><font face="Arial, Arial, Helvetica">'."\n" ;
print '          <p align="right">';
print '<input type="submit" value="Submit">';
print '<input type="reset" value="Reset">';
print '<!--mstheme--></font></td>'."\n" ;
print "    </tr>\n" ;
print '    </table><!--mstheme-->';
print '<font face="Arial, Arial,  Helvetica">'."\n" ;
print "</div>\n" ;
print "</form>\n" ;
print "<!--mstheme--></font></body>\n" ;
print "\n" ;
print "</html>\n" ;
```

LISTING 21.4   continued

```perl
sub PrintError {
print "Content-type: text/html\n\n";
print "<html>\n" ;
print "\n" ;
print "<head>\n" ;
print "<title>Please Log In</title>\n" ;
print '<meta name="Microsoft Theme" ';
print 'content="blank 011, default">'."\n" ;
print "</head>\n" ;
print "\n" ;
print '<body background="_themes/blank/blbkgnd.gif" ';
print 'bgcolor="#FFFFFF" text="#000000" link="#999999" ';
print 'vlink="#990000" alink="#666666"><!--mstheme-->';
print '<font face="Arial, Arial, Helvetica">'."\n" ;
print "\n" ;
print '<div align="left">'."\n" ;
print '<form action="../cgi-bin/login.pl" method=post>'."\n" ;
print '   <!--mstheme--></font>';
print '<table border="0" width="294" height="21" ';
print 'style="border-style: solid; border-color: #000000">'."\n" ;

print "    <tr>\n" ;
print '        <td width="294" height="21" bgcolor="#990033" ';
print 'colspan="2"><!--mstheme-->';
print '<font face="Arial, Arial, Helvetica">'."\n" ;
print '         <p align="center">';
print '<font color="#FFFFFF">$message</font>';
print '<!--mstheme--></font></td>'."\n" ;
print "    </tr>\n" ;

print "    <tr>\n" ;
print '        <td width="294" height="21" bgcolor="#990033" ';
print 'colspan="2"><!--mstheme--><font face="Arial, Arial, Helvetica">'."\n" ;
print '         <p align="center">';
print '<font color="#FFFFFF">Please Log In</font>';
print '<!--mstheme--></font></td>'."\n" ;
print "    </tr>\n" ;
print "    <tr>\n" ;
print '        <td width="91" height="21">';
print '<!--mstheme--><font face="Arial, Arial, Helvetica">User Name: ';
print '<!--mstheme--></font></td>'."\n" ;
print '        <td width="187" height="21">';
print '<!--mstheme--><font face="Arial, Arial, Helvetica">';
print '<input type="text" name="Username" size="23">';
```

21

LISTING 21.4   continued

```
print '<!--mstheme--></font></td>'."\n" ;
print "     </tr>\n" ;
print "     <tr>\n" ;
print '         <td width="91" height="21">';
print '<!--mstheme--><font face="Arial, Arial,  Helvetica">';
print 'Password:   ';
print '<!--mstheme--></font></td>'."\n" ;
print '         <td width="187" height="21">';
print '<!--mstheme--><font face="Arial, Arial, Helvetica">';
print '<input type="text" name="Password" size="23">';
print '<!--mstheme--></font></td>'."\n" ;
print "     </tr>\n" ;
print "     <tr>\n" ;
print '         <td width="91" height="21">';
print '<!--mstheme--><font face="Arial, Arial, Helvetica">';
print '<!--mstheme--></font></td>'."\n" ;
print '         <td width="187" height="21">';
print '<!--mstheme--><font face="Arial, Arial, Helvetica">';
print '<!--mstheme--></font></td>'."\n" ;
print "     </tr>\n" ;
print "     <tr>\n" ;
print '         <td width="91" height="21">';
print '<!--mstheme--><font face="Arial, Arial, Helvetica">';
print '<!--mstheme--></font></td>'."\n" ;
print '         <td width="187" height="21">';
print '<!--mstheme--><font face="Arial, Arial, Helvetica">'."\n" ;
print '          <p align="right">'
print '<input type="submit" value="Submit" name="B1">';
print '<input type="reset" value="Reset" name="B2">';
print '<!--mstheme--></font></td>'."\n" ;
print "     </tr>\n" ;
print '   </table><!--mstheme-->'
print '<font face="Arial, Arial, Helvetica">'."\n" ;
print "</form>\n" ;
print "</div>\n" ;
print "\n" ;
print "<!--mstheme--></font></body>\n" ;
print "\n" ;
print "</html>\n" ;

exit 0 ;
return 1 ;
}
```

LISTING 21.4   continued

```perl
sub GetFormInput {

    (*fval) = @_ if @_ ;

    local ($buf);
    if ($ENV{'REQUEST_METHOD'} eq 'POST') {
        read(STDIN,$buf,$ENV{'CONTENT_LENGTH'});
    }
    else {
        $buf=$ENV{'QUERY_STRING'};
    }
    if ($buf eq "") {
            return 0 ;
        }
    else {
        @fval=split(/&/,$buf);
        foreach $i (0 .. $#fval){
            ($name,$val)=split (/=/,$fval[$i],2);
            $val=~tr/+/ /;
            $val=~ s/%(..)/pack("c",hex($1))/ge;
            $name=~tr/+/ /;
            $name=~ s/%(..)/pack("c",hex($1))/ge;

            if (!defined($field{$name})) {
                $field{$name}=$val;
            }
            else {
                $field{$name} .= ",$val";

            }


        }
    }
    return 1;
}
```

This code does some neat things. First, it validates the entries to make sure that they are not blank. If they are, the PrintError subroutine is called. This routine regenerates the Login.html page with the error message printed at the top. The next bit of code takes the

21

username and password and tries to connect to the database. If everything checks out, the $Username and $Password variables are passed on in the hidden input tags, and the PostAd.html page is created (see Figure 21.5). If a connection is not made, the PrintError subroutine is called. This is a nice little trick to help create a secure environment for your database and provide as little annoyance as possible to the user.

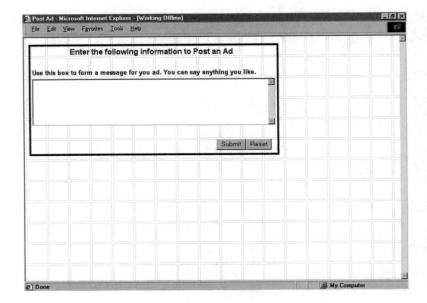

Posting an Ad

The next part of the Web site you'll look at is the search form (see Figure 21.6). The search form will allow the customer to search the ads and registered customers for a suitable date. The user will be able to select options from the Web form on which to base the search. An SQL SELECT statement will be built based on the customer's choices. The resulting Web page will display all the matches in the database. Take a look at the HTML code in Listing 21.5.

FIGURE 21.6

The search form.

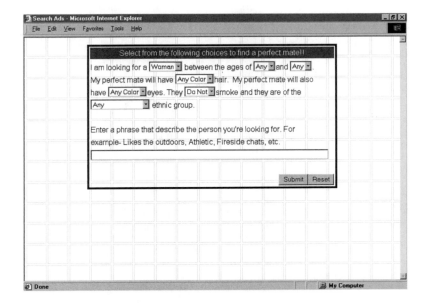

LISTING 21.5 Filling out the Search Form

```
/head>

<body>

<div align="center">
  <center>
<form action="../cgi-bin/SearchAd.pl" method=post>
  <table border="0" width="521" height="25"
style="border-style: solid; border-color: #000000">
    <tr>
      <td width="521" height="25" bgcolor="#990033">
        <p align="center"><font color="#FFFFFF">
Select from the following
        choices to find a perfect mate!!</font></td>
    </tr>
    <tr>
      <input type="hidden" name="Username" value="">
      <input type="hidden" name="Password" value="">
      <td width="521" height="25"></td>
    </tr>
    <tr>
      <td width="521" height="25">I am looking for a
<select size="1" name="Gender">
        <option value="M">Man</option>
        <option value="F" selected>Woman</option>
```

21

LISTING 21.5   continued

```
         </select> between the ages of <select size="1" name="LAge">
            <option value="18">18</option>
            <option value="F">19</option>
            <option value="18" selected>Any</option>
         </select>and <select size="1" name="UAge">
            <option value="1" selected>Any</option>
            <option value="18">18</option>
            <option value="19">19</option>
         </select>.</td>
      </tr>
      <tr>
        <td width="521" height="25">My perfect mate will have
<select size="1" name="Hair">
            <option value="Brown">Brown</option>
            <option selected>Any Color</option>
            <option value="Black">Black</option>
            <option value="Blonde">Blonde</option>
         </select>hair.  My perfect mate will also </td>
      </tr>
      <tr>
        <td width="521" height="25">have <select size="1" name="Eyes">
            <option value="Brown">Brown</option>
            <option selected>Any Color</option>
            <option value="Blue">Blue</option>
            <option value="Green">Green</option>
         </select>eyes. They <select size="1" name="Smoke">
            <option value="Y">Do</option>
            <option selected value="N">Do Not</option>
         </select>smoke and they are of the </td>
      </tr>
      <tr>
        <td width="521" height="25"><select size="1" name="Race">
            <option selected>Any</option>
            <option value="Caucasian">Caucasian</option>
            <option value="African American">African American</option>
            <option value="American Indian">American Indian</option>
            <option value="Hispanic">Hispanic</option>
            <option value="Asian">Asian</option>
            <option value="Other">Other</option>
         </select> ethnic group. </td>
      </tr>
      <tr>
        <td width="521" height="25"></td>
      </tr>
      <tr>
        <td width="521" height="25">
Enter a phrase that describe the person you're
            looking for. For </td>
      </tr>
```

LISTING 21.5 continued

```
      <tr>
        <td width="521" height="25">
example- Likes the outdoors, Athletic,
        Fireside chats, etc.</td>
      </tr>
      <tr>
        <td width="521" height="25">
<input type="text" name="Phrase" size="69"></td>
      </tr>
      <tr>
        <td width="521" height="25"></td>
      </tr>
    </center>
    <tr>
      <td width="521" height="25">
        <p align="right"><input type="submit" value="Submit"
name="B1"><input type="reset" value="Reset" name="B2"></td>
    </tr>
    </table>
  </div>

  </body>

  </html>
```

Listing 21.6 is the complete script for SearchAd.pl.

LISTING 21.6 Processing the Search Form with Script

```perl
#!/usr/local/bin/perl

&GetFormInput;

# The intermediate variables below make your script more readable
# but somewhat less efficient since they are not really necessary.

$Username = $field{'Username'} ;
$Password = $field{'Password'} ;
$Gender = $field{'Gender'} ;
$LAge = $field{'LAge'} ;
$UAge = $field{'UAge'} ;
$Hair = $field{'Hair'} ;
$Eyes = $field{'Eyes'} ;
$Smoke = $field{'Smoke'} ;
$Race = $field{'Race'} ;
$Phrase = $field{'Phrase'} ;
```

21

LISTING 21.6   continued

```
$message = "" ;
$found_err = "" ;


$errmsg = "<p>Field 'Username' must be filled in.</p>\n" ;

if ($Username eq "") {
    $message = $message.$errmsg ;
    $found_err = 1 ; }


$errmsg = "<p>Field 'Password' must be filled in.</p>\n" ;

if ($Password eq "") {
    $message = $message.$errmsg ;
    $found_err = 1 ; }

if ($found_err) {
    &PrintError; }

## Start Building the SQL string

$SQL = "SELECT * FROM Customers as C, Ads as A
        WHERE A.Customer_ID = C.Customer_ID ";

$Build = "AND C.Gender = 'M' ";

if ($Gender eq "M"){
    $SQL = $SQL.$Build;}

$Build = "AND C.Gender = 'F' ";

if ($Gender eq "F"){
    $SQL = $SQL.$Build;}

$Build = "AND C.Age >= $LAge AND C.Age <= $UAge ";
$SQL = $SQL.$Build;

$Build = "AND C.Hair_Color ='$Hair' ";
if ($Hair){
    $SQL = $SQL.$Build;}

$Build = "AND C.Eye_Color ='$Eyes' ";
if ($Eyes){
    $SQl = $SQl.$Build;}

$Build = "AND C.Smoke ='$Smoke' ";
$SQL = $SQL.$Build;
```

LISTING 21.6   continued

```
$Build = "AND C.Race = '$Race' ";
if ($Race){
    $SQl = $SQl.$Build;}

$Build = "AND A.Ad_Text LIKE '%$Phrase%' "'
if ($Phrase){
    $SQL = $SQl.$Build;}

##Connect to the database

$DSN = "DSN:mysql:database=Meet_A_Geek";

$message = "Error Connecting to Database";

my $dbh = DBI->connect($DSN, $Username, $Password)
        or &PrintError;
my $sth = $dbh->prepare($SQL);
$sth->execute();

print "Content-type: text/html\n\n";
print "<html>\n" ;
print "\n" ;
print "<head>\n" ;
print '<meta http-equiv="Content-Language" ';
print 'content="en-us">'."\n" ;
print '<meta http-equiv="Content-Type" ';
print 'content="text/html; charset=windows-1252">'."\n" ;
print "<title>Your Search Produced the ';
print 'Following Results</title>\n" ;
print '<meta name="Microsoft Theme" ';
print 'content="blank 011, default">'."\n" ;
print "</head>\n" ;
print "\n" ;
print '<body background="_themes/blank/blbkgnd.gif" ';
print 'bgcolor="#FFFFFF" text="#000000" link="#999999" ';
print 'vlink="#990000" alink="#666666"><!--mstheme-->';
print '<font face="Arial, Arial, Helvetica">'."\n" ;
print "\n" ;
print '<div align="center">'."\n" ;
print "  <center>\n" ;
print '  <!--mstheme--></font>';
print '<table border="1" width="508" height="17" ';
print 'bordercolordark="#666666" bordercolorlight="#CCCCCC">'."\n" ;
print "    <tr>\n" ;
print '      <td width="507" height="17" bgcolor="#990033" ';
print 'colspan="5"><!--mstheme-->';
print '<font face="Arial, Arial, Helvetica">'."\n" ;
```

21

LISTING 21.6   continued

```
print '          <p align="center"><font color="#FFFFFF">';
print '<b>Your Search Produced the'."\n" ;
print "          Following Results</b></font>\n";
print "<!--mstheme--></font></td>\n" ;
print "     </tr>\n" ;
print "     <tr>\n" ;
print '          <td width="507" height="17" ';
print 'bgcolor="#FFFFFF" colspan="5">';
print '<!--mstheme--><font face="Arial, Arial, Helvetica"> ';
print '<!--mstheme--></font></td>'."\n" ;
print "     </tr>\n" ;
print "     <tr>\n" ;
print '          <td width="186" height="17" bgcolor="#FFFFFF">';
print '<!--mstheme--><font face="Arial, Arial, Helvetica">';
print '<font color="#666666"><b>Name</b></font>';
print '<!--mstheme--></font></td>'."\n" ;
print '          <td width="52" height="17" bgcolor="#FFFFFF">';
print '<!--mstheme--><font face="Arial, Arial, Helvetica">';
print '<font color="#666666"><b>Age</b></font>';
print '<!--mstheme--></font></td>'."\n" ;
print '          <td width="98" height="17" bgcolor="#FFFFFF">';
print '<!--mstheme--><font face="Arial, Arial, Helvetica">';
print '<font color="#666666"><b>City</b></font>';
print '<!--mstheme--></font></td>'."\n" ;
print '          <td width="41" height="17" bgcolor="#FFFFFF">';
print '<!--mstheme--><font face="Arial, Arial, Helvetica">';
print '<font color="#666666"><b>State</b></font>';
print '<!--mstheme--></font></td>'."\n" ;
print '          <td width="95" height="17" bgcolor="#FFFFFF">';
print '<!--mstheme--><font face="Arial, Arial, Helvetica">';
print '<font color="#666666"><b>View'."\n" ;
print "          Ad</b></font><!--mstheme--></font></td>\n" ;
print "     </tr>\n" ;

## This bit of code generates the grid.
## It uses the mod function to test\
## if a row is even or odd. It adjusts the colors accordingly.

while($ref = $sth->fetchrow_hashref()){

    if($x % 2 > 0){
        $bg = "#666666";
        $ft = "#FFFFFF";}
    else{
        $bg = "#FFFFFF";
        $ft = "#000000";
     }
```

LISTING 21.6   continued

```
print "     <tr>\n" ;
print '        <td width="186" height="17" bgcolor=$bg>';
print '<!--mstheme--><font face="Arial, Arial, Helvetica">';
print '<font color=$ft><b>$ref->{'First_Name'} $ref->{'Last_Name'}';
print '</b></font>';
print '<!--mstheme--></font></td>'."\n" ;
print '        <td width="52" height="17" bgcolor=$bg>';
print '<!--mstheme--><font face="Arial, Arial, Helvetica">';
print '<font color=$ft>$ref->('Age'}</font>';
print '<!--mstheme--></font></td>'."\n" ;
print '        <td width="98" height="17" bgcolor=$bg>';
print '<!--mstheme--><font face="Arial, Arial, Helvetica">';
print '<font color=$ft><b>$ref->{'City'}</b></font>';
print '<!--mstheme--></font></td>'."\n" ;
print '        <td width="41" height="17" bgcolor=$bg>';
print '<!--mstheme--><font face="Arial, Arial, Helvetica">';
print '<font color=$ft><b>$ref->{'State'}</b></font>';
print '<!--mstheme--></font></td>'."\n" ;
print '        <td width="95" height="17" bgcolor=$bg>';
print '<!--mstheme--><font face="Arial, Arial, Helvetica">'."\n" ;
print '          <p align="center"><font color="#000000">';
print '<b><a href="../cgi-bin/viewad.pl?ref->{'Customer_ID'}&';
print 'Username=$Username&Password=$Password">Ad</a>';
print '</b></font><!--mstheme--></font></td>'."\n" ;
print "     </tr>\n" ;

    $x = $x +1;

}


$sth->finish();
$dbh->disconnect();

print "     <tr>\n" ;
print '        <td width="186" height="17" bgcolor="#FFFFFF">';
print '<!--mstheme--><font face="Arial, Arial, Helvetica"> ';
print '<!--mstheme--></font></td>'."\n" ;
print '        <td width="52" height="17" bgcolor="#FFFFFF">';
print '<!--mstheme--><font face="Arial, Arial, Helvetica"> ';
print '<!--mstheme--></font></td>'."\n" ;
print '        <td width="98" height="17" bgcolor="#FFFFFF">';
print '<!--mstheme--><font face="Arial, Arial, Helvetica"> ';
print '<!--mstheme--></font></td>'."\n" ;
print '        <td width="41" height="17" bgcolor="#FFFFFF">';
```

LISTING 21.6 continued

```
print '<!--mstheme--><font face="Arial, Arial, Helvetica"> ';
print '<!--mstheme--></font></td>'."\n" ;
print '        <td width="95" height="17" bgcolor="#FFFFFF">';
print '<!--mstheme--><font face="Arial, Arial, Helvetica"> ';
print '<!--mstheme--></font></td>'."\n" ;
print "    </tr>\n" ;
print '  </table>';
print '<!--mstheme--><font face="Arial, Arial, Helvetica">'."\n" ;
print "  </center>\n" ;
print "</div>\n" ;
print "\n" ;
print "<!--mstheme--></font></body>\n" ;
print "\n" ;
print "</html>\n" ;

##In case of an error throw the user back to the log in page

sub PrintError {
print "Content-type: text/html\n\n";
print "<html>\n" ;
print "\n" ;
print "<head>\n" ;
print '<meta http-equiv="Content-Language" ';
print 'content="en-us">'."\n" ;
print '<meta http-equiv="Content-Type" ';
print 'content="text/html; charset=windows-1252">'."\n" ;
print "<title>Please Log In</title>\n" ;
print '<meta name="Microsoft Theme" ';
print 'content="blank 011, default">'."\n" ;
print "</head>\n" ;
print "\n" ;
print '<body background="_themes/blank/blbkgnd.gif" ';
print 'bgcolor="#FFFFFF" text="#000000" link="#999999" ';
print 'vlink="#990000" alink="#666666"><!--mstheme-->';
print '<font face="Arial, Arial, Helvetica">'."\n" ;
print "\n" ;
print '<div align="left">'."\n" ;
print '<form action="../cgi-bin/login.pl" method=post>'."\n" ;
print '  <!--mstheme--></font><table border="0" width="294" ';
print 'height="21" style="border-style: solid; ';
print 'border-color: #000000">'."\n" ;

print "    <tr>\n" ;
print '      <td width="294" height="21" ';
print 'bgcolor="#990033" colspan="2">';
print '<!--mstheme--><font face="Arial, Arial, Helvetica">'."\n" ;
```

LISTING 21.6 continued

```
print '            <p align="center">';
print '<font color="#FFFFFF">$message</font>';
print '<!--mstheme--></font></td>'."\n" ;
print "      </tr>\n" ;

print "      <tr>\n" ;
print '            <td width="294" height="21" ';
print 'bgcolor="#990033" colspan="2">';
print '<!--mstheme--><font face="Arial, Arial, Helvetica">'."\n" ;
print '            <p align="center">';
print '<font color="#FFFFFF">Please Log In</font>';
print '<!--mstheme--></font></td>'."\n" ;
print "      </tr>\n" ;
print "      <tr>\n" ;
print '            <td width="91" height="21">';
print '<!--mstheme--><font face="Arial, Arial, Helvetica">';
print 'User Name: ';
print '<!--mstheme--></font></td>'."\n" ;
print '            <td width="187" height="21">';
print '<!--mstheme--><font face="Arial, Arial, Helvetica">';
print '<input type="text" name="Username" size="23">';
print '<!--mstheme--></font></td>'."\n" ;
print "      </tr>\n" ;
print "      <tr>\n" ;
print '            <td width="91" height="21">';
print '<!--mstheme--><font face="Arial, Arial, Helvetica">';
print 'Password:   <!--mstheme--></font></td>'."\n" ;
print '            <td width="187" height="21">';
print '<!--mstheme--><font face="Arial, Arial, Helvetica">';
print '<input type="text" name="Password" size="23">';
print '<!--mstheme--></font></td>'."\n" ;
print "      </tr>\n" ;
print "      <tr>\n" ;
print '            <td width="91" height="21">';
print '<!--mstheme--><font face="Arial, Arial, Helvetica">';
print '<!--mstheme--></font></td>'."\n" ;
print '            <td width="187" height="21">';
print '<!--mstheme--><font face="Arial, Arial, Helvetica">';
print '<!--mstheme--></font></td>'."\n" ;
print "      </tr>\n" ;
print "      <tr>\n" ;
print '            <td width="91" height="21">';
print '<!--mstheme--><font face="Arial, Arial, Helvetica">';
print '<!--mstheme--></font></td>'."\n" ;
print '            <td width="187" height="21">';
```

21

LISTING 21.6   continued

```perl
print '<!--mstheme--><font face="Arial, Arial, Helvetica">'."\n" ;
print '          <p align="right">';
print '<input type="submit" value="Submit" name="B1">';
print '<input type="reset" value="Reset" name="B2">';
print '<!--mstheme--></font></td>'."\n" ;
print "    </tr>\n" ;
print '  </table>';
print '<!--mstheme--><font face="Arial, Arial, Helvetica">'."\n" ;
print "</form>\n" ;
print "</div>\n" ;
print "\n" ;
print "<!--mstheme--></font></body>\n" ;
print "\n" ;
print "</html>\n" ;

exit 0 ;
return 1 ;
}

sub GetFormInput {

    (*fval) = @_ if @_ ;

    local ($buf);
    if ($ENV{'REQUEST_METHOD'} eq 'POST') {
        read(STDIN,$buf,$ENV{'CONTENT_LENGTH'});
    }
    else {
        $buf=$ENV{'QUERY_STRING'};
    }
    if ($buf eq "") {
            return 0 ;
        }
    else {
        @fval=split(/&/,$buf);
        foreach $i (0 .. $#fval){
            ($name,$val)=split (/=/,$fval[$i],2);
            $val=~tr/+/ /;
            $val=~ s/%(..)/pack("c",hex($1))/ge;
            $name=~tr/+/ /;
            $name=~ s/%(..)/pack("c",hex($1))/ge;

            if (!defined($field{$name})) {
```

LISTING 21.6   continued

```
                $field{$name}=$val;
        }
        else {
                $field{$name} .= ",$val";

        }


    }
  }
  return 1;
}
```

There is a lot of code in this listing. The interesting part is the building of the SQL statement. This statement is generated based on the values the user chose. Simple `if` statements control what goes into the SQL statement. The SQL statement is a simple `SELECT` statement that joins on the `Ads` table. You do this because you only want customers who have posted ads. This guarantees it. The resultset is stored in the `$sth` variable. If there were no errors, the code continues by building the result page. This page will contain a grid of data with alternating row colors. This is made possible by checking to see if a row is odd or even. If the row is odd, the background color is turned to a dark gray and the font color is turned to white. If the row is even, the background color is white and the font color is black. This neat little trick is simple to do, and it greatly enhances the page that is returned to the user.

The cells in the table are filled with the values contained in the record set. The `while` loop allows you to walk through the resultset and post the values that were returned in the `SELECT` query.

21

FIGURE 21.7

Search ad results.

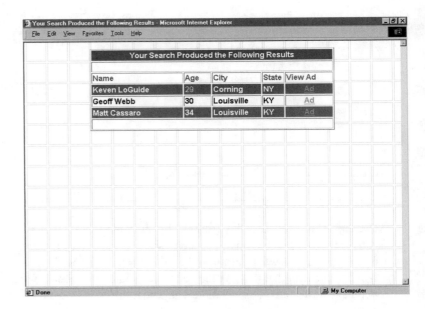

Test and Deploy

The final steps in the creative process are to test your code and then put it into production. When you are finished thoroughly testing your code, give it to someone else. You can bet that 9 times out of 10 he or she will find something that you missed. Programmers, as a rule, don't make very good testers. We know how our product is supposed to work, so that's how we test it. We don't try the unexpected. Users will. Test your scripts well before you deploy them. Also test your Web pages (or the output of your scripts) using Internet Explorer as well as Netscape Navigator. You may be surprised at how well things turn out in one browser and look terrible in another. Finally, test your output using various screen resolutions. The user's screen resolution greatly affects how your Web page looks.

The final step is deployment. This is where you take your system and put it into production—your ultimate goal. The hard work and hours of design are all for this crowning moment. There should be no surprises at this point. You should know before your product ever reaches this point whether it will be a success or a failure. If you followed the creative process, along with the database design process, you can almost beguaranteed your system will be successful.

Summary

Today, you learned about the creative process and the steps that are involved. You saw how the database design process meshed with the creative process to help you reach your goal. You also learned the importance of design; with proper planning, it is an easy transition from an idea to a working system.

You also reviewed the key events that took place on your three-week journey. You reviewed how to create a database, as well as the supporting tables and columns. You saw how to import data from an existing database, and you also went over security and how to implement it. Finally, you created a series of Web pages and Perl scripts that took your design and made it reality.

Q&A

Q **The Products table had a picture column in it. How are images stored in MySQL?**

A MySQL can store images as BLOB types. They first must be escaped before they can be stored. There has been much debate in the newsgroups as to whether it is better to store images in the database or to store a link to a directory where the file is located instead. The argument is that BLOB types are inefficient. They take up too much space and cannot be OPTIMIZEd. However, the file system is probably the best place to store files. Your best bet is to store images in a directory outside your database.

Q **How often should I OPTIMIZE my database?**

A You should OPTIMIZE your database regularly, especially when your database is young. The OPTIMIZE command is needed when a large number of records have been either deleted or inserted into your database.

Exercises

1. There are two scripts that you did not create on the flow chart—the script to display items from the Products table and the script to create an order. Create these scripts using Perl and the DBI/DBD.
2. The same task as the first exercise, but this time use ADO and ODBC.

21

WEEK 3

In Review

You have finished your third and final week of learning MySQL. You started the week with a look at a highly-used interface. In the middle of the week, you covered a lot of database administration tasks. You ended the week with a full review of what you have learned by building a Web site using MySQL from the ground up. You now possess the basic knowledge to go out and fully deploy MySQL in real-life situations.

15

16

17

18

19

20

21

APPENDIX A

SQL Syntax and Commands

This appendix will provide you with a list of SQL commands for your reference. The commands are listed in alphabetical order. The command will be followed by a list of possible parameters. Optional parameters will be enclosed by brackets[]. Examples will be provided where appropriate.

ALTER [IGNORE] TABLE table_name specification [, specification]

Specifications] can be

- ADD [COLUMN] column name (column definitions) [FIRST or AFTER column_name]
- ADD INDEX [index_name] (column_list)
- ADD PRIMARY KEY (column_list)
- ADD UNIQUE [index_name] (column_list)

- ALTER [*COLUMN*] *column_name* {SET DEFAULT *default_value* or DROP DEFAULT}
- CHANGE [COLUMN] *old_col_name create_definition*
- DROP [COLUMN] *col_name*
- DROP PRIMARY KEY
- DROP INDEX *index_name*
- MODIFY [COLUMN] *create_definition*
- RENAME *new_tbl_name*

This is a ton of information, but it is really straightforward. The IGNORE keyword causes rows with duplicate values in unique keys to be deleted; otherwise, nothing happens. Any one of the previous specifications can be used in the ALTER TABLE statement.

Examples:

```
ALTER TABLE Customers ADD COLUMN Account_Number INT

ALTER TABLE Customers ADD INDEX (Customer_ID)

ALTER TABLE Customers ADD PRIMARY KEY (Customer_ID)

ALTER TABLE Customers ADD UNIQUE (Customer_ID)

ALTER TABLE Customers CHANGE Customer_ID Customer_Number INT

ALTER TABLE Customers DROP Customer_ID

ALTER TABLE Customers DROP PRIMARY KEY
```

The previous command does not require the column name because there can be only one PRIMARY KEY in a table.

```
ALTER TABLE Customers DROP INDEX Customer_ID

ALTER TABLE Customers MODIFY First_Name varchar(100)

ALTER TABLE Customers RENAME] Customer
```

CREATE DATABASE *database name*

This simple command creates a database. The database name must be well formed or this statement will generate an error.

Example:

```
CREATE DATABASE Meet_A_Geek
```

CREATE [*AGGREGATE*] FUNCTION *function_name*, RETURNS {*STRING* | REAL | INTEGER} SONAME *shared_library_name*

This function causes a function that you have created to be loaded into the func table of the mysql database. The function_name is the name you want to use to call this function from an SQL statement. You must also indicate what type of value your function returns after the RETURNS keyword. The options for this value are either STRING, REAL, or INTEGER. The SONAME refers to the shared library name of this function.

If you use the optional keyword AGGREGATE, MySQL treats this function as though it were part of the aggregate functions, such as SUM(), AVG(), or MAX().

CREATE [UNIQUE] INDEX *index_name* ON *table_name* (*column_list*)

This command creates an index on a given column in a given table.

Example:

```
CREATE INDEX idx_cust_ID ON Customers (Customer_ID)
```

CREATE [TEMPORARY] TABLE [IF NOT EXISTS] *table_name table_definition* [*table_options*] [[IGNORE or REPLACE] *select_statement*]

This statement will create a table. The table definition is a list of column names and types.

CREATE TABLE has the following optional parameters:

- CREATE TEMPORARY TABLE Temp_Customers (Cust_ID INT)   This statement creates a temporary table that will automatically be deleted when the connection that created it drops.

- CREATE TABLE IF NOT EXISTS Customers (Cust_ID INT)   This statement will only create the table if the table does not currently exist.

- TYPE = {ISAM or MYISAM or HEAP}   Used to set the type of table that is created.

- The tables options can be any of the following:

  - ISAM is the original table type.

  - MYISAM is the newer storage type. This is used by default.

  - HEAP tables are stored in memory only. They have the following constraints:

HEAP tables do not support AUTO_INCREMENT columns.

Only = or < = > can be used with indexes.

HEAP tables use a fixed record length format.

HEAP tables do not support an index on a NULL column.

HEAP tables do not support BLOB or TEXT columns.

You can have non-unique keys in a HEAP table (not that normal with hashed tables).

Example: CREATE TABLE Customers (Cust_ID INT) TYPE = HEAP

- AUTO_INCREMENT = X   Sets the starting point of an AUTO_INCREMENT column.

  Example: CREATE TABLE Customers (Cust_ID INT AUTO_INCREMENT) AUTO_INCREMENT = 90000

- AVG_ROW_LENGTH = X   Rarely used. Sets the length of a table row in variable length columns.

- CHECKSUM = {0 or 1}   Adds a performance hit, but allows the myisamchk utility to spot tables with corrupted data easier.

- COMMENT = "comment to be made"   Allows you to add a comment to a table. The limit is 60 characters.

- MAX_ROWS = X   Sets the maximum number of rows that will be stored in a table. May increase performance.

- MIN_ROWS = X   Sets the minimum number of rows that will be stored in a table. May increase performance.

- PACK_KEYS = {0 or 1}   When set to 1, will make your indexes smaller and faster. Updates will take longer.

- PASSWORD = "password"   This will password protect the .frm file.

- DELAY_KEY_WRITE = {0 or 1}   When set to 1, all updates to the table will occur when the table is not in use.

- ROW_FORMAT= { default or dynamic or static or compressed }   Determines how the rows will be stored in a table.

Example of a CREATE TABLE statement:

```
CREATE TABLE Customers
(Customer_ID INT NOT NULL AUTO_INCRMENT PRIMARY KEY,
First_Name VARCHAR(20) NOT NULL,
Last_Name VARCHAR(35) NOT NULL,
Address VARCHAR(100) NOT NULL)
```

DELETE [LOW PRIORITY] FROM *table_name* WHERE *conditions* [LIMIT n]

The delete command deletes values from a given table based on the conditions expressed in the WHERE clause. The DELETE statement has the following optional parameters:

- LOW_PRIORITY   Delays the deletion until the table is not in use
- LIMIT X   Limits the number of deletions to X

Example:

```
DELETE FROM Customers WHERE Customer_ID = 3
```

To delete all rows from a table without actually dropping the table, use the following command:

```
DELETE FROM Customers
```

DESCRIBE *table_name* [*column_name*]

This statement will show a detailed definition of the columns in a table.

To see a description of all the columns in a table, use the following:

```
DESCRIBE Customers
```

To see a description of a specific column, use

```
DESCRIBE Customers Customer_ID
```

DROP DATABASE [IF EXISTS] *database_name*

The DROP DATABASE statement will delete a database. There are no warnings or questions, so be careful when you issue this statement.

Example:

```
DROP DATABASE Meet_A_Geek
```

DROP FUNCTION *function_name*

Deletes a user-defined function from the func table in the mysql database. See CREATE FUNCTION.

DROP INDEX *index_name* ON *table_name*

This statement will delete a given index on a specific table.

Example:

```
DROP INDEX idx_cust_id ON Customers
```

DROP TABLE [IF EXISTS] table_name [, table_name] ...

This statement will delete the specified table. Again, with all DROP and DELETE statements, be careful, there are no warnings or hesitations.

Example:

```
DROP TABLE Customers
```

EXPLAIN {select_statement or *table_name*}

This command will display the query plan for the select clause. It displays the same results as the SHOW. See SHOW.

Example:

```
EXPLAIN SELECT C.First_Name
FROM Customers AS C, Orders as O
WHERE C.Customer_ID = O.Customer_ID
```

FLUSH *flush_option*[, *flush_option*] ...

This statement will clear the cache MySQL uses. The possible options are

- HOSTS   Clears the hosts cache tables. Use this option if one of your hosts IP addresses change or if the local IP address changes.
- LOGS   Closes all open logs.
- PRIVILEGES   Use this when you add a new user or change information in the MySQL database. Reloads the grant tables.
- TABLES   Closes all open tables.
- STATUS   Resets system status variable to 0.

Example:

```
FLUSH PRIVILEGES
```

More than one option can be stated at a time.

```
FLUSH PRIVILEGES, TABLES
```

A

GRANT *privilege* ON *database_object* TO *user_name* IDENTIFIED BY *password* [WITH GRANT OPTION]

This command grants user privileges. This is the preferred method of adding users. The administrator may grant one, some, or all of the following privileges:

ALL PRIVILEGES	ALTER	CREATE
DELETE	DROP	FILE
INDEX	INSERT	PROCESS
REFERENCES	RELOAD	SELECT
SHUTDOWN	UPDATE	USAGE

The database object can be a column, table, or database.

The password is encrypted automatically. Do not use the password() function.

Remember to reload your grant tables after making changes using the FLUSH command.

Using the WITH GRANT OPTION option gives the user the ability to grant options to other users.

Wildcard characters can be used when specifying a host.

The IDENTIFIED BY clause is optional, but, to ensure the security of your database, it is highly recommended.

Example:

To grant a user all privileges to all databases and also give them the ability to grant privileges to others, use the following:

```
GRANT ALL PRIVILEGES ON *.*
TO mark@localhost IDENTIFIED
BY "dinosaur"
WITH GRANT OPTION
```

To grant a user SELECT and UPDATE privileges to a specific database, use the following:

```
GRANT SELECT, UPDATE ON Meet_A_Geek.*
TO sydney@localhost
IDENTIFIED BY "toys"
```

To create a user with no privileges, use the following:

```
GRANT USAGE ON *.* TO user@localhost
```

INSERT [LOW_PRIORITY or DELAYED] [IGNORE] [INTO] table_name [(column_list)] VALUES(value_list), INSERT [LOW_PRIORITY or DELAYED] [IGNORE] [INTO] table_name [(column_list)] SELECT ..., INSERT [LOW_PRIORITY or DELAYED] [IGNORE] [INTO] table_name [(column_list)] SET column_name = expression[, column_name = expression] ...

These statements add new rows to an existing table. If no column names are used, the values in the VALUES list must match up to the table's columns by type, position, and number. If the column names are used, the values in the VALUES clause must match up to the column list by position, type, and number.

If using the SELECT clause, the results of the SELECT clause must match by type, position, and number of columns in the table; If a column list is used, the results must match up to it.

The optional LOW_PRIORITY will cause the insertion to be delayed until the table is not in use.

The DELAYED option causes the insertion to be delayed until the table is free. It will also bundle multiple statements together and write them all at once, improving performance.

Example:

```
INSERT INTO ]]Customers
(Customer_ID, First_Name, Last_Name)
VALUES (NULL, 'Scott', 'Johnson')
```

KILL thread_ID

This statement kills the process identified by the thread. This can also be accomplished using the mysqladmin command. The thread's ID can be seen after a SHOW PROCESSLIST command.

Example:

```
KILL 18
```

LOAD DATA [LOW PRIORITY] [LOCAL] INFILE *'file name'* [IGNORE or REPLACE] INTO *table name*, [FIELDS TERMINATED BY *symbol*] [ENCLOSED BY *symbol*], [ESCAPED BY *symbol*] [LINES TERMINATED BY *symbol*],[IGNORE *n* LINES] [(*column_list*)]

This statement causes a text file named *'file name'* to be loaded into a table.

If the optional keyword LOCAL is used, MySQL will look for the file on the client machine. If this word is absent, the file will be loaded from the server.

A full path must be given for the filename.

The table must have the proper number of columns with matching data types. If not, errors similar to those in an INSERT statement will occur.

Example:

The following example will load a comma-delimited text file, named accessdata.txt, into the Customers table. The fields are enclosed with quotation marks.

```
LOAD DATA INFILE '/home/mark/accessdata.txt' INTO Customers
FIELDS TERMINATED BY] "," ENCLOSED BY """
```

LOCK TABLES *table_name* {READ or WRITE}[, *table_name* {READ or WRITE}] ...

This statement locks a table for the named process. When locking tables, it is important to lock all the tables you are going to use.

The LOCK remains in effect until either it is unlocked or the thread that issued the lock dies. See UNLOCK.

Example:

```
LOCK TABLES Customers READ, Orders WRITE
SELECT C.* FROM Customer AS C, Orders AS O WHERE O.Customer_ID = C.Customer_ID
UNLOCK TABLES
```

In this example, the Customers and the Orders table had to be locked because the SELECT statement used both tables.

OPTIMIZE TABLE *table_name*

This statement frees up the dead space that is held by deleted records.

This statement should be used when large numbers of records have been deleted or variable length fields have been altered.

The table is read-only until this operation is completed.

Example:

```
OPTIMIZE TABLE Customers
```

REPLACE [LOW_PRIORITY or DELAYED] [INTO] *table_name* [(*column_list*)] VALUES(*value_list*), REPLACE [LOW_PRIORITY or DELAYED] [INTO] *table_name* [(*column_list*)] SELECT ...,REPLACE [LOW_PRIORITY or DELAYED] [INTO] *table_name* SET *column_name* = *expression* [, SET *column_name* = *expression*] ...

This statement is identical to the INSERT statement, and has all the same options as the INSERT statement. The only difference is that this statement will delete a record before it is inserted if the old record has the same value in a unique index.

Example:

```
REPLACE INTO Customers (Customer_ID, First_Name) VALUES(12, "Jason")
```

REVOKE *privilege_list* ON *database_object* FROM *user_name*

The REVOKE statement takes away the privileges given in the GRANT statement.

The grant tables must be reloaded for any changes to take effect. See the FLUSH command.

See the GRANT statement for the privilege list.

The following example takes away all privileges for the user mark at localhost. It does not delete the user from the MySQL grant tables.

Example:

```
REVOKE ALL PRIVILEGES ON *.* FROM mark@localhost
```

SELECT [DISTINCT] *column_list* **[INTO OUTFILE** *'file_name'* *export_options*] **FROM** *table_list* **[{CROSS or INNER or STRAIGHT or LEFT or NATURAL} JOIN** *table name* **[ON** *join condition*]], **[WHERE** criteria]**[GROUP BY** *column names*] **[HAVING** *criteria*]**[ORDER BY** *column names*]**

This statement will return a resultset based on the criteria provided.

The DISTINCT keyword will return only unique values from a given column.

The clauses after the WHERE clause provide additional filtering.

Example:

```
SELECT * FROM Customers WHERE Last_Name
LIKE "Paul%"
ORDER BY Last_Name
```

SHOW parameter

The SHOW statement returns a resultset based on the parameter provided. The following are the allowable parameters:

- COLUMNS FROM *table_name* [FROM *database_name*]

  or

  COLUMNS FROM *database_name.table_name*   Provides a detailed list of information based on the table name
- DATABASES   Shows a list of databases
- GRANTS FOR *user_name*   Displays the privilege information for the given user.
- INDEX FROM *table_name*   Returns information on all the indexes in a table
- PROCESSLIST   Shows a list of processes and IDs that are currently running
- STATUS   Shows server status variables
- TABLES FROM *database_name*   Shows the list of tables in a database
- TABLE STATUS FROM *database_name*   Shows a detailed account of the actions taken in a table
- VARIABLES   Provides a list of system variables

Example:

```
SHOW COLUMNS FROM Meet_A_Geek.Customers
SHOW PROCESSLIST
```

UNLOCK TABLE *table_name* or UNLOCK TABLE

This command releases all locks held by the client.

UPDATE [LOW_PRIORITY] *table_name* SET *column_name* = *value* [WHERE *criteria*] [LIMIT *n*]

The UPDATE statement allows the user to edit the values contained in a database.

The optional LOW_PRIORITY keyword causes the UPDATE to occur only when the table is not in use.

Example:

```
UPDATE Customers SET First_Name = "Geoff" WHERE Customer_ID = 12
```

USE database name

The USE statement causes the named database to be the active database. Other databases are still accessible using the dot (databasename.tablename) format.

Example:

```
USE Meet_A_Geek
```

APPENDIX B

Current MySQL Functions

This appendix contains a list of current MySQL functions that can be performed within an SQL SELECT statement. The functions are in alphabetical order, followed by a brief description and an example. There cannot be any whitespace between the function and the parenthesis.

ABS(*x*)

Returns the absolute value of *x*.

Example:

```
SELECT ABS(-2)
```

Result:

2

ACOS(*x*)

Returns the arc cosine of *x*. Returns NULL if *x* is not between −1 and 1.

Example:

```
SELECT ACOS(-0.653644)
```

Result:

2.283186

ADDDATE(*date*, INTERVAL *interval expression*)

Returns the result of the date plus the interval expression. Returns NULL if the given date is not a true date. This function is the same as DATE_ADD().

Possible INTERVALs:

YEAR, DAY, HOUR, MINUTE, SECOND

Example:

```
SELECT ADDDATE("1969-04-29", INTERVAL 1 YEAR)
SELECT ADDDATE("1969-04-29", INTERVAL 1 DAY)
SELECT ADDDATE("1969-04-29", INTERVAL 40 DAY)
```

Results:

"1970-04-29"

"1969-04-30"

"1969-06-08"

ASIN(*x*)

Returns the arc sine of x. Returns NULL if x is not between -1 and 1.

Example:

```
SELECT ASIN(0.987)
```

Result:

1.409376

ASCII(*x*)

Returns the ASCII code of the first character in a string.

Example:

```
SELECT ASCII("A")
```

Result:

65

Example:

```
SELECT ASCII("Abc")
```

Result:

65

ATAN(*x*)

Returns the arc tangent of *x*.

Example:

```
SELECT ATAN(3)
```

Result:

1.249046

ATAN2(x, y)

Returns the arc tangent based on the signs given in the arguments to determine the quadrant.

Example:

```
SELECT ATAN(2,2)
SELECT ATAN(-2,2)
```

Results:

.785398

-.785398

AVG(*expression*)

This function returns an average of the numbers given in the expression provided in the argument. Only non-NULL values are used in the average.

Example:

```
SELECT AVG(Price) FROM Customers
```

Results:

23 (Given that Price is a column in a table)

BENCHMARK(*count, expression*)

Performs the *expression* given in the argument *count* times. The value that it returns is always 0. The important thing is the elapsed time that is given in the end. This allows you to judge how quickly the server evaluates your queries.

Example:

```
SELECT BENCHMARK(20000, SELECT * FROM Customers)
```

Results:

The results will vary depending on certain key factors, such as server load. The results will always be 0 with an elapsed time.

BIN(*x*)

Returns a binary value of *x*, where *x* is a BIGINT. The return value type is a string.

Example:

```
SELECT BIN(3)
```

Result:

"11"

CEILING(*x*)

Returns the smallest integer value that is not less than *x*. The return value is converted to a BIGINT. See FLOOR().

Example:

```
SELECT CEILING(4.56)
```

Result:

4

Example:

```
SELECT CEILING(-4.56)
```

Result:

-4

CHAR(*x*, *y*, *z* ...)

Returns a string of values based on the ASCII code values of the arguments provided. NULL values are skipped.

Example:

```
SELECT CHAR(65, 78, 87, 100)
```

Result:

ANWd

CHARACTER_LENGTH, CHAR_LENGTH

See LENGTH().

COALESCE(*expression1*, *expression2*)

Returns the first non-NULL value in the given list of expressions.

Example:

```
SELECT COALESCE(NULL, 345, 56)
```

Results:

345

CONCAT(*x*, *y*, *z*, ...)

Returns the result of combining the arguments into one string. If a NULL value is used for any of the arguments, a NULL value will be returned.

Example:

```
SELECT CONCAT("Sydney", " ", "Renee")
```

Result:

Sydney Renee

Example:

```
SELECT CONCAT("SO", NULL, "0987")
```

Result:

NULL

B

CONV(*x*, from base, to base)

Converts a number from one base to another. The return value is a string.

Example:

```
SELECT CONV(3, 10, 2)
```

Results:

"11"

COS(*x*)

Returns the cosine of *x* where *x* is in radians.

Example:

```
SELECT COS(4)
```

Result:

-0.653644

COT(*x*)

Returns the cotangent of *x*.

Example:

```
SELECT COT(5)
```

Result:

-0.29581292

COUNT(*x*)

Returns the of non-NULL values in a resultset. If an * is used, it returns the number of rows in the resultset.

Example:

```
SELECT COUNT(Smokers) as Smokers FROM Customers WHERE Smoker = "Y"
SELECT COUNT(*) FROM Customers
```

Results:

129

300

CURDATE() and CURRENT_DATE()

Return the current system date.

Example:

```
SELECT CURDATE()
```

Result:

"2000-01-30"

CURTIME() and CURRENT_TIME()

Return the current system time.

Example:

```
SELECT CURTIME()
```

Result:

'23:49:00'

CURRENT_TIMESTAMP()

Returns the current date and time. See NOW(), SYSDATE(), and CURTIME().

Example:

```
SELECT CURRENT_TIMESTAMP()
```

Result:

'2000-01-30 23:49:34'

DATABASE()

Returns the name of the current database.

Example:

```
SELECT DATABASE()
```

Result:

'Meet_A_Geek'

B

DATE_ADD()

See ADDDATE().

DATE_ADD(*date*, INTERVAL *value Type*) and ADD_DATE (*date*, INTERVAL *value Type*)

Adds the value to the date argument. The word INTERVAL is a keyword and must be used in the function. The *Type* can be one of the types shown in Table B.1.

TABLE B.1   Time/Date Types

Type	Expected Value
SECOND	SECONDS
MINUTE	MINUTES
HOUR	HOURS
DAY	DAYS
MONTH	MONTHS
YEAR	YEARS
MINUTE_SECOND	"MINUTES:SECONDS"
HOUR_MINUTE	"HOURS:MINUTES"
DAY_HOUR	"DAYS HOURS"
YEAR_MONTH	"YEARS-MONTHS"
HOUR_SECOND	"HOURS:MINUTES:SECONDS"
DAY_MINUTE	"DAYS HOURS:MINUTES"
DAY_SECOND	"DAYS HOURS:MINUTES:SECONDS"

If you use one of the types in the first column, the value must match the format in the second column. See DATE_SUB().

Example:

```
SELECT DATE_ADD("2000-01-27", INTERVAL 4 DAY)
```

Result:

2000-01-31

Example:

```
SELECT DATE_ADD("2000-04-23 23:59:59", INTERVAL "1:1" MINUTE_SECOND)
```

Result:

2000-04-24 00:01:00

DATE_FORMAT(*date*, *format_symbol*)

Formats the given date according to the format given in the *format_symbol*. More than one symbol can be used to describe a format. Table B.2 lists the acceptable format symbols.

TABLE B.2   Format Symbols

Format Symbol	Meaning
%M	Full month name
%m	Month—numeric
%b	Abbreviated month name
%W	Full weekday name
%D	Day of the month
%Y	Year—4 digit
%y	Year—2 digit
%j	Day of the year—numeric
%a	Abbreviated weekday name
%d	Day of the month—digit
%r	Time—12 hour clock
%T	Time—24 hour clock
%H	Hour 00-23
%h	Hour 01-12
%"i"	Minutes 00-59
%S	Seconds

Example:

```
SELECT DATE_FORMAT('2000-02-27', '%M %D %Y')
```

Result:

February 27th 2000

DATE_SUB(*date*, INTERVAL *value Type*) and SUBDATE (*date*, INTERVAL *value Type*)

Subtracts the value from the date argument. The word INTERVAL is a keyword and must be used in the function. See ADDDATE() for the types and related values.

Example:

SELECT DATE_SUB(2000-01-01, INTERVAL 1 DAY)

Result:

1999-12-31

Example:

SELECT DATE_SUB(2000-03-10 00:00:00, INTERVAL 1 MINUTE)

Result:

2000-03-09 23:59:00

DAYNAME(*date*)

Returns the name of the day given in date.

Example:

SELECT DAYNAME('2000-01-27')

Results:

"Thursday"

DAYOFMONTH(*date*)

Returns the day of the month given in the date argument.

Example:

SELECT DAYOFMONTH('2000-01-27')

Result:

27

DAYOFWEEK(*date*)

Returns the index of the day of the week that is given in the argument. See the following list for the correct index for the corresponding day.

1 = Sunday

2 = Monday

3 = Tuesday

4 = Wednesday

5 = Thursday

6 = Friday

7 = Saturday

Example:

```
SELECT DAYOFWEEK('2000-01-27')
```

Result:

5—Corresponds to the Thursday index.

DAYOFYEAR(*date*)

Returns the day of the year for date. This is the Julian date.

Example:

```
SELECT DAYOFYEAR('2000-01-27')
```

Result:

27

Example:

```
SELECT DAYOFYEAR('2000-04-23')
```

Result:

114

DECODE(*binary_string*, *encrypt_string*)

Returns the decrypted results of the *binary string*. The *encrypt_string* must be the same string used in the encryption process.

DEGREES(*x*)

Returns the value of *x* given in radians as degrees. See also RADIANS().

Example:

SELECT DEGREES(4.345)

Result:

248.950162

ELT(*X*, *a*, *b*, *c*, ...)

Returns the string whose position in the argument list matches *X*. See FIELD().

Example:

SELECT ELT(3, "Sam", "Ken", "Mark", "Scott")

Result:

"Mark"

ENCODE(*word*, encrypt_string)

Returns an encrypted binary string based on the *encrypt_string*. See DECODE().

Example:

SELECT ENCODE('tacobell', 'taco')

Result:

ENCRYPT(*word*[, *seed*])

Returns an encrypted string. Uses the UNIX crypt() function. The optional *seed* can be a 2-letter string.

Example:

SELECT ENCRYPT('tacobell', 'sa')

Result:

saAUT2FASzS2s

EXP(*x*)

Returns the value of the base of natural logarithms, raised to the power of *x*.

Example:

```
SELECT EXP(5)
```

Result:

148.413159

EXTRACT(*value* FROM *date*)

Returns the value given from the given date. The *value* must be in one of the following formats:

Accepted values:

SECOND

MINUTE

HOUR

DAY

MONTH

YEAR

MINUTE_SECOND

HOUR_MINUTE

DAY_HOUR

YEAR_MONTH

HOUR_SECOND

DAY_MINUTE

DAY_SECOND

See ADDDATE( ), and DATE_SUB( ).

Example:

```
SELECT EXTRACT(DAY FROM "2000-01-27"
```

B

Result:

1

Example:

```
SELECT EXTRACT(DAY_SECOND FROM "2000-01-27 12:01:45"
```

Result:

10145—returned in DAY/HOUR/MINUTE

FIELD(x, y, z, ...)

Returns the position in the argument list where x and the string match. See ELT().

Example:

```
SELECT FIELD("Mark", "Sam", "Ken", "Mark", "Scott")
```

Result:

3

FIND_IN_SET(x, stringlist)

Returns the position in the string list where x is found. If x is not in the string list, 0 is returned. The string list is a list of string values separated by a comma.

Example:

```
SELECT FIND_IN_SET("Mark", "Mark, Stan, Ken")
```

Result:

1

FLOOR(x)

Returns the largest integer value that is not greater than x. The returned value is converted to a BIGINT. See CEILING().

Example:

```
SELECT FLOOR(4.56)
```

Result:

4

Example:

```
SELECT FLOOR(-4.56)
```

Result:

-5

FORMAT(*NUM*, *DEC*)

Returns the number given in *NUM* formatted to '*x,xxx,xxx.x*' rounded to the decimals given in DEC. If DEC is 0, no decimal part will be returned.

Example:

```
SELECT FORMAT(12345.45, 1)
```

Result:

12,345.5

FROM_DAYS(*days*)

Given a day number (from TO_DAYS()), will return a date.

Example:

```
SELECT FROM_DAYS(694734)
```

Result:

1902-02-13

FROM_UNIXTIME(*unix_time*[, *format_symbols*])

Returns a date based on the given *unix_time*. The optional parameter provides formatting.

Example:

```
SELECT FROM_UNIXTIME(951631200, '%M %D %Y')
```

Result:

February 27 2000

GREATEST(*x*, *y*, ...)

Returns the largest valued argument. Uses the same rules as LEAST for comparisons. See LEAST().

Example:

```
SELECT GREATEST(45, 222, 3, 99)
```

Result:

222

Example:

```
SELECT GREATEST("A", "B", "C")
```

Result:

C

Example:

```
SELECT GREATEST("Mark", "Sam", "Ken")
```

Result:

Sam

HEX(*x*)

Returns a hexadecimal value of *x*, where *x* is a BIGINT. The return value type is a string.

Example:

```
SELECT HEX(15)
```

Result:

"F"

HOUR(time)

Returns the hour given in time.

Example:

```
SELECT HOUR('11:45:01')
```

Results:

11

IF(*expression1, expression2, expression3*)

If *expression1* evaluates to True, *expression2* is returned. If *expression1* is False, *expression3* is returned.

Example:

```
SELECT IF(1, "This", "That")
SELECT IF(0, "This", "That")
```

Results:

"This"

"That"

IFNULL(*expression1*, *expression2*)

If *expression1* is NULL, *expression2* is returned. If *expression1* is not NULL, *expression1* is returned.

Example:

```
SELECT IFNULL(Favorite_Movie, "None")
FROM Customers
WHERE Customer_ID = 5567
```

Results:

If the column Favorite_Movie is NULL then the word "None" is returned. If Favorite_Movie is not NULL then the value for that column is returned. This is a handy function in case you must have something returned in a resultset.

ISNULL(*expression*)

Returns 1 if the given *expression* is NULL. Returns 0 if it is not.

Example:

```
SELECT ISNULL(Favorite_Movie)
FROM Customers
WHERE Customer_ID = 2322
```

Results:

If the Favorite_Movie column is NULL then a 1 is returned. If not, a 0 is returned.

INSERT(*x*, *y*, *z*, *j*)

Returns the string *x* with *j* replacing the characters starting at *y* for a length of *z*.

Example:

```
SELECT INSERT("Database", 5, 4, "ware")
```

B

Result:

"Dataware"

INSTR(*x*, *y*)

Returns the value of the position of string *y* in string *x*. This is the reverse of LOCATE(*x*, *y*) and POSITION(*x*, *y*).

Example:

```
SELECT INSTR("Mark", "M")
```

Result:

1

LAST_INSERT_ID()

Returns the last sequence number of an inserted record in an AUTO_INCREMENT column. This number is stored based on the connection. So, if two records were inserted into the same table from two different connections, the last number for the first connection would be the record it inserted, and the number for the second connection would be the number that it inserted.

Example:

```
SELECT LAST_INSERT_ID()
```

Result:

15

LCASE(*x*)

Returns the string *x* with all characters in lowercase. See LOWER(), UCASE(), UPPER().

Example:

```
SELECT LCASE('MARK')
```

Result:

"mark"

LEAST(*x*, *y*, *z*, ...)

Returns the smallest valued argument. The following rules are used for comparisons:

- If all values are integers, they are compared as integers.
- If the argument is a case-sensitive string, they are compared as case-sensitive strings. Otherwise, they are compared as non–case-sensitive strings.

See GREATEST().

Example:

```
SELECT LEAST(9, 45, 12, 34, 6)
```

Result:

6

Example:

```
SELECT LEAST("A", "B", "C")
```

Result:

A

Example:

```
SELECT LEAST("Mark", "Sam", "Ken")
```

Result:

Ken

LEFT(*x*,*y*)

Returns the number of characters from *x*, starting from the left until it reaches a length of *y*. See RIGHT().

Example:

```
SELECT LEFT("Database", 4)
```

Result:

"Data"

LENGTH(*x*)

Returns the length of string *x*.

Example:

```
SELECT LENGTH("The Quick Brown Fox")
```

Result:

19

LOAD_FILE(*filename*)

Opens the file and returns the contents as a string. The file must reside on the server, and the user of this function must have FILE privileges.

Example:

```
UPDATE Products SET Picture = LOAD_FILE("/home/pictures/Flowers.gif") WHERE
Product_ID = 12
```

Result:

This command will load the contents of the Flowers.gif into the Picture column of the Products table. The column must either be a BLOB or TEXT type column.

LOCATE(*x*, *y*, *z*)

Returns the position of the string x in string y starting at z. Returns 0 if it is not found.

Example:

```
SELECT LOCATE("M", "Mark", 2)
```

Result:

0

Example:

```
SELECT LOCATE("M", "Mark", 1)
```

Result:

1

LOG(*x*)

Returns the natural algorithm of the argument x.

Example:

```
LOG(5)
```

Result:

1.601438

Example:

LOG(-5)

Result:

NULL

LOG10(x)

Returns the base 10 algorithm of the argument.

Example:

LOG10(1000)

Result:

3

Example:

LOG10(-1000)

Result:

NULL

LOWER(x)

Returns the string x with all characters in lowercase. See LCASE(), UCASE(), and UPPER().

Example:

SELECT LOWER('MARK')

Result:

"mark"

LPAD(x, y, z)

Returns the string of x left padded with the string z until the length of the return string is equal to y. See RPAD().

Example:

SELECT LPAD("Mark", 8, "OK")

Result:

"OKOKMark"

LTRIM(*x*)

Returns *x* without leading spaces. See RTRIM() and TRIM().

Example:

```
SELECT LTRIM("   Mark")
```

Result:

"Mark"

MAX(*expression*)

Returns the maximum value of the given expression.

Example:

```
SELECT MAX(Customer_ID) FROM Customers
```

Results:

387

MID(*x*, *y*, *z*)

Returns a string *z* characters long from string *x*, starting at position *y*.

Example:

```
SELECT MID("Database", 4, 4)
```

Result:

"base"

MIN(*expression*)

Returns the smallest value (minimum) of the given expression.

Example:

```
SELECT MIN(Customer_ID) FROM Customers
```

Results:

1

MINUTE (*time*)

Returns the minute given in *time*.

Example:

```
SELECT MINUTE('11:45:01')
```

Results:

45

MOD(*x*,*y*)

Returns the remainder of *x* divided by *y*. The symbol % can also be used.

Example:

```
SELECT MOD(13,2)
```

Result:

1

Example:

```
SELECT 19 % 7
```

Result:

5

MONTH(*date*)

Returns the index for the month given in *date*.

Example:

```
SELECT MONTH('2000-01-27')
```

Result:

1

MONTHNAME(*date*)

Returns the name of the month given in *date*.

Example:

```
SELECT MONTHNAME("2000-05-10")
```

Result:

"March"

NOW()

Returns the current date and time. See CURTIME(), CURRENT_TIMESTAMP, and SYSDATE().

Example:

SELECT NOW()

Result:

'2000-01-30 23:51:00'

OCT(x)

Returns an octal value of x, where x is a BIGINT. The return value type is a string.

Example:

SELECT OCT(10)

Result:

12

OCTET_LENGTH()

See LENGTH().

PASSWORD(password)

Returns an encrypted string of the given password string.

Example:

SELECT PASSWORD('tacobell')

Result:

35decd2c4ab0f0c1

PERIOD_ADD(x, y)

Returns a value resulting in the sum of y months added to period x. x is not in date value.

Example:

SELECT PERIOD_ADD(9910, 4)

Result:

200002

PERIOD_DIFF(*X*, *Y*)

Returns the number of months between *x* and *y*. *x* and *y* should be in either YYMM or CCYYMM format.

Example:

```
SELECT PERIOD_DIFF(200010, 199804)
```

Result:

30

PI()

Returns the value of PI.

Example:

```
SELECT PI()
```

Result:

3.141593

POSITION(*x*, *y*)

Returns the position of the first occurrence of *x* in *y*. Returns 0 if *x* is not found in *y*.

Example:

```
SELECT LOCATE("fox", "The quick brown fox jumped")
```

Result:

17

Example:

```
SELECT POSITION("ox", "The quick brown fox")
```

Result:

18

POW(*x*, *y*) and POWER(*x*, *y*)

Return the result of *x* raised to the power of *y*.

Example:

```
SELECT POWER(2,3)
```

Result:

8

Example:

```
SELECT POW(9,2)
```

Result:

81

QUARTER(*date*)

Returns the quarter of the year given in *date*.

Example:

```
SELECT QUARTER('2000-06-22')
```

Result:

2

RADIANS(*x*)

Returns the value of *x* given in degrees as radians. See DEGREES().

Example:

```
SELECT RADIANS(248)
```

Result:

4.328417

RAND() and RAND(*seed*)

Returns a random float type number in the range 0 to 1. If an argument is provided, it is used as the *seed*. (A *seed* is used to generate the random number. The same *seed* will return the same series of random numbers—making them not random but predictable.)

Example:

```
SELECT RAND()
```

Result:

.6847

Example:

```
SELECT RAND()
```

Result:

.1067

Example:

```
SELECT RAND(3)
```

Result:

.1811

Example:

```
SELECT RAND(3)
```

Result:

.1811

REPEAT(*x*, *y*)

Returns a string of *x* repeated *y* times. If *y* is less than 0, an empty string is returned.

```
SELECT REPEAT("Mark", 4)
```

Result:

"MarkMarkMarkMark"

REPLACE(*x*, *y*, *z*)

Returns the string *x* with all occurrences of *y* replaced with *z*.

Example:

```
SELECT REPLACE("The Brown Cow", "The", "A")
```

Result:

"A Brown Cow"

REVERSE(*x*)

Returns string *x* in reverse order.

Example:

```
SELECT REVERSE("Mark")
```

Result:

"kraM"

RIGHT(*string, length*)

Return the rightmost *length* of characters from *string*. A NULL will be returned if the string is NULL.

Example:

```
SELECT RIGHT("Super", 2)
```

Results:

"er"

ROUND(*x*)

Returns the argument rounded to the nearest whole number (integer). See ROUND(*x,y*).

Example:

```
SELECT ROUND(5.374)
```

Result:

5

Example:

```
SELECT ROUND(-5.374)
```

Result:

-5

ROUND(*x,y*)

Returns the argument x, rounded to the decimals specified in y. See ROUND(*x*).

Example:

```
SELECT ROUND(4.345, 1)
```

Result:

4.3

RPAD(*x*, *y*, *z*)

Returns the string of *x* right padded with the string *z* until the length of the return string is equal to *y*. See LPAD().

Example:

```
SELECT RPAD("Mark", 8, "OK")
```

Result:

"MarkOKOK"

RTRIM(*x*)

Returns *x* without trailing spaces. See LTRIM() and TRIM().

Example:

```
SELECT RTRIM("Mark      ")
```

Result:

"Mark"

SECOND(*time*)

Returns the second given in *time*.

Example:

```
SELECT SECOND('11:45:01')
```

Result:

1

SEC_TO_TIME(*seconds*)

Returns the time in hh:mm:ss format based on the number of seconds given in the argument.

Example:

```
SELECT SEC_TO_TIME(56789)
```

Results:

"15:46:29"

SESSION_USER()

Returns the user of the current connection.

Example:

```
SELECT SESSION_USER()
```

Result:

'mark@localhost'

SIGN(x)

Returns the sign of x. If x is negative, a −1 is returned. If x is 0, a 0 is returned. If x is positive, a 1 is returned.

Example:

```
SELECT SIGN(-14)
```

Result:

−1

Example:

```
SELECT SIGN(0)
```

Result:

0

Example:

```
SELECT SIGN(45)
```

Result:

1

SIN(x)

Returns the sine of x where x is in radians

Example:

```
SELECT SIN(7)
```

Result:

.656987

SOUNDEX(*x*)

Returns a SOUNDEX string from *x*.

Example:

```
SELECT SOUNDEX("George")
```

Result:

"G620"

SPACE(*x*)

Returns a string with *x* number of spaces.

Example:

```
SELECT SPACE(12)
```

Result:

"   "

SQRT(*x*)

Returns the square root of *x*.

Example:

```
SELECT SQRT(9)
```

Result:

3

Example:

```
SELECT SQRT(-16)
```

Result:

NULL

STRCMP(*string1*, *string2*)

Returns 1 if *string1* is the same as *string2*. If they are different, this function returns 0. A NULL value is returned if either string is NULL.

Example:

```
SELECT STRCMP("Sandy", "Sandy")
```

Results:

1

Example:

```
SELECT STRCMP("Sandy", "Sandra")
```

Results:

0

Example:

```
SELECT STRCMP("Sandy", "sandy")
```

Results:

0

STD(*expression*) or STDDEV(*expression*)

Returns the standard deviation of the given *expression*. Only non NULL values are used to compute this value.

Example:

```
SELECT STD(Quantity) FROM Orders
```

Results:

2.435

SUM(*expression*)

Returns the total sum of the given *expression*. Only non-NULL values are used to compute this value.

Example:

```
SELECT SUM(Cost) FROM Orders
```

Results:

10234.34

SUBSTRING_INDEX(*x*, *y*, *z*)

Returns a string from *x* after *z* occurrences of *y* have been found. If *y* is positive, everything to the left of the final delimiter is returned. If *y* is negative, everything to the right is returned.

Example:

```
SELECT SUBSTRING_INDEX("mysql.3-23-3.Linux.tar.gz", ".", 3")
```

Result:

'mark@localhost'

Example:

```
SELECT SUBSTRING_INDEX("mysql.3-23-3.Linux.tar.gz", ".", -3")
```

Result:

"Linux.tar.gz"

SUBDATE()

See DATE_SUB()

SYSDATE()

Returns the current date and time. See also CURTIME(), NOW(), and CURRENT_TIMESTAMP().

Example:

```
SELECT SYSDATE()
```

Result:

'2000-01-31 23:54:34'

SYSTEM_USER()

Returns the user of the current connection.

Example:

```
SELECT SYSTEM_USER()
```

Result:

'mark@localhost'

TAN(x)

Returns the tangent of x where x is in radians.

Example:

```
SELECT TAN(12)
```

Result:

−0.635860

TIME_FORMAT(*time*, *format_symbol*)

Returns the given time in the specified *format_symbol*. The *format_symbol* can only be the time-related symbols in the table under DATE_FORMAT(). See DATE_FORMAT().

Example:

```
SELECT TIME_FORMAT('2000-01-23 00:34:33', '%H %i')
```

Result:

00 34

TIME_TO_SEC(*time*)

Returns the number of seconds based on the time given in the argument.

Example:

```
SELECT TIME_TO_SEC("15:26:29")
```

Results:

55589

TO_DAYS(*date*)

Returns the number of days from the year 0 to the given date. See FROM_DAYS().

Example:

```
SELECT TO_DAYS('1902-02-12')
```

Result:

694733

TRIM([[BOTH or LEADING or TRAILING][*x*] FROM] *y*])

Returns the string *y* with the specified string *x* removed from the beginning, end, or both of the string *y*. If no options are used, spaces are removed from the front and back of the string. See LTRIM() and RTRIM().

Example:

```
SELECT TRIM(" Mark ")
```

Result:

"Mark"

Example:

```
SELECT TRIM(LEADING "M" FROM "Mark")
```

Result:

"ark"

Example:

```
SELECT TRIM(BOTH "X" FROM "XXXFILE.XXX")
```

Result:

"FILE."

TRUNCATE(x,y)

Returns the argument x truncated to y decimal places. If y is 0, no decimal places will be returned in the result.

Example:

```
TRUNCATE(3.4567, 2)
```

Result:

3.45

Example:

```
TRUNCATE(3.4567, 0)
```

Result:

3

UCASE(x)

Returns the string x with all characters in uppercase. See UPPER(), LOWER(), and LCASE().

Example:

```
SELECT UCASE('sam I am')
```

Result:

"SAM I AM"

UNIX_TIMESTAMP([*date*])

Without the optional date argument, returns a UNIX timestamp. If a date is given, it will return the date as a UNIX timestamp.

Example:

```
SELECT UNIX_TIMESTAMP()
```

Result:

949301344

Example:

```
SELECT UNIXTIMESTAMP('2000-02-27')
```

Result:

951631200

UPPER(*x*)

Returns the string *x* with all characters in uppercase. See UCASE(), LOWER(), and LCASE().

Example:

```
SELECT UPPER('sam I am')
```

Result:

"SAM I AM"

USER()

Returns the name of the user for the current connection.

Example:

```
SELECT USER()
```

Result:

'mark@localhost'

VERSION()

Returns the server version as a string.

Example:

```
SELECT VERSION()
```

Results:

"3.22.23b"

WEEK(date [, *start*])

Returns the week number given in the date argument. The optional parameter *start* indicates on which day the week starts. If 0 is used, the week starts on Sunday. If 1 is used, the week starts on Monday.

Example:

```
SELECT WEEK('2000-04-29')
```

Result:

17

Example:

```
SELECT WEEK('2000-04-29', 1)
```

Result:

17

WEEKDAY(*date*)

Returns the index for the day of the week given in the argument. The following list identifies the index to use for the corresponding weekday.

0 = Monday

1 = Tuesday

2 = Wednesday

3 = Thursday

4 = Friday

5 = Saturday

6 = Sunday

Example:

```
SELECT WEEKDAY('2000-01-27')
```

Result:

3—Corresponds to the Thursday index

YEAR(*date*)

Returns the year given in date.

Example:

```
SELECT MINUTE YEAR('00-01-27')
```

Result:

2000

APPENDIX C

Answers to Exercises

Day 1

1. Compare the prices of several other databases that have the same feature set as MySQL. These would include SQL Server, Oracle, Adaptive Server and DB2. See how much MySQL is really worth.

    You will find that MySQL is priced well below its competitors. At the time of this writing, Microsoft's SQL Server is priced at $28,999.00 for the Enterprise Edition with an unlimited number of clients. The Enterprise Edition of Sybase Adapter 12 with a 10-seat license sells for $1,650.00 for Windows NT. The Linux version of Sybase Adaptive Server sells for $995. MySQL, on the other hand, is at most $200.

2. Go to Web sites or test some products that use MySQL. (Some are included on the CD-ROM.) Seeing MySQL in action can really change one's mind about open source products.

    Support Wizard is a great example. It uses MySQL very efficiently.

Day 2

1. Using the command line, display all the data in the `mysql` database.

    You can do this by using the following SQL command:

    ```
    SELECT * FROM mysql;
    ```

2. You can also use the `SHOW` command. This will show all the tables in the database (`SHOW TABLES FROM database_name`).

    Check to see if the `mysqld` is running using two different methods.

    The first way is to use the `mysqladmin` command.

INPUT   `bin/mysqladmin -p ping`

    The other way is to `grep` (on Linux and UNIX machines) or to look at the processes or services that are currently running by pressing Ctrl+Alt+Delete (in Windows).

INPUT   `ps -aux | grep mysqld`

3. Telnet to a remote site and start and stop the MySQL server.

    From the command line, start a Telnet session connecting to the computer that is currently running MySQL. After you have established a connection, change directories to the `mysql` installation directory (`/usr/local/mysql`, by default). You must have MySQL `root` privileges to start and stop the server. To do this, use the `mysqladmin shutdown` command. To start it up again, use the `safe_mysqld&` command.

4. Use the MySQL monitor remotely

    This can be accomplished by using Telnet to connect to a remote MySQL server.

Day 3

1. In the Meet-A-Geek project, we defined several business objects. Can you define any more objects?

    Based on interviews with the client, you can develop more business objects. For the `Meet_A_Geek` database, they might be a `Shipper` object, `Advertisement` object, `Coupon` object, or maybe a `Credit Check` object.

2. Come up with the rest of the business rules for the Meet-A-Geek project.

    Additional business rules would also depend on interviews with the client or further study of the business process. Some rules might include "A transaction cannot be committed until a form of payment is verified." Another possible rule could be that an item will not be shipped unless the item is available in inventory.

Day 4

1. Create and drop databases using the mysqladmin utility as well as using the monitor.

    To create the database, use the following:

INPUT
```
bin/mysqladmin -p CREATE DATABASE TestDB
```

To drop the database, use the following:

INPUT
```
bin/mysqladmin -p DROP DATABASE TestDB
```

To experience the same results using the MySQL monitor program, use the following commands:

INPUT
```
CREATE DATABASE TestDB;
```

INPUT
```
DROP DATABASE TestDB;
```

2. Add a couple of users to the database, and try using these accounts.

    The easiest way to add users is to use the GRANT statement. This can be accomplished by issuing the following commands:

INPUT
```
GRANT ALL ON *.* TO mark@% IDENTIFIED BY "thor2000";
```

Day 5

1. Describe some benefits of normalization.

    Normalization helps create a flexible, efficient database that lends itself to easy reporting and manipulating.

2. Identify areas that may not need to be normalized.

    Items such as two columns to hold addresses or zip codes may not need to be normalized. Also, if you are going to capture a small amount of data, maybe one table would be more efficient.

Day 6

1. Create the schema for the Meet_A_Geek project. Base the schema on the blueprint that was developed on Day 3.

   The following could be placed in a text file and redirected into the mysql command:

```
CREATE DATABASE Meet_A_Geek;
USE Meet_A_Geek;
CREATE TABLE Customers
(Customer_ID INT NOT NULL PRIMARY KEY AUTO_INCREMENT,
                    First_Name VARCHAR(15) NOT NULL,
            Last_Name  VARCHAR(30) NOT NULL,
            Address VARCHAR(100) NOT NULL,
            City VARCHAR(30) NOT NULL,
                    State VARCHAR(20) NOT NULL,
            Zip VARCHAR(15) NOT NULL,
            Email VARCHAR(20) NOT NULL,
            Age TINYINT NOT NULL,
            Gender CHAR(1) NOT NULL,
            RACE VARCHAR(15) NOT NULL,
            Eye_Color VARCHAR(20),
            Hair_Color VARCHAR(20),
            Activity VARCHAR(100),
            Movie VARCHAR(50),
            Occupation VARCHAR(50),
            Smoker ENUM('Y', 'N') DEFAULT "N");

CREATE TABLE Shippers
(Shipper_ID INT NOT NULL PRIMARY KEY AUTO_INCREMENT,
            Name VARCHAR(100) NOT NULL,
            Location VARCHAR(100) NOT NULL,
            Shipping_Method VARCHAR(40) NOT NULL,
            Active CHAR(1) NOT NULL);

CREATE TABLE Orders
(Order_ID INT NOT NULL PRIMARY KEY AUTO_INCREMENT,
            Shipper_ID INT NOT NULL,
            Transaction_ID INT NOT NULL,
            Customer_ID INT NOT NULL,
            Order_Date DATETIME NOT NULL,
            Customer_Message VARCHAR(255),
            Amount_Due FLOAT(5,2) NOT NULL);

CREATE TABLE ProductionOrders
(ProductionOrders_ID INT NOT NULL PRIMARY KEY AUTO_INCREMENT,
            Product_ID INT NOT NULL,
            Order_ID INT NOT NULL);
```

```
CREATE TABLE Transactions
(Transaction_ID INT NOT NULL PRIMARY KEY AUTO_INCREMENT,
                Transaction_Date DATETIME NOT NULL,
                Amount_Paid FLOAT(5,2) NOT NULL,
                Ship_Date DATETIME NOT NULL);

CREATE TABLE Products
(Product_ID INT NOT NULL PRIMARY KEY AUTO_INCREMENT,
                Name VARCHAR(100) NOT NULL,
                Description VARCHAR(255) NOT NULL,
                Price FLOAT(5,2) NOT NULL,
                Manufacturer VARCHAR(255) NOT NULL,
                Picture VARCHAR(100));
```

2. Create indexes for the Meet_A_Geek database. Use the lessons you learned here to determine which columns should be indexed.

   An index should be placed on the following columns:

   Customer_ID in the Customers table.

   Shipper_ID in the Shippers table.

   Product_ID and Order_ID in the Production_Orders table.

Day 7

1. Using the knowledge you have gained here, go back and redefine all the column values of the Meet-A-Geek project.

   See exercise 1 of the previous day.

2. Practice inserting rows into a table using the SET and ENUM column types.

   The following are a few examples:

   ```
   INSERT INTO Customers (Smoker) VALUES('Y');
   ```

   ```
   INSERT INTO Customers (Smoker) VALUES(NULL);
   ```

   The first example will insert a Y into the table. The second example will insert the default value, which, in your database, is N.

Day 8

1. Use the `mysqlimport` command, with the proper options, to complete the following task:

   You need to import a spreadsheet from the shipping department. The shipping department gives you a worksheet to import into the database that keeps track of all the orders that have been shipped. The fields are separated by forward slashes and the data is enclosed by single quotes. Everything that is on the sheet is new data; no old data has been updated. Import the file.

   To accomplish this, use the following command:

   `INPUT` `bin/mysqlimport -p -i -fields-enclosed-by=' -fields terminated-by=/`

2. Use the `mysqldump` command properly in the following scenario:

   The boss wants to give a report to the accountants based on the Orders table. The accountants need the quantity and price of every item that was ordered to figure out commissions. They do not need the DDL, but they do need the report to be comma-delimited. Create the report.

   To accomplish this, use the following command:

   `INPUT`
   ```
   bin/mysqldump -p -t --fields-terminated -by=,
   Meet_A_Geek Orders >> Report.txt
   ```

Day 9

1. Translate the following into SQL statements:

   1. View all the records of customers from the `Customers` table who have placed an order.
   ```
   SELECT * FROM Customers WHERE Customer_ID = Orders.Customer_ID
   ```

   2. View all shippers that have been used in the past month.
   ```
   SELECT Shipper_Name FROM Shipper as S, Orders as O
   WHERE O.Order_Date >= '2000-01-01'
   AND O.Order_Date <= '2001-01-31'
   AND O.Shipper_ID = S.Shipper_ID
   ```

   3. View all customers.
   ```
   SELECT * FROM Customers
   ```

2. Create an SQL statement that accomplishes the following:

   Add the following information to the Customers table:

   First Name: Brent

   Last Name: Jacobs

   Address: 123 N. Hampton Lane

   ```
   INSERT INTO Customers (First_Name, Last_Name, Address1)
   VALUES('Brent', 'Jacobs', '123 N. Hampton Lane')
   ```

3. Change the name of the last record you added from "Jerry" to "Sam."

   ```
   UPDATE Customers SET First_Name = 'Sam'
   WHERE Customer_ID = LAST_INSERT_ID()
   ```

4. Delete all records from the Customers table whose first name is Jerry.

   ```
   DELETE FROM Customers WHERE First_Name = 'Jerry'
   ```

5. Create an SQL statement that returns the number of customers whose names begin with M.

   ```
   SELECT COUNT(Customer_ID) as Cust_Count
   FROM Customers
   WHERE First_Name LIKE "M%"
   ```

6. Create an SQL statement that returns the average number of products each customer purchases. (Hint: use the quantity column.)

   ```
   SELECT AVG(Quantity) FROM Orders
   ```

7. Create an SQL statement that returns all the customers who have placed an order in the past month, sort it in ascending alphabetic order, and group the records by date.

   ```
   SELECT C.* FROM Orders as O, Customers as C
   WHERE O.Order_Date >='2000-01-01'
   AND O.Order_Date <= '2000-01-31'
   AND C.Customer_ID = O.Customer_ID
   ORDER BY C.Last_Name
   GROUP BY O.Order_Date
   ```

C

Day 10

1. Use some of the functions you learned today in queries using the `Meet_A_Geek` database.

   The following are some examples:

   ```
   SELECT SUM(Amount_Paid) AS Total FROM Transactions;
   SELECT MAX(Customer_ID) AS Top FROM Customers;
   ```

2. How would you get the total number of transactions that occurred on March 1, 2000?

   ```
   SELECT COUNT(Transaction_ID)
   FROM Transactions
   WHERE Transaction_Date = '20000301";
   ```

Day 11

1. Imagine that you have a table called `Orders`, and you want to update it while no other threads can read from it. You also have a table called `Products`, which you want to read from but not update. Write the syntax for appropriate locking and unlocking of these tables.

   ```
   LOCK TABLES orders WRITE, products READ;
   ...
   UNLOCK TABLES;
   ```

2. Consider each of the following scenarios. In which would you consider applying a key to the table? Would you use a unique or non-unique key?

   1. A table containing the birthdays of all of the people you know. Your computer accesses it once a day to see if it's anyone's birthday today, and, if so, emails him or her a greeting.

      A non-unique key

   2. A table of products available to order from your online shop. Duplicates are not allowed.

      A unique key

   3. A table that records the sales tax applied to products sold. It is written to each time a product is sold, but read from only once per quarter.

      No key

Day 12

1. List the advantages and disadvantages to using an interface as opposed to the MySQL Monitor program.

   - Advantages:

     Interfaces allow you to perform complex database operations programmatically.

     They allow you to control what is entered into your database and perform error checking.

   - Disadvantages:

     You have to know a programming language to create the interface.

     The development cycle is long.

2. What are the basic requirements for a database connection?

   Server name or IP address, username and password, database name.

Day 13

1. Using ADO, connect to the MySQL database and optimize your tables.

```
Dim mConn as Connection
Dim mCmd as Command

With mConn
    .ConnectionString = "Server=10.1.1.20;driver=MySQL;" &_
"db=Meet_A_Geek;uid=mark;pwd=my2000"
    .Open
End With

With mCmd
    .ActiveConnection=mConn
    .CommandType = adCmdText
    .CommandText = "OPTIMIZE TABLE Customers"
    .Execute , , adExecuteNoRecords
End With

mConn.Close
```

2. Create an ASP that allows a user to edit data from the Customers table.

   The answer to this question can be found in the Appendix C directory located on the CD-ROM that accompanies this book.

Day 14

1. Create a Perl script that takes a request from the user and displays values from the database based on the given value. For example, with the Meet_A_Geek database, create a Web page that allows a person to see a list of customers based on the state the customer is from. Pass this value to a Perl script that uses that parameter in a SQL SELECT query.

   The answer to this question can be found in the Appendix C directory located on the CD-ROM that accompanies this book.

2. Create a Perl Script that adds a user to the database. Hint: use the GRANT statement.

```
#! /usr/local/bin
use DBI;
$DSN = "DBI:mysql:Meet_A_Geek:10.1.1.50";
$dbh = DBI->connect($DSN,"mark","tacobell");
$dbh->do("GRANT ALL ON *.* TO Joe@% IDENTIFIED BY "thecircus");
$dbh->disconnect();
```

Day 15

1. Write the PHP syntax for connecting to a MySQL database and doing a SELECT on a table called products. The table includes the fields *name* and *price*. Your query should retrieve all products whose price is less than $50. You should allow for an error condition and, if need be, call the user-defined error_report function.

```
<?php

function error_report () {
    echo "Error: ".mysql_errno()."; error description:
".mysql_error()."<br>\n";
}

$sql = "SELECT name, price FROM products WHERE price < 50";
if ($result = mysql_query ("$sql")) {
    while ($row = mysql_fetch_array ($result)) {
        echo "Product: ".$row[name]." price $".$row[price]."<br>\n";
    }
} else error_report ();
```

Day 16

1. Write a SELECT statement to output the current time in the format 'hour:minute am/
    pm weekday nth month year'.

    ```
    SELECT DATE_FORMAT(NOW(),'%r %W %D %M %Y');
    ```

2. Write a SELECT statement to find which weekday the 4th of July will fall on in 2010.

    ```
    SELECT DAYNAME('2010-07-04');
    ```

3. Write a SELECT statement to add 1,000 days to 1 April 2000 and return the date. On
    what weekday will the subsequent day fall?

    ```
    SELECT DATE_ADD('2000-04-01',INTERVAL 1000 DAY);
    ```

    The day is a Friday. You can get the second result using

    ```
    DAYNAME(DATE_ADD('2000-04-01',INTERVAL 1000 DAY)).
    ```

Day 17

1. Add several users to the Meet_A_Geek database using the techniques that were
    discussed on this day. Add one using the GRANT statement, one using the
    mysql_setpermission utility, and one where you actually manipulate the grant
    tables manually.

    Using the GRANT statement:

    ```
    GRANT ALL ON *.* TO Paul@% IDENTIFIED BY "horatio";
    ```

    Use the mysql_setpermission command (if you get stuck, use the -help option).

    To manipulate the GRANT tables, you must have the proper authority. To add a user,
    use mysql:

    ```
    INSERT INTO user VALUES("%","mark", password("cougar")
    ,"Y","Y","Y","Y","Y","Y","Y","Y","Y","Y","Y","Y","Y","Y");
    ```

    You would then need to give the user access to a database by manipulating the db
    table.

2. Revoke the privileges you granted the users you created in exercise 1 by using the
    REVOKE statement.

    ```
    REVOKE ALL ON *.* TO Paul@%;
    ```

3. Delete the users from the database.

    ```
    DELETE FROM user WHERE User="Paul" AND Host="%";
    ```

Day 18

1. Go to the crash-me Web site and compare MySQL against your favorite database.

   The crash-me Web site is linked to the MySQL Web site. It shows a statistical comparison of many popular databases.

2. Create a user-defined function similar to the one in this day.

   Implement the function in your MySQL database following the instructions in this day.

   To implement your new function, you will have to add this function to the grant tables. To do this you will use the CREATE FUNCTION statement. The syntax for the CREATE FUNCTION statement is as follows:

   INPUT
   ```
   CREATE FUNCTION function_name RETURNS return_type "compiled file name"
   ```

   After you have added the function to the grant tables, you should be able to use it like any other intrinsic MySQL function.

Day 19

1. Write the syntax for checking a table called my_table for deleted blocks.
   ```
   isamchk -r my_table
   ```

2. Give the syntax for showing the current list of active threads on a MySQL server.
   ```
   mysqladmin -u username -p processlist
   ```

3. Write the function call for encrypting the string 'my string' with the salt in 'ht1QbxA2IJPhU'.
   ```
   SELECT ENCRYPT('my string,','ht');
   ```

Day 20

1. Perform the recovery option of the myisamchk utility on all of the Meet-A-Geek tables.

   To accomplish this task, type the following command:

   INPUT
   ```
   bin/myisamchk -r *.MYI
   ```

2. Get the specifications for a server to use for the Meet_A_Geek database, knowing that this database will be accessed around 10,000 times a day via the Internet.

MySQL runs best on UNIX-based systems. For the Meet_A_Geek database, a high-end UNIX server would be best. But again, this is very subjective. You probably could get away with running it on an Intel system running Linux.

Day 21

1. There are two scripts that you did not create on the flow chart—the Script to display items from the Products table and the script to create an order. Create these scripts using Perl and the DBI/DBD.

    The answer to this question can be found in the Appendix C directory located on the CD-ROM that accompanies this book.

2. The same task as the first exercise, but this time use ADO and ODBC.

    The answer to this question can be found in the Appendix C directory located on the CD-ROM that accompanies this book.

C

INDEX

Symbols

+ (addition operator), 276
& (ampersand), 25
&& (ampersands), 165
* (asterisk), 136, 148, 161
* (multiplication opera-
  tor), 276
. syntax, 328
{} (braces), 279
[] (brackets), 274, 433
, (comma), 162
. (dot), 326
'' (double quotation
  marks), 272
= (equal sign), 148, 274
! (exclamation point), 165
% (modulo operator), 276
( ) (parentheses), 159
% (percent sign), 322

|| (pipe symbols), 165
"" (quotation marks), 248
; (semicolon), 28, 63, 79,
  82, 271
' (single quotation mark),
  217, 272
- (subtraction operator),
  276
<% tag, 220
$dbh-
  disconnect statement>, 249
  do(SQL statement)>, 249
-#, - -debug=... option
  (mysqladmin), 362
-#=debug_ options,
  - -debug=debug_option
  (isamchk), 369
- -add-drop-table option
  (mysqldump), 124, 349
- -add-locks option
  (mysqldump), 124, 348

- -big-tables parameter,
  379
- -debug option (mysqld),
  356
- -delayed-insert option
  (mysqldump), 124
- -enable-locking para-
  meter, 379
- -fields-enclosed-by=char
  option (mysqlimport),
  125
- -fields-enclosed-by=
  'delimeter' option
  (mysqldump), 349, 354
- -fields-escaped-by=char
  option (mysqlimport),
  125
- -fields-escaped-by=
  'escape_ char' option
  (mysqldump), 349, 354

Numbers

A

M

Other Related Titles

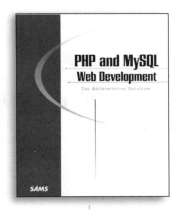

PHP3 and MySQL Web Development
William Jason Gillmore
ISBN: 0-672-31784-2
$39.99

Sams Teach Yourself Active Server Pages 3.0 in 21 Days
Scott Mitchell
ISBN: 0-672-31863-6
$39.99

Roger Jenning's Database Developer's Guide with Visual Basic 6
Roger Jennings
ISBN: 0-672-31063-5
$59.99

Writing Stored Procedures with Microsoft SQL Server
Matthew Shepker
ISBN: 0-672-31886-5
$49.99

Sams Teach Yourself Microsoft SQL Server 7.0 in 21 Days
Richard Waymire
ISBN: 0-672-31290-5
$39.99

SQL Unleashed, Second Edition
Sakhr Youness
ISBN: 0-672-31709-5
$49.99

All prices are subject to change.

Windows 95/98/NT/2000 Installation Instructions

1. Insert the CD-ROM disc into your CD-ROM drive.
2. From the Windows 95 desktop, double-click the My Computer icon.
3. Double-click the icon representing your CD-ROM drive.
4. Open the `readme.txt` file for descriptions of third-party products.

Linux and UNIX Installation Instructions

These installation instructions assume that you have a passing familiarity with UNIX commands and the basic setup of your machine. As UNIX has many flavors, only generic commands are used. If you have any problems with the commands, please consult the appropriate man page or your system administrator.

1. Insert CD-ROM in CD-ROM drive.
2. If you have a volume manager, mounting of the CD-ROM will be automatic. If you don't have a volume manager, you can mount the CD-ROM by typing

   `mount  -tiso9660  /dev/cdrom  /mnt/cdrom`

3. Open the `readme.txt` file for descriptions of third-party products.

Note

/mnt/cdrom is just a mount point, but it must exist when you issue the Mount command. You can also use any empty directory for a mount point if you don't want to use /mnt/cdrom.